CITIZENSHIP AND
EMPLOYMENT

CITIZENSHIP AND EMPLOYMENT

Investigating Post-Industrial Options

JOCELYN PIXLEY

School of Sociology, University of New South Wales

Published by the Press Syndicate of the University of Cambridge
The Pitt Building, Trumpington Street, Cambridge CB2 1RP, UK
40 West 20th Street, New York, NY 10011-4211, USA
10 Stamford Road, Oakleigh, Melbourne, Victoria 3166, Australia

Printed in Hong Kong by Colorcraft

National Library of Australia cataloguing in publication data
Pixley, Jocelyn F. (Jocelyn Florence), 1947–   .
Citizenship and employment.
Bibliography.
Includes index.
ISBN 0 521 41793 7.
ISBN 0 521 44615 5 (pbk.)
1. Manpower policy. 2. Full employment policies. I. Title.
331.12042

Library of Congress cataloguing in publication data
Pixley, Jocelyn, 1947–
Citizenship and employment: investigating post-industrial options
Jocelyn Pixley.
Includes bibliographical references and index.
ISBN 0 521 41793 7
ISBN 0 521 44615 5 pbk
1. Unemployment. 2. Full employment policies. 3. Income
maintenance programs. 4 Producer cooperatives. 5. Communal
living. I. Title.
HD5707.5.P567 1993   92-19634
339.5--dc20   CIP

A catalogue record for this book is available from the British Library

ISBN 0521 41793 7 hardback
ISBN 0521 44615 5 paperback

Contents

Contents

Acknowledgements

The idea of the lone author is a wonderful fiction conjured up by visions of a pen dripping in blood. It is true and of course not true. This book began as a PhD, and my thanks for the encouragement and stimulation from my supervisor, Maria Markus, are rather a small effort in reciprocity. (Mayby reciprocity of this kind can only be 'generational'.) Maria did more, though, by calling for determination and imagination even while our discussions were always good fun (to me). On a different note, the civil servants who gave such long interviews were most helpful, despite knowing that I disagreed with their strategy. Thanks also to the ABC for their kind permission to quote from the 1979 Boyer Lectures of R.J.L. Hawke.

From Michael Pusey came the initial enthusiasm for insisting that I press on to turn the thesis into a book: for this, too, I want to thank John Keane, Anna Yeatman, Lois Bryson and some anonymous readers for invaluable criticisms that gave the argument a sharper focus. The thesis would not, however, have become a book without the decision of Robin Derricourt, Editorial Director of Cambridge University Press who is himself rather sceptical of PhD to book transitions. If a PhD has to convince examiners that apprenticeship is over, a book must aim to convince a public. I have been determined to do that mainly because I was maddened that the opposing arguments were still in safe soil while unemployment rose to more depressing heights.

And on the sort of tenacity needed to see the process through, many more thanks are due, although personal and intellectual support frequently overlaps: to Elizabeth Fulop, Ian Flett, Joe O'Donnell, Diana Shaw and Jennifer Wilkinson for reading many drafts and for giving comforting, but not too soothing help, and to my children, Sam Dawson and Louisa Dawson, who had to 'wear it'. The responsibility for the argument rests with me.

JOCELYN PIXLEY

·Introduction:
Developing a case against 'alternative work'

This work began from an irritation. Just when the employment situation was deteriorating further in the early 1980s, a number of books adding a new twist to the issue appeared. Attention was drawn to the benefits of 'work' other than 'employment'. A progressive solution to joblessness, we were told, would emerge if we all engaged in an 'informal economy' and self-provisioning within a convivial environment. Such a trend might be more satisfying and less eco- logically damaging than creating more conventional jobs.

For those feminists trying to expand opportunities for women in the workplace, and themselves searching or clinging to their paid work, this message was perplexing. Instead of a difficult mix of household and paid work, the future, according to this line, lay in domestic work and vegetable gardens. Housework was exactly what we had been trying to leave and we had been successful in creating a political agenda around this issue. Now it seemed that what we had been arguing against was being put forth as the most eco- nomically and environmentally sound pathway to a healthier, 'post- industrial' future.

This political message appeared to me to be suspect for a number of reasons – and not only in regard to women. In various countries low-income teenagers were facing a future where they would never find a job. Adult workers were being told they were 'too old' at forty- eight. It seemed at the time that if an 'informal economy' offered nothing to women who were trying to gain independence and support their children – and who already possessed work skills – its promise to jobless school leavers or anyone else was clearly an even more empty one.

My project thus began as a criticism of this idea that an 'informal economy' might be better than searching for what might merely be low-paid and environmentally destructive jobs. But in 1982 I could

1

not make many new suggestions in mounting a case for employment. It could be argued that new jobs need not damage but could enhance the environment, and a rapidly expanding literature existed on the detrimental effects of unemployment. What more could be said? A year later, the 'informal work' solution was partly discredited, especially in Britain, although not before the Thatcher government had used these vague ideas to promote 'self help'. That same year in Australia, however, a far more ambitious program to find specific alternatives to employment was suddenly launched by a new federal Labor government. A party of the left was sending bureaucrats off to northern New South Wales communes, Israeli kibbutzim and co-operatives in Mondragon. Unemployed teenagers, it was hoped, would move to rural communes and retrenched workers would buy up failed enterprises with their redundancy pay, and convert them into worker co-operatives. It seemed that a good deal more needed to be said on the subject.

Now, as I conclude in the early 1990s, a few of those who argued that industrial society was over and, more seriously, that 'post-industrial' societies did not need to foster full employment, have lately changed tack. Some admit that jobs are important, though the majority have not changed from the line that a state-guaranteed income for all would be preferable to policies aiming for full employment. I take the stronger argument, that mass unemployment is not open to a progressive solution unless a return to job creation is at the forefront of any attempt to find one. In the meantime unemployment is growing again in many OECD countries.

My argument, as events unfolded, came to be about the intellectual climate that accepted joblessness by neglecting the role of the state. While professing to accept a need for 'alternatives' to conventional employment, the failure of certain governments to actually convert this into a workable policy has resulted in growing segments of populations being told they are not wanted unless their labour is cheap. Further, if they do not offer their labour to the lowest bidder, the dole-work threat is trundled out. This suggests a return to a climate like Britain's of the 1840–80s, by which time the workhouse became truly operative.

It is time the employment debate was thought out again. This book presents a feminist approach to the idea that unemployment for women or men could be desirable. It is difficult for women, and far more obviously so, for men, to feel enthusiastic about domestic work and economic dependence, even if such a future is framed as an 'alternative to wage labour' and a 'guaranteed income'. If women were still the dependants of men there would be less official unemployment, but what would be the consequences of (re)constituting not only women but other less powerful segments of the population as dependent? What is to happen to what are now marginalised populations in post-employment societies? The post-industrial utopia has not created this polarisation, but it has provided a soft, if not flabby, intellectual climate unable to withstand the current dry winds.

This book consists, then, of practical evidence and theoretical arguments against the notion that the separation of income from work is timely or desirable. The first part looks at the theory that underpins proposals for breaking the cash/work nexus. Post-industrial intellectuals argue this could be a progressive solution to unemployment, but a close inspection (in chapter 1) of their various assumptions about governments suggests it is highly unlikely. The policy proposals are theoretically flawed by tendencies either to ignore the state's potential roles or to assume somewhat naively that future government might take a benign role regarding those facing lifetimes of unemployment.

Chapter 2 considers the imposition of the cash/work nexus during industrialisation, emphasising the key strategies of collective resistance last century. One major attempt to escape from the wage labour nexus (mainly through rural subsistence) gradually became impossible for increasing segments and categories of populations. Another option, to weaken the cash/work nexus through resistance from within, by union movements and their related political parties, became more prevalent and effective for white men.

From the 1960s onwards, the relatively comfortable position of organised workers in many countries was challenged from below and above. During the turbulent time when Blacks and women, in particular, made their own claims and various 'wars on poverty' were launched (with some success), the counter culture staked out a radical position meant to *break* rather than further weaken the cash/work nexus. Post-industrial approaches have their basis in the theory and practice of the counter culture, as chapter 3 explains. Although the alienation of prevailing authoritarian work structures was their core political focus, some elements of the counter culture began to query why people should work at all; others marginalised themselves from mainstream activism in communes.

A decade later post-industrialists became enthusiastic about breaking the cash/work nexus in a new context of developing unemployment, recession, global relocation of industry and rapid technological change. Fatalism was widespread. The vision became one that aimed to establish this break more thoroughly, with extensive underpinning from governments in providing guaranteed incomes and institutional supports for all kinds of 'work'. The claim was that such an alternative to wage labour would empower the newly called underclass and draw them into political activism and work activities more rewarding than conventional employment.

The second part of this book compares such theoretical projections with practical evidence of those governments that have already implemented or proposed exactly the same policies for various segments of the unemployed. The three chapters of this part are offered, therefore, as *test cases* for the post-industrial strategy, regardless of whether it is proposed for countries in Europe, Australasia or north America. While there are significant variations in the historical and policy contexts of OECD countries' experiences of unemployment, the strategy presumes a relatively high level of state intervention for proper implementation. The test cases come mainly from exactly that type of government, namely Australia's.

These cases of alternatives in practice demonstrate that guaranteed incomes have been proposed by Australian and United States governments not so as to *extend* institutional support to the most powerless but in order to *withdraw* whatever may be available. Worker co-operatives and communes were promoted by Labor governments in Australia that were ostensibly committed to *improve* the situation of the unemployed, but which used these schemes to achieve the opposite. In practice the post-industrial strategy is shown to be seriously flawed, wherever it might be implemented.

The final part of the book explores the nexus between citizens and work. The issues not only concern present economic contingencies but also encroach on far more fundamental questions about the constitution of citizenship and the marginalisation of those excluded. The result of pursuing the post-industrial strategy in Australia led directly to proposals for dole-work, internationally a popular conservative theme. Politically acceptable levels of unemployment grow higher and higher as chapter 7 recounts. Citizens' rights are only available for the employed: the rest face imposed duties and heightened state surveillance.

Chapter 8 considers the pessimism about curing chronic unemployment and related optimism about breaking the cash/work nexus, and finds both to be unjustified. Comparative studies emphasise different experiences of unemployment rather than a uniform, post-industrial global order. In chapter 9, the nature of collective and individual participation in the numerous modern arenas is evaluated. The question here is whether political engagement, leisure pursuits, domestic tasks and informal work activities are only potentially satisfying, or possible at all, when governmental or personal dependence is not imposed. In the light of the evidence, it seems that those who are excluded from mainstream work become more powerless and experience a more meaningless life than those who are included. Likewise, governments become less accountable to and more authoritarian in their dealings with those categories already excluded. Expectations that people will experience an enhanced policial life using the free time they gain through being unemployed are unfounded. Instead of these post-industrial dreams, it is time, the book concludes, to renew a political commitment to job creation by searching for new ways to give universal opportunities to take on responsible forms of publicly visible and socially useful employment.

PART I

Breaking the Nexus in Theory

CHAPTER 1

The Post-industrial Strategy:
Alternatives to Wage Labour as Policy?

Contemporary experience has been marked in many places by the gradual acceptance of chronic unemployment as a basic facet of modern life. New and old terms have appeared to describe the phenomenon – a *dualised* society has emerged, with a permanent *underclass* of out-of-work populations at one pole and the more fortunate, *tax-paying* citizens of the workforce at the other. The *core* populations are separate from those on the periphery, the marginalised people who move in a nether world between the *contingent* workforce and the status of welfare client. In many OECD countries the number of homeless and the extent of begging have increased, as has the use of these invidious distinctions.

At the same time, long-term unemployment has been accompanied by an apathy and a fatalism which have (further) marginalised unemployment as an issue. Moreover, newly popular perceptions have also *devalued our understanding of work* in capitalist societies, particularly in its mainstream form of protected wage labour. Where striving for full employment was formerly regarded as a duty for a society to uphold, its supporters are now few and seen as passé and ignorant of 'post-industrial trends'. The resurgence of laissez-faire economics has boosted utilitarian conceptions of work – we work merely to buy goods and leisure – while justifying unemployment and deregulated wage labour under the banners of efficiency and inflation.

Political and intellectual responses to these socio-economic conditions, while extremely diverse, have nevertheless made the prevailing climate in many OECD countries one where high rates of unemployment are politically acceptable. The basic concern in this book is with a range of responses to structural unemployment from both governments and intellectuals; responses that bear certain similarities but have quite different motivations behind them.

9

On the one hand, post-industrial intellectuals have been motivated to defend the unemployed. Even more, they propose certain provisions for those outside the mainstream of wage labour that they believe would *challenge* the prevailing political–social system. They claim that it is time for a thorough separation of income from work, so as to overturn present conservative tendencies and enhance political participation. According to this position, *alternatives to wage labour* are preferable to demanding jobs, because employment is merely a discipline that prevents citizens from engaging in the politics of their society: indeed, employment is quite unrelated to citizenship.

On the other hand a number of state policies directed at implementing such post-industrial schemes have been formulated in several countries. The political motivation for such policies by no means involves an acceptance of the aims of the post-industrial challenge to the political–economic system. To the contrary, these governments have been interested in the schemes merely as potential *solutions to problems faced by the state* in dealing with the growing underclass of unemployed. The impact of this government interest has yet to be faced by those post-industrial theorists who, under present conditions, take refuge in a total rejection of the idea of full employment. The critical problem is that governments (in Australia in particular) have been able to transform the proposals (as potential challenges to wage labour) into *a further marginalisation* of the poor and unemployed. The implications of these government designs for alternatives to mainstream work provide, therefore, a counterfactual argument against the likelihood that the unemployed could become politically active. In effect, the post-industrial strategy of alternatives to wage labour has failed to consider that governments have already taken on similar positions to legitimise a form of non-participation in no way connected with ameliorating the situation of the unemployed.

The aim of this book is to defend the idea of full employment, without being utopian about any restoration of some 'Golden Age'. My defence is based on asking whether there is an alternative to wage labour that does not seriously weaken the citizenship of whole categories of the population. The answers – to be found especially in state activities – demonstrate that there is none. Over the years, it will be demonstrated, particular governments have attempted to introduce a range of alternatives, not in order to undermine wage labour, but as alternatives to income support or to finding proper employment for marginalised groups. Indeed, far from being influenced by post-industrial intellectuals, governments have used similar schemes to render the unemployed more powerless. For example, President Nixon nearly introduced a guaranteed income scheme designed to reduce the number of female welfare claimants and to force male Black populations into low-paid sectors of the labour market. Other governments favoured guaranteed incomes to cut back welfare services. In Australia, although recent Labor governments insisted that they were committed to full employment, this supposed commitment in fact began with a pursuit of 'alternatives to paid work' (their phrase). Young unemployed were to learn how to survive on communes, and redundant adult workers were to purchase the folding or bankrupt enterprises that formerly employed them and convert them into worker co-operatives. Rather than promoting a post-industrial vision, such attention to 'alternatives' only served to further marginalise and silence the unemployed, and to trim welfare budgets.

What I aim to demonstrate, therefore, is that post-industrial claims to empower the unemployed are fundamentally flawed. Now that governments have formulated employment (or rather employment free) policies based on proposals such as those outlined above, we can see the practical implications of the post-industrial utopia. It is clear that very similar schemes or strategies supported by governments have themselves been to the detriment of the unemployed. While job creation is a difficult issue, the proposition that full employment is undesirable and should not even be an *aim* in policy has further eroded the rights to and chances of political participation of those already excluded from the labour market.

The arguments supporting my claim point out serious fallacies in this wishful thinking and show that a reassessment of the employment debate is long overdue. I argue that, contrary to post-industrial assumptions, employment is very much a part of being a citizen and that the issue of employment must be cast in terms of rights and obligations that make it possible to participate in the life of the society. The case is not that wage labour is so good, or that the meaning of citizenship should be reduced to membership of the workforce. Far from these limitations, the issue is rather that exclusion from the mainstream of economic life cannot even allow for the possibility of developing an inclusive, active citizenry.

What are the key arguments in this contemporary employment

debate? During this lengthy period of unemployment, the most progressive debates on the issue have been sharply divided about the status of work. One school of thought, supported by a new generation of post-industrial writers which emerged as the recession set in, has moved beyond the futurologists of the previous boom years – like Daniel Bell and Alvin Toffler with their optimistic, if simplistic, predictions about the end of industrial society. Writers like Barry Jones, Andre Gorz, Bill Jordan, Fred Block, John Keane and Claus Offe broadly agree about how the changes wrought by the slump are apparently hastening the trend towards a post-industrial future. Full employment will not return, they argue, mainly because new technology has decisively displaced labour. They urge that the dearth of jobs, the cause of such wasted lives in the short term, could be the basis of a societal transformation in the long term. In their view, it was time for 'sleepers' to wake and take the path to 'liberation from work', for a revolution is inaugurating a structural or even 'system' change to post-industrial society.[1] Alternatives to wage labour are preferable to futile attempts at job creation, they suggest, as long as the unemployed are supported financially by governments, since with greater free time they are likely to become politically active and thus to transform these societies.

The opposing school refuses to accept that unemployment is a permanent fact of life. The situation facing the unemployed could at least be improved by political will and, if the old Keynesian strategies are insufficient and problematic, by various schemes for creating jobs.[2] Though both sides deplore the effects of chronic unemployment, those favouring full employment seriously doubt that the unemployed could participate actively in politics, on the grounds that people who are excluded from mainstream work are likely to be marginalised from society.

This basic disagreement between the post-industrial school and the full employment school has produced a succession of claims and counter claims ever since the prevailing political message in much of the OECD world began to be that unemployment must be tolerated to cure inflation. What can we make of these claims, given that unemployment rates have barely improved in the meantime? In this book we will see that various government 'employment' strategies have been closely related to the post-industrial position. The results, in each case, are that the unemployed – the weakest group in the society – are in an even worse position than before and, far from participating actively in political life, are more and more facing the authority of governments as powerless clients.

My chief criticism of this utopian intellectual response is that it fails to consider how similar schemes have been instrumentalised by governments and how this is an inevitable outcome. This contemporary, progressive, intellectual culture – a very influential one – has not been prepared to reject such government policy proposals, in the distant hope that the alternatives might still have subversive effects. But no existing government will permit this possibility.

THE POST-INDUSTRIAL CLAIM

The post-industrial debate has had a many sided, if not tortuous, development. By looking briefly at the origins of the general idea, the premises involved in the later challenge to work and the work ethic are more easily scrutinised. For a start, the notion that modern societies could be moving beyond an industrial logic to a *post-industrial* one became popular in the United States during the 1960s, on the grounds that mass universities, the service sector and the number of white collar workers were all increasing rapidly. The emphasis was no longer on the production of manufactured goods but far more on the provision of services. Attendant upon this new emphasis, many predicted the end of industrial class conflict, especially during the decade of student unrest throughout the West, and argued that traditional proletarian politics were now over. The right wing version of the post-industrial thesis, such as that of Daniel Bell, saw a growth in professional autonomy and job satisfaction for all these service sector workers, accompanied by social decisions being reached harmoniously through 'scientific' and technical means. A left wing European version, as represented by neo-Marxist Alain Touraine, presented a bleaker post-industrial vision of emerging transnational managers of change and technocratic controllers with increased powers based on new communications technology. Those critical of the notion at the time questioned whether these changes amounted to a transformed post-industrial society or a deeper continuity. They pointed out that the service sector consisted primarily of jobs like cleaning and secretarial work that suffered the same industrial discipline and conditions as the manufacturing sector, and that the projections from Toffler and Bell (among others) served in fact to mask a further concentration of capitalist corporatist power.[3]

After the collapse of the long boom, a new generation of post-industrial theorists emerged to tackle the issue of unemployment, with none of the earlier, simplistic faith in technical solutions to the now rapid decline of industrial employment. Their line, in very broad outline, is that the contraction of the industrial sector and the concurrent micro-electronic revolution are irreversible, while the service sector, particularly according to Barry Jones, is incapable of generating a job growth to make up for the loss of manufacturing jobs. Although their position is sympathetic with the situation of the unemployed, it opposes all proposals for a new commitment to full employment on the grounds that such policies can only lead to an increasingly authoritarian and unworkable defence of the status quo. In this view, unemployment is permanent.[4] An actual breaking of the cash/work nexus is, however, considered potentially desirable and preferable to devising futile and punitive job schemes. John Keane, for example, argues that the cash/work nexus is a key characteristic of modern employment societies because the possession of a job is the only (or predominant) way to secure the right to an income. Jobs, however, are based only on their profit-making potential, which entails constant moves to drive down wages and control the work process. Unemployment is, and always has been, endemic in societies where profit is the sole determinant of an investor's calculation about whether or not to buy labour power.

Most post-industrialists assume the possibility that the inequities of employment societies would be undermined by the separation of income from work. Aware that the existing form of unemployment cannot achieve this transformation, Keane and Claus Offe especially emphasise *two conditions* that are necessary for such a change. The first would provide an alternative source of income. Hence, wage labour should be abandoned only if an income could be guaranteed for all, irrespective of 'activity'. Second, 'work' should be redefined to include housework, hobbies, informal work, subsistence farming, do-it-yourself projects (such as home building) and gardening, through the more autonomous self-regulation of these activities within communes, co-operatives, and other modes of household or neighbourhood networks and self-help organisations. This non-mainstream work (which is quite distinct from 'employment') should be institutionally supported by the state; recognition should be given to useful work irrespective of remuneration.

Following from all this, they assert that the unemployed would be *likely* to use their free time to be politically active if their incomes were guaranteed (by the state). The result would be a societal transformation that would *challenge the political system* and enhance personal autonomy. These changes would also reduce the centrality of the mainstream commodity markets because the numbers of commodity buyers and sellers would decline as alternative 'economies' proliferated. It would, therefore, serve as a solution both to the structural problem of an over-supply of labour and to the situation of the unemployed. Different post-industrial authors present different versions of this utopia. In arguing for 'a more relaxed and more frugal way of life',[5] some have favoured leisure as a genuine alternative (Andre Gorz), since they see nothing liberatory about paid work and argue that most people are 'allergic' to jobs. Others are more aware that the trauma of unemployment is related to a human need for work (Claus Offe; John Keane), or simply want us to recognise that housewives, students and hobbyists are usefully 'employed' (Barry Jones).

Nevertheless, all emphasise alternative ways of living and working, drawing implicitly upon the earlier debates and experiments of the counter culture, with its rural communes and worker co-operatives. Most also demonstrate an awareness of the feminist movement's drive to politicise domestic labour, by recognising that it is necessary and useful work that is seen as of little value because it is unpaid. They have been unanimous in demanding the right not to engage in paid work. The assumption is that the exclusion of a significant number from the workforce can be ameliorated and even improved by other forms of societal participation, especially in the stress on liberation from the cash/work nexus and, as Gorz puts it, the 'politics of free time'.

The work ethic, or celebration of work as a goal in life, is regarded as reactionary (Gorz) and a 'moribund chain' that still binds people to work. Barry Jones suggests that we should 'abandon the masochistic doctrine of work for work's sake'.[6] The work ethic is a ruling class ideology, according to most post-industrialists, that maintains relations of domination by inculcating a moral commitment to paid work and an appreciation of industriousness. This ideological hold is therefore the main reason why the unemployed are so deluded in wanting paid work, even if their incomes could be guaranteed. The separation of income from work would, however, challenge the value structure of modern societies, especially this work ethic.

The post-industrial position regarding the service sector, in contrast to Daniel Bell's optimistic vision of autonomous professionals, is now completely pessimistic about its future, especially since it presently consists so largely of unskilled, poorly paid and insecure jobs. Contemporary post-industrialists insist that the micro-electronic revolution displaces not only manufacturing labour but also service labour, like that in retailing, storage, maintenance and information processing.[7] The rest of the labour-intensive service sector is assumed to exist only as long as servile labour is available. They point to the futility of so-called junk jobs and argue that there are few creative or meaningful areas of paid work left where jobs could be created.

Although in most cases the post-industrial strategy is a sympathetic attempt to confront these serious contemporary problems in an innovative manner, its claim to actually offer progressive solutions is questionable.

A PROGRESSIVE SOLUTION OR A FLAWED POLICY? POST-INDUSTRIAL ASSUMPTIONS ABOUT THE STATE

What are the major problems with this diagnosis and strategy? One of the most important flaws is its neglect of the role of governments. The strategy needs state intervention, yet what government would ever genuinely accept a challenge to the political system? The state, in fact, can easily ignore these progressive goals and use exactly the same proposals to further marginalise the powerless. In existing contexts, the provision of lifelong guaranteed and adequate incomes by the state is unimaginable virtually anywhere in the world.

Furthermore, post-industrialists assume that the unemployed might become politically active if their incomes were guaranteed. They present an attractive utopia of co-operatives, informal networking and mutual aid between households, although they admit that the whole scheme requires governmental underpinning. But government schemes to provide alternatives to employment, far from solving the problems facing the unemployed, let alone politicising them, only further weaken their rights as citizens.

How, then, can the flaws be identified? The assumption is that alternatives to wage labour would transcend mere employment and enhance citizenship. This is the critical hypothesis, and yet, because state support is required (especially to guarantee incomes), the role of governments in these strategies is critical. It is necessary to examine, therefore, the main post-industrial approaches to the state.

IGNORING THE STATE

The idea of separating income and work gained (renewed) currency as part of the theoretical reaction to a range of social problems emerging from the world recession of the 1970s. It was a time when rethinking 'work' became popular. An early influence on the idea came from research by Ray Pahl and Jonathon Gershuny, which hardly considered the state at all. Pahl suggested (for example), when unemployment initially became entrenched in Britain, that the growing importance of householders' self-provisioning, self-service and moonlighting was creating an important, 'productive' new sector, an 'informal economy', such that a shift from 'employment' to 'work' could prove 'more satisfying and rewarding': 'unemployment could, under certain specified conditions, be a positive benefit'.[8]

This was instantly popularised, and sparked lengthy debates and significant government interest. The conservative Ivan Illich was influential with his ideas about 'shadow work', convivial tools and the right to 'useful unemployment'.[9] Business professors argued that

> Universal employment is not only a dubious privilege, but one we cannot afford. Today there is a physical and psychological flight from modern employment. The growth of the informal or free economy offers a way forward. It promises greater opportunities for women, those with manual skills, and the permanent resident, although there is not much in it for the mobile executive on the make.[10]

Pahl himself later retracted the idea that the unemployed can survive without money, after finding that the opportunities for informal self-provisioning did not extend to unemployed households. He also admitted that 'an embarrassing amount of attention' had been devoted to his and Gershuny's earlier 'good news' about an 'informal economy' developing to save an ailing capitalism.[11]

Interest in the idea then turned to stress a need for state support for alternative forms of work through guaranteeing basic incomes. Little more was said about why governments had found the informal economy idea so attractive. Only the more traditional Marxists criticised the Pahl and Gershuny proposals. Their approach to the state is well known.

THE STATE AS RULING-CLASS TOOL

The Marxist view is that states act almost automatically to *incorporate* any oppositional tendency or optimistic strategy (such as Pahl's informal economy idea), due to an inescapable logic of ruling class interests. Conflict and change are explained mainly from this logic of capital–labour relations at national and international levels.

This approach was well represented by Enzo Mingione's assessment that the 1970s recession was effecting a trend towards 'neo-dualism' in Western societies. In 1978 he explained the marginalisation of large sections of these labour forces in terms of a contradictory policy 'implemented by capitalism' in order to squeeze wages further.[12] The contradictions for capitalism from mass unemployment, like the reduction of effective demand, were convincingly identified. Such frameworks, however, present capitalism as a conscious actor and give little room for the state's role in general, let alone exceptions to 'neo-dualism' such as are found, in particular, in Norway, Sweden or Japan. (To be fair, the same neglect of comparative analysis is common among post-industrialists.) Indeed, if dualism, where the marginalised unemployed are left to fend for themselves, is contradictory for a capitalist economy, it is far more so for the state.

State interest in alternatives to paid work is also more attributable to state problems than to ruling-class interests. The issue of the state was subsequently alluded to by Redclift and Mingione in 1985, in a critical review of the then fashionable preoccupation with studying informal or domestic forms of production, 'beyond employment'. They suggested that the rhetoric of self help, used to legitimate 'Rightist policies' of a reduced welfare state in the early eighties, had been directly derived from that earlier optimism of writers like Pahl about the efficacy of alternative or household survival strategies.[13] While such Marxists were understandably concerned with social dislocation and growing polarisation as unemployment set in, they tended merely to set down the state incorporation of the informal economy idea to an 'irony'.

Less concerned with this problem of state incorporation was Andre Gorz who, at much the same time, analysed the decline of the French industrial working class, and farewelled the Marxist hopes for a revolutionary proletariat by welcoming a new revolutionary subject, the 'non-class of non-workers'.[14] His views were the most popularly read of all among progressives, and thus launched the wishful thinking surrounding Gorz's rather vague idea that a benign state could develop from a 'non-class' revolution.

THE STATE AS 'STEERING' THE SYSTEM

Most post-industrialists, however, reject traditional Marxist explanations either of the potential for a revolution – whether of a class or a non-class – or of inevitable incorporation. If the modern 'capitalist state' is neither determined by class power nor a mere tool of the ruling class, then a revolution will not necessarily solve the problem of state power. Post-industrialists mostly take a 'system' approach. This position is represented especially by Claus Offe, Jurgen Habermas and Fred Block who, during the 1980s, became the most influential proponents of the separation of income from work.

Habermas and Offe provide many fruitful paths for explaining modern Western developments. Both insist upon an analytical distinction between 'state and society' for a more adequate understanding of modern societies than that provided by traditional Marxism, and for finding paths beyond the present structures. They posit certain differences between state power and class power. Habermas uses an engine metaphor, where the two 'steering mechanisms' for 'the system' are 'power and money'. They also qualify the popular liberal view that 'the state' is all-pervasive.[15] Since legitimation is partly derived from the state's supposed impartiality, both argue that the state cannot act directly as a class agent, but neither is it a neutral arbiter. The state is dependent upon taxes and finances from the capitalist economy and, despite its increasing involvement in the economy during this century, it is not in a position to organise the accumulation process itself. Therefore the state has an 'institutional self-interest' in maintaining and facilitating the expansion of the capitalist economy. This state interest does not necessarily mean an 'alliance' with the ruling class, nor is it *always* linked with capitalist 'class pressure' upon the state.[16] Rather, it is for the state's own sake.

If Western democratic states, in this view, still reproduce capitalism, these efforts are continually contradicted by other functions facing states, above all by the necessity to maintain the legitimacy of this process. It is within these contradictions, moreover, that Habermas and Offe can readily identify 'state problems'. With the advent of a 'historic compromise' between capital and labour, social welfare and mass democracy became the two legitimating planks of Western states. And yet the power of the state remains limited by being basically excluded from the economic system but simultaneously dependent upon the movements of the economy. As the twentieth century progressed, the state had to ensure government finances and electoral success by increasingly intervening to manage economic (accumulation) crises and to provide cash transfers and social wages, or goods for use value not exchange value. But such decommodification by the state, especially of commodities such as labour, continually undermines market movements.

Hence, from this system point of view, unemployment is a state problem for many reasons. In accordance with classical economics, if unemployment meant facing the alternatives of starvation or the workhouse, the labour market would be naturally corrected since wages would be driven down and inflation cured, so the demand for labour would rise again. Struggles against these punitive alternatives were linked with the advent of popular democracy, and job creation and unemployment benefits do indeed decommodify labour power or weaken the cash/work nexus (since the human beings attached to labour power can survive without selling it to the lowest bidder). Liberal democracies have found unemployment a problem, not just because of effects on state budgets and on the economy of diminishing consumer demand, but also in the perennial problems for the state of legitimation from below at election times. Such governments (in general) are forced to maintain the unemployed with cash transfers rather than risk an increase in violence or allow embarrassing scenes of public starvation. But this does not allow the 'cure' of unemployment prescribed by classical economic theory to be effected. Budget deficits become larger and larger, partly from increases in social security cash transfers, while the corporate sector, in supposed alliance with tax payers, frequently uses the country's deficit as a further tool to blackmail governments. Consequently, governments become further dependent upon 'business confidence' about new investment, since their basic revenue comes from taxation and finances from the capitalist economy.[17] Indeed, to push this 'system' line further, marginalising sections of the unemployed away from labour-force participation (that is, from claiming unemployment benefits) without risking unpopularity with voters, is therefore a state interest (a point I will return to later).

This critical perspective takes into account the 'reality' of state power, which liberals criticise as though it inevitably intervenes effectively (for state purposes) against the operation of the market. The liberal position against the state's involvement in social justice, and against bureaucratic encroachments of all kinds, offers a return to market distribution with its resultant 'dualising' effect of chronic unemployment. While readily acknowledging the 'invasion' of state 'steering mechanisms' into public and private spheres of everyday life, Habermas and Offe demonstrate that the state, *even when* it is attempting to pursue a social democratic path, is continually thwarted by having no option but to maintain accumulation. As James O'Connor pointed out in the 1970s, this maintenance hardly represents an 'encroachment' on the economy but rather a necessary but inexorable source of state debt. The process should not be seen as the inevitable 'logic' of state domination but as a problem of contradictory policies. In this view, the state has a limited range of actions with which to intervene in the economy, and these would remain limited even if its own dynamic were more accessible to oppositional and popular demands. In the face of accumulation problems, it is also a state interest to avoid being accessible and accountable.

The explanatory potential of these theories to account for contemporary social developments is quite significant. Both Habermas' and Offe's work are useful for identifying 'systematic limitations' of contemporary welfare states and their internal contradictions by showing the main forms of contemporary crises occurring between the separate but interconnected subsystems.[18] The employment crisis is considered very carefully by Offe. Nevertheless, their system-oriented perspective is too global and insufficiently comparative. It does not allow criticism of particular state actions since, if one follows their logic, the use of alternatives to employment (which they propose) indeed coincides with current state interests, at least in countries that have accepted high levels of unemployment.

This problem becomes clear when one considers Offe's rationale for the guaranteed income position he has maintained for some time.[19] Offe presents late twentieth-century society as a system comprising four subsystems, those of 'material production, cultural reproduction, political public sphere and state domination'. He argues that a major problem facing 'the system' is that only the subsystems are really 'open for options'. The relations between the subsystems are, however, 'rigid, fatal and sealed off from any freedom of choice', and the co-ordination between them is also grossly inadequate.[20] He mentions several options for overcoming this problem, such as redesigning the co-ordination or making state administration more efficient, but suggests that the only effective solution would be to *reduce* the demand for co-ordination by 'unburdening' each subsystem's 'social steering mechanisms' (by reducing 'steering needs').[21] What would this entail? Offe singles out the problem of unemployment.

The subsystem, state, is 'overburdened' by demands from the unemployed for paid work (and, it has to be said, for unemployment benefits), but the only existing mechanism for providing jobs is for the state to foster more economic growth. The economy (material production) is as dependent on state policies as the state is on the economy, but state decommodification only creates the above market problems. The possibility for 'unburdening' these two subsystems that Offe proposes is to 'uncouple' income and work through a guaranteed income. It would, he argues, give relief to 'substantial economic and socio-political steering problems'. He bases this possibility on the grounds that commodity production is sufficiently modernised already. The implication is that the two subsystems could only 'renounce' further modernisation if those demanding paid work were instead guaranteed an income. 'The system' would function better if co-ordination and compatibility between sub-systems were improved by making them less dependent upon each other. This would – it is implied – reduce the number of contradictory policies that the state has to pursue.

Despite Offe's qualifications,[22] a guaranteed income scheme considered from this systems approach can really only ease the dysfunctions, especially of unemployment, arising from contradictory policies – it is a form of 'crisis management' from above. Jean Cohen suggests that Offe inadvertently supports a 'technocratic illusion' that steering mechanisms can be autonomous,[23] or separate from the values and norms entrenched in all subsystems. In this case, it means that he is asking us to accept that the state should ignore demands from below and, for that matter, struggles over the definitions of norms themselves, which Offe himself would see as central to new social movements.[24] But why should demands (like those for jobs) be ignored? What might be the effects of merely meeting 'system requirements'?

The problem here is that if the state is meant to act as an autonomous entity and in this way to correct dysfunctions, there is no assurance that it will not marginalise people to suit its own interests. Although the motivating force for theorists like Offe and Habermas is the potential for democratic changes, the proposal that the state should ignore demands (and thereby invalidate them) would result in there being no checks on the state from outside its own field of action, nor any reason for it to act in a democratic manner.

And where unemployment is concerned, in fact, it is in the state's interest to marginalise sections of the unemployed away from labour force participation (or from claiming unemployment benefits), while not appearing to be that harsh. This is because it may reduce the budget deficit and inflation, if those so marginalised have to take any work at any price. In this sense, Offe's post-industrial strategy in a number of points coincides with state interests in a manner which seems to defeat his own democratic ideals.

In addition, applying Offe's 'unburdening' proposal to reduce demands for co-ordination is hardly appealing as a democratic method of easing dysfunctions in the subsystem of the 'political public sphere'. It suggests an autonomy – if not futile isolation – of public demands far removed from the other subsystems. But from the state's point of view it would, no doubt, reduce the 'demand overload' and the 'legitimation deficit' which confront it. Here again, where Offe is concerned, this deficit is seen in a one-dimensional manner which involves insufficient 'mass loyalty'.

The problem, as Cohen argues,[25] is that Offe's theory can only identify behaviour that is functional or dysfunctional for the maintenance of the system, by showing how interest conflicts are actually created by 'crisis management' or structural reform. It is difficult from his perspective to assess social action or social movement conflicts that are not based solely on capital or labour interests, but on wider social struggles that can and do emerge from below. (This is despite Offe's recognition of new social movements.)

Fred Block has pursued a similar path in his post-industrial assessment of new 'macroeconomic management problems'. The idea of 'reindustrialisation' is, for Block, an impossible myth, because, he argues, the modernised economy has reached saturation limits.

This may well be so but, like Offe, he proposes reshaping state-society relations through a 'disburdening' or a 'debureaucratization of the state' by, for example, freeing the poor from state regulation. For example, if the dole were given in a lump sum, individuals could start their own small businesses or provide non-profit services.[26] Unlike Habermas, Block concedes a potential for politicisation within existing workplaces, and he does favour government provision of incentives to conserve jobs. Nevertheless, a guaranteed income would serve as a 'final cushion' and state support should be given for worker co-operatives and so forth.[27] Unlike Offe, he insists that the state's 'capacity for effective action' can only be increased if 'nonstate actors' are mobilised and political participation revived, but he also suggests a need for the state to mobilise actors as well.[28] But why would the state mobilise political struggles from below unless forced to respond? Again, Block offers an unintended top down approach which contradicts his proposed 'debureaucratization'.

Habermas' crisis theory does not intend to exclude the conflictual aspect of social action from below, as expressed in 'new' social movements (but not the labour movement).[29] In contrast to Offe's interest-based criteria, Habermas aims to assess 'genuine loyalty' or legitimacy of the political system,[30] as well as the claims of social movements, through communication criteria. Social action is analysed from the perspective of communicative interaction rather than the instrumental action which is, for him, the basis of and key problem with the Marxian emphasis on work and production.

Habermas justifies separating income from work with a diagnosis that the present limitations of the welfare state are due to its feeding on the image of 'laboring society'.[31] The European workers' movements were inspired by a utopian ideal of independent producers. But its inherent 'productivist' vision of progress has subsequently magnified the distortions of instrumental rationality to the point of endangering the world. Similarly, the social democratic reformism it also inspired has now resulted in a welfare state paternalism that is no longer acceptable. Habermas suggests that 'dissidents of industrial society' recognise that it is insufficient to control the capitalist economy but that the 'project' of the welfare state has the additional task *now* to contain the state itself.[32] To do this, 'it would obviously lose labor as its central point of reference', partly by a guaranteed minimum income that would shield the 'lifeworld' from both the 'employment system's inhuman imperatives' and from the counterproductive effects of 'administratively providing for human life as a whole'.

This proposal is a logical outcome of Habermas' long-held position that the potential for emancipation lies not in the instrumental activities of work but in radical discourse or 'ideal speech-situations'. Social action is assessed according to criteria of a counterfactual, consensual nature: these are 'idealisations' yet they occur in 'everyday practice'.[33] Since communicative interaction is oriented to reaching an understanding, whereas strategic or instrumental action aims at influence over others, Habermas suggests that the repression and rigidity of distorted communication patterns would decrease through wider realisation of the former. Such claims are posited as values,[34] but his interpretation is, nevertheless, made from a utopian position. Explanation of the present – such as the reasons for particular demands being made – is also difficult, for the claims made by Habermas for communicative interaction are not grounded in actual social developments. Instead, he maintains that the necessary although insufficient conditions for the extension of interpretive understanding can be found everywhere.

The only link between these communicative criteria for analysing social movements – or actual social or historical agents,[35] making demands at a particular time – is his 'colonisation–decolonisation' model of systemic crises. But here, too, historical agents are difficult to identify. Habermas argues that the 'system', with its two specific steering mechanisms of money (economy) and power (state) are increasingly invading or 'colonising' the sphere of symbolic reproduction or the public and private arenas of everyday life ('lifeworld'). Communicative interactions are constantly being replaced with strategic interactions. Social movements contest this process of 'colonisation' by the state or the economy.[36] These criteria lead Habermas to regard feminism as the one modern social movement that is emancipatory and offensive, rather than merely defensive or retreating into 'particularism',[37] only because feminism appears to affirm enlightenment values, such as universalism and freedom, while also articulating protests and needs made public through systemic crises.[38] But the crises and protests, and especially the reasons for their emergence, are far from clear since they can only be interpreted through his communicative perspective. Even within feminism, this approach neglects the historical contexts and the gains and losses of early feminism, as well as the disputes *within* feminism.[39]

More to the point here, it can easily be agreed that Habermas' proposal that both economy and state should be 'contained' is certainly important, if that means rendering both of them more accountable, just and democratic. But from which arenas and in what historical contexts could such containment take place? Because a guaranteed income requires state implementation, the issue is whether such a policy is likely to 'contain' the state at all, let alone the commodity markets. Is it possible, in other words, that the state could be democratised through this process? A further question is whether a guaranteed income in principle offers any source of community whatever, or any identity from which demands could emerge.

Indeed, by applying the system approach, the opposite tendency is found more easily than that suggested by Habermas (or Offe). The post-industrial proposal to seek alternatives to wage labour coincides very easily with state interests, in marginalising the unemployed further. As will be demonstrated, it has legitimised redefinitions of work by governments and provided a simplistic and popular 'solution' to the very real problems of low paid, dull and routine jobs (a consequence of workers' lack of control in most workplaces), as well as of unemployment itself. On the question of a guaranteed income again, the assumption that a government might guarantee a *generous* income in the contemporary context, or give proper support to alternative structures, is questionable even from a system view of state 'steering mechanisms' acting strategically.

Other problems cannot be very adequately dealt with from a system framework. Even if, as the following chapters will show, many government schemes for alternatives to employment were eventually not implemented because of contradictory demands, the governments involved still did achieve relative success in redefining work, removing rights and, indeed, taking welfare paternalism to new extremes. Offe's explanation of the successes and failures of state strategies according to the 'functional imperatives' of accumulation and legitimation neglects what has been called the 'strategic intelligence' that state agencies can display.[40] (So here the alternative schemes were worth pursuing for other state reasons.) Furthermore, the social-historical context in various Western countries, both of struggles and of state responses, are more specific than that allowed by the system crisis perspective. If Sweden has maintained a 3 per cent unemployment rate for some time, why has the Swedish state not faced the same contradictions as other states? If state actions are not always due to contradictions, other explanations of state responses must be found.

Post-industrialists point out that a full employment scheme is likely to increase state authoritarianism. This is a possibility, although there seems to be a failure on their part to recognise that citizens have no control over an income set by the state. For example, other proponents of a guaranteed income, notably John Keane, follow Habermas' and Offe's opposition to full employment on the grounds that such labour market decisions would be made by a strong bureaucratic state. Like Fred Block, the method of allocating labour power that Keane favours is one that is directed through decisions by 'individuals, co-operatives and trade unions'.[41] What we must query, however, is whether those individual decisions could change the structure of the labour market to the benefit of the segments at the bottom.

Some writers have subsequently modified their stand on abandoning full employment. Andre Gorz, in particular, having argued that people are deluded in wanting jobs, underwent a sea change in his 1989 proposal that people *should* retain the private property of their labour power through securing the opportunity to sell it on the market.[42] Yet there are new and equally influential adherents of the post-industrial view. Bill Jordan, in particular, has costed a basic income scheme for Britain and endorses its potential to foster the 'common good' of all citizens.[43] By 1989 this basic income idea was seen by Stuart Hall and David Held as an element in reviving citizenship in Britain.[44] Offe, Habermas and Block have not, so far as I am aware, changed their positions, although Block recently stressed that work has intrinsic benefits if it is a 'good job'. In the meantime he still urges a basic income for everyone else, and assumes like Keane and Jordan that it would improve workers' ability to reject poor jobs and lead to greater leisure.[45] Jordan is bemused that women seem to prefer and even enjoy being in the world of paid work, despite jobs being hardly, in his view, 'good'.[46] Few ask whether an entitlement to receive cash from the state might be a rather poor source of solidarity or inclusiveness.

THE STATE AS AGENT OF CHANGE

Alain Touraine is possibly the only post-industrialist who has not entered this employment debate (or proposed a guaranteed or basic income scheme). Touraine's action or conflict-oriented framework does not permit a technocratic approach. He originally defined post-industrial society as an extension and *broadening* of technocratic control in a pessimistic prognosis quite at odds with that of Daniel Bell.[47] Because his theory is concerned with struggles for self-management that emerge from below, it avoids (mostly) the system-oriented approach exemplified by Offe. It constantly asks who has control over social change, rather than assessing whether oppositional movements are carriers of a communicative utopia. Habermas and Offe regard the subsystems of state and economy as acting strategically (whether successfully or not) only in the face of systemic contradictions. This does not always help to account for specific social changes that may vary in different societies. Touraine, by contrast, attempts to explain social change by providing a model with which to analyse particular contests for control between a particular state and both dominant and subordinate groups. It is from these relations that the kinds of change that occur can be identified. And where Habermas (or Offe) defines the state according to its steering capacity, where it may be reactive, adjustive or manipulative, Touraine defines it as an 'agent of change'. He sets up a model of state versus society, emphasising their continual effects upon each other while refusing to regard society as an harmonious, unified entity. In addition, Touraine proposes that since norms are defined institutionally, and imposed from above on organised everyday life, contesting a norm is always a political act. His model can help to explain the continual processes of conflict, as they affect the paths taken by a particular state. Indeed, such a notion of the state being the 'agent of change' illuminates some of the modern dilemmas involved in the concept of state sovereignty.

Assessing alternatives such as guaranteed income schemes through an action framework concerned with struggle from below is more fruitful, I propose, than using Habermas' problematic communication criteria, even though Habermas and Offe are more useful in *identifying* systemic 'state problems', such as unemployment. In addition, although Touraine recognises that union conflicts can often be regarded as demands for self-management, and that conflictual participation in work structures provides some of these possibilities while exclusion gives none (*contra* any basic income scheme), Touraine himself has hardly justified his selection of one exclusively oppositional movement per 'type' of society. Hence the labour movement should be regarded as one movement among several in either industrial or post-industrial societies and it may, one day, revive or 'move' again.

Broadly speaking, Alain Touraine is a representative of the so-called neo-Marxian school. Like many social theorists,[48] Touraine has repeatedly emphasised his efforts to transcend, analytically, the 'old dualisms', particularly between 'structural objectivism' and 'revolutionary subjectivism' (in this respect, at least, his is rather like Anthony Giddens' approach[49]). As we saw, traditional Marxism tends to a structural determinism, while a liberal perspective on radical alternatives would ignore the evidence of the case studies, where continual struggles over oppositional demands were transformed in various ways by governments and distorted into demands for market liberation by sections of the dominant economic class.

Touraine does not define social movements in economic or systemic terms at all, although his perspective retains a concept of class relations, something which is lost from Habermas' and even Offe's perspective. Class relations are not used as an automatic explanatory device, however, and society is not seen as a social system with an 'inner logic' as in the engine metaphor, but primarily as a field of social action.[50] He rejects both economic determinism and teleological theories of change, choosing what he calls a 'sociology of conflicts' rather than a 'philosophy of contradiction' by questioning the wisdom of combining 'the contradictions of a system' with social action. Even if class domination has its own logic – capitalists seek profits – a social situation cannot be reduced to the *internal logic of domination*. As he argues,

> a social situation is also based on a *culture*, i.e. on the construction of the norms which determine the relations between a community and its environment and which, instead of representing the ideology of the dominator, actually define a social field; at the same time, a social situation is activated by social struggles which challenge, restrict or overthrow this domination and the repression it inflicts.[51]

Action is defined according to different levels of analysis whereby, for example, the individual actor is constrained and circumscribed in interactions at the level of everyday life. She or he may contest the prevailing norms but can only (collectively) become an 'historical actor' through social movements. At this level, however, the social relations and not individuals are the object of study.[52] In this way, according to Touraine, people do make history.

For Touraine the state is – through time – the chief agent of order (using a Weberian definition) but also of historical change.[53] While the *type* of change depends on the specific shape of class conflict, the state, seen as 'external' to class relations, ushers in the change. The state does not *serve* the 'ruling class' as a mere tool, but provides the principles of economic organisation whereby it may be defending the power of some 'partly archaic dominant class' or drawing support from 'the thrust of new forces'.[54] The state is the agent at the level of historical development – *not* of social evolution – so if the state dominates change, there is no unique principle that would explain the kind of change that may occur. Change, according to this 'statist' conception, is unpredictable and entirely contingent. It depends on an outside stimulus, and the direction the change takes depends on the form of the social structure or the types of historical alliances existing at any time, and the way these impact on or against the state. Social movements are not the actors of change, but what Touraine calls the 'catalytic agent of the force of change'.[55] They cannot be such actors because only the state has sovereignty, meaning both the appropriate means and the legal right to institutionalise social change.[56]

Accordingly, the state should be a central consideration in proposals for the future because the state is the predominant and unified entity in modern societies that is in a position to implement social change. (If sovereignty is further centralised to the new institutions of the European Community (EC), the argument still remains, as it does if new nation states emerge from present independence movements.) The qualitative *kinds* of change and order imposed by the state, however, are contingent upon the strengths and relative weaknesses of popular movements (or historical alliances) at any time. The social compromises that ensue can range, therefore, from being even more than now or, at the least, slightly less in the interests of the dominant economic class. To express this bluntly, whether the state is more open to the right or to the left, it will still manage change or maintain order.

What is useful from Touraine's approach, when we attempt to assess all the alternatives to wage labour, is especially the insight that the role of the state cannot be ignored. Whether democratic or not, the state will intervene in some way, and the less democratic, the more likely it is to distort proposals for alternative ways of living and working. In the 1990s, many liberal democracies are increasingly undemocratic, and the power of dominant groups is more concentrated. If the separation of income from work is possible, especially when employment trends may well become much worse, it still has to be asked whether alternatives to wage labour can be realised in a form that is desirable and acceptable for the society.

These are the questions that this book will attempt to answer. The assumptions about the state will be tested by looking at the various occasions when specific governments have tried to introduce alternatives via policy options like communes, worker co-operatives and guaranteed incomes. It will investigate, therefore, the general results of the post-industrial separation of income from work. This proposal is virtually indistinguishable from the state's interest in developing *non-participation,* which aims at the further marginalisation of the poor and unemployed, whose claims on the state will thus be rendered less visible and in that sense will actually subside.[57] There is now a widespread acceptance of punitive action against the unemployed, as the popularity of dole-work schemes demonstrates. They are blamed when they have no other option but to survive on a meagre income from the state. Yet their chances for political protest are extremely limited from a position of exclusion, where it is very difficult to develop a consciousness of subordination or for a real adversary to emerge. The feminist movement, for example, re-emerged when women's work participation was expanding rapidly. But our chief historical examples of action by those with the self-created identity of unemployed, are of the 1930s hunger marches. It does seem to me that the only content possible for demands 'from without' is the demand for inclusion, for jobs and for the opportunity to participate. Restructuring work from within work, which also involves the politicising of new needs from work has, as I see it, more potential than the abandonment of employment, and the related supposition that the unemployed might become politically active if only governments would guarantee their financial security. In contrast, governments, in an environment like that, will guarantee as little income as possible.

Employment should not be a *privilege,* however, because the labour market is stratified. The issue that remains is how society should continue to try to define work, rather than have definitions imposed from above. It seems fair to say that the meaningless and dull aspects of many kinds of paid work, that both exist now and could be created in the future, can only be transformed by actually participating in the work. For, although my defence of paid work may appear from an emancipatory viewpoint to be a defence of dull, powerless work – and more of it, they say – the onus is on the post-industrialists to show that the flight from wage labour will not make the situation worse. My position only recognises that alienation within work is never absolute. If *being there* by no means guarantees the possibility of active and conscious participation in paid work and, even less, any control over the process, the problem is that *being absent* or excluded from it makes this quite impossible. This is the paradox: work structures cannot be transformed through concerted, collective action, unless one is employed in them. Entry into a multiplicity of other spheres of life is, moreover, closely connected to one's participation in the everyday work structure.

The problem, therefore, is the post-industrial assumption that future governments will be benign and more accountable to the 'work-free'. It appears, rather, that whether the state is democratic or not, it will intervene, and the more powerless the citizens, the fewer defences they will have in checking the authoritarian and non-democratic tendencies of governments, as well as the dull compulsion of the market.

NOTES

1. For a summary of the post-industrial debate of the 1960s, see K. Kumar (1978). The most well known representatives are Daniel Bell (1973) and Alvin Toffler (1970). The shift in the position, after the recession, is shown by the titles chosen by, for example, Andre Gorz, *Paths to Paradise: On the Liberation from Work* (1985) and Barry Jones, *Sleepers Wake! Technology and the Future of Work* (1982).

2. An opposition to the post-industrialists emerged in debates in the United States, Europe and Britain by the mid 1980s, with representatives such as the following: Michael Rustin (1985); Goran Therborn (1986); Juliet Schor (1985), (1985a). In Australia, the most well known employment advocate, Keith Windschuttle, while not addressing the post-industrial argument, has a full employment position that could be termed as 'realistic' as that of Michael Rustin. He is, for example, no more optimistic about Keynesian strategies than John Keane, and sees them as labour displacing and as more expensive than other job creation schemes. See Windschuttle (1986).

3. A. Touraine (1971). Apart from Kumar's criticisms, see also the critique of the 'new' post-industrialists by Boris Frankel (1987).

4. More recent arguments, while similar to Barry Jones' earlier suggestions, are even more adamant that full employment is impossible and undesirable. See J. Keane & J. Owens (1986); J. Keane (1988), chapter 3; A. Gorz (1982); F. Block (1985); C. Offe (1984), (1987).
5. A. Gorz (1985), p. 37.
6. B. Jones (1982), p. 200
7. *ibid.*, pp. 65-7. Teaching is an example of 'information processing'.
8. Among many articles written on this at the end of the 1970s, see for example J.I. Gershuny (1979). The quotations are from R.E. Pahl (1980), p. 5. S. Burns (1975); and C. Handy (1982) were other proponents.
9. I. Illich (1981). Illich's *Tools for Conviviality* and *The Right to Useful Unemployment* appeared in 1973 and 1978 respectively.
10. D. Pym (1980), p. 223.
11. R.E. Pahl (1984), pp. 10-11. Pahl and Gershuny are critically considered by L. Morris (1988).
12. E. Mingione (1978) p. 212.
13. N. Redclift & E. Mingione (eds) (1985), p. 4.
14. A. Gorz (1982).
15. See B. Frankel (1978), pp. 28-42, for this point in a comparison of Marxist theories of the state, and also D. Held & J. Krieger (1983).
16. C. Offe & V. Ronge (1979).
17. This, in other words, is one of the legitimation problems stemming from fiscal crises facing Western governments. See J. Habermas (1975); J. O'Connor (1973).
18. See J. Keane, in C. Offe (1984a), pp. 11-34.
19. C. Offe (1987).
20. *ibid.*, p. 16.
21. *ibid.*, p. 19.
22. C. Offe (1984). Offe's qualifications therein are discussed in chapter 9.
23. J. Cohen (1982), pp. 25-6. Such a charge was the nub of Habermas' argument against Luhmann. See J. Habermas (1975), pp. 130-5.
24. For example, C. Offe (1978).
25. J. Cohen (1982).
26. F. Block (1987), pp. 29-33.
27. *ibid.*, pp. 138-40. This article was initially published in 1984.
28. *ibid.*, pp. 32-3.
29. J. Cohen (1982), pp. 26-7.
30. see Keane in C. Offe (1984a), p. 23.
31. J. Habermas (1986), p. 7.
32. *ibid.*, p. 14.
33. J. Habermas (1982), p. 235.
34. For example, *ibid.*, p. 237.
35. S. Benhabib (1981), p. 55.
36. See, for example, J. Habermas (1987), pp. 318-23.
37. J. Habermas (1981), p. 34.

38. S. Benhabib, p. 55.
39. Early feminism made substantive gains that were also ascriptive, though understandable in the context. See J. Pixley, (1991). Modern feminism is by no means a homogeneous movement.
40. D. Held & J. Krieger (1983), p. 491.
41. J. Keane & J. Owens (1986), p. 119.
42. See A. Gorz (1989).
43. B. Jordan (1987), (1989).
44. S. Hall & D. Held (1989), p. 23.
45. F. Block (1990), pp. 204–8. As Block says, the latter claims are very similar to Robert Theobald's argument of the 1960s: see chapter 3.
46. B. Jordan (1987), pp. 115–23.
47. A. Touraine (1971).
48. Especially French social theorists. See C. Lemert (1981).
49. Giddens' structuration theory is equally concerned to escape this dualism. A. Giddens (1984), p. 2.
50. J. Cohen (1982), p. 30.
51. A. Touraine (1981), p. 58, his emphasis.
52. A. Touraine (1977), pp. 276, 344, 358.
53. A. Touraine (1981), pp. 76, 102–4.
54. A. Touraine (1977), p. 366. There are, in some respects, similarities between Touraine's concept of historicity and Gramsci's notion of historical bloc, especially of unified blocs defined not by objective sociological categories but by their concrete political expression at specific historical periods. See, e.g., A. Gramsci (1971), p. 83; C. Boggs (1976), pp. 80–1.
55. A. Touraine (1977), p. 411.
56. Touraine himself does not use the term 'sovereignty', but throughout he implicitly refers to it.
57. I am grateful to Anna Yeatman for this formulation in her examiner's report on my earlier PhD dissertation.

CHAPTER 2

The Cash/Work Nexus:
Past Struggles, Same Problems?

Most people agree that a modern state consists of centralised and complex institutions performing a vast range of tasks within a society. It is not clear where limits exist to its capacity for oppressing powerless groups. The post-industrial proposal to separate income from work involves, I have argued, some critical and possibly unwarranted assumptions about the state. But what of the related theoretical assumptions that the market would decline in importance if the cash/work nexus were broken and, following from this, that such a contracted market would enhance the power of excluded groups? Are these assumptions reasonable ones? Many take the view that no prediction is safe; in line with this it seems to me that the only way to test the post-industrial thesis is by examining the existing conditions of political participation at the end of the twentieth century. Consequently it is necessary to consider the influence of market participation on the nature of modern citizenship.

This chapter will analyse, from various historical and theoretical perspectives, previous struggles over the cash/work nexus as the labour market evolved. The aim is not to provide an exhaustive survey but to isolate several basic developments in the labour and commodity markets in order to understand the present context of possible outcomes if the cash/work nexus were somehow broken. This will give the background in which to then assess, in later chapters, how the proposed alternatives to employment – as actual state policies in relation to today's markets – might affect the marginalisation experienced by those sections of populations already excluded. Depending on the answer, it may be possible to identify which strategy might best improve their position – the politics of full employment or the separation of income from work.

THE CASH/WORK NEXUS

The modern state is, therefore, not the sole consideration in any attempt to analyse the proposal to break the cash/work nexus. The assumption made about the contemporary labour market by these theorists, is that it is feasible and desirable to leave it, as long as the state guarantees some 'cash' to individuals. But is now an auspicious time to abandon the labour market unharmed, either politically, economically or in our individual identities?

This question should be considered with a clear understanding of the term 'cash/work nexus' (or the bond between income and work). What does it mean to break the cash/work nexus, or to separate income from work? What is the difference between *breaking* and *weakening* the nexus? Needless to say, the answers to these questions are not simple. What is often neglected in the more romantic post-industrial visions is that a precise definition of the nexus depends on specific historical contexts.

The link between income and work is more or less tight and more or less universal, in accordance with numerous factors. The *extent* of markets in goods and services, land and labour is a major set of factors. Another is the *manner* in which political forces shape the labour, commodity and capital markets, and make available (more or less) goods, services and land through diverse non-market avenues. Contrasts between pre-industrial and industrial societies provide the most well known understandings of the cash/work nexus, but modern variations also abound. The type and extent of market regulations, the amount of goods, cash and services provided by a government, whether these are universal entitlements or selective, stigmatising 'hand-outs', and the depth of class, gender and ethnic stratifications in a society are just some of the factors that shape the nexus.

The cash/work nexus is *tight* when the following conditions obtain. Goods, services and land must be available only as commodities, and the cash with which to purchase these commodities must be obtainable only by selling the single alienable commodity that is 'owned' by the vast majority, namely labour power, to the few buyers who own capital.

The above tight nexus, however, is a myth promoted by economic liberalism and it exists nowhere. Even in a liberal dystopia, children are required to attend school, at least to render their capacity to work saleable in a modern society, and therefore children cannot sell their labour power and others are needed to support them. Education could be a commodity but, by and large, it is state run. Armies and police are required to protect private property – there are private security firms but again, like much infrastructure, it is more profitable for these national and international tasks to be left to the state.

The list of non-commodities and non-market activities is endless. Nevertheless, the cash/work nexus is *weakened* by every pathway available to the population *to withdraw* – as other needs dictate – from selling their labour power and *to obtain* or produce some goods and services through non-market sources. Withdrawal from the labour market is made possible by unemployment and sickness benefits, sick leave, maternity and parental leave, holiday time and holiday pay loadings, disability and retirement pensions (or insurantial techniques), long-service leave, student or child allowances and also full employment. The more generous the income support, the more weakened the nexus, while the same applies with full employment, which, by improving the labour sellers' position, provides greater choices and options to leave particular jobs. Obtaining non-market goods and services weakens the nexus by obviating the necessity to find cash to pay for items such as transport, healthcare, housing, education and so forth. Producing goods to use directly (such as food, shelter, clothing) requires the availability of arable land, skills, tools and/or material.

The nexus would be *broken* in a modern society if a secure income were available not just to a few via wealth but to all via the state *and* if that income were sufficiently high to provide a genuine choice about whether or not to sell one's labour power. That is, the nexus between income and work would be separated if the whole population had sufficient income never to take up employment. The nexus would not be broken at all, but reinforced, if the income guaranteed were set below minimum wage levels, or rather below an income providing the bare essentials of modern life.

The relation between income and work in modern societies does not just involve the extent of the imposed duty to work, and the question of whether the income is socially acceptable as adequate or otherwise. The nexus also involves control over the work process. Wage labour offers no control over the work process, though this is qualified in times of full employment, as well as by successes or failures of labour movement conflicts and particular positions in the labour market, and whether there are options to withdraw from it. Other work structures, like communes and worker co-operatives, provide greater control over the work process than wage labour and, rather than an imposed duty to work, there is a freely assumed obligation towards fellow workers. The 'whip of hunger' may still operate, however, for they do not always provide a socially acceptable income, though this is the intention of a guaranteed 'maximum' income in which there would be no duty to work of any sort imposed from above.

Hence, the other way the cash/work nexus would be *broken* is if a subsistence form of work were successful enough to obviate the need to gain an income (or very much income). This pathway has been exemplified by experiments with rural communes. Is it, however, possible to gain a socially adequate subsistence by avoiding all markets in modern societies?

The next section will consider the basic organisation of labour markets up until the challenges to them during the 1960s, by briefly reviewing the key developments in modern labour markets and the previous struggles over the cash/work nexus up to that time. It may be that the pessimism, say of Habermas, that the workplace is irredeemably 'productivist', or that wage labour developed solely to the advantage of the buyers, is not entirely justified. Similarly, we may question the popularity over the past two decades of rethinking 'work' and denigrating full employment as a utopian dream, and of unearthing earlier forms of 'work' or finding women's traditional household work somehow more liberating than paid employment. Even if alternatives, out of their historical context, appear to be an improvement on wage labour, it may also be the case that in the contemporary context certain aspects of the market are more or less permanent.

PAST STRUGGLES AGAINST THE LABOUR MARKET

In this brief review of struggles against the developing labour market during the nineteenth century, I will identify two major strategies. One comprises collective attempts to *escape* the cash/work nexus by trying to retain or regain access to the means of subsistence through farming small-scale units of land or by small cottage production. The other is the labour movement strategy to *weaken* the nexus from within and via political means.

The imposition of wage labour as the predominant form of work occurred in varying ways in the industrialising world. One thing is clear. No human population would continue to offer its capacity to labour for sale and wait to find its price on the market, as if it were just another commodity, until access to other ways of surviving, particularly from living off the land, was blocked. The enclosure movements in Europe provided this necessary condition but, as Polanyi shows, this was insufficient. The transformation of peasants, artisans and 'vagabonds' into free wage labourers in nineteenth-century Britain required fifty years of government planning, restrictions, new laws, discourses and regulations, as well as the establishment of a vast number of state disciplinary institutions (asylums, schools, workhouses and prisons), facts conveniently denied by the liberal conception of the minimal state. In Britain the constitution of unemployment as the clearing mechanism of a national labour market was only possible when paternalistic and patriarchal forms of government, such as 'outdoor relief' (guaranteed 'minimum' incomes as with Speenhamland) were abolished and new disciplines of 'self-responsibility' imposed by introducing the threat of starvation.[1]

This transformation was catastrophic, and it is understandable that today's post-industrial writers urge that labour will never find its price and should not *have* to find its price. If there *can* be alternatives to wage labour in today's societies, however, this may involve turning back the clock. We first need to know if the latter is possible, or if some developments are irreversible. The issue here is that the transformation was not simply accepted passively; in the process of countless resistances, new structures and identities were forged.

The major struggles against the cash/work nexus comprise two basic forms. As I said, one strategy has been to avoid the labour market altogether, at one extreme. At the other has been resistance within the labour market aiming to weaken the cash/work nexus through the collective action of labour sellers. Of course for the populations involved, simply 'getting by' has been the predominant and continual problem in the face of the newly instituted whip of hunger. Getting by for individuals or households was never a 'strategy', as Ray Pahl assumes, although the methods of survival in a new structure of constraints were certainly various – seasonal paid work, domestic production of some food, local barter of skills or goods – especially while the commodity markets were still limited.[2]

ESCAPE FROM WAGE LABOUR

Avoidance strategies basically arose from collective attempts to prevent the growth of factories or the far more common efforts to secure control of land, and hence the means of subsistence, or other productive property. Prevention is most famously represented by the Luddites, the machine breakers who made repeated, highly organised attempts to preserve their own cottage production and to revive the paternalist legislation which protected artisans from being free wage labourers. As E.P. Thompson recounts, these efforts in Britain during 1811–17 ended in hangings or starvation for many, though some Luddites later became Chartists or joined the Ten Hour Movement to weaken the nexus.[3]

In most parts of Europe all the traditional legal and political arrangements of feudalism were abolished, bit by bit, to make land alienable. Peasant movements resisted the liberal revolution on the land and the prospects of wage labour or commercial farming wherever they could. Those peasants who became confirmed in land possession, notably in France, parts of Germany and Scandinavia, held fast to their social security and whatever economic security could be had amidst the remnants of feudal traditions.[4] This strategy was not available in Britain or Ireland, where enclosure had earlier been more thorough, if not totally brutal. Migration was the chief form of escape.

The successive invasions, primarily undertaken by Britain, which made land alienable in the Americas, Australasia, parts of Africa and elsewhere, involved total destruction: American Indians and Australian Aborigines are still trying to regain control of minute segments of the land they had worked for thousands of years. Wars and genocide resulted in an intended final solution: so-called protected reserves. These were concentration camps, and it is a moot point whether the populations of the hunting and gathering societies were denied the private property of their labour power or attempted to resist its imposition. Through the twentieth century, labour markets spread to the rest of the world, except in the state socialist countries which are just now introducing clearing mechanisms, or in South Africa where a police state still administers a range of assigned, indentured or 'coolie' labour. For the underdeveloped countries of today, the option of migration is not available (as it was from Europe in the nineteenth century). Those who do migrate to the overdeveloped world enter at the lowest level of fully developed labour markets.

By contrast, the previous voluntary migration movements from Europe, particularly to the Americas and Australasia, were primarily motivated to gain access to land. The migration option was Europe's safety valve, as in the United States the westward settling of owner-occupying commercial farmers was likewise for the industrialising eastern states. During the nineteenth century, as C. Wright Mills puts it, nearly four-fifths of the free people 'owned the property with which they worked'.[5] The mass of smallholdings in the United States did not decline permanently until the 1930s depression, farmers having become 'the tool and victim' of the rise of American capitalism, after which Roosevelt's New Deal contrived only to subsidise larger farmers and hence aid the concentration of consolidated farming and rural corporations.[6]

Yeoman or subsistence movements in Australia never stood a chance, though it was not for lack of trying. Pastoral capitalism was developed by colonial governments soon after the British invasion. Crown land was regularly set at prices too high for most migrants in order to create labour markets, for without labour the land from which Aborigines were driven could not become capital. Squatting on pastoral land was only successful for those already equipped with money and labour.

In Australia the repeated struggles to secure land and attempts at small-scale cultivation, inspired by rural radicalism, were based, as in the United States, mainly on a wish to escape from urban industrialism and labour markets generally, rather than to challenge individualistic capitalist enterprise.[7] Irish immigrants had the strongest desire for land in Australia, influencing the radical Land Conventions of 1857–59. After the goldrushes, stronger calls to 'unlock the lands' led to the Free Selection Acts of the 1860s and 1870s, where governments conceded small and unworkable pockets of land, which discriminated against small selectors and merely encouraged existing squatters to become landowners, thereby extending property relations in the pastoral industry.[8]

During the same period, pastoralists had made repeated efforts to retain the convict system. They also imported indentured labour or slaves ('blackbirding') from British India and the Pacific region. Although itinerant free wage labour gradually replaced convicts, by initially providing and permitting cheap or convict labour, colonial governments created the pastoral class that dominated for most of the century.

The yeoman movements, in which land was worked by individual households, were not the only efforts to survive from the land. In Australia a commune 'fever' broke out during the 1890s depression, following massive unemployment, strikes, lockouts and army violence. After the failure of the strikes, a majority in the embryonic labour movement began to place their hopes on the parliamentary road to reform, and Labor parties were established in that decade. Land, however, was still an important issue: the unions had favoured land taxes in 1888 and the first New South Wales Labor Party platform (1891) included American economist Henry George's idea of a single tax on unimproved land values.[9] But while some unionists were turning to the parliamentary path, rural demands of various state socialists and utopian socialists inspired other unionists to give up these fledgling union struggles as futile, and turn away from wage labour towards communal and co-operative principles.

The first experiment occurred during the shearers' strike in 1891, when a hundred strikers formed a co-operative settlement in Queensland, financed from union funds.[10] By then, utopian socialists like William Lane, who had demanded 'village settlements' for years, had become convinced that a 'co-operative socialist life' was not attainable in such hostile surroundings as Australia. For him, colonial governments had ignored the idea for too long and the remaining arable land was insufficient.[11] In 1893 about 600 Australians departed to set up a socialist colony in Paraguay under Lane's leadership.

In that same year, a 'fever' of agrarian utopianism broke out, mainly aroused by the hardship of the depression. Even worse, the fever was to be fanned by state support.[12] In no state was there any provision of relief for the unemployed. Usually, when there were lay-offs, unemployed men could only send deputations to plead with the colonial governments or, if times were more severe, take to street marches or invade public offices in order to force governments to respond. What they expected was provision of local relief work (work, not support). The state usually responded by offering rail passes to all men prepared to go up country to try their luck, which resolved the issue if enough accepted the offer.[13]

This time, the depression was more severe. In addition, rural radicalism still seemed pertinent. In a mercantilist, pastoral economy such as that of nineteenth-century Australia, the prime way to contest the control over society was through demands for land. If large numbers of people owned land, the social order of pastoral capitalists' domination through the convict system and later indentured or free wage labour could perhaps be broken. The commune fever was in fact the dying spark of that old male rural unionist radicalism, which glowed briefly after the failure of the strikes. For, despite the effort put into the communes, the amount of land and capital was never sufficient for unemployed, debt-ridden people, and none survived the decade. Exceptionally, South Australian settlements along the Murray River began from the principle that the land should be for 'industry and workers' and not for 'rent and landlords'. Some settlers had themselves applied for land expressly to escape from 'wage servitude and landlordism' rather than actual unemployment.[14] Most planned to combine principles of 'co-operation and communism' with their working and living, though others did so by necessity.[15]

The worst threat to the rural utopians' schemes was the problem of state intervention. Every colonial government had faced riots and protests from growing numbers of desperate, unemployed men demanding relief work – anywhere. In the space of one year (1893) four colonial governments reversed the previous policies of indifference towards the demands for 'village settlements'. The radical demands for communal land were implemented as state labour farms, where meagre savings were lost, although frugal relief accrued to the starving. Several private charity schemes operated more as 'anti-utopias' like those in Germany at the time, designed expressly to 'solve' unemployment by circumventing socialist claims to a right to work guaranteed by the state. 'Labour colonies' would prevent further state intervention, set the unemployed to work out of harm's way and provide a test for 'idlers', as well as morally improve all concerned. In the event, the most successful Australian labour colony, at Leongatha, was run by the Victorian colonial government, although in all other respects it paralleled the charities' original purposes completely. It supplied temporary work at subsistence wages to men driven there chiefly by the prospect of starvation.[16] Even for those started more 'spontaneously', land had to be granted from the state, so governments could easily redefine needs, set work tests, reduce food rations and turn co-operation into a discipline of labour.

More broadly, these experiments failed because new alliances were forming. Militating against the interests of the pastoralists (who vehemently opposed 'state aid' to extend land ownership, even for labour farms), was a small group of industrialists whose rising influence permeated state apparatuses or who achieved notoriety through their own charities. The old rural radicalism was also useful for these industrialists, and for governments keen to avert the more dangerous threats from the excluded.

While so many of the unemployed had been in no position to reject the experiments, the emergent union movement quickly rejected this strategy of communal co-operation via land reform. Unions turned to the state to press for industrial advantages from the rising manufacturing groups, who needed support against pastoral dominance. Communes were soon forgotten.

Interest in rural life was later revived by conservative and fascist groups. The twentieth century version of rural populism in Australia took the form of post-World War I soldier settlements – a gross failure[17] – and government-sponsored 'closer settlement' schemes. Various religious communes also rose and fell, most notably the 'wretched experiments' of the Catholic Rural Movement.[18] During the 1930s, a few rural labour camps set up by wealthy graziers were inspired by Nazi schemes for the young.[19] In sum, one of the few historians who has studied communes without the later impetus and research sponsorship from the Hawke Labor government argues that 'Australian history is littered with failed rural experiments'.[20]

The other notable way of avoiding wage labour that emerged last century was through collectively owning, controlling and working productive industrial property. Worker co-operatives reverse the wage labour relationship because, in principle, labour hires capital. Nevertheless, just like peasant or owner-worker farming, self-employed shops or businesses and rural communal forms of work, worker co-operatives have only managed to weaken the cash/work nexus in specific economic and political contexts. They have never risen successfully out of the depths of recession, despite the numerous grass roots attempts to convert failed enterprises through collective self-exploitation. Italy and France have the most successful tradition. Some skilled workshops set up in Paris as an *ad hoc* strike tactic during 1833 were so successful against existing employers that they were consciously adopted as a mechanism to escape the wage system. In both countries, builders' co-operatives secured government contracts and have played a lasting role in public works. The top down experiments, notably from those of Robert Owen and Charles Fourier, which were attempted in Europe and the United States, typically ended in failure although in general, the ideology of co-operation was an important influence within the working class against the dominance of competitive individualism.[21]

The principles of mutual aid were practised far more successfully within consumer co-operatives and friendly societies, particularly in Britain, Germany, the United States and Australia. Consumer co-operation and friendly societies do not, of course, represent any escape from wage labour to other forms of work, although they do *weaken* the cash/work nexus, either by reducing prices or by permitting members to opt out of work when it is necessary. Their origins lie partly in the feudal town practices of corporate societies of artisans that monopolised entry, membership, prices and production. After guilds were abolished in Europe, aspects of these precommodity arrangements were favoured by conservative and aristocratic groups, and by the Catholic Church.[22] The ideas were also revived by 'respectable' male skilled workers, and in Australia friendly societies strongly resisted the threat of state control through subsidies. They stressed that their members' gainful employment was the way to avoid the state-induced pauperisation of the Speenhamland system (with its guaranteed minimum income) or the hated English workhouses.[23] The societies had few female members but, by 1913, a full 46 per cent of the Australian population were 'beneficiaries', with sick pay for the men, and medical care and funeral expenses extended to their families.[24] The consequence was a flourishing trade in life insurance and banks geared to the 'little man'.[25] (This development throws light on the wages strategy taken by Australian unionists later, since if workers could maintain high wages and pay for their own co-operative services, they would not press for universal statutory services.) The legacy from the societies was female care for children and dependence on husbands, along with male independence from either charity or explicit state social policy like health or housing. In Australia the societies' real independence was lost after a long battle against the increase in monopoly power of the medical profession during the 1920s. In their opposition to national schemes, the societies were not just protecting their own co-operative insurance, but also defending the principle of consumer control over the standards and costs of medical care, a control previously asserted through each society's contractual relations with doctors.[26] The British consumer co-operatives likewise insisted on controlling the quality of goods sold, thus preventing unscrupulous adulteration. Prices were controlled to the extent that profit was removed from the retailing of goods.

RESISTANCE WITHIN WAGE LABOUR

Although there are exceptions, most of the attempts to avoid wage labour during the nineteenth century failed. The more well-organised movements (such as Luddism or Utopian Socialism), however, often turned to other decommodifying strategies and developed new precedents and ideologies to weaken the cash/work nexus *within* the labour system. Indeed, as the commodity markets became more centralised, as small-scale units of production were destroyed or gradually eroded and as capitalist control replaced aristocratic forms of domination, attempts to create alternatives to wage labour and to retrieve feudal protective principles became increasingly romantic and futile. Participation in civil society through gaining the rights to organise open trade unions and to vote and form political parties were the predominant and most bitterly fought strategies.

It must be stressed, however, that variations in the 'historic compromise' between capital and labour around the 1900s are so numerous that the concept is virtually useless as an explanatory device. Governments played a key role, a point emphasised by Polanyi, although Esping-Andersen goes so far as to maintain that the historical origins of modern social policy have entirely conservative foundations: it was not just Bismarck who systematically and deliberately attacked the liberal driven commodification of labour, but other autocratic governments too, at least in Europe.[27]

Such weakening of the cash/work nexus when introduced from above usually has disciplinary and conservative effects, although similar paternalism may result from bureaucratisation even when a protective measure has been generated from demands from below. Distinctions are also blurred, which can be seen in struggles to reduce working time, like that which produced the Ten Hour Bill (passed in 1847 in Britain). This may well be regarded, as Marx did, as 'the political economy of the working class' for the first time attacking that of the middle class.[28] Yet the state was also acting as a 'collective capitalist' and for its own population interests to prevent the working class from being worked to its destruction.[29]

But the fact that conservative and capitalist interests may also be served is not an argument against *the principle* of weakening the nexus. The decisive problem, of which the above is but one example, was that in the liberal attempt to regard and to use labour as a pure commodity, the humans attached to this commodity faced extinction. Polanyi points out, however, that liberals never admitted that labour combination for labour strikes (with strike funds) are, in principle, the means for labour to act as a commodity waiting for its preferred price.[30] Capital strikes, more damaging and effective against humans than labour strikes, are similarly in accordance with the market principle. (In contrast, lock-outs are not market but power operations on the part of owners.) Nevertheless, the cash/work nexus *had* to be weakened, whether from above or below, because, as Polanyi argues, no society can survive on pure market principles. Possessive individuals own their own labour power and must continually sell themselves: they owe no obligation to anyone, the future generation in particular. During the nineteenth century, children were abandoned by wage labourers, infanticide was common and child labour was worked to death. Hence, whether democratic or not, governments stepped in.

The kinds of protective measures and 'social citizenship rights' (or the type of welfare package) brought in by Western states depended on the shape of alliances between dominant groups, the strengths and weaknesses of oppositional movements and the particular political–institutional structures of the state. Touraine's unifying perspective holds, to an extent, in explaining how, after the 'transitional' types of resistance recounted above failed, the various workers' movements truly emerged, in that they accepted the new economic, scientific and ethical patterns (industrialisation), but opposed *capitalist control* over industrialisation. That is, the opposed social movements became oriented towards the same cultural patterns.[31] But Touraine's dubious identification of one oppositional movement with 'industrial society' does not square with some 'grand facts'. In some countries, notably the United States and Australasia, feminist and temperance movements also contested control over the process of industrialisation. (Since the Woman's

Christian Temperance Unions had two million world members, it may be that the Wobblies – International Workers of the World – are remembered too selectively.) Of equal significance was the near uniform exclusion or marginalisation of women from workforces and the opposition to feminist movements by most elements of labour movements.

Even T.H. Marshall saw that the British Factory Acts of the 1860s curtailed the new civil right of concluding a free contract.[32] Henceforward women and children could not unrestrictedly sell their labour. The effects of social citizenship rights were similarly ambiguous for organised labour, let alone everyone else.[33] Education Acts further removed children from the labour market and, by extending childhood dependency, placed impossible burdens on women. Women were not everywhere passive victims of this process, however. Although women's exclusion was as much a tactic of state policies as of male unionism, the former to reduce the death rate and the latter to prevent employers' use of cheaper female and child labour, men refused to share financial resources (however meagre) with women, yet they still demanded 'conjugal rights' (marital rape). It is understandable, then, that first-wave feminism and women's temperance attacked 'rapacious male sexuality' by glorifying purity, motherhood *and* family limitation – their only bargaining counter with governments anxious to preserve and increase populations. Cash transfers 'targeted' at mothers and children reflected these struggles, as did 'homemaking' supported by 'breadwinning', which women used as best they could in their collective efforts to *avoid* the labour market. Cash protection for unemployed or sick men, for old age and disability, whether through insurance or from state revenue, were the gendered result of ameliorating the commodity form. Government approaches to housing, health, transport and so forth were also various, but these kinds of social rights, when provided directly by the state, removed the cash/work nexus from these basic requirements for survival, while creating new conflicts between the relevant bureaucracies and their 'clients'.

To take just a few national variations, the weakness of local industrialists and a strong workers' alliance with a radical farmer movement *and* temperance is what made Sweden's decommodification so thorough and distinctive.[34] In the United States, conversely, the fact that the labour movement never developed a national political party along European or Australasian lines was not due only to chronic ethnic and gender divisions and labour market segmentation. As happened earlier in Britain with laws against combination, the American labour movement suffered a century of violent repression inflicted by the state and by employers who were free to do likewise with private police, espionage forces and arsenals, until a more 'legalistic amelioration' was introduced in 1935–37.[35] In the United States to this day, the cash/work nexus is weakest for those sectors most comfortably tied to paid work, while those who can receive cash transfers and food stamps cannot afford to work, so low are minimum wages.

In Australia, a weak industrialising class formed a loose alliance with the labour movement when the pastoralists' dependence on British capital, disrupted by the 1890 collapses, momentarily reduced their influence on colonial governments. The Woman's Christian Temperance Movement, the largest body of women demanding the vote, also helped to effect a temporary defeat of pastoralism, as represented by the vote for federation and a permanent decline in itinerant rural wage labour. The sober, industrious male labourer who gained a 'family wage' was exactly what many women – as well as industrialists and bureaucrats – wanted.[36]

The labour movement demanded that the pastoralists' option of importing cheaper indentured labour be outlawed, in order to improve workers' bargaining strength through labour supply shortages. Their new political party, the Australian Labor Party (ALP), thus embarked on a battle for white 'wage-earner' welfare to weaken the employment nexus.[37] A trilogy of arbitration, tariff protection and immigration controls was implemented by the new commonwealth government. Male wages, jobs and living standards were to be protected from the discretion of capitalists by a centralised arbitration system, which imposed definitions of breadwinner need and set low wage levels for women;[38] by tariffs (to establish and maintain Australian industries); and by an Immigration Restriction Act which excluded non-whites and hence indentured labour. Nevertheless, this strategy of a rather exceptional system of income distribution for whites through a regulated wage system rather than through state welfare was never solely about more equitable incomes.[39] The Australian labour movement equally emphasised the nature of social participation in the belief that men should achieve such participation – and hence be the primary members – through paid labour. The union movement maintained a long hostility to dependence on the state and its accompanying degradation by consistently demanding paid work, not 'doles', during recessions.[40] Not only that, but the centralised wage system enabled a growing number of men to achieve other kinds of independence from the state, to buy their own houses and pay for private services or use the friendly societies. Retirement on the pension (1909) was the only universal gain, women being regarded more as wornout breeders than as workers.[41] This relatively gender-neutral policy left a different legacy to that of the United States, however, where cash transfers remain sharply gender divided to this day.[42]

All these variations in types of welfare packages and hence of options for withdrawing from the labour market at certain life stages (or from personal incapacity or market failure), as well as protected jobs, wages and conditions, or a system of social wages (health, housing, education) more common in Europe, may reduce a person's reliance on employment. While they have been more extensive in some countries than others, a few generalisations are possible. The first is that during the first half of the twentieth century most women became increasingly dependent on employment (indirectly) and more directly dependent financially upon men. That is, while men's employment situation was improving, women's lack of employment opportunities became increasingly unviable and inequitable. The second is that whenever there was a viable chance, women opted for employment.

After World War II, the dependence of women and children on male wages intensified in new directions. Very broadly this was due to the following. After labour markets had adjusted to the specific state regulations or enticements, a declining number of women could join the workforce. Despite this lengthy segregation, the limited nature of commodity markets until the 1950s meant that many women had greater opportunities to produce use values within households than was the case afterwards. That is, an 'informal economy' did exist that is not available today. Women's unpaid work weakened the cash/work nexus for men and, cultural beliefs and political rights permitting, enabled women in some places to claim a measure of independence. As part of women's response to industrialisation, caring for the next generation through quality not quantity and the maintenance of workers were the twin bases of first-wave feminism's claims for women's social and political participation. Although this 'separate but equal' strategy has proven unreliable (motherhood and homemaking were imposed by the state; home chores proliferated and became newly ascribed), it is also the case that market forces shape households as well. Women's skilled household work was often a potential source of bargaining strength with individual men, as long as such work was not cheapened by the commodity form. Hence, bread and cake making, fruit and meat preserving, vegetable and allotment gardens, dairy or at least poultry produce, the sewing of children's clothes and soft furnishings, candle making, midwifery and other nursing expertise were significant contributions for about half a century. The privilege of a wife exclusively working unpaid at home did not just accrue to husbands. Nevertheless, women's unpaid work often helped prolong male strikes and, as Young and Wilmott found in London during the 1950s, working-class women often created their own solidarity, down among the women, within a 'proto-trade union' of female kin and neighbours.[43]

A deskilling process and serious redundancy in the material if not emotional purpose of home production began when a majority of goods formerly produced by women at home became cheaper to purchase ready-made, and when the medical profession monopolised more health services. As food processing and garment factories multiplied, the previous *money-saving* work of home-baking, pickling or sweater-knitting thus became a luxury of the rich. The unpaid housewife's financial dependency henceforward became complete, as *cash* was needed to put into effect the new managerial, transporting, consumer and caring (or educational and negotiating) skills required to operate a modern household. These skills, and male dependency on them, remain unrecognised.

This further commodification of goods and services was also a function of women's low pay (first in the West, and now elsewhere). The male unions' battles against female labour did not prevent women's employment, but segregated their much cheaper labour away from male-dominated areas. The strata who were formerly domestic servants started the trend towards pricing married women out of informal or household work (by entering, for example, food-processing industries like canning). In the nineteenth century, domestic and personal services were not just the major source of paid work for women: they were also, as late as the 1891 census in Britain, the largest single occupational group along with 'agriculture, horticulture and forestry'. In the censuses of both 1851 and 1911, domestic servants comprised 14 per cent of the workforce.[44]

After that, domestic service declined rapidly. In Britain the first exodus was into the armament industries during World War I but, as food and other domestic provisions were commodified and the care of humans was also being institutionalised, the opportunities for female employment in factories, health, education, commerce and finance expanded. As soon as it was available, women fled from domestic service, mainly because it was not wage labour. The worker was not hired for a specific portion of her time but the 'person of the worker' was hired, argued an American reformer attacking domestic service in 1901.[45] Domestic service was often lonely, sexual harassment was common, and generally the hours were excessively long, the pay poor due to trucking of bed and board, the supervision continual and the work physically demanding. In Australia in 1901, of the 46.42 per cent of women in the workforce, 30.61 per cent were in private domestic service. By 1947, of the 18 per cent of women in employment, the percentage of domestic servants had dropped to 5.84.[46] Arbitration commissioners in 1908 and 1911, in trying to prevent women from working in factories, expressed surprise when female witnesses claimed that they preferred factory work to domestic work. The commissioners nevertheless pressed on, setting women's wages at 50 per cent of the male living wage in 1918.[47]

Although there are national exceptions, especially on the European continent, after the 1950s women's labour force attachment rose again. No longer a reserve army, women joined the permanent workforce, but were weakly attached, partly because of the legacy of segregation and low pay which naturally suited employers, and partly because the bulk of their work is still counted as non-employable, unskilled and unnecessary. That is, their ascribed responsibilities do not provide them with a protected option to withdraw temporarily from the labour market, but the reverse – they are forced into temporary employment. Secure employees may withdraw to be ill but not to care for an ill child. Hence new forms of casual, part-time and insecure employment for women developed apace.

In liberal democracies by the 1950s, therefore, the option of trying to escape from wage labour (without wealth) was gone. Even in the United States, where small farms continued long after industrial-isation, that avenue closed, and only France is notable for its inability to undermine the peasant sector. In Australia, concentration of land ownership was facilitated far earlier by government policies. The commune experiments here were possibly the worst excesses in futility (though other small farmer settlements were also bleak), especially because governments had used the ideas to marginalise the unemployed and to convert the schemes into rural 'workhouses'. The option facing most women – financial dependence on a male 'breadwinner' – provided a measure of *independence* in avoiding wage labour only when domestic production was cheaper than equivalent commodities. After these commodities out-priced household or 'informal' provision, the cash/work nexus operated, indirectly, as a tight private control. Independent employment was thereafter a vital necessity for women.

In contrast, a strategy of resistance within wage labour proved to be the only viable avenue for the majority of men. Yet these efforts to weaken the cash/work nexus were accomplished largely at the expense of women and also, if not more so, of particular ethnic groups, a marked phenomenon in the United States. This left a legacy of male–female relations where women's ascribed status – albeit in new forms with intensified and isolating responsibilities – remained intact, and where segmented labour markets became impervious to women's entry into employment.

Certain aspects of these developments are by no means incapable of change. Labour market segmentation is one, and it is not uniform. But it is necessary, however, to recognise that once wage labour became a defining characteristic in modern societies, a new social order was created that permeated all other aspects of these societies. New values emerged as new institutional structures were established, so much so that the formal sphere of wage labour has become the principal sphere of social participation today. The old structures of land division and the social relations that went with them are gone. This means, therefore, that when we consider the possible alternatives for the future, we have to think about *moving beyond* the present, and not about any form of returning to the past. In this sense social trends are irreversible. The economy no longer consists of small-scale units of production, but of labour, commodity and capital markets that are highly concentrated. Equally the modern state is complex and centralised. It is now very difficult to participate in such a society without participating in both arenas. Women came to this recognition during the boom years.

In so far as markets had solidified by the 1950s, this was also when white male unions were at their peak: most OECD countries had brought in commitments to full employment for men. There was an economic boom, and populations were told that they had never had it so good. And yet poverty was rediscovered soon after, presenting a new set of challenges during the 1960s.

NOTES

1. K. Polanyi (1957). A recent study by Mitchell Dean (1991) sets the 'event' of constituting poverty between 1795 and 1835, culminating in the Poor Law Amendment Act.
2. R.E. Pahl (1984); L. Morris (1988).
3. E.P. Thompson (1968), especially pp. 569–604.
4. E.J. Hobsbaum (1962), pp. 186–96.
5. C. Wright Mills (1956), p. 7.
6. *ibid.*, pp. 13–44; J.T. Patterson (1986), p. 61.
7. H. McQueen (1970), p. 46.
8. R.W. Connell & T.H. Irving (1980), p. 107.
9. B. Fitzpatrick (1944), p. 99.
10. M. Munro Clark (1986), p. 51.
11. G. Souter (1968), p. 22.
12. R.B. Walker (1970); R.E.W. Kennedy (1968); M. Munro Clark (1986).
13. S. Macintyre (1983), p. 20.
14. M. Davitt (1898), pp. 73–4.
15. R.B. Walker (1970) p. 30.
16. R.E.W. Kennedy (1968) pp. 54–8.
17. K. Fry (1985) p. 29.
18. 'History is threatening to repeat its sad failures', *The Australian*, 25.6.83.
19. J. Shields (1982).
20. 'History is threatening to repeat its sad failures', *The Australian*, 25.6.83.
21. M. Mellor *et al* (1988), pp. 1–34.
22. G. Esping-Andersen (1990) p. 39.
23. D. Green & L. Cromwell (1984), pp. 24–5.
24. *ibid.*, pp. 221, 14, 69.
25. J. Roe (1976), p. 17.
26. D. Green & L. Cromwell (1984), p. 176.
27. G. Esping-Andersen (1990), pp. 40–1.
28. cited in E.P. Thompson (1968), p. 603.
29. For example, K. Marx (1954), pp. 229, 257–8, 271–3.
30. K. Polanyi (1957), p. 148–9.
31. A. Touraine (1984), p. 7.
32. T.H. Marshall (1965), pp. 88–9.
33. J. Pixley (1992).
34. G. Esping-Andersen (1990), p. 30.
35. J. Barbalet (1989), pp. 249–56.

36. J. Pixley (1991).
37. F.G. Castles (1985).
38. See E. Ryan & A. Conlan (1975).
39. K. McDonald (1990).
40. S. Macintyre (1985), pp. 59–68.
41. L. Tierney (1970), p. 211.
42. See the debate in *Thesis Eleven*, no. 17, (1987) between Nancy Fraser, Lois Bryson and Sheila Shaver.
43. M. Young & P. Wilmott (1973). Also see A. Summers (1975), p. 443, and Connell and Irving (p. 280) on women's efforts to prolong strikes.
44. B. Jones (1982), p. 18.
45. S. Strasser (1977), p. 239.
46. B. Kingston (1977), p. 61; S. Siedlecky and D. Wyndham (1990), p. 11.
47. E. Ryan & A. Conlan (1975) pp. 75, 111.

CHAPTER 3

Challenging the Employment System: The Counter Culture and Reforming Governments

A rediscovery of poverty and the eruption of movements other than the labour movement preoccupied the 1960s. During the long boom, organised labour movements in many OECD countries had been economically powerful although politically weak, especially in the United States, Britain and Australia.[1] Alliances between fractions of the dominant class were stable and conservative parties dominated the state. Of course there were exceptions but it seemed that the Adenauers, Eisenhowers, Menzies, de Gaulles and Macmillans would stay forever; they represented an anti-communism that brooked no internal criticism. Censorship was common and public life shrank as the privatised, suburban nuclear family was further emphasised as the only acceptable household type. A rapidly growing number of students was evidence of Western productivity and wealth. Students were meant to be grateful for their fathers' hard work and wartime sacrifice. Existing stratifications of class, gender and race were as they should be, according to the new TV boxes which promoted women's expanded role as consumers. Daniel Bell proclaimed the end of ideology and the prevailing message emphasised how the post-colonial world could 'catch up' with the West. Where there was concern, pessimism was uppermost. Hence, Erving Goffman's *Stigma* (1964), was exemplary in showing how impossible it was for stigmatised groups to redefine their imposed identities.

At just that time, however, challenges broke out. The Black movement in the United States sent shock waves across all these paternalist regimes and ignited Blacks in other parts of the world.[2] In protesting the Vietnam War, middle-class students too found that the white world was not so beautiful. Public life became highly volatile, and the status quo was sometimes defended with violence.[3] Several elements of what was initially and broadly called the counter culture turned to attack the sexism, racism, attendant poverty and

56

environmental degradation involved in the various compromises between labour, capital and governments. Feminist, gay and environmental movements emerged partly from this. Other sections of the counter culture, in criticising what they called 'the system', argued that authoritarianism was intrinsic to governments, private enterprise, trade unions and nuclear families. In opposition to traditional forms of left-wing politics, many proposed a rejection of wage labour as the only way to undermine the dominant culture, and turned to the self-marginalisation exemplified by the commune movement. The present post-industrial position has drawn very much on this latter counter culture theory and practice of redefining work and attempting to *break* the cash/work nexus. To the extent that this latter element challenged the established order, however, it lasted only until commune living got under way, as this chapter argues. At that stage, the ideas were no test case for the post-industrial strategy because governments did not become interested in communes until the next decade.

In contrast to communes, the new 'discovery of poverty' was immediately a mainstream political issue. Ensuing struggles from below to extend social wages and increase cash transfers resulted in a further *weakening* of the cash/work nexus, and more inclusive forms of citizenship began tentatively to embrace Blacks, immigrant workers and women. The main examples to be discussed herein are President Johnson's 'war on poverty' in the United States and the Whitlam government's reforms in Australia. These two OECD countries provided very little in social wages (along with Canada, Japan and New Zealand). The United States and Australian governments also came closer than those elsewhere to implementing guaranteed income schemes after this 'discovery of poverty' and the welfare 'explosion' of the 1960s. They therefore provide the evidence for the first test case of alternatives in practice. As will be discussed in the next chapter, some of the groups involved in formulating new welfare policies or in criticising government measures had raised the notion of a guaranteed income for totally different purposes than those of United States and Australian policy makers. The potential of a guaranteed income for separating the connection between income and work (or the reverse) became *the* contested issue for a time. Some radicals argued against including the poor in the employment system; and, in a similar strategy, parts of the new feminist movement lobbied for wages for housework. It is necessary to consider the specific contexts of these emerging theoretical positions before recounting their later fate in government hands.

The whole period of cultural change was a time of crisis, when the dominant economic classes became fragmented and pressed for contradictory changes to their economies. Governments' responses to these challenges and demands from both dominant groups and oppositional movements were extraordinarily mixed. The 'new' social movements emerged in a general context of inertia at the political–institutional level. The two issues of interest here, the struggles against poverty and the debates over counter culture strategies, both involved radical attacks on the employment system. Governments dealt with the poverty debate promptly; the counter culture challenges through communes were anathema to them for another ten years.

POLITICAL STRUGGLES 1960s: THE 'DISCOVERY OF POVERTY'

THE UNITED STATES

In the case of the United States, the background to the new 'discovery of poverty' was an increase in rural poverty following the concentration and mechanisation of farms during the 1940s and 1950s, and subsequent demographic changes when southern Blacks migrated to swelling northern ghettos. White southerners had consistently rejected those welfare and employment components of the New Deal that might have raised labour costs or emancipated the Black population.[4] Accordingly, tenant farmers and sharecroppers, who were basically indentured plantation labour, faced a further demise in their conditions or enforced migration north. The civil rights movement was not primarily directed at poverty, however, but at the southern apartheid system. Bus boycotts, marches and demonstrations during the 1950s generated white antagonism and police and mob violence in the south, although before 1964 Black leaders mainly pursued a non-violent, integrationist path and the ghettos were quiet.[5]

The visibility of poverty was politicised during the early 1960s. In 1960 the Democratic Party, having lost white support in the south, turned to attract the growing Black vote in the industrial states by promising to deal with civil rights and poverty. Michael Harrington's

The Other America was published in 1962. Read by President Kennedy himself and later to become a best-seller, it found a 'new' poverty in ghettos, and rural areas, and among the elderly and the minorities who faced 'a wall of prejudice'. It was the catalyst for an outpouring of theories and research on poverty, especially after poverty became front-page news.[6] According to Piven and Cloward, as the white south became increasingly disaffected, cultivating the Black urban vote became more urgent for the Kennedy and Johnson administrations.[7] Even so, Kennedy's planners themselves considered poverty to be more a rural than a Black problem. In addition, and instead of viewing poverty as an economic condition, many social scientists and administrators became deeply concerned with 'illegitimacy', female-headed households or 'broken families', especially among the Black population, and with identifying an unshakable 'culture of poverty'.[8]

Whether the civil rights movement itself was the more influential catalyst, with the Kennedy and Johnson administrations genuinely keen for liberal reforms, or whether the Democrats were merely desperate for this new northern vote, the situation was certainly an open one. In 1964 President Johnson announced a 'war on poverty' whose controversial programs were later criticised for fiscal mismanagement and embezzlement, and for inciting demonstrations, protests and riots.[9] The latter reached 'unprecedented heights' between 1965 and 1968, with Black riots in the biggest cities in the United States. An attendant popular fear of dangerous mass unrest grew so much that even corporate leaders lent some support to Johnson's reforms.[10] Organised pressure groups developed too, aided by radical activists trying to foster the political power of the poor. The civil rights movement was undoubtedly important in mobilising Blacks and prompting direct action, such as that led by the National Welfare Rights Organization, which was formed in 1966. This was a short-lived but vocal and highly political women's liberation movement which lobbied around class and gender issues. At its peak the 22 000 members, consisting of AFDC mothers (Aid to Families with Dependent Children), staged hundreds of sit-ins and confrontations at welfare offices, demanding increased benefits, jobs and sexual freedom (by removing the 'man in the house' rules from single mothers' eligibility criteria). They encouraged poor people to take advantage of aid and to remain on the welfare rolls as long as they were in need: the view was fostered that welfare was not a privilege but a right. This led to a fantastic jump in the participation of those eligible for AFDC.[11]

Hence, the liberalisation and expansion of the old New Deal programs, as well as the introduction of new ones in housing, health and nutrition, resulted in an explosion of the numbers receiving income maintenance. Even granted that the poverty line was drawn particularly bluntly in the United States (set at one-half of median family income in 1959, it dropped to one-third in 1974), the aged, for example, dramatically improved their status after huge increases in social security benefits. (From 40 per cent in poverty in 1959, only 16 per cent were poor in 1974.) These measures weakened the cash/work nexus: in 1948, one-half of all men over sixty-five were in the labour force; with social security expansion the proportion dropped to 20 per cent.[12]

Many of the United States programs are means tested or unemployment tested, as they are in Australia, although the difference in the United States is that low-paying employment has consistently been a key source of poverty. The American labour movement was never in a position to gain protection from centralised wage fixing or minimum wage regulations. The labour federations in the monopoly or corporate sector did, however, secure high wages, and employee-benefits like private health care and occupational pensions also expanded during this time.[13] But when a federal minimum wage law was enacted in 1966, it only covered one in three southern farm workers. Those tenant farmers whose labour price did rise tended to lose their jobs and their access to patches of land for subsistence farming, as machines replaced them.[14] The wage law could hardly be called effective: in 1967 over 14 million people in poverty lived in households whose head was employed or underemployed. The Great Society likewise made little difference to the poverty of female-headed households, whose numbers remained stable, comprising 40 per cent of the poverty population in 1969.[15]

The distribution of social benefits in the United States remains biased regarding gender and race. Means tested social assistance programs, like the AFDC, mainly support women, whereas the more generous, non-means-tested entitlement programs like old age insurance allow men greater access to benefits and reward them more generously. The inferior labour market position of Blacks is partly a reflection of the use of Black workers to undercut high-paid labour and of organised labour's exclusion of Blacks. It is also due to the political suppression of Blacks, especially through the southern planter class' control over welfare.[16]

Nevertheless, although radicals claimed at the time that welfare expansion served merely to control the temporary outbursts from below, the war on poverty and the economic growth up until the early 1970s still saw a 'fantastic drop' in the number of poor.[17] Indeed, it was the Nixon administration which extended the social wage, legislating between 1969 and 1972 for huge increases in social security benefits, indexation and a guaranteed pension.[18] This was, however, despite Nixon's efforts to control the explosion. The standard trade-off, by which unemployment in the United States was consistently used to drive down wages and prices, disappeared by then too. That is, the employment nexus was substantially weakened by the explosion of income maintenance, because the availability of unemployment benefits, food stamps, housing subsidies and so forth could, in some sectors and regions, moderate the requirement to take any job on any terms. Despite high levels of unemployment, wage and workplace demands and price growth were not affected.[19]

It was during the Nixon administration, however, that guaranteed income plans were also proposed, especially in order to stem this growing strength of the weakest segments of the population. In the next chapter we will investigate the different contexts in which these plans were introduced, and then rejected. The possible effects on the cash/work nexus would have been various, but their attraction for governments in both Australia and the United States lay in halting what were seen as growing demands from below.

AUSTRALIA

The 'discovery of poverty' in Australia created one of the first public debates of the 1960s which questioned the stifling order of twenty-three years of conservative rule. Conservative governments had fostered a political and social denial of new and old categories of poor – the historical outcome of the Australian 'wage earner welfare' system (as discussed on page 49). Federal ministers would declare the non-existence of poverty with impunity and, even when the evidence mounted against this rosy view, clung to the 'pocket' approach – if there was poverty, it only existed in smaller and smaller pockets.[20]

As in the United States, the presence of what was later described as an underclass of permanent poor was a 're-discovery', but this time 'the poor' lacked traditional (Anglo, male) allies who were now 'upward borne, hard-pressed and deeply committed to consolidation'.[21] In Australia, the relative emancipation of the working class over a century was such that the post-war workforce no longer faced insecurity and deprivation. At a time of full employment, wages and salaries were high but services in kind so limited and cash transfers at such a low level that poverty was extreme for welfare beneficiaries. For those facing life on a pension in the 1960s the 'level of cash social services . . . [represented] not so much a defence against poverty, but their first real encounter with poverty'.[22] Before Aborigines gained Australian citizenship in 1967, they and newly arrived migrants were mostly prevented from claiming even these benefits.

The official 'rediscovery' of poverty in Australia occurred much later than in the American or British case. It had to wait until the ALP's electoral triumph in 1972 seemed inevitable. The delay has been attributed to Australian myths of egalitarianism supposedly veiling the realities of wealth distribution. The British research of Titmuss and Townsend had raised no more than academic interest, despite Australia's lack of a national health service or housing provisions like those of Britain. President Johnson's war on poverty had only confirmed Australia's self-satisfied conviction that it was free of this problem.[23] And yet the reasons for poverty becoming 'visible' in the United States were different to those in Australia. The United States had higher unemployment levels and greater numbers of 'working poor',[24] and particular demographic changes and the civil rights movement were also specifically American phenomena.

In Australia, by contrast, it was not simply right wing propaganda that delayed the issue's emergence. (Macmillan had tried suggesting that 'the British' had 'never had it so good', yet Labour again took power in 1964.) It was equally the case in Australia that poverty had simply been swept under the political carpet. The preoccupation of the Australian labour movement with the wage regulation strategy and with real wage levels as a defence of living conditions always relegated other social needs to the status of emergency or extraordinary;[25] this was less the case in Britain. Such a 'labourist tradition' (compared to the low levels of unionism in the United States) was still the main oppositional force during the boom time, and therefore little public attention had been paid to the fact that 'basically, the poor today are those who fall outside the established system of wages and salary regulation (or the 'perks' system)'.[26]

During the fifties, only the aged, of all the scattered, heterogeneous groups in poverty in Australia, were able to politicise their needs to any effect. Old people *outside* the pension system became more vocal as inflation grew. Interestingly enough, instead of left wing arguments against the means test on the grounds of its social stigma – a major stand of most European socialists – in Australia critics did not usually aim to abolish the means test but to extend it, for those who wanted to achieve eligibility. The main criterion for relaxing the means test or raising the pension rate was not a matter of principle but of whether electoral gain would ensue.[27] Though pensioners as a whole suffered a lower degree of hardship than all other income security recipients,[28] the residualist perspective was overwhelming in government, which considered that pension increases discharged its total welfare responsibility.[29] Prime Minister Menzies in 1963 clearly saw a pension as 'something for nothing'. When asked whether he could live on the age pension, he replied: 'Never having had any money I didn't work for, I wouldn't know'.[30] Although Gorton has been considered a more compassionate Liberal prime minister, his hopes for Australia in 1968 included no more than that pension rates should ensure 'at least a modest standard of living so that they do not need blankets to be provided for them in the winter, so that they at least have enough to eat and a roof over their head'.[31]

Why did the concern with poverty emerge then? Jill Roe, at the time, argued that the 'third historical acknowledgement' of poverty was started by 'international comparisons and carried through by interested professional groups, semi-autonomous Institutes and an enlarged welfare lobby (by the seventies a welfare industry)'.[32] She was sceptical of linking the opposition to the Vietnam war to anything more novel than opposition to conscription. A sense of 'national shame', as expressed in the first public shock to Australia's smugness – the erection of the Aboriginal Embassy (a tent outside Parliament House) – was considered unlikely to have had much bearing on the new official concern with poverty. The debate started quietly in 1964, but reached a crescendo in 1974, when the federal Labor government asserted that it would 'restore Australia to a position of leadership in the provision of welfare services', as Treasurer Hayden put it.[33] At the time, many agreed that the whole issue had been brought up by a few experienced welfare experts, a 'concerned core' of 'well-meaning people' speaking up at 'crucial moments' against the general hostility at any suggestions that tax payers' pockets might be affected. Lois Bryson suggested the United States' war on poverty had some influence, although in Australia the debate was 'very little affected by the actions of the poor themselves'.[34] This was indeed so, and for Roe, too, Labor's electoral slogan of 1972, 'It's Time', was successful because more than the 'debatable poor' would benefit from a social wage, rather than the wages strategy, when high health costs, pressure on private school intakes and remote and expensive housing threatened far more comfortable groups. 'The poor', in this reading, had become politically useful.[35]

This last factor suggests more general reasons why the whole poverty debate cropped up at this time. Just when the debate got going, Arthur Calwell was replaced by Gough Whitlam as the leader of the ALP after its electoral defeat in 1966. Under Calwell, the social services platform of the Labor Party had been only marginally different from those of the Liberal-Country Party governments.[36] By 1968 a new kind of ALP leadership with an educated, professional background began reformulating the party package in a turn away from the previous 'labourist' tradition of male wages. The new policies comprised a moderate nationalism and, as a young Labor politician had it (in 1973), 'governmental planning and intervention to revitalize and refurbish Australian capitalism in order to secure efficiency and growth and thus provide the resources for *ambitious social programmes*. And . . . no single reference to socialism'.[37]

What this turn away from the 'labourist' tradition of the ALP meant, let alone whether *socialism* had ever been more than rhetoric, is still debated.[38] And yet, rather like the radical critique (later to be recanted in bleaker times)[39] that Johnson's war on poverty was merely a technique to control the unruly poor, the new ALP was described as a party keen to listen to experts who were similarly keen to be heard. Such a position was exemplified by Catley and McFarlane's 'technocratic labor' thesis.

As Catley and McFarlane depict it, discontent in the ranks of domestic industry became increasingly directed against conservative governments. The huge inflow of foreign capital was, by the end of the 1960s, used less for direct ownership and construction of capital resources than for speculation. Extensive state subsidies were, however, still being poured into the only dynamic (but mostly foreign owned) sector, namely the mineral and energy industries. In relation to domestic industry, serious questions were being raised about the level of protection and tariffs in specific business and bureaucratic quarters. To cap it all, there was a breakdown in wage fixation in 1969 which the Liberal government was unable to control, leading to faster rises in real wages during 1969–72 than those during the Whitlam years. For these reasons there were a variety of business leaders, conservative academics, especially economists, and civil servants calling for some effective co-ordinating planning machinery, a notion overtly rejected by the Liberals and their traditional supporters, because planning smacked of socialism.[40]

With the hindsight of the 1990s, however, the welfare radicalism prompted by new social movements, as well as the social democratic program of the new ALP, were also responses to demands from below. Moreover, in contrast to Catley and McFarlane, there was no reason to assume that the ALP's move against protectionism would inevitably result in favour of multinational capital, for example, let alone that the state could easily implement changes, *or* do so purely on behalf of monopoly capitalism.[41]

Looking back, the range of issues, the demands made and the numbers involved in protest movements, frequently in opposition to the trade union movement, were major signs that a transitional period in Australia's history was underway. This rapid politicisation included strenuous attacks on the woeful inadequacy of the existing welfare system. Hence, the poverty debate was not just between economists with a conscience and welfare 'experts', though even they were later ignored. The new welfare lobby was not merely an interest group: it contained diverse radicals who created new public forums; experiments from grass roots social workers were reported by sympathetic journalists, who shocked their readers with the poverty findings, even if this caused little more than 'vague unease' among the public, or a 'sense of sin' among those enjoying the fruits of the boom.[42] Perhaps it was merely another attack on the Liberals, who had presided over what was called the 'Ice Age'.[43] Nevertheless, poverty became a public issue, and it was the state to which critical attention was turned in the demand for change. The revamped Labor Party was at least listening to this spectrum of protest and opposition, as well as to the conflicting demands from domestic industry, multinational capital and economists. But such an ill-fated party (as in government it later proved to be) could hardly be accused of planning a new capitalist order, or, in a cynical technocratic manner, *using* the poverty debate, as some implied. Distinctions between what might be radical and what might merely strengthen the capitalist economy, however, were not always easy to draw among the strategies of that time.

How the poverty debate actually got underway is an easier question to follow. Several welfare experts set it off in 1964 with a tentative 'pockets of poverty' approach. Being a year of full employment, with a stable economy and a growth rate at 7 per cent, it was greeted with public disbelief.[44] Even this pockets approach, explaining poverty as a dispersed and individualised phenomenon (as radicals pointed out), was not itself granted official recognition until 1969. Meanwhile John Stubbs' *The Hidden People* of 1966, (modelled on Michael Harrington's *The Other America*, 1963) continued the pockets theme but gave a number – half a million – to the incidence of poverty. More explicit evidence came in 1970 when a Melbourne poverty survey demonstrated an inescapable percentage rather than a pocket. Welfare expert Professor Ronald Henderson found that the 4 per cent 'in need' suffered 'disabilities' of 'old age, lack of a male breadwinner, a large number of dependent children, recent migration to Australia, or prolonged illness'.[45] Although this survey's conservatism, its austere minima and its underestimation were soon attacked, this disabilities approach at least made a vital connection between poverty and the fate of those not in the workforce. It was also important in publicising the issue, since by then 'the measurement debate was on'.[46] Conservative governments tried to halt this outpouring, but ignoring the debate was proving counter productive. With an election imminent, Prime Minister McMahon reluctantly bowed to the demands for a national inquiry into poverty in Australia, now the subject of major newspaper editorials. In August 1972 a Commission of Inquiry into Poverty was begun, chaired by Professor Henderson.

Such a concession by the conservative coalition was totally ineffectual in the face of all the criticisms and protests against the old order, and soon after the McMahon government met with electoral defeat. The poverty inquiry was, of course, only one of the vast number of strategies attempted by the state once the ALP took office in 1972.[47] One of the early achievements (in 1973, before unemployment levels rose) was to raise the rate of unemployment and sickness benefit payments substantially, to the level of pensions. Instead of ignoring *the actual needs* of beneficiaries and thus enforcing the employment nexus via extreme hardship, there was now an element of need included. The Opposition, with its traditional conservative position that people would not work if given half a chance, argued that this change would generate 'idleness'. Even the Minister for Social Security, Hayden, justified the undoubted liberalisation by insisting that the work test still 'effectively controls the work-shy'. It was in that year that the term *dole bludger* was introduced to the press by a Liberal Party free trader, Bert Kelly.[48]

Ceaseless criticisms and internal doubts about the effect of welfare benefits on work incentives served as continual harassments for the more conservatively minded in the welfare field. In the Department of Social Security's own journal, a defence of the raised benefits set up a pathological model in which a majority of registered un-employed were cast as 'socially disabled', which was contrasted reassuringly with an estimated tiny number of 'work-shy'.[49] Others had higher hopes: the government also set about decentralising the Department of Social Security, in order to encourage the 'involvement of the people of the area in social planning and social action at the local level'.[50] Generally, it was a period of 'movement and optimism in welfare', later 'fatally weakened' by inflation, unemployment and economic decline, the more so since welfare expansion relied heavily on increasing economic growth rather than taxes.[51]

Ill omens and a plethora of counter attacks emerged while Labor was still honeymooning. A well known conservative journalist emphasised the importance of a survey by the OECD called 'Australia', particularly because its prognosis was so different from 'the contemporary conventional wisdoms of the local intelligentsia – currently preoccupied by the horrors of poverty, pollution and international companies and convinced that economic development and population growth need to be curtailed'.

The OECD was proposing 'more people, capital and technology from abroad', quite the opposite to the 'negative intellectual fashions' favouring 'selfish' barriers against immigration and inter-national capital, all 'done in the name of humanism'. Armed with quotes from the rising neo-conservative backlash in the United States (such as Irving Kristol's condemnation of 'the preoccupation with redistribution of income'), the position taken was that those who talk 'fervently' about equality are using it as a propagandist cover in a 'new class war' between 'the professional classes and the business community for status and power': 'Welfarism involves a rapid growth in job opportunities and incomes of social workers, nurses, teachers and public servants of all kinds and this has to be at the expense of business *and* industrial workers – and to the extent it is inefficient – at the expense of the underprivileged themselves'.[52]

It was from these sorts of arguments that 'neo-libertarian' support arose for a negative income tax. Yet in the face of the dole bludger backlash, radicals who had initiated the poverty debate themselves came to support a guaranteed income. Indeed, left wing elements had not been slow to criticise the proliferation of poverty inquiries. At the same time there were only a few efforts to recruit the poor to say something on their own behalf. Age and mothers pensioners' groups were set up in 1972, largely by social workers, but 'contrary to experience in America, it seems that the voice of the poor' was diminished rather than amplified by the proposals of the time to 'assist' Australians.[53]

The issue of who might be benefiting from the welfare explosion became controversial later on in the debate, when the alleged lack of participation by 'the poor' (compared with articulate middle income groups) in the Labor government's Australian Assistance Plan was seen as a reason for more direct cash transfers rather than services in kind.[54] That is, it was a further argument for other radical welfare groups, who began to formulate proposals for a guaranteed income in Australia. It was in complete opposition to the negative income tax envisioned by the 'neo-libertarians', let alone the other conservative elements rising against the possibility of a more progressive society. As will be seen, the motives for promoting and opposing the plans in both the United States and Australia were multifarious.

THE COUNTER-CULTURE VERSUS LEFT-WING POLITICS

During the same ten years of ferment, and much more widespread and oppositional than many of the key actors in the poverty debate, the Australian counter culture emerged, again later than the overseas trend. This section will deal exclusively with the Australian developments, only because the chief example of governments attempting later to use the counter culture challenges to the wage labour system arose here, when ALP governments in the 1980s promised to 'solve' unemployment with rural communes. By contrast the United States and Britain were by then in the grip of the more thoroughgoing conservatism of Reagan and Thatcher who, unlike ALP Prime Minister Hawke, did not bother meddling with the old counter culture communes.

As briefly mentioned before, the 1960s was a time when Australian unionists were economically militant and their wage demands increasingly successful. As elsewhere, most were still privately consolidating the suburban dream. Although rising numbers of women and migrants were entering the labour market, they were still politically quiet. The rapid expansion of high schools and tertiary institutions was also a significant post-war development. This ambiguous exclusion of the young from the workforce and the poor quality of the education provided, gave some content to their protest. Another issue was the control of young men through conscription to fight in Vietnam. Their protests erupted before the more explicitly excluded groups became politicised.

Although it was largely a student phenomenon, the counter culture was short-lived for other reasons as well. Soon after, significant numbers turned either to the activism of 'new' social movements (feminists, gays, environmentalists) and related alliances (notably in the green bans of the New South Wales Builders Labourers Federation), *or* took an exit path to communes. What was the motivation behind the commune movement? More recent literature on Australian communes tends to explain this flight as a cultural lag, deriving from American communitarianism, combined with a widespread sense of disillusionment following the failure of anti-Vietnam campaigns.[55] Those involved at the time stressed specific disappointments, such as the students' energetic campaign for the ALP in 1966 and police brutality towards anti-Vietnam demonstrators, which undermined students' previously growing confidence that they were the 'conscience of society'. Cultural values were henceforward regarded as too conservative and well entrenched to maintain the view that students' political role as the social conscience could have any efficacy as a strategy for change. Consequently, a new 'separatism' emerged.[56] Amidst the affluence of full employment, those who felt dissatisfied with their society also despaired that radical change could be brought about by revolutionary parties. To them this strategy was discredited by Stalinism on the one hand and the pervasiveness of Western consumerism on the other. Pessimism like this was widespread in the counter culture, due to cross-fertilisation and the importation of ideas from the United States and Europe.

There had been an outpouring of literature, poetry, underground newspapers, films and theoretical debates in the 1960s. Paris of May 1968 was one of *the* events, though there were many others. Allen Ginsberg, Hermann Hesse, Paul Goodman and exponents of the Russian anarchist tradition were just a tiny fraction of the popular heroes. Analysis of the counter culture's position against left wing strategies was exemplified by Murray Bookchin,[57] while theoretical celebrations like Theodore Roszak's *The Making of the Counter Culture* were very influential in expressing the new tendency:

> How often have we heard old-line radicals condemn the bohemian young for the 'irresponsibility' of their withdrawal into kooky communities of their own? Instead, they are advised to 'grow up' and 'be responsible'. . . . Give your energy to political action . . . plan political coalitions . . . find a project; agitate; sit-in; come to the demonstration. . . . The activities are noble enough. But they are at best, only episodic commitments. Run them together as one may, they have not the continuity and comprehensiveness demanded by a way of life. And it is a way of life the young need to grow into. . . . The trouble is, many of the young are just too alienated even for the intelligent compromise, with its inevitable disciplines, its taxed paycheck. . . . The answer is: you can make up a community of those you love and respect, where there can be enduring friendships, children, and, by mutual aid, three meals a day scraped together by honourable and enjoyable labor. . . . There are not many reliable models. . . . Maybe none of them will work. But where else is there to turn? And where else can one any longer look for the beginnings of an honest revolution except in such 'pre-revolutionary structure-making' (as Buber calls it)?[58]

Although such ideas for communes as a program for progressive change were widely popular in many Western countries,[59] the Australian commune movement arose from specific political and structural circumstances as well. Similarly, there was a specific context for the Australian government's considerations, a decade later, about the potential of communes as a state policy.

Australia's second drive to industrialise did not occur until after the war, so the promotion of household consumerism developed slightly later than in the United States. Education also expanded then, and the rising numbers of immigrants were allowed to have little cultural impact on the basically homogeneous and largely intolerant majority. In the context of Australian politics, neither the strong labourist flavour of the formal left wing parties nor the ambivalence towards Stalinism of the revolutionary parties appealed to students. These marginal left parties were trying to regain credibility, but not to the extent of accepting growing numbers of educated, middle-class students, unless they were revolutionaries. Since the far left still focused mainly on a proletarian revolutionary consciousness, via a 'strategic' unionism, students could play little part. Students themselves rejected such strategies. Not yet wage labourers, but disliking the new consumerism of most wage labourers (let alone of their own families), students turned to remaking their own lives in a way that was more oriented towards the *rejection* of the existing society than towards its *remodelling*.

A brief look at the directions of Australian radical thought at the time, particularly the debates about the potential of the counter culture's turn to communes, demonstrates this more clearly. In this context, the student movements' widespread rejection of electoral strategies in favour of 'cultural radicalism' came just before the ALP restructure. Traditional labourism with its attendant racism was replaced by what, retrospectively, could more adequately be regarded as a brief glimmer of social democratic programs and interests (such as those regarding poverty) than a 'technocracy'.[60] The ALP was and still is the only Australian mass-based party of the left, especially following the weakening of the Communist Party of Australia (CPA) after 1956. A variety of new left groups emerged in the universities during the 1960s: rarely debating with the ALP, most were dedicated to somehow 'detonating' a mass movement for radical change. As small cliques, however, such hopes for wider support were ruined by their tendency to compete against each other rather than engage in dialogue with the general student body.[61]

In comparison with the old left intellectual tradition, which was largely a selective celebration of male working-class myths, simultaneously pursuing a unionist strategy and following either the Moscow or the Peking line, the new left led a revival of radical intellectual thought. It turned to various continental strands of neo-Marxist theory, such as Gramsci and the Frankfurt School, and at the same time was frequently contemptuous of working class politics.[62] The old left's vision of socialism was criticised for resting too much on mateship and nationalism, as well as relying on the simplistic attribution of socialism's failures to betrayal by leaders.

Some new leftists (like Humphrey McQueen) took eclectic positions by criticising Australian working class values for being racist, jingoistic and bourgeois in aspiration,[63] while agreeing with the CPA that the Labor Party was committed to capitalism and always had been. McQueen at the time set this down to the 'petit-bourgeois consciousness' of the working class. A revolutionary or 'proletarian consciousness' had emerged more from the Wobbly traditions and the CPA's anti-racist campaigns, and was again discernible in the extensive strike actions of workers who opposed industrial arbitration in the late 1960s.[64]

The old parties responded by trying to shake off the statist assumptions of traditional dogmas. Even though the CPA retained its opposition to reform through parliament, the notion of a revolutionary subject required rethinking. Whether to find another social base – possibly in the new student protest movements – or to analyse more carefully whether the working class had indeed been 'integrated', were the main dilemmas. By 1970 Althusserian Marxism was also becoming influential and the CPA was urged to find 'a strategy which recognised the irreducibility of levels of struggle . . . [while] criticizing the collapse of political perspectives into an undifferentiated ethical struggle against "capitalist values" '.[65]

In other words, if these new theoretical influences, in the face of political bankruptcy, led the old left to reformulate policies and strategies, it did not mean that the cultural radicalism inspiring so many middle class university students was to be welcomed. And, by and large, both the new and the old left tended to reject what they saw of student movements. While being self-critical about their own failures towards students, many new left intellectuals considered, for example, that

> the student radical left has demonstrated a partial capacity . . . to break through the prevailing consensus (to which the old left contributes), . . . to activate new areas of concern, dissent and resistance. Yet the movement's potential as a powerful oppositional or revolutionary force is threatened by its own lack of concern for the formulation and articulation of relevant theory. Political radicalism is undermined by cultural continuity.[66]

This questioning the potential of the student movements was exemplified in the disapproval meted out by the left to Dennis Altman, who in 1970 wrote a series of articles on the counter culture in the United States and Australia. I will discuss this debate at some length, because Altman's was the most prominent attempt to develop an Australian theory of the counter culture and of radical change through alternative structures of everyday life. It came just as the commune movement was beginning.[67]

Altman's celebration of the counter culture was used as evidence that important changes in people's behavioural habits were taking place. He argued that the causes of student revolt should have been attributed not just to the Vietnam issue, but to far more encompassing social change: students should have been seen as the 'barometer' of what he diagnosed as a transition to post-industrial society. The counter culture was neither a class revolt nor directed at economic inequalities, but a cultural revolt 'of the favoured against the system that increasingly favours them', asserted Altman. Technological change was very likely to increase 'bureaucratic order', but it might equally open up 'possibilities for clashes on values'. Since it carries its own internal contradictions, post-industrial society is not an end to history, as posed either by Bell's 'end of ideology' or by Marcuse's 'one dimensional society'. The counter culture was 'post-literate, post-Protestant and post-liberal'; it combined an anarchic strain with a search for community: ' "Doing your own thing" and the need for community are the two planks of the counter culture, and if their synthesis is not easily achieved there are steps towards this in experiments with communal living and community self-government'.[68]

Altman considered his analysis less applicable to Australia, which had neither a Marxist cultural heritage like that of continental Europe nor the liberal rhetoric of the United States. The Australian respect for authority and 'repression of self-expression' were not mitigated by any ideology of freedom or natural rights, as in the United States. Without an 'intellectual counter culture', the tension between new and old in Australia was more between *life-styles* than between *forms of thought*. But if the counter culture rejected establishment policies, it also rejected traditional left values: 'puritan/specialised/positivist/linear values'.[69] Altman stressed the need for a 'cultural revolution', since if scarcity had been overcome, repression had not: only if values were changed would elites lose support. In Australia, although a Labor government was preferable to a Liberal one, only 'limited progress' was possible through party politics: real social change occurred through cultural change. This was not a simplistic reversal of Marx (social being is the key to consciousness), because the counter culture had developed out of the new technological changes. For Altman, 'the socio-economic structure acts as a broad limitation on possible developments of consciousness – counter culture is in some ways a dialectic product of the modern industrial state – but not, surely, as a determinant of automatic and inevitable reflexes'.[70]

Neither development was pronounced in Australia – yet. Even so, if the counter culture were to provide an alternative model and shake large numbers out of apathy, Altman warned that there was no guarantee that it would not be co-opted and merely result in bolstering the status quo.

Altman's presentation of this latter argument drew a hostile reaction from both the old and the new left.[71] He was accused of 'mechanistic determinism', since the change from industrial to post-industrial society was attributed not to capitalist relations but merely to the forces of production. Altman was transforming 'the contradictions of capitalism' into 'a clash of cultural values, and, at this point, mechanistic materialism turns into simplistic idealism'.[72] He was denouncing the producer ethic as it was becoming obsolete; hence the counter culture occurred 'because the functional requirements of capitalism are in a flux'. Although the counter culture detached the young from established values it did not offer a 'firm alternative', and therefore was not a 'revolutionary subject'. Australian Marxists must not fall for every 'passing fad', but, nevertheless, the counter culture might have efficacy as a 'point' where revolutionary ideas could enter popular consciousness.[73]

These kinds of criticisms give some idea of the theoretical positions of the time. Altman himself was later to be more explicit about the statist consequences of either the reform path or the notion of a revolutionary subject. Other left criticisms were more ambivalent. One welcomed the fact that Altman had initiated a debate on these issues at all, for the 'institutionalised Marxists' in Australia were also limited in accepting 'the narrow bourgeois definition of politics as 'something out there' and separate from the 'rest of one's existence'.[74] They viewed politics merely as 'violence, power and organisation'. Nevertheless, both the left *and* the counter culture tended to separate politics from culture, for if the Marxists were too dogmatic in rejecting culture, Altman and Roszak also deserved criticism for neglecting politics. They failed to see that the counter culture myopically over-values itself in rejecting politics so as to change the 'wicked' dominant culture. Moreover, Altman's contradiction between a 'technocratic lifestyle' and the subjectivity of liberated hippie movements confuses 'abstract categories' with 'living reality'. This reasserts bourgeois social theory's separation of public and private, which counter culture theory was combining as 'technocracy'. For Peter O'Brien, 'it is not simply a pragmatic question along the lines "will a hippie commune work?" Rather, it is a serious conceptual confusion between the bourgeois "hypostasization of individuality" and what is in reality the social construction of the "individual".' In this way, Altman makes 'a similar mistake to the "solely political" revolutionaries – a denial of the dialectical nexus between political, cultural and individual liberation'.[75]

Hence where 'vulgar' Marxists argue that social liberation must precede individual liberation, and Altman merely reverses the equation, both have separated the two processes.[76] Altman's originality lay in his attack on the puritanism and bourgeois culture of many 'new Left revolutionaries', as well as the CPA attitude to revolution as an 'externalised happening, a swift, sudden displacement of power relationships'. The new liberation movements, according to O'Brien, were responding to 'the totality of bourgeois repression . . . rooted in the *instinctual* structure of every individual within capitalist society'.[77] Some Marxists' superficial dismissal of cultural revolution as merely a hip capitalism of drug and rock consumerism, as opposed to 'the real political struggle', revealed their own 'repression'. Moreover, counter culture issues should not be regarded as good organising concerns for a *vanguard* although, *contra* Altman, a 'revolutionary culture' would 'lead to the realisation' that *both* the actor and the social structure have to be transformed. These criticisms of both positions were apposite, as an exchange between Altman and a Marxist-Leninist student group reveals. In retrospect, the left was correct in fulminating against the counter culture's failure to analyse even 'the hip capitalism of drug and rock consumerism'. Altman himself remarked on these problems, but the other side's narrow intolerance was exemplified in this left group's view of the counter culture as 'objectively counter-revolutionary'.[78]

Altman's continuing attempts to develop a theory of the counter culture led him to a conception of politics broad enough to include social movements other than the labour movement. While recognising that hedonism is by no means revolutionary, Altman could now see a theory and practice far more revolutionary than Marxism and the traditional working-class movement developing in the women's and gay liberation movements emerging from the counter culture. He still supported communes as one form of the 'alternative institutions' being developed, not from an economic perspective, but as an attempt to reconstruct a family as a form based on association, not birth, and to reconcile the need for autonomy and community. As for its middle-class white basis, Altman considered that the working class – with the exception of the 'sub-proletariat' such as the Aborigines or unskilled migrants – had been assimilated 'as is': 'Whether it be the Communist Party in Italy or France, the "hard-hats" in America, or the union movement in Australia, they represent groups who may not always support the status quo, but who nonetheless are very unlikely to support any sort of revolutionary strategy'.[79]

Even the 'embryonic' counter culture in Australia faced attempts at direct repression from 'established authority', with police action and official hysteria in response to protests, hippies and the 'drug culture', along with censorship trials. According to Altman, while the counter culture was ignoring 'economic wo/man', it was far worse that Marxists were ignoring 'the non-economic needs of wo/man'.[80] By this stage, Altman's analysis was less optimistic about the potential for change coming out of the commune movement.

Yet these disputes between the more organised intellectual left groups, the theoretically mostly inconsistent counter cultural movements and their qualified defence by figures like Altman, was only part of the legacy taken up by later post-industrialists. The fact was that the counter culture spontaneously acted *again*, as Altman recognised, but in quite divergent directions. The commune movement emerged as the element representing disillusionment with the possibility of transforming society. The previous political struggles, as we saw, had been further handicapped by hostility about the issue of *culture* on the part of the left wing parties and the wider 'labourist' tradition. If the 'new' social movements thereupon became one way of politicising needs (especially of women and gays) that had been so totally ignored by this tradition, pessimism about changing the system and rejection of student activism was another widely followed option. Instead of fighting for change in the public arena, this group set out on their own challenge against wage labour.

For a significant group of students in Australia, the turning point away from old-style political clubs *and* mainstream participation in the workforce, towards concerns with personal expression, community and personal relationships came around 1971. It was reflected in the Nimbin Festival of 1973, which was sponsored by the Australian Union of Students and partly aided by the new ALP government. The festival resembled a Woodstock or an Isle of Wight; it exemplified the main characteristics of counter culture 'happenings' throughout the West. Politics had by now become the 'politics of cultural change'.[81] It was Nimbin (in balmy northern New South Wales) that first witnessed the mushrooming of communes in Australia.

THE SELF-IMPOSED DECLINE OF RADICALISM

Conscious and widespread self marginalisation followed immediately after the Nimbin festival, and encompassed far more than earlier experiments with urban communal housing. By 1974 the 'rural utopian back to the land' movement was being described as 'one of the most significant and seriously motivated elements of the counter culture' in Australia.[82] A year later *The Way Out*, a selection of influential commentaries on the phenomenon, was published. It gives numerous indications of the decline of radicalism involved. The emphasis, following Altman's earlier work, was on a celebration of changed consciousness being effected within alternative lifestyles. Foremost among the commune enthusiasts in Australia was Peter Cock, who was one of the many from the original counter culture to become involved in government plans for communes in the 1980s.[83] Writing of an alternative strategy in *The Way Out*, he represented a view promoting the independence of individuals from institutional structures. The need for certain 'social forms' was accepted, but these must be 'facilitative of personal powers'.

The pathway to radical change rejected revolution as well as reformism, because the demands of the 1960s had meant asking change of the despised policy makers whose manipulation was 'inevitable'. The effective way to change the 'corporate state', according to Cock, must begin with the micro-structures,[84] for by creating alternatives like communes 'we can experience right now in concrete form the meaning of a civilisation of interacting persons'. The middle class could begin change, since the 'reactionary' working class was only concerned with distributive consumerist struggles. It was important to create the alternatives first, because the participants would then have 'new life and power to be able to tackle the social order'.[85]

The editors of *The Way Out* were more cautious about the turn to self marginalisation, and their warnings exemplify the decline of the counter culture as an oppositional movement. It was necessary to redefine goals since many could now see that 'being an outgroup' did not solve either their own or their society's problems. They called for more honesty about the problem that communes were merely a fashionable alternative: the underprivileged did not have the option of dropping out, and regarded the anti-materialist philosophy as middle-class self-indulgence that cheated them of rights they had not gained. Despite the warnings, the editors still attempted to suggest that the social order *could* be challenged by rural communes: 'Moving to the country might solve some people's particular hassles, but unless you move somewhere like Nimbin . . . where people are trying to communicate with the larger community and the local district, you will be doing very little to change the direction of society, and the oppressive nature of many people's lives'.[86]

By contrast, the few critical comments, for example, on the insufficiency of changing 'people's heads', since external structures and relations of power were more important,[87] were by now of little concern to the commune movement. This was clearly evident in *The Way Out*, where accounts of communes, self evolution, spirituality, alternative schools, living styles and health by far outnumbered the articles on radical politics, such as the anti-Vietnam campaigns of nearly a decade previously and the then current green bans in Sydney.

In addition, a different political element in the volume highlighted the Whitlam government's sympathetic approach to the separatist movement (along with the original anti-Vietnam position). Cabinet member Moss Cass, for example, argued that 'political action and power' were needed to deal with social and institutional forces, but he recognised that politics could not reach the whole 'human spirit', and that alternatives to the conventional 'dead-end future' sprang from times of 'profound cultural turmoil'.[88] Others in the Whitlam government proposed a 'legitimate role for government' in the commune movement. Although an ALP Conference submission on encouraging 'less materialist lifestyles' had been narrowly defeated in 1973, progressive support was considered 'inevitable': 'Without buying out the converted, a government can assist them make their point of view more effective'.[89]

By this stage, when the commune movement was becoming so popular, Altman was much more critical of the notion that marginalisation could be a strategy for social change. This part of the counter culture was merely returning to traditional rural values, he argued, save for the emphasis on breaking away from the consumer ethic. But the experiments in personal relationships, although inspired by resentment of monogamy, were only proving that traditional sex roles 'appear more difficult to escape in the confines of a closed group than in the midst of anonymous urban living'. There was also a new and strangely pervasive 'puritanism', and a problem that a radical break with the nuclear family frequently required authoritarian direction. Against the commune movement's faith in small groups being exemplary alternatives, Altman was now stressing the counter culture's challenge – through the 'sexual liberation' movements – to the beliefs and values legitimating the existing social order.[90]

Altman also suggested that a new problem was becoming apparent in ecological concerns. This ironically showed the counter culture representing the direction that Western society might have to follow out of *necessity* rather than a conscious *rejection* of the previous affluence.[91] As a measure of his disillusionment with the commune strategy, Altman warned of the dangers of the incorporation of counter culture ideas, citing the governmental encouragement included in *The Way Out*. His fear of state interest in communes was, in fact, to prove well founded only in the case of the Hawke government.

Although the bias was towards communes at the time, there were some experiments with other alternative structures. Disagreement with the commune strategy led to suggestions, for example, that 'co-operative workplace ideas' were far superior to small group communes, since 'they can be adopted by a huge range of ordinary people within our society, but because they change the nature of one of the fundamental bases of society, they cannot be co-opted by society as it is'.[92] But in fact only a few 'pure' worker co-operatives were set up in the early 1970s, arising also from the spontaneous enthusiasm of the middle class 'drop outs' in the commune regions.

For the next decade, communes remained isolated, while some communal groups attempted to battle against local regulations on their own. It was not until Australian governments attempted to formulate post-industrial policies on unemployment in the 1980s, that the commune movement became implicated in quite different designs of the state. This will be later discussed in detail as one of the test cases. During the 1970s, however, communes gradually lost their shock effect to become occasional objects of derision in mainstream political debates in spite (or because) of several Whitlam government ministers' tolerance of the counter culture. Indeed, mainstream animosity against 'dole-bludging hippies' provided part of the promise for progressive post-industrialists. More seriously, the supposedly radical experiments with redefining work, and the theoretical position that wage labour was so dehumanising that it was altogether better avoided, were very influential.

By the time the federal government became interested, the impact of the counter culture, as such, was well over. Having excited the imagination or indignation of so many in Australia for a few years, existing communes would later shake off their counter culture origins.[93] Worker co-operatives, by contrast with communes, never appeared as so 'radically' alternative to mainstream participation in the workforce. They could not contest the cash/work nexus by rejecting it by *choice*, because most experiments began only after the recession, through various internal responses to state 'employment' strategies. By the mid-1970s, guaranteed income proposals were part of a major attempt to roll back the radical tide of the 1960s. On the whole, it proved to be relatively successful, even though the guaranteed income idea eventually became unnecessary. After the world recession gradually deepened, alternatives to wage labour became redefined as alternatives to paid work, and then appeared (to governments) in a different light.

NOTES

1. S.A. Marglin (1990), p. 5.
2. D.J. Rothman (1985), p. 108.
3. This period covers the ten years prior to the election of the Whitlam government in 1972, and the Kennedy and Johnson administrations in the USA. Police forces were repeatedly drawn out during the anti-Vietnam demonstrations, students were shot dead at Kent State University; and drug and censorship trials were common.
4. G. Esping-Andersen (1990) p. 166.
5. F.F. Piven & R.A. Cloward (1971), pp. 202–5, 253; J.T. Patterson (1986), p. 111.
6. Harrington, cited in J.T. Patterson (1986), p. 99.
7. F.F. Piven & R.A. Cloward (1971), pp. 255–6.
8. J.T. Patterson (1986), pp. 101–15, 134–6.

9. *ibid.*, p. 111; F.F. Piven & R.A. Cloward (1971), p. 256.
10. J.T. Patterson (1986), p. 245; F.F. Piven & R.A. Cloward (1987), p. 10.
11. A participation rate of 33 per cent of eligible families in the early 1960s rose to more than 90 per cent in 1971. J.T. Patterson (1986), pp. 178–81; J. Quadagno (1990), p. 16.
12. J.T. Patterson (1986), pp. 158–9; F.F. Piven & J.T. Cloward (1987), p. 20.
13. G. Esping-Andersen (1990), p. 174.
14. F.F. Piven & R.A. Cloward (1971), pp. 202–5.
15. J.T. Patterson (1986), pp. 159.
16. J. Quadagno (1990), pp. 14–5.
17. J.T. Patterson (1986), p. 157.
18. G. Esping-Andersen (1990), p. 175.
19. F.F. Piven & R.A. Cloward (1982), pp. 14–32.
20. G. Elliott (1978), p. 35.
21. J. Roe (1975), p. 148. This underclass comprised Aborigines, single parents, large families, recent migrants, the young and the unskilled – categories which had either existed in the long term or were created as a consequence of post-war drives to industrialise, using high migrant intakes.
22. L. Tierney (1970), p. 217.
23. W. Higgins (1978), p. 142.
24. P. Stricker & P. Sheehan (1981), p. 40; R.F. Henderson (1971), pp. 113–4.
25. F.G. Castles (1985), p. 99.
26. J. Roe (1976), p. 323.
27. F.G. Castles (1985), p. 101; R.F. Henderson *et al* (1975); S. Horne (1970).
28. M.T. Lewis (1975), p. 15.
29. G. Elliott (1978), p. 34.
30. Cited in L. Tierney (1970), p. 220.
31. Cited in M.T. Lewis (1975), p. 5.
32. J. Roe (1976), p. 320.
33. Cited in J. Roe, *ibid.*, p. 315.
34. P. Hollingworth (1975), p. 5; L. Bryson (1977), p. 197.
35. J. Roe (1975), p. 147.
36. T.H. Kewley (1980), p. 37.
37. N. Blewett (1973), p. 363, my emphasis.
38. For example, for various discussions about the nature of the ALP both past and present see P. Beilharz (1986); S. Macintyre (1986).
39. F.F. Piven & R.A. Cloward (1982), p. 29. They had also, in *Regulating the Poor* (1971), accused the Democrats of having a Machiavellian plan to win Black support: see J.T. Patterson (1986), pp. 133–5.
40. R. Catley & B. McFarlane (1983), pp. 91–3.
41. See B. Frankel (1978), pp. 15–16, for a criticism of Catley and McFarlane on this issue.
42. J. Roe (1975), p. 147; G. Elliott (1978), p. 35.

43. R. Ward (1973).
44. Experts such as Mendelsohn - see J. Roe (1976), p. 317; R. Catley & B. McFarlane (1983), p. xvii.
45. Henderson *et al* (1975), p. 196-7.
46. See J. Roe (1976), pp. 316-8.
47. R. Mendelsohn (1979), p. 322.
48. Hayden, 28.2.73, cited in M.T. Lewis (1975), p. 16; A. Farrar (1987), p. 26.
49. S. Spooner (1973), p. 22.
50. Hayden, cited in T.H. Kewley (1980), p. 41.
51. P. Tulloch (1983), p. 265; R. Catley & B. McFarlane (1983), p. 125.
52. Peter Samuel, *The Bulletin*, 24.2.73. my emphasis.
53. J. Roe (1975), pp. 318-19.
54. For example, M. Jones (1974/5).
55. E.A. Sommerlad, *et al* (1985), p. 30; M. Munro Clark (1986), p. 54.
56. R. Gordon & W. Osmond (1970), pp. 25-30.
57. See, for example, his collection of essays in M. Bookchin (1971).
58. T. Roszak (1970), pp. 201-3.
59. The criticisms, for example, by P. Abrams & A. McCulloch (1976) and J. Case & R. Taylor (1979) are also relevant to Australian communes.
60. For example, S. Macintyre (1986).
61. R. Gordon & W. Osmond (1970), p. 8.
62. *ibid.*, pp. 11, 38; W. Higgins (1974), p. 165.
63. Patrick O'Brien (1973), p. 122.
64. H. McQueen (1970), pp. 59-65; R. Catley & B. McFarlane (1983), pp. 92-3.
65. W. Higgins (1974), pp. 166, 177, 179; also see Peter O'Brien (1971), p. 31.
66. R. Gordon (1970), p. vii.
67. The titles partly reveal his arguments: 'Students in the Electric Age' in R. Gordon (1970), 'The Politics of Cultural Change' (1970a), later followed by 'Revolution by Consciousness' in H. Mayer and H. Nelson (1973), among a number of other studies.
68. D. Altman (1970), pp. 130-1, 135, 141.
69. D. Altman (1970a), pp. 23-6; (1970), p. 146.
70. D. Altman (1970a), p. 27.
71. Peter O'Brien (1971), p. 23.
72. K. Rowley (1970), pp. 148, 156.
73. *ibid.*, pp. 158-61.
74. Peter O'Brien (1971), p. 22; (1970), p. 163. O'Brien was critical of the limitations of historians like Brian Fitzpatrick and Ian Turner, as well as the new approach of McQueen and Terry Irving.
75. Peter O'Brien (1970), pp. 24-5.
76. Peter O'Brien (1971), p. 165. Most orthodox Marxists in fact agree with 'vulgar' Marxists on this point. For an elaboration, see A. Heller (1976).

77. Peter O'Brien (1971), pp. 26, 27, my emphasis.
78. *ibid.*, pp. 26–9. Flinders University Marxist-Leninists (1973), p. 720.
79. D. Altman (1973), p. 723.
80. *ibid.*
81. D. Altman (1977), p. 460.
82. G. Gill (1974), p. 7.
83. Cock later wrote his PhD thesis on communes.
84. Here Cock was following Marcuse's stress on liberating 'our inner subjective condition'. P. Cock (1975), p. 5.
85. He argued, for example that the least dehumanised can 'provide a lead to the down-trodden' while the final strategy would 'deal with those most resistant to change'. *ibid.*, pp. 5–11.
86. M. Smith & D. Crossley (1975), pp. 1–2.
87. C. McGregor (1975), pp. 16–17.
88. Moss Cass, then a federal Minister, provided the foreword to the Smith & Crossley volume.
89. P. Ellyard (1975), pp. 205–7.
90. D. Altman (1975), p. 14; (1977), p. 457.
91. D. Altman (1977), p. 463.
92. D. Bisset (1975), p. 169.
93. By the time of the Hawke government interest, it became known more mildly as the 'alternative lifestyle' movement.

PART II
Alternatives in Practice

CHAPTER 4

Guaranteed Income Schemes:
The Success of the Backlash

In the first part I suggested that post-industrial arguments about subverting the 'employment system' involve three main theoretical assumptions. The first is that a policy aiming to break the cash/work nexus would be properly implemented by governments. Second, that the market is more effectively contracted, controlled and reformed by reducing rather than increasing market participation. Third, the counter culture's theoretical rejection of wage labour demonstrates the subversive, 'radicalising' nature of the strategy were it to be generalised. Consequently, the separation of income from work is only progressive if all three assumptions are well founded.

The context for the emergence of this theory has also been laid, to the point where these assumptions will now be tested. This second part consists of evidence of several governments that formulated three major strands of the proposal into concrete policy – namely, guaranteed income, commune and worker co-operative schemes.

Even though other governments would naturally operate differently and face specific circumstances other than those considered here, the test cases are generalisable in the following respects. The policies incorporated the exact content of the post-industrial strategy in numerous ways. In every case, countless dilemmas or contradictions appeared in these policy-formulating processes, and the resolutions and debates around them therefore reveal the practical implications of a broad spectrum of potential policy directions. Finally, post-industrialists themselves argue that unemployment is no temporary phenomenon confined to specific (although numerous) OECD countries. Rather, it is a permanent, inevitable 'fatality' for all, better met – across the board – by implementing their strategy. That is, they claim it is generalisable within a relatively uniform environment of post-industrial societies.

I will now return to the context where the governments in question set out on 'post-industrial' paths. Of note, the political and cultural challenges between the 1960s and the early 1970s involved, from one corner, many demands on states to *weaken* the employment nexus. Raised levels of unemployment benefits and age pensions, and expanding social wages like health, housing and educational opportunities did, in fact, considerably enhance the ability of organised labour to improve its position in the labour market. With hindsight, it is generally agreed that this period of reform served to decommodify wage labour to a much greater extent than previously, especially in countries like the United States and Australia.

Yet the challenges from below had been initiated by activists from those sections of the population historically excluded from the specific institutional structures of either the American or Australian labour movements, and the effects for them were more mixed than for groups within these structures. Blacks in the United States, women and students in both countries, and Aborigines and recent migrants in Australia had, during this decade, made various attempts to emerge out of these situations of segregation and political marginality. Some elements managed to form large popular movements while others became more or less politicised. Although a few movements arose directly from the counter culture, the resurgence of activism in itself had probably been inspired by the civil rights movement.

By the 1970s, however, the politicisation of these formerly excluded segments had resulted in only a few institutional victories. Women, Blacks and recent migrants still predominantly occupied the lowest paid and least secure end of the labour market. They remained like-wise predominantly the stigmatised clients of the welfare state, for even if unemployment benefits enabled more to wait for a better price or choice of employment, and even if AFDC or 'widows' pensions' became more widely available to Blacks or single women generally, these rights were not firmly accepted, as this chapter will show.

By contrast, in 1973 James O'Connor predicted a fiscal crisis of the state. His diagnosis involved comparing, first, the growth in budget expenditures of states trying to maintain both accumulation and legitimisation (or 'mass loyalty'), second, the inability of states to collect sufficient taxes from the corporate sector and third, the new demands of the 1960s that, unlike those arising from capital–labour disputes, were directed solely against the state. He predicted that a fiscal *crisis* would ensue because states would be unable to buy social peace in the face of escalating demands from below. Twenty years later it is clear that the term 'crisis' is inapplicable: states proved to be more adaptable than had been predicted. Many governments took on conservative and authoritarian positions vis-à-vis marginal populations at the same time as they removed various controls on markets. Hence, while demands abated, budget deficits did not.

Moreover, after the 1973 oil shock, unemployment took off in numerous OECD countries and those previously excluded Blacks and women were joined by other young people and those over fifty. The assumption (made by Habermas and other post-industrialists) that states merely respond in an environment neglects not only government adaptability or management of change but also the contingent nature of reactions from below. There were infinitely changing alliances and splits; strategies were piecemeal and unpredictable. In the 1990s there is still no 'crisis' and unemployment is still politically acceptable, despite the fact that such a long period of recession, cutbacks and increasing marginalisation was unthinkable in the early 1970s.

The first case study gives counterfactual evidence about the separation of income and work, taken from those governments that seriously proposed alternatives to employment as state policies. None of the proposals – the guaranteed income plans, the so-called 'informal economy' proposals, the Australian schemes for communes and worker co-operatives – was ever broadly implemented, certainly not at a national level. Nevertheless the practical implications are clearly evident in the scope of policy formulation, of experiments and of national debates. Moreover, as *policies* they are noteworthy in their similarity if not faithfulness to post-industrial theory. The truly damning factor in this evidence concerns the *motives* for state involvement. While governments positively enthused over the schemes, none ever aimed to defend the unemployed or in any way enable a challenge to be mounted against the existing economic and political system. Indeed, far from these post-industrial intentions, the opposite was accomplished. As we will see, the impetus for government interest arose from conservative or economic libertarian motives intended to stem the 'demand overload' and ameliorate fiscal and electoral problems in relation to unemployment and increased welfare provision. The *similarities in content and differences in motive* will be carefully investigated. The processes that *led* to state interest in alternatives to existing forms of paid work provide the central counterfactual evidence, but the subsequent effects *live on* in the countries concerned.

The first concrete proposal for a guaranteed income came the closest of all to implementation. It emerged in the United States during 1970, and by 1972 it had been defeated. In Australia, 1974 saw major recommendations for guaranteed income schemes from a handful of key government bodies, which were rejected by 1975. The plans emerged when the oppositional movements were still highly visible, and when extended accountability structures and wider definitions of citizenship had reached many OECD governments' agendas. If a guaranteed income were not necessarily progressive even in times when those governments were relatively liberal in their dealings with the least powerful parts of society, it is fair to be even more cautious in the present context of chronic unemployment and political conservatism. The commune and worker co-operative policies did not arise until the 1980s, when conservatism was more entrenched, even in the case of Australia's new Labor government.

In all cases (although to a greater or lesser extent), the proposals did not originate in state departments or come from technocratic planners, but initially came to public light through the protests and experiments of the social movements and radicals of the 1960s. Their demands were about subverting, not preserving, the status quo, and they occurred when the level of debate was unusually open to oppositional groups. Moreover, the negotiations and disputes between the various groups involved in these counterfactual cases followed no easy path. This throws light on the difficulties that constantly befall any effort to formulate needs from below. Finally, although the rationales behind the radical challenges and the state proposals were so totally different, *the similarities between the alternatives* hinge on the question of the cash/work nexus, similarities which ultimately support new right or economic rationalist policies.

FROM SOCIAL MOVEMENTS TO STATE POLICIES

The evidence of the last chapter shows that one part of the radicalism of the 1960s attempted to oppose the strong tradition of Australian labourism or American individualism by breaking the cash/work nexus. Such counter culture ideas became integral to the post-industrial vision. *Alternatives to wage labour*, therefore, describes a radical idea with the explicit aim of transforming existing social relations. By contrast, the conservative interest in alternatives, as alternatives to *existing and accepted unemployment*, was oriented solely towards maintaining the status quo. The very nature of state interest means that the adoption of such alternatives as concrete policy could never be more than partial. All the alternatives under review here have a tendency to break the cash/work nexus to a greater or lesser extent (see figure 1, p. 92). As a radical idea, each proposal comprises different levels of formulating needs to provide greater control over working than over wage labour, as discussed in chapter 2.

The following counterfactual cases show that state interest in the alternatives cannot break the cash/work nexus *in practice*, since this would create other state problems. The rationale behind the state policies, therefore, was never to embrace the proposal that would break the cash/work nexus most radically, yet this is the one alternative that above all requires state implementation. A *universal* guaranteed income set at socially acceptable levels would enable all members of the society to avoid meaningless work. No Western state has introduced this policy, and its future implementation is most unlikely given the nature of these governments and their negative reactions to date towards providing an income above minimum wage levels. On this, even post-industrialists, like Bill Jordan, agree. An income set below socially accepted income levels is a different matter, as we will see. All the other radical proposals for breaking the cash/work nexus as a reforming prescription are of interest to the state, since income provision is not inherently a part of the plans and universal implementation is unnecessary. Hence, the separation of income from work – a grim reality for the already excluded and unemployed – could possibly be rendered ideologically more attractive if various groups were provided with alternatives, such as a commune or a worker co-operative. The fact that they *might* provide an alternative source of subsistence or *possibly* some money, would ease the state problem of providing incomes. Governments wanted to avoid maintaining the marginalised population through cash transfers or job creation schemes, and thus to drive down the price of labour.

Although none of the schemes were, in the event, implemented, the governments involved derived considerable gains. It is to these

The Relation of Income and Work in Modern Societies: Subversion of, or subordination to, the employment system?

	Socially acceptable as adequate income	Control over work process	Duty to work	Freely assumed obligation	Rationale of state policies
Guaranteed income	Yes	*	No	?	State never introduces policy.
Worker co-operatives	Maybe	Yes	Yes	Maybe	State policy for unskilled, unemployed and the redundant.
Communes	No	Yes	Yes	Maybe	State proposal for unskilled, unemployed. No choice, survival work.
Unemployment benefits	No	*	No	Maybe	State reduces or redefines benefit, tightens work test.
Wage labour	Yes	No	Yes	No	State to keep wages down, threat of unemployment.
Guaranteed minimum income	No	No	Yes	No	Proposal to deregulate labour market and reduce social wage. May lower minimum guarantee.
Work for the dole	No	No	Yes	No	Vertically imposed duty to work.

*Depends on the demand for labour.

Breaking cash/work nexus

Enforcing cash/work nexus

Possibility to avoid meaningless work, and therefore relative control over life.

Adequate income if viable. Control and horizontally accepted obligation.

Self-sufficient if productive aim, and/or ability to claim benefits. Arable land and skills required.

Tendency to loosen nexus only if benefits sufficient, and work test allows choice.

Income and relative control depend on labour market position.

In principle not in labour market but forced to search for any work.

Compulsory and meaningless work.

Figure 1 The relation of income and work in modern societies: subversion of, or subordination to, the employment system?

contrasts, distortions and difficulties, as revealed in the debates of the time, that I shall now turn. As we saw, the period up to the mid 1970s was a time of crisis to which most governments were unable to respond effectively except by conceding a presence to oppositional groups in the political arena. The guaranteed income scheme was one of the many debates, as well as being the first post-industrial alternative, that was seriously considered as policy by at least two different kinds of states. As policy, President Nixon used it as an initial counter response to the reforms of President Johnson's administration which (like the Whitlam government in Australia) had been central in the early stages of debate. The kinds of changes that might have been implemented, from reform to deregulation and welfare cutbacks, depended on the outcomes of these struggles. The changes that ensued from the interplay between radicals and conservatives are described here in some detail, since the cases illuminate the dilemmas facing social movements and hence the key problems with the post-industrial strategy. The state is the central issue here, since only the state can implement the changes; but in these respects also, only the state can distort the intended effects.

GUARANTEED INCOME SCHEMES IN THE UNITED STATES

The guaranteed income idea represents an alternative to paid work. An income is guaranteed by the state, irrespective of a citizen's activity, once her or his income falls below a specified level. The specification of the level is crucial as it involves two completely different standpoints towards the operation of guaranteed income schemes: a maximum level determines the opposite trajectory to a minimum level. These two positions can most clearly be discerned in the work of two major contributors to the guaranteed income debate in the United States.

In 1965, Robert Theobald – a left liberal – proposed a guaranteed income from the perspective of then popular predictions about the effects of cybernation and abundance. According to his view, it would serve as a short-term solution to technological unemployment, and a long-term solution to breaking the cash/work nexus, because a guaranteed income set *above* minimum wage levels would destroy the financial incentive that forced people to sell their labour power, and would thereby achieve 'full *un*employment'. The resulting social justice would undermine the labour market and remove the constraints of wage labour, where social need is limited by earning power. Instead of meaningless types of employment, incomes would be assured and people could choose not to work, or to work in groups (which Theobald described as 'consentives') on 'custom made products' or in communication and information activities, as described in Marshall McLuhan's vision of all-round interaction in a 'global village'.[1] This is generally the 'maximalist' position.

The 'minimalist' position is represented by, among others, Milton Friedman, who suggested a negative income tax in *Capitalism and Freedom* (1962). Friedman's intentions for a guaranteed minimum income set *below* minimum wage levels were to *preserve* and *restore* the market, both in recommodifying and further spreading the commodity form. This would, he argued, strengthen the freedom to choose one's own work, goods and services, and to exercise one's own judgement instead of being subject to the prescriptions of welfare services, with their implicit assumptions that the poor are somehow inadequate. It would encourage greater consumerism, protect the incentive to work, prevent further growth of government services and eliminate or at least minimise public welfare costs. Where Theobald favoured retaining other forms of welfare, and spoke of 'entitlements' for all, Friedman talked about abolishing 'bureaucratic excess' and granting 'benefits' to 'the poor' through Internal Revenue. Hence, Friedman's further premise was that with a minimum income guaranteed to all, the government would (and should) stop intervening in the economy. As such, negative income tax – or a guaranteed *minimum* income – represents cash against public services, the individual as against the collectivity, a minimum of equality of opportunity as against egalitarianism, and the marketplace instead of the political arena.[2]

There was initial enthusiasm for both positions, partly as a response to early optimistic post-industrial arguments about automation. But the popularity of either Theobald's viewpoint or Friedman's perspective (the latter especially among economists) was also a reaction to President Johnson's war on poverty, with its proliferation of federally funded services. Criticism from the left as well as the right suggested that the middle class fared better from a submission system; and that professional research flourished while the poor got little cash and much less of the benefits of education.

It was, however, the Friedman idea that reached the level of political and practical experimentation. Barry Goldwater used it in the 1964 presidential campaign, while Daniel Moynihan (who had taken an intense interest in Black 'families') 'sold it' to President Nixon.[3] Proposals for a negative income tax emerged not just in the United States during this time, but also in Canada, Australia and several European countries, while in Britain the Conservative Party pressed for it under the banner of 'Down with the Poor'.[4]

The Nixon administration was, of all the interested governments, the most closely identified with a disguised version of a negative income tax, although one aimed only at families with children. In 1969 Nixon proposed a Family Assistance Plan (FAP), the fate of which has been critically analysed by Jill Quadagno in an argument stressing the importance of recognising how social policy is organised by race and gender as much as by class. She shows that Nixon's FAP had the intention of forcing young Black males into the labour market and mothers into unpaid housework and private dependence. The FAP was, however, finally rejected, mainly because in the south the income guaranteed would have exceeded minimum wage levels for Blacks and therefore threatened the entire structure of the Black labour market in the South.[5]

There are more precise reasons for its failure after three years of 'ugly, mean' skirmishing.[6] Nixon's plan was designed to stimulate work by using market incentives rather than compulsory work requirements. It proposed abolishing Aid to Families with Dependent Children (AFDC), the means tested cash transfer for poor women and children, and replacing it with a negative income tax for poor working families with children under eighteen. The combination of set payments to each member of a family, an annual earnings exemption and a 50 per cent marginal tax on non-exempt earnings would have meant that a family of four with no working members could receive a guaranteed income floor of $1600 a year, whereas a similar family with an employed household head could still receive benefits until its income reached $3920. A 'workfare' element was added that required adult recipients to register for 'suitable' training or work, or forfeit their welfare subsidies.[7]

The implications of the FAP in the north were vastly different from those in the south. In the north, as we saw, there had been an explosion in AFDC, a welfare program that did not enforce a male breadwinner/female caregiver family type. Far from it. AFDC was 'wrong and indefensible', according to Nixon, for it 'makes it more profitable for a man not to work than to work, . . . [and it] encourages a man to desert his family rather than stay with his family'.[8] Quadagno argues that if there was a 'legitimation crisis' of the state when the urban riots were at their height, it is important to remember that the rioters were primarily young Black males. How would this insurgency be contained by Nixon's proposed expansion of welfare to employed household heads? Policy makers, according to Quadagno, did not focus on the state of the labour market and Black unemployment as the source of civil disorder, but on the state of the Black family. Many agreed with Moynihan's well publicised arguments that the disintegration of the Black family was the ultimate cause of riots. His prescription was to re-establish male dominance in the Black family by guaranteeing that 'every able-bodied Negro man was working': 'Ours is a society which presumes male leadership in private and public affairs', but in the 'Negro' family 'the dependence on the mother's income undermines the position of the father'.[9]

Hence, although Nixon tried to sell the FAP with promises to increase AFDC mothers' workforce participation, there were no programs to provide for this and the childcare provisions were negligible. Subsidising the low wages of Black males in their role as breadwinner and removing the program that paid benefits to single women were therefore the chief objects, in order to resolve, indirectly, the turmoil in urban ghettos. In Quadagno's words,

> neither welfare mothers nor women in working-poor households would have gained autonomy. Designed by white males, the FAP also would sustain a racially segregated labor force and do nothing to increase the occupational mobility of black males.[10]

The response to the proposal was mixed, although not divided so much by class as by race and gender. Representatives of the big corporations, for example, typically favoured a more limited version that removed eligibility for anyone involved in a labour dispute. Representatives of more labour intensive small businesses vehemently opposed the threat that the FAP posed to their labour supply. The small service-sector firms, many in the south, were well aware of the feminisation of the labour force, and wanted to preserve their supply of low-wage labour from welfare mothers. The FAP would reduce southern women's incentive to take this work.

As far as organised labour was concerned, racially motivated resentment had developed against the explosion of AFDC and other benefits to the 'non-working poor', in a defence of the 'working poor' (who were 70 per cent white). Some powerful unions protested against civil rights gains and turned from the Democrats to George Wallace's segregationist ticket. The traditional concerns of labour emerged too, however, over the potential of FAP to undermine union wage levels and to flood the market with low-wage workers, hence intensifying the competition between the working poor and welfare recipients for a fixed number of jobs. Despite this, organised labour accepted the FAP bill with minor changes because they had little concern for the non-unionised Black and female low-wage service workers: they were not in the same labour market. Unionists had also campaigned to maintain gender and racial barriers, particularly during the 1960s, when the American Federation of Labor opposed the Equal Rights Amendment for women, as well as government attempts to desegregate the construction industry. Unionists were alarmed at the threats posed by the social protest, fearing both the high costs of welfare expansion and the erosion of their market privilege. By contrast, FAP was not seen as a threat because the split labour market would remain.

The south generated the greatest political opposition to FAP, since its introduction would have raised the entire southern wage base and revolutionised its economy. Where FAP would increase the number of welfare beneficiaries in the north by 30 to 50 per cent, the welfare rolls in the south would rise by 250 to 400 per cent. Most Blacks in the south did not work at minimum-wage jobs, but were marginally employed (as maids and seasonal farm hands), and FAP would have equalised the earnings at the bottom of the scale between men and women, Blacks and whites, and minimum and non-minimum wage workers. It would have removed political power from whites as well. This was because, first, the southern welfare system was manipulated to give planters cheap farm labour, in that it provided federal welfare in the winter and forced workers into the fields during spring and summer. Second, any political activity could threaten welfare recipients, to the extent that Blacks in the deep south were denied welfare for engaging in civil rights activities or even registering to vote. The extent of Black voter turnout was determined by the source of livelihood. In counties where Blacks were dependent on white landlords, white employers and white sources of credit, political participation by Blacks remained low.[11]

Any implementation of the Family Assistance Plan in the south would have reduced Black people's economic dependence on whites, by freeing them from the necessity to accept the lowest wage work and enabling greater political participation. Senator Russell Long of Louisiana, one of the many who opposed the reduction in the cheap labour supply, exclaimed at one stage in the debate in Congress, 'I can't get anybody to iron my shirts'. The southern Democrats were hence the most determined opposition, although the bill was defeated by additional influence from an entirely different protest from below, namely the welfare (AFDC) women in the northern ghettos who said, 'We ain't gonna clean it'. The National Welfare Rights Organisation lobbied 'liberal' Senators about the threat to their economic security, the workfare requirements, and the total inadequacy of the minimum floor (in the north), and proposed to 'ZAP FAP' as it would force northern recipients to take any low-paid work.[12] Hence, as Quadagno suggests, despite the support for the plan from big business, organised labour and state bureaucrats, the combination of those who opposed it, for quite different reasons, proved more powerful. Southern conservatives, Northern liberals, urban welfare mothers and the Chamber of Commerce were the most outspoken, and Congress scuttled FAP in 1972.

There were several experiments with guaranteed income schemes in a number of states, but by 1978 Moynihan announced that, since the experiments had proved 'calamitous', he had been mistaken about the proposal. According to Moynihan, the scheme had increased 'family dissolution by some 70 per cent', had 'decreased work' and so forth.[13] Rather than being a vindication of Theobald's claims for the 'maximalist' position, however, evidence suggests it merely reduced wives' workforce participation far more than husbands', thus enhancing male authority in the household. Moreover, the case may well have been that even the minimalist proposal, with its aim to reduce the social wage, was by then unnecessary after the oil shock (1973) and the subsequent welfare 'backlash' that deepened with President Reagan's election in 1980.

GUARANTEED INCOME PLANS IN AUSTRALIA

A rather different set of conflicts occurred in Australian debates over a guaranteed income. It was a time of full male employment, high wages and salaries, but very limited services-in-kind and low levels of cash transfers. The oppositional groups involved in the poverty debate had tried to redefine and formulate new needs, and demanded that welfare provisions be improved. This politicisation of formerly ignored needs resulted in certain changes in the state, though the changes that were effected drew other state responses and created further conflicts with increasingly militant conservative groups. By the years 1974 and 1975, four major federal documents had recommended variations on a guaranteed minimum income, while two reports had rejected the scheme. After the Whitlam government was sacked, however, official debate was hastily closed by the Fraser government.[14] But for five years a range of groups representing many interests and political views supported either the maximalist or minimalist standpoints, opposed both, or reversed their previous opposition to guaranteed income schemes.

Such schemes were opposed mainly by two kinds of positions.[15] Those taking the first, anxious to promote raised cash transfers and the establishment of social services like housing and health, were fearful that any guaranteed income would prevent such reforms to the male wage-earner form of welfare (which consisted mainly of arbitration and tax concessions) in Australia. These welfare reformers and welfare radicals included the new oppositional groups, such as the feminist movement, as well as welfare agencies, welfare experts and bureaucrats, and Labor politicians, from the paternalistic to those promoting greater participation. The second position opposed the guaranteed income on the grounds of the work incentive. *Any* guaranteed income would obviate the need for the able-bodied to work or, at least, suffer the work test. The authoritarian conservatives promoting this argument claimed support from a huge cross-section of wage and salary earners: the so-called taxpayers.

The earliest promotion of the minimalist position came from the fledgling neo-libertarian movement, attracted to the Friedman vision. As a consequence of welfare demands, neo-libertarians were alarmed at the imminent growth of services and promoted the negative income tax as cheaper than and preferable to an increased welfare state. These and other aspects of the neo-libertarian vision were not just opposed by welfare radicals and reformers, but also by entrenched dominant groups from the rural and manufacturing sectors (the old authoritarians). Neo-libertarians wanted reduced protection and reduction of government regulations in order to permit freer movement of capital and of multinational corporations. The negative income tax would also drive down wages (and hence inflation) and undermine union strength. Welfare 'experts' and welfare reformers, exemplified by Henderson, chair of the Poverty Commission, were partially implicated here as well, since their later minimalist position was mindful of taxpayers' political strength. They were concerned, however, about the effects of wage earner status in Australia, which marginalised and impoverished *all* cash-transfer categories. A guaranteed minimum income, as a right accorded to all citizens, would help to undermine this marginalisation. Other voluntary welfare bodies were concerned with shaking off entrenched paternalism and stressing the right to define one's own needs.

Support for the maximalist position was more a response to the increasingly aggressive work incentive position of authoritarian conservatives, when unemployment benefits were raised in 1973. Attendant upon the attacks on beneficiaries, various welfare radicals turned to this view, particularly left wing intellectuals then associated with the Australian Council of Social Services (ACOSS). Their position was similar to that of Theobald, in questioning the 'work ethic' and revaluing women's unpaid work.[16] Along similar lines the 'wages for housework' debate among Marxist-feminists occurred at much the same time.

THE PROMOTIONAL CAMPAIGNS:
GUARANTEED INCOMES VERSUS WORK INCENTIVES

Guaranteed income plans were probably discussed first in Australia in about 1969, well before poverty was officially acknowledged.[17] Some, taking inspiration from sources such as Theobald's *The Challenge of Abundance* (1962), pointed out that 'the popularity of this idea of an automatic and impersonal guarantee of an adequate income is owed to the fact that it provides a vision of a system of social benefits which will not consign beneficiaries to second class citizenship'.[18]

The poverty debate became an increasingly significant public issue. In the face of the conservative government's refusal to acknowledge the issue, ACOSS, a peak body formed in the 1950s to represent national voluntary welfare agencies, was moving away from a patronising charity ideology towards a radical welfare position against the state and began to lead the demands for the poverty inquiry in 1972.[19] In 1970 ACOSS launched a discussion about Nixon's Family Assistance Plan, where sharp disagreement was expressed against the negative income tax. The position was that if a guaranteed income were meant to 'most help those who needed it most', Australia's pension scheme already did that. In addition, given the history of pensions being regarded as a right and not a charity in Australia, the idea that a guaranteed income would prevent recipients from being stigmatised was inappropriate. Instead, 'the chief threat to human dignity in Australian income security comes from the inadequacy of rates of benefit for those without other resources – that is, the guaranteed minimum'. The overriding problem here was that even if a negative income tax were instituted there was no certainty that it would set an adequate minimum.[20]

The inadequacy of President Nixon's scheme was therefore a further reason for rejecting the negative income tax idea as irrelevant for Australia. In 1971 Henderson, for example, asked whether the 'sweeping measures' proposed in the United States would be any more effective than a 'piecemeal' approach for the Australian case. Friedman's solution for the United States was irrelevant because, unlike Britain and Australia, the United States had no system of family allowances to households with children, and also had 'considerable unemployment and under-employment and substantial areas of low wages and earnings'. He considered that the merit of the minimum income scheme in the United States was that every dollar would go the poor and none wasted on the 'comfortably off'. But there were defects: 'without an *unacceptably high rate of effective taxation* and at reasonable cost, the minimum income provided can only be about half the poverty line'. Also, the negative income tax was stressed as a substitute for other welfare services. As Henderson put it, 'obviously it is not a complete substitute so long as it only provides an income half of the poverty line'.[21]

This understatement highlights Henderson's classical economic perspective of defending low tax rates. The economies supposed to be gained from sweeping away welfare apparatuses seemed to him 'exaggerated' claims. More seriously, a negative tax would be inflexible in the face of the need for immediate help in cases like bereavement, desertion and accident, where social services would still be needed.[22]

Henderson's austere poverty line and tendency to 'blame the victims' were understandably criticised at the time,[23] yet his emphasis on the importance of raising minimum or basic wages was more interesting. Comparing the wide discrepancy between British and

Australian minimum wages over the previous twenty-five years, he defended the Australian Arbitration Commission's role in effectively raising the real wage of unskilled workers (including male migrants). Its 1969 judgement had given a larger percentage increase to wage earners at the bottom of the scale than to those higher up. This was, he considered, 'a valuable approach to the reduction of poverty'.[24] Henderson suggested that the two outstanding problems in the Australian welfare system were the failure by migrants to take up existing services and the poverty of those paying market rent for accommodation.

Such reservations about guaranteed income schemes were at least partly a function of the boom conditions still obtaining in Australia. More to the point, though, was that welfare reformers and radicals were at the forefront of public campaigns to extend social services and the actual level of cash transfers. The growing enthusiasm for a guaranteed minimum income was based more on the new economic libertarianism and was mainly connected with attacking the mounting poverty debate. Negative taxation first received promotion from the Taxpayers' Association. Similar to Friedman's idea, it was a version of the tax rebate system, with the tax-value rebate fixed for everyone, regardless of their income. Low income earners, instead of paying no tax at all, would receive the tax value of the wife deduction, for example, as a refund or subsidy. By relieving 'some of the taxation pressure' for those on low incomes, wage and price rises would be reduced. The 'utopian aim' was to achieve such 'stability' as to minimise wage rises altogether and to keep down prices.[25]

Clearly these views opposed those of Henderson's on the 1969 wage rise as a method of relieving poverty. Fears about inflation were directed to the control of wages and not prices. The relative strength of labour vis-à-vis profit shares at the time, and the fact that inflation benefits the poor more than the rich (by and large), meant that support for negative income tax was in the interests of dominant groups.

At this stage, however, such discussions were only a prelude to the forthcoming struggles. By 1972, action on guaranteed incomes became more concrete. After much agitation Henderson began the poverty inquiry, and his terms of reference expanded after the Whitlam government took office at the end of the year. When the inquiry was over, Henderson emerged as a guaranteed minimum income supporter. In the meantime, a modest guaranteed income experiment was conducted by the Brotherhood of St Laurence, in an explicit effort to publicise poverty as a social rather than an individualised phenomenon. The Brotherhood also moved to support full government implementation of a guaranteed income scheme.[26]

In 1973 unemployment and sickness benefits were raised considerably and the dole bludger campaign was immediately launched by conservatives. Accordingly, libertarians supporting negative tax felt duty bound to use the flimsy evidence of experiments in the United States to justify their position that negative tax did not affect work incentives[27] – or, to be more precise, depending on the tax level and income floor set, *should* not affect them. A quite different response to the growing dole bludger campaign was to ignore incentives. Indeed, rather than being concerned about the possible deleterious consequences of a guaranteed income on attitudes to work, a tiny minority of welfare radicals suggested far more dramatically that the work ethic itself should be questioned.

The most influential work from this approach was carried out by Margaret Lewis, a member of ACOSS. She criticised 'the work value' as having an 'inflated' position over other values informing the Australian income security system. 'Equality of economic well-being' was of little interest to either the government or the community at large, because it contradicted 'the principle of contribution to national wealth' so entrenched in the Australian system. This resulted in the stigmatising of groups such as supporting mothers, 'whose social behaviour is considered deviant by middle class norms'.[28] The constraints imposed by wage earner welfare denied others a right to income security, because such a right related only to 'previous contribution to national wealth and productivity'.[29] Lewis argued that this should be the object of criticism. It led to problems even with the newly raised level of unemployment benefits, because the new commitment did not mean that the ALP government was rejecting the value of the work ethic. As she said, the new ALP government philosophy merely presupposed 'that a person will *choose to work* rather than choose *not* to work; it is not a rejection of the value of the work ethic, although it is suggested by the Opposition that the new policy will have this effect'.[30]

While Labor was not really rejecting the work ethic, it was ignoring the contradictions inherent in 'the traditional view' of self

help, namely that all the able bodied should contribute to the productivity of the community, which in turn should *enable everyone*
to make such a contribution. This notion of reciprocal obligation
was contradicted by the profit motive, where work is just a means
to an end which is continually adjusted to achieve the least cost. Since
this 'business orientation' towards work was also a deeply embedded
one, for those subjected to it 'the instability of employment sometimes compares unfavourably with the stability of income security
programs'. It was possible to preserve the work ethic and achieve
greater equality by combining a guaranteed income with social
assistance and universal payments to specific categories (such as
child endowment). But Lewis questioned whether a guaranteed
income should be related only to traditional social contingencies.
'Because of low wages and unstable employment conditions many
people may have a greater need for an adequate and stable income
than a need for work as such'.[31]

As the attacks on 'dole bludgers' mounted, the promotion of a
guaranteed income, which would attack work incentives and erode
employers' prerogatives, developed rapidly.[32] Some suggested that,
since the working poor's jobs were ill paid, dull and offered little
chance of 'advancement', many might well prefer a social benefit.
The protestant ethic was only a rationalisation for society's need to
scapegoat the poor. It was predicted that work disincentives would
be only temporary, because 'the market would react by making the
range of dreary jobs more attractive' and, as 'futurists' argue, 'automation will make work unnecessary for most people'.[33]

Months later, just when the government's commitment to full
employment was being abandoned, stronger statements about
breaking the nexus between work and income mounted. ACOSS
formed a taskforce recommending an 'adequate minimum income'
as a right for all citizens. The assumption here was that as long as
people were *forced* to work in meaningless or demeaning employment, there was 'no compulsion in improving the quality of jobs
made available'. ACOSS pointed to numerous anomalies. First, the
community feared the provision of adequate welfare lest jobs go
wanting, although it desperately sought 'to create new jobs, however
socially worthless or ecologically destructive, as old ones disappear'.
Second, the tradeoff between inflation and unemployment, where
government policy made it necessary for a certain percentage of the
population to be unemployed, contradicted the work ethic. Instead,

'if the community can only absorb a certain number in the work-force then it should allow some other groups to drop out'. Finally,

> viewing work in terms of pay alone has produced a synonymity of 'pay' and 'worth'. We come closer to a multi-dimensional definition of work if we define it as 'an activity that produces something of value for other people'. This definition broadens the scope of what we can call work and places it within a social context. Housework, care of children and 'voluntary' work for instance, are seen to be work since they are being productive for other people.[34]

This radical thread of the guaranteed income debate (one that was making explicit use of the Theobald maximalist position for full *un*employment, but also with new feminist strands), emerged at the same time as several *official* recommendations for a guaranteed *minimum* income. A thinktank set up by the Whitlam government, the Priorities Review Staff (PRS), entered the field first with its report: 'Possibilities for Social Welfare in Australia'. It was far from sympathetic to welfare recipients and to the expansion of services under the Whitlam government. First, the generosity of the minimum income was tied to the amount of social services and welfare payments it would *replace*. Second, the proposed income of $28.84 per week with a 50 per cent tax rate, was only slightly better than the $23 per week a single unemployed person received in 1974. The qualifications and justifications provided by the PRS indicate the types of changes it envisaged:

> Payments to 'idlers and dropouts'. The scheme would carry an incentive for those able to work. For many the incentive may not be adequate. In order to gain political acceptance, it may be necessary to incorporate tests of willingness to work, or to be retrained, into the scheme.
> Entrenched interests. Many well-intentioned providers of social services may feel threatened by obsolescence, and working in the (negative) Taxation Department may not appeal. . . .
> Paternalism. The view that the poor do not know what is good for them (or their children) is widespread and, particularly where children are concerned, may be justified in some cases. A compromise here could be vouchers for particular services.
> (Further) while we do not see income redistribution as a panacea, the general thrust of our argument is that if direct transfers are feasible, it will help more of the poor, more efficiently, than provision of services. But we recognise complications. Direct transfers may not always be allocated in ways which alleviate poverty (eg. booze instead of food) and this argues for a minimum income system supplemented by residual

personal benefits, including health and education, rather than for a system of broad and inevitably paternalistic social services.[35]

This report was greeted with a variety of responses, and the mass media turned to the debate and attendant bureaucratic rivalries with relish.[36] It was hailed as a 'blueprint for radical social reform in Australia' in a grand splash in *The National Times*, and was initially supported by various conservatives.[37] Neo-libertarian positions were even more favourable to the idea of negative income tax. For example:

> If everyone's incomes were raised by this means to a *reasonable level*, there would be no pressing case for the continued existence of the State Housing Commissions, which confine the poor to ghetto housing estates where the vicious circles of low expectations and low performance interact to ensure the maintenance of social problems. Education and health should also be able to be priced so that competition and choice and innovation are restored. *These services are too important to be left to the dead hand of government monopoly,* and NIT *would ensure that inability to pay was no longer an excuse* for this . . .[38]

In a similar fashion, *The National Times* drew its own conclusions from the report: 'The proposals on social welfare are aimed at slimming the *great welfare bureaucracy* and providing a more efficient and just service. The proposals on the economy and business are clearly committed to a free enterprise market system which would bring approval from OECD'.[39]

The PRS report was, therefore, closely connected with the renewal of economic libertarianism and the concomitant opposition to the Whitlam government's reformist path. The report had ignored the problem that housing, health and education would all have to be paid for from an extra $5.84 per week. Moreover, housing and health had never been 'government monopolies' in Australia. (The ALP government faced strenuous opposition even to the Medibank public health scheme.) For libertarians the risk that recipients would spend their money on 'booze and pokies' was preferable to the paternalism of welfare, and certainly to its expense.[40] Apart from the paltry nature of the 'great welfare bureaucracy' in Australia – despite the efforts of the poverty debate – the arguments about paternalism also wilfully disregarded the question of 'discretional income'. Below a particular income there is little control over consumption: if the dollar a week saved is never going to be sufficient to enable a mortgage to be taken out, for example, there is no choice between saving or spending.

The PRS report was released in 1974, a few months before unemployment actually started to rise. The campaign against 'dole bludgers' had become more hysterical and vicious. In opposition to the views of the PRS, the paramount concern in the 'bludger' campaign was to control those who had apparently chosen to evade the discipline of work and 'live off' the rest of the community, especially 'hippies' on communes. As we saw, the 'debate' grew from the virulent campaign against the ALP government's substantial liberalisation of unemployment benefits.[41] Now, arguments to the effect that 'only the human vegetables should get aid handout' filled the press.[42] Wild estimates of the numbers of 'no-hopers', 'loafers' and 'slackers', were made in a 'perfect blizzard of denunciations' by Liberal politicians, according to a *Herald* editorial. The *Herald* itself argued that 'the general, and eminently justified view is that people have a right not to work, but no right to taxpayers' support in choosing idleness'. The Labor government's response was to 'tighten up' the benefits system quite harshly, while maintaining that 'we can't force people to work against their will'.[43] Some Labor leaders also joined the general attack.

Amidst all this rhetoric, when unemployment suddenly rose in the middle of 1974, its causes were frequently attributed solely to the rise in benefit payments. By then, the ALP government was the subject of increasing attacks. Overshadowed by the far more significant transformations of the time, the debate about the guaranteed income continued, along with the other recommendations from the many commissions and committees still in progress.[44] In the context of the 'bludger' campaign and the sudden rise in unemployment, the guaranteed income debate became more complex. Henderson's own attitude had changed during the course of the Poverty Inquiry. He now believed that 'piecemeal' reform would not work, and that a 'sweeping reform', which he believed his proposed guaranteed minimum income would prove to be, was the better approach in order for income transfers to be regarded as an automatic *right*.[45] To talk of rights amid this new 'dole cheat' media beat up, was another response to campaigns against the Whitlam government's expansion of welfare. Henderson's interim report, recommending a guaranteed minimum income fairly similar to that of the PRS scheme, was also released in 1974.[46]

The first 'official' rejections of guaranteed minimum income schemes were published that year as well. The Asprey Committee, which reviewed taxation, disposed of negative income tax schemes summarily. Instead, its main proposal suggested swinging the whole tax system towards the indirect taxation of goods and services. The Asprey Committee was only interested in whether a 'primary test of eligibility' would be applied, since it could only approve of tests 'recognising *particular* causes of need' – age, unemployment or sickness. Whenever these 'primary' tests were discarded and replaced by 'the sole tests of income and family size', such an income guarantee was stepping right over their dividing line. Negative income tax schemes proposed to pay an income 'irrespective of whether the recipients have genuinely sought work and been unable to find it or are genuinely sick or disabled or have any other valid reason for not earning their own livings. In the Committee's view, such schemes seem likely to have consequences for incentives to work and save which make it impossible to consider them seriously'.[47] In effect, the Asprey Commission insisted that poverty should never be the criterion for an income guarantee, only inability to work. Following this opposition and Treasury's unsurprising dislike of the expense of even a bare minimum guaranteed income,[48] the official debate quietly wound down and was buried with the sacking of the government in November 1975.

The guaranteed minimum income idea was not entirely lost in Australia. A few years later, a far more radical economic libertarian vision proposed deregulation of all markets, reduction of government services and, consistent with *pure* liberalism, a 'resolute application of anti-monopoly and restrictive trade practices legislation'. In this version, a negative income tax would forestall moves to raise the minimum wage, because of the supposed benefits of an income guarantee to 'part-time and seasonal workers, self-employed workers earning less than the minimum wage and the unemployed'. These groups would form the lower level of a two-tiered labour force. The higher level would be privileged by the introduction of 'worker-capitalism' via superannuation funds. (Some of these predictions are now fact.) The scheme would guarantee full employment to a reduced percentage of a unionised workforce, while the guarantee would be 'made explicitly dependent on stability-conforming wage behaviour'. A more recent, and even harsher position is defended by certain economists, while in 1989 a new guaranteed minimum income scheme was included in a left program as well.[49]

There were other versions debated during the Whitlam government years which focused exclusively on women. The wages for housework debate appeared, initially, to be the most radical of all the suggestions, since, by its reckoning, the capitalist system was underpinned by the unpaid domestic labour of women.

The housework campaign was conducted between 1972 and 1975 by several feminist groups in Europe and North America, as well as Australia. In 1972, Selma James demanded equal pay, childcare and a guaranteed income 'for women *and* for men, working and not working, married or not'. 'All housekeepers are entitled to wages (men too)'.[50] Later, wages for housework became the single strategy, mainly because it embodied an insistence for greater control over all aspects of women's lives.[51] It was assumed that if the creation of surplus value depended upon women's unpaid labour, then wages for housework would undermine capitalist production. Critics, especially other feminists, quickly suggested that rather than challenging the sexual division of labour it would institutionalise women as housewives, with the spectre of the state as employer. The general character of the guaranteed income does not necessarily contain these implications. The debate petered out by 1975, when it was demonstrated that surplus value was not *necessarily* dependent upon unpaid housework.[52]

Another proposal of the time, similar to the wages for housework campaign, was an idea for mothers' wages. This was justified quite differently by, for example, David Gil in the United States. Gil argued that the consequences of wages for mothers would be an increase in the bargaining power of women at the segregated end of the labour force – there would be a shortage of women because of those who had withdrawn onto mothers' wages, while those still in the labour force could in turn threaten to withdraw. The wage would end women's economic dependency and families would gain 'economic strength and related political power'.[53]

In Australia at that time, the feminists' successful fight for equal pay had only improved a very limited number of job categories. Equal pay in fact revealed more starkly the sex-segregated nature of the labour force, particularly marked after seventy years of the family wage. Accordingly, the main projects of the 1970s were affirmative action to break down traditional barriers, and demands for childcare and the eradication of sexism in schools.

In 1973, in answer to the demands for child care, the Department of Social Security (DSS) addressed the issue merely by suggesting the payment of mothers' allowances. Feminist groups like Women's Electoral Lobby (WEL) showed a brief interest before flatly rejecting the idea, the chief defect of the proposal being that the DSS never suggested that men might do such chores. The DSS had opposed spending government money on 'substitute care' rather than mothers' allowances, because childcare encouraged 'maternal employment' and 'deprived' mothers of the choice of working or staying at home.[54]

Feminists, mainly from WEL, opposed this for being discriminatory in that working mothers would be paying for those not at work, and that the dual workload would also be reinforced. Moreover, the element of choice in this allowance would be negligible for most women, who either worked or stayed at home not by choice but because of a host of other compelling reasons – economic hardship, housing conditions, inadequate childcare and traditional social attitudes.[55] The allowance would not be generous enough to approach a real wage: the DSS offer amounted to half the current female factory wage rate, and this would only reinforce the lowly rating of childcare and housework. In any case, the Minister for Social Security (Hayden) had rejected even that.

Meredith Edwards also suggested that if it *could* be proved that mothers actually do make a contribution to the whole economy through their domestic duties, it could result in 'making the value to the family of these services subject to income tax', because fairness would dictate that a larger personal tax exemption should be provided to working couples. Concerning childcare, if a society were to pay mothers to stay at home, the quality of the care would be difficult to assess. Women's contribution to the economy could be far greater if they worked, while economies of scale and specialisation could be effectively achieved in childcare services. In this sense, society might easily face greater costs by inducing women to stay at home.[56]

Some right wing women's organisations supported mothers' allowances, however, and the ACTU included it in its policy. It was especially backed by Catholic, Democratic Labor Party (DLP) unions.[57] Hence, while Australian Marxist-feminists were considering wages for housework,[58] WEL was just refuting mothers' allowances. WEL had perceived no relation between unpaid domestic labour and its benefits to capital, but the wages for housework debate never considered the state, or not until the full implication of the state as husband/employer was realised. The ascriptive nature of wages for housework was quickly recognised and the idea abandoned, although in terms of feminist theory, the policy discussions from ACOSS and these radical debates enabled a much clearer distinction between work and employment to emerge.

DILEMMAS

In analysing the further fate of guaranteed income plans, several issues should be addressed. The first concerns dilemmas or implications if any had been implemented. Questions to be considered here are what sort of gains and losses might have accrued, and to whom. The second is the role of the state in these particular struggles to publicise new needs from below, the mounting opposition from above and the diverse support, in the Australian case, for the various versions.

Both issues are related: in considering the gains and losses, one of the chief problems inherent in any guaranteed income is that it requires state implementation. Furthermore, the historical problem was that any possible effect on the market could not be predicted, except by considering the particular context and structure of the labour market for different groups, such as the case of Blacks in the southern United States.

For any guaranteed income, the predictions about market reactions comprised the following options. Would a right to income seriously affect the work ethic or even break the 'income/work cash nexus'? If so, would this actually result in gains (money, dignity, power or some combination of these) for those outside the unionised labour force? And would it force the labour market to improve the quality of jobs on offer, or to automate even faster, or conversely, hire at cheap rates those supplemented by a guaranteed income? If it cannot really weaken the cash/work nexus, would a guaranteed income result in an increase or a decrease in wage bargaining power for all those people presently without such leverage, and/or threaten those already possessing some bargaining potential? These were the conjectures that in the United States applied differently to Blacks in the north and south, and in Australia applied variously to women, migrants, Aborigines and the unemployed.

In the case of Australia, radical libertarians had certainly seen the potential for wage reduction in the negative income tax.[59] Nevertheless, other gains might have accrued to the powerless. The potential effect that a guaranteed income might have for women, in the sense of their gaining the status of citizen rather than being treated as a category – woman-as-mother or woman-as-houseworker or woman-without-male-breadwinner — was radical. By contrast, this was the chief drawback with the wages for housework debate, and hardly new in the history of Australian income security and arbitration, where women were always a separate category. Yet the radical ACOSS position for a generous guarantee that would sever the cash/work nexus, as well as both debates about payments to women, suffered from the chief defect that if the state was going to reject a minimum guarantee, it would never agree to a maximum. Nevertheless, even a relatively 'frugal' income floor, and Henderson's disappointing retention of 'categoricals' in his guaranteed minimum income,[60] had one advantage. It would still dismantle the chief principle of the seventy-year-old income security system in Australia, namely that security was a right only if contributions to 'national wealth' (of either wage labour or babies) had been made previously. Poverty and citizenship were to be the chief criteria or, as the Poverty Commission put it, the new aim was 'to emphasise that the right to a minimum income and the obligation to pay tax are but two sides of the same coin'.[61]

Of course, there were still dangers in relying on market predictions, especially ones so contradictory and dependent upon the current political and economic situation. After the Australian government abandoned full employment and moved to the right, the beneficial effects of a guaranteed minimum income looked, from the ACOSS position, far more doubtful.[62] Many on the left thereupon felt constrained to prove that everyone, given a chance, would prefer to work. The income/work nexus had been broken forcibly, and oppositional groups were pressed into continual denials that unemployment was a matter of individual choice, as the 'bludger' campaign insisted. But the previous radical position – in favour of a guaranteed income set above minimum wage levels – also included issues similar to new right fulminations against self-serving welfare experts. Some left perspectives especially criticised the short-lived Australian Assistance Plan for increasing the powerlessness of the poor to the benefit of the articulate middle class, and for the dangers of 'comprehensive social planning'.[63] Direct distribution of Aboriginal welfare expenditure, for example, would have given Aborigines double the basic wage if welfare workers' wages were subtracted. As Bryson noted, the 'poor' usually receive only 'a small proportion of any money ostensibly spent on their behalf', when slum clearances mainly benefit investors, retraining schemes aid employers, and rent subsidies line landlords' pockets.[64]

By contrast, one welfare expert opposed the guaranteed income by dismissing the work ethic 'problem' as merely the paternalist conservative position that would inevitably prevail against libertarian right enthusiasts. According to Patricia Tulloch, the weakening of the income–work bond was 'a single and uneasy exception' to the *liberal* nature of any guaranteed income scheme, in that they all reinforce market principles and retain the basic structure of inequality.[65]

A slightly different position was taken by Jill Roe. In 1976 she argued that 'the relatively recent notion that poverty would be eliminated by industrial arbitration and social services', as originally propounded by Henderson, had been contradicted by the rising demand for benefits from people now called 'clients'. That was the reason for Henderson's subsequent guaranteed minimum income proposal, which, if implemented, might have 'transformed' the history of social policy. But as she said, that would have depended upon the terms. 'To be more than *a convenient bureaucratic arrangement, which also stifled dissent* neatly, it would need to be accompanied by *a statutory right to work without eligibility tests.* It would also need to be accompanied by a genuinely controlled distribution of income (from all sources)'.[66] In other words, Roe applied far more stringent qualifications to the market predictions so popular in the earlier days, making it clear that none of the proposals met them.

For all that, the 'preferred proposal' in Henderson's Poverty Report was not as elitist as some argued,[67] given that the scheme had been based largely on assumptions of full employment, of the vast majority of wage earners being union members, and of an arbitration system that continued to protect and narrow wage differentials by raising the wages of the unskilled. Of course, the first condition was not to be met, the second had been eroded over some time, especially with the entry of women and migrants into a secondary non-unionised labour market; and the third can always be threatened whenever there is more emphasis on free collective bargaining or new laws are introduced to restrict union rights. It could be argued – given that boom conditions were still, if only *just,* obtaining – that it had been a well meaning attempt to raise the incomes of 'categoricals', the chief groups to be found 'in poverty' in Australia. Also, it did not suggest, as the PRS report had, that a guaranteed minimum income would be a *substitute* for services-in-kind.

But the proposal was attached to the proviso that a guaranteed minimum income would never gain acceptance if the rest of the population had to suffer income reductions in order to transfer money to 'poor people'. Tulloch pointed out that the predicted resentment was accepted as a political fact, and the commission tended to be apologetic about the redistributive aspects of its proposals.[68] It was not just a matter of the tradition of selective policies, or of the high costs of home ownership and other self help which made protected wage earners so antagonistic to further redistribution. Nor was it a matter of Henderson's frequent argument that more universal provision would spread resources too thinly to be of any real help to those in severe need – though this was a significant reason for the reluctance of the Poverty Commission to be less selective.[69] Henderson was also the classical economist who believed that the only incentive for the rich to invest and 'work' (and *not* evade taxes), should be their vast income unfettered by heavy taxation. (The incentive for the poor to work was the equally classic view that they should barely survive on a frugal welfare income.) Since the commission was only investigating the poor, and not the rich, its claim that 'there simply are not enough rich people for even total expropriation of their incomes to go very far' was slightly ingenuous. The guaranteed income was only marginally above Henderson's own poverty line, and although there was some redistribution down, that was to come mainly from groups like married working couples who were childless. As the commission stated, the scheme was meant to operate 'without markedly worsening the position of any person compared with the present system'.[70]

As for the effects on work incentives, this problem seemed insoluble. Henderson was committed to the ALP government's view that the unemployed were just as needy as pensioners. Therefore their guaranteed minimum was to stay the same. But since they suffered no personal disability which would prevent them from working, they should not be in 'a better position than the full-time worker', and would lose a dollar for every dollar earned (100 per cent tax rate on guaranteed income compared to 40 per cent for the 'permanently disabled').[71] In opposing this, ACOSS was concerned,[72] for example, that there would be even more emphasis placed on the work test than before – a fairly justified fear given the 'bludger' campaign. A government could set harsh work tests, yet the unemployed might have less monetary incentive to work than the disabled – unless full-time wages were far higher than the guaranteed minimum income. In the secondary labour market, this was increasingly unlikely.

As with the Nixon plan's effects on AFDC mothers in the north, the Poverty Commission's guaranteed minimum income offered little guarantee of security. Also it would not necessarily guarantee a more generous income, it would just change the system of income security. What it might guarantee was a further entrenchment of existing relations of inequality.

When assessing the Henderson scheme, it is interesting to note that in a paradoxical way it was more radical than the wages for house-work proposals, despite its being supported or even formulated by more heterogeneous and less radical groups. Although the domestic labour argument for wages made assumptions about the strong link between the family and capitalism, these assumptions were quite simplistic – as was quickly agreed in the feminist movement – and would give women even less choice to be other than houseworkers. The hopes that a guaranteed minimum income would raise 'the poor' above the disputed poverty line and *at most* weaken the work ethic were more modest. The Henderson package also treated the family as the income unit. Had this been otherwise, there were possibilities of a long-term change in the position of women – which few noticed at the time – vis-à-vis protected male wage earners.

Edwards was one of the few who suggested that a guaranteed income should treat everyone as a citizen while arguing against payments for housework. Criticising the Henderson proposal, she pointed out that if the payment went to the individual who earned no income, whatever the household type, a guaranteed income would 'provide an excellent opportunity to reduce the financial dependence of many women regardless of whether they be classified as poor'. Her idea of an individual payment was not as a reward for household and childcare functions performed in the home, but simply 'in recognition of the possible hardship that is caused by financial dependence of one adult on another'.[73]

By contrast, in the Henderson and PRS proposals – just as in the existing income security system – spouses were denied the privilege of individual cash transfers that accrue to the elderly or other individuals sharing the same household. Both policies, and those that tax the family unit, assume that 'family' resources are pooled fairly between spouses. While no evidence existed at the time to support this, Edwards later proved the assumption erroneous. But as she said then, the reports had ignored that numbers of women may be in poverty, or with no choice but to put up with 'intolerable marital strains'.[74] In view of the stigma faced by single parents and the unemployed, and the state's rejection of all guaranteed income schemes, it need hardly be added that such a view was ignored.

The various dilemmas and failures described above ensued not because the radical demands were co-opted by the state, but more as a result of the visibility of oppositional movements and the openness and pressures on the state to accede to popular demands. At the time of the poverty debate, the various neo-libertarian groups imported the Nixon/Friedman negative tax idea as a strategy to ward off imminent welfare reforms. In the face of the challenges from below, the Australian government, when still in Liberal-Country Party hands, was primarily concerned with maintaining order and rule. The whole political arena was more than usually autonomous, as dominant groups were deeply divided at the time. This was partly due to the way economic control was passing out of Australia, which enabled the union movement to reap economic advantages although it took little part in the political activism.[75] The state's only response was to try to stifle increasingly widespread dissatisfaction. So it was at this time, as we saw, that some of the radical counter cultural groups came to reject a wide range of traditional political protest, after state repression against the anti-Vietnam movement, and the commune movement emerged.

The situation of crisis and conflict gradually became difficult to control, and the state eventually intervened to implement change (for the duration of the Whitlam period). The level of popular mobilisation had heightened, and increasing dissensions were splitting the different dominant groups. It could not, however, be predicted whether the state would bring in reformist changes and accede to popular demands, or implement quite different changes more in line with the growing economic libertarianism. Conversely, none of these newly visible groups could effect their desired changes without state intervention.

Within such a climate the guaranteed income proposals were

responses to efforts by oppositional groups to place poverty on the public agenda. Attendant upon the politicisation of the poverty of excluded groups, especially with the drives to improve the social wage, some of the earliest attacks against the increase in welfare services came armed with the negative income tax proposal. The interests involved were concerned *to remove the poverty issue from the public agenda* and put it back in the private sphere of family and market, the 'reprivatisers'.[76] Bureaucratic simplicity, the 'liberation' of market forces and the abolition of services were the chief benefits for the radical 'neo-libertarian' position. Other traditionally more authoritarian 'reprivatisers' preferred to continue blaming the victims and disciplining the 'work-shy'. A prevalent argument was that poverty was due to psychological defects.

In the face of proposals for the negative income tax, in a climate still of full employment and high male wages, many oppositional groups (for example, the early ACOSS position) refused to countenance a guaranteed minimum income or a negative income tax, since all the other efforts to politicise poverty and define needs from below would have been silenced. Struggling against the entrenched male wage earners' welfare was difficult enough: the private nature of housing, health, childcare and so forth was particularly the case in Australia. How would a guaranteed income help when the only poor were those already receiving cash transfers from the state? These arguments were stronger before the ALP's election in late 1972, when the reform and construction of new social services (such as Medibank) were still open, vital questions. (I will disregard, for this analysis, the undoubted problem that welfare empire builders were also involved. More problematic were the low numbers of 'poor' people involved in the Australian debate.)

At the same time, Henderson, institutionalised expert, supported wage earner welfare while admitting to housing related poverty. His work exemplified the way the definition of 'poverty' was continually renegotiated, with new vocabularies constructed in the process. If 'pockets of poverty' was a last defence of a state still trying to maintain the status quo, Henderson's own disability approach and his poverty line were the subjects of continual criticism from oppositional groups. Whether poverty should be equated with financial poverty and whether the 'austere' line was 'fair' or merely pragmatic vis-à-vis the administrable concerns of the state and taxpayers were highly contested issues.

On this last point, support from male Anglo wage earners for the groups in poverty became increasingly problematic. Once poverty was successfully politicised, the issue became a candidate for legitimate state intervention. But how was it to be defined? The new Labor government not only started a vast translation of newly publicised issues and needs into needs that would be administered in one way or another (hence the conflicts between the PRS Review, the Poverty Inquiry and the Asprey Committee – let alone the rest), but it also, along its reformist, high spending path, raised the income of the unemployed to that of pensioners.

The 'dole bludger' campaign against the raising of unemployment benefits had to be answered by the state. If specific categorising of cash transfer recipients was not to become administratively meaningless and politically unpopular with taxpayers, the work test for unemployment benefits should remain. In the face of other new discourses, like the 'dole bludger' term itself, the Labor government tightened measures to prevent dole *cheats*. In response to these attacks, welfare radicals had little option but to turn to a *generous* guaranteed income that might break the cash/work nexus and improve the quality of jobs in the labour market. For these oppositional groups, the removal of categories became an urgent strategy to prevent new definitions of need being imposed by the state and by reprivatisers. To speak of 'citizens' and 'rights' would remove the stigma or 'disability' of being unemployed, a migrant, or a woman. Wage earner status would be undermined if category definitions were replaced by the sole one of 'citizen'. People would be able to define their *own* needs through money; this would oppose the institutional language of experts and the definitions of the state. By contrast, 'reforming' economists, obsessed by the effects that the chief form of state welfare in Australia, arbitration, has on the ability of the state to raise further taxes from protected wage earners, turned to proposing only a very minimum income to emphasise the 'right' to income security.

As to this question, even if a guaranteed income had been implemented, one must still ask how could anonymous, categoryless citizens be able to ensure that their income remained at all adequate. What might have been the social costs and gains? The guaranteed income by definition required the state to set a standardised level of need. How could citizens collectively take any part in defining their particular needs? How could they resist the state's interpretation? Given the lack of services-in-kind, many would be increasingly vulnerable to labour, land and commodity markets.

The promoters of radically increased welfare were – in any case – beaten on every front. They had faced the threats to welfare services posed by a negative income tax, as well as threats from reprivatisers where authoritarian conservatives were joined (electorally) by male wage earners. Those outside the labour force would be historically constrained by their problematic relation to labour force participants, who became increasingly constituted as taxpayers. Yet even the draconian radical right libertarian proposals (negative income tax), with the definition of need expressed for their own interests, were far too radical for state bureaucracies vis-à-vis the work incentive argument. Eventually, the failure of the negative income tax proposal with its concomitant service cuts was a small price to pay for more significant changes effected by the state.

After the Whitlam government was sacked in 1975, the guaranteed income proposals were dropped, along with many other schemes. If the Henderson scheme had gone ahead, certain benefits would have accrued to dominant groups. As in the northern United States, a guaranteed *minimum* income would have marginalised further the excluded categories who, with their categorisation thus removed, would have had less chance of organising into specific protest movements concerned with specific needs. Cheap, unprotected labour would have been more readily available.[77] The market would have been reinforced at the expense of the social services and welfare professionals who had gained such a threatening prominence during the Whitlam era. All this, it could be argued, is in the interests of the new libertarian, dominant groups. But the policy could not be implemented. There were the traditional themes, especially work incentives, which could not be undermined, and the inertia of various mechanisms. There were other groups with relative influence and cross-cutting alliances.

If the policy could not be implemented in the interests of dominant groups, who have the greatest influence, it was unlikely that anti-establishment groups would succeed with their more generous versions. But to talk of anti-establishment groups suggests unity whereas, far more than in dominant groups, there are always divisions and competition. Those actually in poverty were not even involved: the newly emerging welfare lobby was itself divided. Middle-class groups – not the poor – had benefited from the greater welfare participation encouraged by the ALP government. Eventually even they wanted an end to inflation and were joined by protected labour in favouring tax cuts.

As we saw, the state shifted from maintaining the previous order in a more or less intact form to managing change without endangering the system. The old nationalism and strength of wage earners, from the viewpoint of new (still rising) dominant groups, could not be undermined without state action. Conservative parties were too linked to old national capital, which strongly rejected the removal of state regulatory bodies or the institution of a more libertarian economic order. Oppositional groups demanded change too: repressive police action and censorship trials were also fought with libertarian arguments. The Whitlam period itself was a situation of crisis *created* by the level of rifts and debates in and between oppositional groups contesting control. Though the period witnessed the creation of a national movement by Aborigines, the mobilisation generally emerged from middle-class elements. Against the old repression, the state interpreted this popular pressure coming from the growing solidarity of feminists, students and others excluded from wage earner welfare and rights. Greater participation and public accountability, let alone the state's attempts to address poverty were, however, of little interest to the old national capital and the labourist tradition. The reformist path of social democracy apparently only benefited the rising professional middle classes. When neo-libertarian positions – such as that of the PRS – eventually managed to suggest that neither the poor *nor* wage-earners *nor* multinational mining interests were being served by a reformist path, and then offered the temptation of a negative tax, the end was near, though not without further intense conflicts. It was then that the state abandoned Keynesian policies (to the long-term detriment of wage earners) and the attempt to nationalise Australia's mineral resources.

The argument that dominant groups coalesced to sack the ALP government is persuasive,[78] yet one needs to remember that the state had already instituted the major changes that were to facilitate the rise of new sections of the dominant economic class: protection had been reduced long before, full employment was abandoned, and foreign capital was accepted. The international slump that occurred just at this brief flowering of popular mobilisation cut across what slim chances the ALP may have had to bring in reform, though interpretations of the recession were also crucial. The right wing gave the Whitlam government full responsibility for the slump and the new wave of unemployment. Inadvertently, by finding no option other than to attack wage earner status, the radical welfare position on the guaranteed income, along with parts of the counter culture, also gave credence to the deindustrialisation and unemployment then underway.

Far more importantly, deindustrialisation had taken place as part of the now defeated reformist path for the state. While this path had been an attempt to reintroduce a strong form of state intervention, unlike the wage earner and tariff protection and state racism of the past, this time it was to be achieved via state control of mineral investment, a widening of democratic participation and greater state investment in social services. These plans failed, although the restoration of 'order' was not accomplished until the constitution was used to expel the Whitlam government. The electoral defeat of the ALP that followed demonstrated the lack of commitment by many of the working class to the ALP's redistribution plans – another instance of the long-term effects of arbitration. Higher taxes would erode the welfare of wages. In this way the regrouped dominant forces, by appealing (for a time) to other popular groups – namely working class male voters – were able to cement the new changes via the state. The irony is that an interventionist state, relying firstly on middle-class mobilisation during the Whitlam period and later on the support of male industrial workers during the Hawke era, came to deindustrialise and further lose its interventionist mechanisms.

Ultimately the problem of order had become more important, but only after macro changes were already set in place during the turmoil of 1975. If a guaranteed income was dubious, to say the least, even in that relatively open climate where the scheme *might* have been cushioned with greater political defences against possible distortions, governments soon became less accountable. This leads to the conclusion that a guaranteed income *in general*, or in any context, offers no progressive solution for marginal populations. In the context of 1975–6 in Australia, any more institutional changes and 'modernisations' of everyday life (as promised, for example, with a guaranteed income) were less possible, and less *necessary* for the newly dominant groups, once the state had carried out changes. These were ones which in any case further reduced its capacity to intervene, since they involved a devolution of state sovereignty. Following the international slump, the state's legitimising and integrating roles were stressed by closing debates at the institutional level, effected with the election of the Fraser government. No major changes occurred until the next Labor government, which drew on the impetus of the Whitlam period and revitalised some of its ideas, but mostly in quite different ways.

NOTES

1. R. Theobald (1967); M. McLuhan (1967).
2. N. Furniss & T. Tilton (1979), pp. 65; J.T. Patterson (1986), pp. 187–8.
3. P. Steinfels (1979), p. 7.
4. See N. Furniss & T. Tilton (1979), pp. 186–7; A. Graycar (1978), p. 14; P. Polanyi (1971).
5. J. Quadagno (1990), p. 11.
6. J.T. Patterson (1986), p. 194.
7. J.T. Patterson (1986), p. 193; J. Quadagno (1990), p. 11.
8. Cited in J. Quadagno (1990), p. 15.
9. Cited in J. Quadagno (1990), p. 17.
10. *ibid.*, p. 19.
11. *ibid.*, pp. 19–25.
12. Cited in J.T. Patterson (1986), p. 194.
13. Cited in P. Steinfels (1979), p. 159. See also F.F. Piven & R.A. Cloward (1987), p. 22.
14. T.H. Kewley (1980). The proposals for guaranteed minimum income schemes were contained in the Henderson Report on Poverty (1975), the Woodhouse Report on Compensation (1974), the Hancock Report on Superannuation (1976) and the Priorities Review Staff report, 'Possibilities for Social Welfare in Australia' (1975). The Asprey Committee's Taxation Review (1974) and Treasury (1974) both rejected the schemes. See Graycar (1978), p. 14; P. Saunders (1978).
15. All these viewpoints are cited with references further on.
16. For example, M.T. Lewis (1975), p. 18.
17. At an APSA Conference of 1969, and an Australian Council of Social Security (ACOSS) conference, published in May, 1970, there was support for the notion of a 'frugal' negative income. See K. Hancock (1970), p. 29.
18. L. Tierney (1970), p. 222.
19. The information about ACOSS's radicalisation during that time was obtained from Adam Farrar (personal interview, 7.9.87), then editor of *Australian Journal of Social Issues*, ACOSS's journal.
20. S. Horne (1970), p. 118; I. Braybrook (1970), pp. 127–8.
21. R.F. Henderson (1971), pp. 108–9, my emphases.
22. *ibid.*, pp. 110–1.
23. See J. Roe (1976), pp. 316–18.

24. R.F. Henderson (1971), pp. 113–14.
25. E. Risstrom (1972), pp. 17, 27.
26. J. Salmon (1975), p. 85. The results of the Brotherhood's scheme were presented to the Poverty Commission (Resources for Poor Families, 1974) and were carefully studied by such bodies as ACOSS.
27. P. Tulloch (1979), p. 151.
28. This was in Lewis' research report for the Poverty Commission (1975), pp. 36–7.
29. 1944 House of Representatives Debates, Cited Lewis (1975), p. 8.
30. *ibid.*, p. 17, my emphasis.
31. *ibid.*, p. 18.
32. This occurred especially within ACOSS and the Brotherhood of St Laurence. J. Salmon (1975), p. 53.
33. P. Smith (1974), pp. 35–40.
34. ACOSS (1975), pp. 31–41. The reference to full unemployment is on p. 49.
35. Quoted in *The National Times*, 18.2.74.
36. *Sydney Morning Herald*, 19.2.74.
37. *The National Times* (18.2.74). Conservatives such as the Liberal Victorian Premier (Hamer), and the Deputy Leader of the Federal Opposition (Lynch) spoke in its favour, *Sydney Morning Herald*, 19.2.74.
38. P. Samuel, *The Bulletin* 2.3.74 (my emphases).
39. *The National Times* 18.2.74.
40. *Sydney Morning Herald* 18.3.74.
41. A. Farrar (1987), pp. 26–8.
42. *The Australian* 10.6.74.
43. *Sydney Morning Herald* 18.3.74.
44. Official discussion about new forms of welfare lasted as long as the Whitlam government (after which, many of the inquiries were terminated). T.H. Kewley (1980), p. 45.
45. As reported by P. Saunders SWRC, in answer to a question put to Henderson at the time, as to why Henderson had changed his mind (personal interview 7.3.86).
46. The research reports funded via the Poverty Commission which recommended such schemes included ACOSS, the Australian Red Cross, the Brotherhood of St Laurence and the ACTU. Australian Council of Trade Unions (1975), p. 24.
47. Australia. Taxation Review Committee (1974), 7.85; 14.5.
48. *Sydney Morning Herald* 7.11.74.
49. W. Kasper, R. Blandy, *et al* (1980), pp. 213, 243; A. Hawke & D.E. Lewis (1989); J. Camilleri, P. Christoff *et al* (1989).
50. Cited in E. Malos (1982), p. 22, my emphasis.
51. C. Burton (1985), p. 63; E. Malos (1982), p. 34.
52. E. Malos (1982), pp. 32–3.

53. D.G. Gil (1973), p. 95.
54. J. Mahony & J. Barnaby (1973), p. 6.
55. M. Edwards (1975), p. 90; E. Windschuttle (1974), pp. 15–16.
56. M. Edwards (1975), pp. 92–4.
57. L. Rubinstein (1976), p. 14.
58. The Australian feminist movement discussed the idea when it was still current overseas. For example, T. Brennan (1977), M. Campioni, E. Jacka *et al* (1975). Burton points out that they followed Dalla Costa in arguing that women constitute a class (a line taken also by B. Cass (1978), and that domestic work is an integral part of the capitalist mode of production, a 'major contribution', although 'indirectly productive of surplus value' – a modification of the Dalla Costa argument (C. Burton [1985], pp. 65–6).
59. E. Risstrom (1972); W. Kasper, R. Blandy *et al* (1980).
60. ACOSS (1976); W. Higgins (1978).
61. Australia. Commission of Inquiry into Poverty (1975), p. 70.
62. ACOSS (1977).
63. L. Bryson (1977a), p. 202; M. Jones (1974/5).
64. L. Bryson (1977), p. 13.
65. P. Tulloch (1979), pp. 151–2.
66. J. Roe (1976), p. 324, my emphases.
67. W. Higgins (1978), pp. 145–157; ACOSS (1977), pp. 6–10.
68. P. Tulloch (1979), p. 153.
69. F.G. Castles ((1985), pp. 36–7.
70. Australia. Commission of Inquiry into Poverty (1975), pp. 70–8.
71. *ibid.*, p. 75.
72. ACOSS (1976), p. 12.
73. M. Edwards (1978), pp 202–3.
74. *ibid.*, p. 202.
75. A. Touraine (1977), pp. 184–90. Such a thesis is supported, as we saw, by much of Catley and McFarlane's (1983) analysis of this time: e.g. chapter 4.
76. N. Fraser (1987).
77. See W. Kasper, R. Blandy *et al.* (1980) for their libertarian vision of this.
78. Taken especially by A.C. Theophanous (1980).

CHAPTER 5

State Promotion of Communes: Austerity and Alternative Lifestyles

The commune movement was the counter culture's most serious challenge to the Western employment system, in that communes became the major established alternative to wage labour. Worker co-operatives, while also popular as counter culture experiments, were less prevalent or remarkable. And unlike guaranteed income schemes, which are totally dependent on government policies, there is no need for state support to set up a commune. In fact the opposite occurred with the 1960s communes, since they emerged from the grass roots and aimed to challenge authoritarian definitions of ways of living and working.

In this sense, the idea that a government might attempt to promote communes seems far fetched. Yet during the 1980s, over a decade after the counter culture phenomenon, it happened in Australia. Where new right groups had been interested in guaranteed income schemes because of their potential to undermine demands for welfare, government interest in alternative work structures developed later, when the employment situation, after a further deterioration in various countries, was apparently in permanent decline. Worker co-operatives, communes and informal economy ideas suddenly became attractive policy options because they did not require state income provision. In the case of communes, Australian governments were by far the most deeply implicated of any OECD country. State intentions here, as with other post-industrial policy options, were far removed from the idea of radical transformation. Instead, communes would be alternatives to the existing and accepted levels of unemployment *and* to government job creation.

In 1983, unemployment reached 10 per cent in Australia and a new kind of Labor government took office. For four years after, the idea of communes for the unemployed and homeless was seriously considered by numerous federal and state departments. Although no 'state commune' eventuated from this effort, the employment problems of Australian governments did gain some resolution, but in no way to the benefit of the unemployed. Instead, by the 1990s, unemployment and underemployment became more entrenched and taken for granted, and governments now do not bother even to seek such 'solutions' to unemployment (as the Labor government called its commune strategy). The story of how communes were used by a state (even in supposedly left wing control) is another test case showing that the post-industrialists' assumption that their proposals are potentially radical alternatives to unemployment and wage labour is erroneous.

The following begins with exploring how the then Prime Minister of Australia, Bob Hawke, became closely identified with the post-industrial strategy. His interest developed quite apart from the fact that one Labor Minister for a time, Barry Jones, is a major post-industrialist. Possibly openness to diversity among Australia's political elites and dominant groups (a more common phenomenon in Australia than in Europe), contributed to the interest in communes. More urgently, employment could hardly be ignored by a Labor Party in 1983, when newly outspoken alliances of the unemployed demanded jobs and attacked class privilege. This was one of the key issues that swept Labor into office.

Under these circumstances, a return to full employment seemed possible (although unlikely). But this track was never pursued. Instead, a new round of restructuring of the labour market and capital markets was launched within a corporatist framework. The commune idea should be seen as a diversion from this program, for although it was presented as a 'radical' change to conventional notions of employment, it was the *only* proposal that year to address employment at all. Why did this happen? Interest at the federal level was based on the communes' potential to legitimise and reinforce what the Whitlam government had ended on – previously unthinkable for the Australian Labor Party – namely accepting unemployment. Henceforward, and despite promises, there was no commitment even to a trend towards full employment. Communes *might* reduce unemployment figures, stem the demand for jobs, and reduce the unemployment benefit bill. The more far reaching effects were the new definitions of 'work', 'employment' and unemployment benefits that emerged from this policy process. These new meanings have further marginalised the unemployed in Australia and removed central issues on unemployment from the public agenda.

The process drew many diverse actors into policy debates, research efforts and media reports; not only were original counter culture and newer 'sustainable community' lobby groups involved, but so too were environmentalists, captains of industry, the union movement, politicians and bureaucrats. Communes were scrutinised from every conceivable angle. Other research and more experiments were undertaken at individual state government levels as well, in the contradictory interest (vis-à-vis federal interests) of reducing homelessness and youth violence. The hopes here were that thousands of new kibbutz dwellers would receive the income support of federally funded unemployment benefits and thus relieve state housing and law and order costs, since teenagers would build their own shelters far away in the countryside.

The following evidence also shows that communes cannot be vehicles for wider social change, and that their internal structure is not necessarily more egalitarian or democratic than other household types. More, since communes aim to evade economic and political constraints, but do not accomplish this in fact, the members' need to defend communes as goals in themselves tends to inhibit other political action and social movements. Self marginalisation and austerity were the original choices. Naturally the commune movement did not invite the federal government to reinterpret this into an alternative lifestyle of 'suppressed materialism' designed for thousands of teenagers already marginalised, powerless and without choice. 'Alternative lifestyle' lobby groups did co-operate in drawing up the plans, nevertheless.

The only choice made by the unemployed was to reject the alternative, a choice made when Australian teenagers could still rely on unemployment benefits. Overall, however, the supply-side strategy of pursuing communes as government policy was a success for the state, especially while a casualised secondary market of jobs was emerging. The strategy helped to legitimate long-term unemployment; it paved the way for restrictions on receiving the dole and for later replacing unemployment benefits altogether; and it assisted in redefining employment to mean 'any work', no matter how ill paid and insecure.

STATE INTEREST IN 'ALTERNATIVE LIFESTYLES'

When counter culture communes were established in Australia, most state apparatuses responded negatively. Police raids were authorised and existing laws of land use, ownership and building regulations were upheld by state and local governments. In Queensland, officials burnt some communes to the ground.[1] This local oppression, accompanied by dramatic media coverage, contrasted with the Whitlam government's sympathetic approach. At the ALP Conference of 1973, Tom Uren, then federal Minister for Urban Affairs and Regional Development, recommended that Labor should 'encourage individuals and groups to develop within the law, lifestyles which are less dependent on materialism than are traditional Australian lifestyles'.[2] The proposal was only narrowly defeated, but press reports trivialised it. One federal minister, Moss Cass, was at the time building a mud house in a 'superior hippie commune near Melbourne', and another, Jim Cairns, became even more involved in the commune movement, to put it mildly.[3]

Apart from the Whitlam government's liberal approach, a more prophetic view of the state's later role, well before long-term unemployment, could be found in the Poverty Commission's inquiry into rural poverty in 1974. It found that 'drop-out' children were living in ways similar to the low income, 'low resource' kind of rural life suffered by Aborigines and 'poor whites'. If this 'innovative youth' was 'approached in the right way', they 'could probably do more to help the poor in rural areas to help themselves than could be achieved by the proliferation of a highly paid poverty bureaucracy'.[4] Such a proposal, to say the least, wilfully ignored the fact that Aborigines are rather better informed on communal life than middle-class whites. Nevertheless, ideas like this were still regarded as 'radical' and unthinkable as government policy. But what *was* the federal government doing, as unemployment moved inexorably upwards?

After full employment terminated with Jim Cairns' removal from Treasury in early 1975, the government's main aims were to fight inflation first by using the lash of unemployment, and to create favourable climates for business. As the jobless rate grew, the Fraser government attempted to manage the agenda to influence public perceptions and to prevent the emergence of debate on full employment.[5] Accordingly, it presented fiscal crises and inflation as *the* problems, rather than a lack of government commitment to providing the opportunity for all to work. The fact that work was not available was initially avoided by launching various 'bludger' campaigns. Only with Labor's electoral campaign in 1982–3 was structural unemployment faced squarely, but after that the meanings of 'bludging' and 'working' were recast.

So, in the late 1970s, the definition of unemployment as an individual problem predominated.[6] The first job training schemes (to increase the demand for teenage boys' labour) implied that young people did not look hard enough and were not 'attractive' to employers. Untied subsidies to employers for hiring the young had limited success.[7] In addition, and apart from changing the methods of measuring unemployment rates and the criteria of eligibility for benefits (by tightening the worktest), thus reducing the numbers definitionally,[8] another option available to governments is to reduce the workforce participation rate or the supply of labour. The Fraser government's most concrete strategy here was to return women to housework by raising the real value of the dependent spouse rebate, which temporarily reduced the supply of female labour and thus reclassified more women as 'not in the labour force'.[9] Women can only be accused of selfishly taking jobs from others (e.g. teenagers) when they are denied claims to citizenship other than indirectly, through their male partners, or when it is claimed that they have no right to employment and should be hidden from all government accounts except male tax claims. Liberals stressed traditional family and 'community' self help for young and old, which they freely declared should rightfully depend on women's unpaid household duties.[10]

While in opposition, the Labor Party began to formulate a new corporatist economic approach, and also changed its approach to winning the female vote. It may be that the Fraser government had miscalculated the extent to which women would accept such a blatant revival of the separate spheres.[11] Even so, Labor later retained the dependent spouse rebate,[12] and the expansion of the casual labour market assumed that women would redistribute wealth to men by taking lower paid jobs. Nevertheless, successive Hawke governments did not claim that women's domestic work is useful and exclusively female work, and disallowed it for some sole parents.[13] Before winning office, Labor became aware that the impact of the feminist movement might produce electoral disenchantment which would backfire against the conservative parties' assumptions of 'women's place'.

In 1979 Bob Hawke entered federal politics, after five years as President of the Australian Council of Trade Unions (ACTU). That same year, in his Boyer Lectures (entitled *The Resolution of Conflict*), Hawke paid homage to feminism. Far from the Liberal Party or the traditional labourist type of antifeminist rhetoric, he proposed *increasing* women's labour market participation through legislation and the provision of childcare. Quoting from Simone de Beauvoir's *The Second Sex*, he observed how new social attitudes about the position of women were creating an arena of 'conflict' and 'guilt'. In order to resolve these and other 'conflicts' over the country's economic problems (that is, between capital and labour), Hawke called for a national 'summit' conference as a starting point.[14]

Also unlike Fraser, Hawke *acknowledged* unemployment as a further arena of 'conflict' and 'guilt', but for this Hawke proposed a different solution: not a summit about jobs, but a way to 'thoroughly reappraise the whole concept of unemployment *benefit*'. The reasons he gave are interesting, since they show the extent of his commitment to the separation of income from work – for those already unemployed. Redefining the dole was necessary because:

> the current concept and levels of benefit are still firmly based on the postwar assumption that full employment is the normal condition of our society. According to this assumption the derivation of income for people in that society is perceived in terms of their participation in the production processes. These processes, it has been assumed, operate to provide work for all, and therefore *unemployment benefits* should not and need not be too substantial because they *exist to cope with those who don't want to work or are in transition between jobs.*
>
> The facts quite clearly show that the full employment assumption is not currently valid, and yet as a society we persist with a 'benefit' concept . . . The very word 'benefit' – the dictionary definition 'a kind deed, a favour, gift, advantage, profit, good' – itself reveals the nature of the assumption and the barren inhumanity of its continual application. *While society cannot provide employment for its members, the production/ work/ income nexus has to be abandoned* as a justification of our present parsimony to the unemployed. An assumption cannot be used to justify making second-class citizens of those who are unfortunate enough to constitute the living proof of the inaccuracy of the assumption.
>
> An increasing number of people, . . . [however,] are finding satisfaction and fulfilment from . . . 'the alternative life-style' . . . We in the conventional community tend to be condescending, if not contemptuous, of the alternative community. At present the only formal relationship between the two communities is through the payment of the dole, a totally negative, even destructive, relationship. . . . *Instead of the negative expenditure on unemployment benefits*, the conventional society could

assist in the provision of land and facilities for alternative communities and so establish a much more creative relationship between the two. . . . In this financial year we will be paying more than a billion dollars in unemployment benefits – a necessary but . . . corrosive outgoing. We are . . . unwise not to explore . . . whether there can be some forms of *more constructive expenditure* which can create more happiness and harmony and a closer balance between the supply of, and the demand for, conventional employment. . . . A recognised and assisted minority alternative community . . . would be infinitely more likely to contribute to an harmonious society than the burgeoning of a disaffected body of unemployed to whom society pretends it has discharged its obligation by the signing of a dole cheque. . . .
I am certain that the nature and rate of change of the forces operating within our society, and internationally, are such that it is an exercise in *futility to imagine that we are either experiencing some mere cyclical departure from full employment* or that we will return to those halcyon days simply by the application of cosmetic Band-Aids.[15]

Stressing a need for 'structural adjustment', Hawke called for a re-examination of society's attitudes to work patterns, education and the work ethic. 'A mindless adherence to past assumptions or a blind belief in the adequacy of existing structures', would only 'jeopardise' the welfare of our society.[16]

The reaction to this was shock. The conservative press ran front-page headlines such as 'Hawke Plan: Govt Hippies', 'The saltbush eaters', and 'Idylls for the idle'.[17] Editorials complained that 'we can hardly afford the luxury . . . of establishing two societies when one is not productive enough'.[18] 'Fancy suggesting that those who labor to keep Australia going ought to finance idylls for those who don't. Or won't. . . . These days . . . the not-so Lucky Country needs people who are committed to joining in, not dropping out. Otherwise, we could all find ourselves in an alternative life-style. Poverty.'[19]

The left-wing journal, *Arena*, called the idea 'Ruled Out of Society' although, as with the conservative press, it failed to perceive how the meaning of benefit was being redefined more narrowly. To *Arena*, Hawke merely proposed that financial assistance for people to make their own lives 'freely and actively', should be 'a right rather than a handout'. What did (correctly) concern *Arena* was more the way that Hawke was undermining societal obligations: the new 'push-outs' from the system would join the 'drop-outs' and both would be encouraged to 'accept less', thus accommodating those who might otherwise jeopardise or challenge the system. Decision makers were unlikely to entertain this as a 'programmatic solution', at least not yet. To do so 'would be to admit the depth, the irreversibility and the permanence of the crisis, . . . and to call in question the assumption . . . that there is a place for everyone within the society'. In the long run, though, 'the hippies might turn out to be the biggest boon the system ever inherited: a self-defined and self-selecting out-group so intensely needed by a declining system'.[20]

The following year (1980) the crisis was indeed being presented as 'irreversible', not least at a conference called 'When Machines Replace People. What Will People Do?' None of the papers questioned the title's assumptions of inevitability and social control. Hawke's paper emphasised reducing the 'youth labour supply', partly through extensive training in the 'conventional system', as a 'fair balance' to state assistance for implementing his commune idea. The fact that there are people who can 'find fulfilment' in alternatives 'should be regarded as a plus' from the viewpoint of the 'yawning gap' between available jobs and people wishing to work, he now argued.[21] Other participants gave his commune plan qualified support: a CSIRO scientist noted how politicians often 'cherished illusions' about populating rural Australia, without any idea of the limited amount of arable land and water resources. Despite this caution, the scientist still assumed that if 'potentially' arable land were used intensively at a 'semi-subsistence existence', it could sustain 10 million people and many more, 'if we were to accept' Third World living standards. Furthermore, although the present commune alternative is currently an 'upper middle class' choice, perhaps others might follow, like the 'less fit', unable to 'cope with the work demands' of high technology and anyway being replaced by it. Were they to choose a 'simpler' rural life, 'then we have very little time to waste' for government assistance and planning.[22]

Also involved in the conference was an original intellectual enthusiast for communes, Peter Cock, who addressed issues of alternatives, the unemployed and redefinitions of work. The alternative lifestyle and its do-it-yourself ethic, he argued, could help to remove the 'culture of poverty' from unemployment because it rejected 'economic definitions of one's value'. It was no 'leisure option', however, because it favoured 'different kinds of work' from those 'built on false needs' that produce 'consumer junk and weapons of war'. Restructuring the dole with incentives to gain private income would produce a 'balance between the right to guaranteed survival (given that technology is doing more and more of the work) and the stimulus to create and make a direct contribution to the wellbeing of society'.[23]

Given that the dole provided 'little expectation or opportunity' to contribute at all, Cock suggested that the relation between government and the alternatives must change. Local regulations against communes should be dismantled, but if those whom society rejected turned to violence, the corporate state would have a 'vested interest' in supporting alternatives. The outcome might be 'reformism and co-option of radical ideas' if the scheme became 'a partial isolated solution' and a 'safety valve' to 'divert the rage and sabotage of those rejected'. Cock's more optimistic view was that the alternatives could transform society, rather than being exploited to support the existing one, because he supported the post-industrial thesis that the present crisis was not just one of employment but of 'the whole institutional and cultural fabric of our society'. If the power and size of the 'public realms' were decreased, an alternative society could evolve which consisted of 'a multiplicity of relatively autonomous pluralistic small communities that are interlinked through electronic communication systems'. But he admitted that what was 'required' for this was the 'collapse of existing power bases and the assertion of personal and community power'. Thus an anarchist conclusion to 'Machines Replace People'.

During this time the ALP's new program developed forthwith, aiming to widen existing power bases by including the union movement. Instead of the Whitlam government's independence from the unions (even over tariff cuts, which caused significant unemployment), the ALP/ACTU Accord was to let unions join in formulating macro-plans for the recovery of the economy. The ALP's ambivalence about unemployment took a new turn for, despite the fact that full employment was a non-starter, the labour movement believed that it *was* pursuing full employment. This was because of the union movement's assumption that the industrial sector generates jobs. Hence it was not generating enough jobs because of a downturn in the business cycle. The ACTU was to urge a revival of productive industries, using a post-Keynesian strategy of corporatist management, with wage restraints, investment enticements and other macro-employment policies. Hawke, the exemplar of unionism and mateship, yet also armed with his own contrasting 'post-industrial' position, played a critical role in bifurcating the likely ALP employment strategies.

Hence the concern with redefining work became more and more fashionable among those holding conventional though not exactly inconspicuous jobs over the next few years. In 1982 post-industrial arguments were thoroughly aired with the publication of Barry Jones' *Sleepers Wake: Technology and the Future of Work*. That year's ALP platform included 'encouragement of legitimate new areas of work activity such as self-employment and worker co-operatives'.[24] At a conference on 'The Future of Work',[25] no consensus was reached about the importance of paid work, although all assumed unemployment to be endemic. While every commentator stressed an overwhelming commitment to and need for paid work, only one criticised the prevailing assumption that the shortage of paid work could be solved by persuading people that 'their salvation lies outside paid work'.[26]

Despite the Labor Party's curious ambivalence, it *had* to recognise unemployment by early 1983: overall rates had reached 9.9 per cent, with men now as affected as women.[27] Unemployed workers' unions had formed, and they set up soup kitchens outside Liberal fundraising dinners to embarrass arriving guests. The call for 'Jobs, Jobs, Jobs', endorsed by Neville Wran, then President of the ALP, was chanted at rallies and marches to the cities, one from Wollongong to Sydney, another ending at the Melbourne Club (heartland of the powerful). While no subsequent Labor government has even considered implementing a full employment program, how could Labor avoid upsetting its traditional constituency? Hawke played a critical role in producing a less condescending rhetoric than the Liberals', and in February 1983 he made 'the right of all Australians to a job' his chief electoral promise. The Fraser government's apparent indifference, if not arrogance, towards the unemployed as the 9.9 per cent rate came out, signalled its end: it was one of, if not *the* key issue in Labor's rise to power.

As it turned out, Hawke's election slogan was not repeated once Labor was in power. The Accord contained wage demands, while eventually making improvements to the social wage, mainly through Medicare. At the Economic Summit which launched the corporatist structures, the employment issue was virtually ignored. The policy directions adopted there implied an acceptance of similar levels of unemployment to those of the Fraser years.[28] Instead, in an address to the International Labour Organisation (ILO) in June 1983, Hawke returned to his ideas for 'redressing the imbalance' on both sides of the supply-demand equation for jobs. Arguing that if unemployment was a 'tragedy', 'increasingly over the years I have come to the view that we should do what we can to reduce the demand for conventional jobs . . . by helping to provide socially constructive alternatives'.[29] Here was the first *official* reference to alternatives to paid work, the aim of which was to reduce the labour supply but not, like the liberals, by explicitly concentrating on the female workforce.

In the light of the visibility (short-lived) of the organised unemployed, Hawke's ILO speech on communes at last struck a chord with the conservative press. *The Australian* still opposed taxpayers funding 'hippy colonies', but could now see that Hawke's suggestion represented

> the first serious attempt by any government to face up to the serious issue of how unemployment benefits should be spent. In fact it will force the Government to seriously consider whether there should not be *a form of compulsory occupational activity* for anyone who is fit to work, but unemployed.
> The dole as such, one of the biggest costs in the Government's budget, and paid virtually without any requirement to *contribute* to society, may be at an end. . . . The question of how unemployment benefits should be applied is one that bedevilled the Fraser Government. Some . . . argued that *people should not have a virtually automatic entitlement to the dole*. The Fraser administration was much more timid than its tough image indicated . . . and refused to bite that particular bullet.[30]

Other journalists, however, had more qualms about the issue of compulsion. A *Sydney Morning Herald* editorial argued that New Zealand had tried a similar project in the early 1970s, called 'Ohu', which was designed

> to soften the impact of unemployment for young people. But this sank when the rhetoric stopped. The problem was that the vast majority of those unemployed did not want to drop out. They wanted, in the memorable chant used during the 1983 Federal election in Australia, 'jobs, jobs, jobs'.[31]

Another article recalled previous rural failures in Australia, and criticised the idea of 'shifting the urban unemployed to the countryside' as a sentence 'to a hopeless and miserable future, at huge cost, which will eventually end with them returning to the cities even more broken than before they left'.[32] Similarly, New South Wales Young Labor condemned Hawke's plan as a form of 'economic

apartheid' and was far more concerned that there were no long-
term structural economic policies to solve unemployment.[33] Others
pointed to the Big Brother element. Because Hawke had said
he would not countenance subsidises to 'drop-outs', how would
drop-outs be identified, and what criteria would be used to assess
'deserving' or successful communes? As Geoffrey Laurence warned,
'We have ways of making you self-actualise' may no longer be
science-fiction.[34]

These criticisms were ineffectual in halting the bureaucratic
machinery. They comprised a minority view at the time, anyway.
Other progressives and post-industrialists, while aware of cynical
motives, merely hoped that these government designs might backfire.
This had been Cock's argument, and also environmentalist Ted
Trainer's, who suspected the 'alternative lifestyle movement' could
have 'delightfully subversive effects', since it represented 'the general
alternative' needed to abandon affluence and growth.[35] Whatever the
motive, communal fever suddenly broke out in state arenas and in
public discourse, ninety years after an earlier epidemic.[36] Immediately
following the ILO speech of 1983, press coverage of numerous kib-
butzin plans increased tenfold and did not abate for two years. Not
only were the federal and state governments busy with research, but
various private bodies also drew up plans. The latter disintegrated
before the year was out.

A new charity, innocuously called the Homeless Children's
Association of New South Wales, was the first kibbutz endeavour.
Hawke lent his support and numerous dignitaries, including
Cardinal Freeman, Barry Unsworth (Secretary, New South Wales
Trades and Labor Council), Archbishop Loane, Judge Staunton,
Magistrate C.R. Briese, Charles Lloyd Jones (David Jones Stores)
and the Vice-Chancellor of Sydney University were 'directors'. As a
Herald article suggested, if the dream of the rural idyll was staging
a 'big comeback', the difference this time was its financial backers:
the 'living embodiments of capitalism, the work ethic and the profit
motive'. Large companies like Westpac, TNT, Wormalds, Burns
Philp and Esso gave substantial donations. 'A heavy pall of respectability now hangs over the commune/kibbutz idea.'[37] Bourgeois
philanthropy was back, although most other press reports swallowed
the publicity. A scheme once considered 'deviant' had now won
'public acceptance', according to one article ingenuously headed
'A kibbutz stirs the national psyche'.[38]

The inaugural meeting of the Homeless Children's Association was at the Sydney Hilton. The source of the directors' concern was this: by 1983 a majority of unemployed teenagers were located in New South Wales, with half in Sydney's western suburbs – far from the Hilton. The numbers of homeless were rising rapidly, and half of all teenagers incarcerated in Australia were located in New South Wales.[39] Ignoring the fact that unemployed *adult men* had embarrassed the captains of industry, the Association decided to send its executive officer to stay at Mt Druitt for seven weeks to investigate the 'causes' of teenage homelessness, helped by funds from the New South Wales Drug and Alcohol Authority. Next it chose a site for a 'pilot' kibbutz, at Mangrove Mountain near Gosford – reserve land granted in perpetuity by the state Labor government to the Association. Sydney University's School of Architecture provided 15 000 work hours to design a model village to accommodate twenty adults and children who would be 'subsidised' by the equivalent of the dole – although self-sufficiency was expected to follow rapidly. The Association presented Hawke with the plan in July 1983. This saw a future 4000 'kibbutz-style' villages spread across Australia, while its more modest 'three-year pilot program' suggested that twenty would be a good start.[40]

The idea took on, and a group of Melbourne businessmen, advised by Israeli 'experts', announced a similar scheme for the Murray River. Yet again, it was consciously designed as a long-term solution to unemployment.[41] But, barely two months later, a Sydney headline announced: 'Dole Farm in Deep Trouble', and went on to report the resignation of Hawke, Unsworth and 'most of the charity's band of top businessmen' from the New South Wales Association.[42] Gosford Council had refused to rezone the land for a kibbutz, following petitions against it from 'hundreds of angry residents on Mangrove Mountain'. Residents argued they were sympathetic towards homeless teenagers but objected to the project because they knew it would fail, 'leaving drug addicts, prostitutes and delinquents to roam the mountain'. A local farmer declared the site was useless for either agriculture or development and, even if the Association spent thousands (which it claimed it did not have) on development and pumping water, the site would still be 'worthless'. Inevitably 'the young people would become frustrated and abandon the kibbutz'.[43]

The Federal government was undeterred by this fiasco. Hawke's 'notional interest' in alternative lifestyles as an 'option' for the unemployed required 'substantive explorations' of how such a policy might be put into effect.[44] This naturally required much more information if appropriate programs were to be formulated. Just as the Mangrove Mountain plan was swamped, at least five ministries set up new sections to investigate the 'hunt for alternatives to jobs', as announced by the Minister of Employment and Industrial Relations (Ralph Willis). So much for election promises, for Willis admitted here to the 'gloomy reality' that even with a 5 per cent growth rate it would take ten years or so to reduce unemployment to early 1970 levels.[45] The bureaucrats seconded to the 'hunt' suggested that their cautious enthusiasm was due to incoming ministers' insistence, if not panic, that they 'Do something' about unemployment.[46]

In late 1983, the Department of Employment and Industrial Relations (DEIR) presented a paper to the new Economic Planning Advisory Council (EPAC), set up after the Summit, called ' "Supply Side" Approaches to the Unemployment Problem'. (Hawke appeared to have reversed the use of demand and supply terminology. Whereas a 'supply-side' strategy usually means a reduction in the supply of labour, Hawke called it a reduction in the demand for jobs.) This particular supply-side approach assumed a fixed demand for labour by employers. Expanding on vague suggestions from Hawke and Willis, the paper identified three ways to reduce labour supply, the first being

> encouragement to *alternative modes of living and working*
> * alternative lifestyles in self-sustaining communities
> * establishment of new small enterprises through work co-operatives or income support arrangements equivalent to unemployment benefits.[47]

Other options for reducing labour force participation were to increase school retention rates and foster early retirement, and to redistribute work through reducing the average hours worked by each employee. DEIR was increasingly pessimistic, and the next year Willis made every effort at the ALP Conference 'towards swinging policy towards coping with unemployment', as the *Financial Review* complacently described it.[48]

Meantime, the Department of Prime Minister and Cabinet had Bob Hogg, principal adviser to Hawke, touring Europe to study alternative communities and attend an international conference on 'alternative workstyles and co-operatives' in Israel.[49] Hogg was the least enchanted within the federal departments, insisting that the alternatives were not to be a 'panacea to the unemployment problem' but to encourage 'people's rights to self-management' in co-operatives.[50]

'Alternative lifestyle' groups rapidly became the object of intense government interest, with federal effort and money poured into gathering data and funding numerous reports. One, on 'Sustainable Rural Resettlement', prepared by a unit at the University of New England, gave a laundry list of the ways the state could 'facilitate' resettlement or 'homesteading', from special courses about communal life for high school students, to allowing unemployment benefits to be capitalised.[51] 'Community consultation' with experts in the field (New South Wales communes) led to the constitution of the National Steering Committee on Low Cost Rural Resettlement.[52]

The Office of Youth Affairs was deeply involved. It gave a $5000 grant for a 'rural resettlement' seminar of the Australian Association of Sustainable Communities (the new lobby group), held at Nimbin and attended by officers from Youth Affairs and the New South Wales government.[53] About $20 000 was spent on a feasibility study for an agricultural training co-operative at Healesville, Victoria, home of the commune started by Peter Cock. An analysis of research material was commissioned (at $5875) from academics at Griffith University,[54] which found fifty-eight people, mainly from communes, universities and government departments, all studying alternative lifestyles.[55] The same group was funded for a readership survey of the magazines *Grass Roots* and *Earth Garden*. Readers were asked about government funding of alternatives – they were in favour of it – and about the 'social characteristics of alternative lifestyle participants'.[56] Estimates of numbers planning to move to 'an alternative lifestyle' (e.g. 95 000) and the current commune population (e.g. 60 000) were optimistic. In discussing Australia's 'long and rich history of utopian lifestyle experimentation', the Leongatha labour colony of the 1890s was evidenced, not for its anti-utopian workhouse basis and Victorian government promotion, but for the numbers involved: 4000.[57] Youth Affairs itself was inundated with submissions: pictures of feudal villages, architectural plans and financial submissions for communal housing filled cabinets and lined walls. But Youth Affairs was mindful that making crown land available ran the risk of 'Pitt Street farmers' exploiting the scheme from the city, and therefore favoured pilot projects under the 'community/self-sustainable concept'.[58]

The Attorney-General's Department investigated legal impediments to the formation of communal enterprises, and likewise had pictures of Nimbin lining its walls, as well as a research library on communes. Officials there were critical of Youth Affairs' reliance on biased surveys by those already committed to communes and personally investigated overseas co-operatives, communes and government 'support organisations' in Britain, Sweden, Denmark, Israel and Spain. The advice garnered strongly suggested that communes could *not* be promoted from the top down, although 'active government support' *could* be provided for sound proposals from the grass roots, because 'economic incentives' would result in 'negative recruitment', an inevitable lack of commitment to co-operation, and a repetition of the commune failures of the 1890s.

The source of optimism for the 1980s experiments lay in the anti-consumerist attitudes of environmentalists, who opposed the view that land was just for 'making money'. Hawke was correct in that 'abundant resources of land in congenial environments' were available, but planning had to ensure 'a closer balance between the supply of, and demand for, an alternative but self-supporting lifestyle': a cautious redefinition of Hawke's employment strategy formula. So it was recommended that land be released and training in 'alternative lifestyles' be provided, presumably to inculcate commitment.[59]

These federal plans only lasted another year. Within EPAC, the supply-side strategy of DEIR was completely discounted by the two other partners of the Accord, capital and labour. The union position naturally sought to protect award wages and conditions, and also opposed the implicit denigration of active employment policies. The labour movement's stand will be discussed in detail in reference to worker co-operatives, where the federal government was particularly criticised for combining communes and co-ops as if both should be 'sub-economic' forms of activity,[60] which indeed they were.

The representatives of capital on EPAC regarded supply-side strategies as 'inconsequential' in comparison to 'broad' demand-side strategies for achieving economic growth.[61] Big business was pressing for cutbacks in wages and public spending, and the dismantling of state regulations on capital movements and employers. The question of alternative rural communities for the unemployed was not capital's responsibility (save for private philanthropy). The least powerful groups within EPAC (the welfare agencies), who in certain respects were the only voices for the unemployed, gave modest support to the supply-side option, though their advocacy of government support for the 'alternative modes of living and working' option was not based on labour market considerations.[62]

But of course the labour market consideration was the chief reason the Hawke government pursued the option. DEIR expressed strong reservations about Hawke's plan, sensing that the work test was being ignored on the north coast. It commissioned another report on whether communes *did* create job vacancies.[63] The two enthusiastic departments, embroiled with the Sustainable Communities lobby, attempted to sidestep the issue of labour market effects, despite the warning against 'economic incentives'. Senator Ryan, for example, considered the Youth Affairs survey gave most 'encouraging' estimates.[64] In April 1985, Youth Affairs provided a further $25 000 for a pilot scheme for unemployed people to learn practical and 'self-management' skills on real communes.[65]

But by the middle of 1984 more concrete evidence against Hawke's plan appeared. The first was an opinion poll of young people carried out for the federal government by ANOP. The main finding was a well entrenched work ethic among students, workers and the unemployed. Teenagers thought mostly about money and getting jobs; but it was 'normal' employment they wanted. There was no enthusiasm whatever for commune living, and the unemployed were hesitant to ask for dole increases because they were well aware of the 'bludger' charges.[66]

The next problem involved a conflict between federal, state and local governments. Both federal and state governments were interested in communes for purely pragmatic reasons. But the states are responsible for education, 'law and order' and housing, not unemployment benefits. Hence federal and state governments faced different public and budgetary pressures over unemployment. Commonwealth funding to the states had been drastically reduced since the recession. A state concern, such as homelessness, in a society where the wage earner is supposed to provide privately for housing, becomes acute in times of high unemployment.

The New South Wales situation exemplified these problems. In 1982 the State Council of Youth recommended 'education for constructive leisure', encouragement by schools and the media of 'alternatives to employment', and that 'new employment patterns' such as work co-operatives and subsistence farming be seen as 'equally valid' (by what means, other than propaganda, it did not suggest). In addition, from 1979 onwards the New South Wales government had pressed for a form of communal ownership called 'hamlet development', in opposition to Lismore City Council's threat to demolish fifteen commune houses on the grounds that health and safety standards were being threatened and that it was unfair that other citizens were not allowed to infringe regulations.[67] Tolerance of communes had broken down over a logging dispute in the Terania rain forest. A referendum held by the Council resulted in a 'massive vote' against hamlets.[68] Armed with experience from the Terania protest movements, commune lobby groups approached the state about this local harassment in 1982. The following year the New South Wales Land Commission tried to purchase a property on the north coast for a pilot commune, but was opposed by Kyogle Shire Council.[69] Then, mounting a larger campaign with more commune experts, the Land Commission prepared a feasibility study on multiple occupancy (1984), at much the same time as the Victorian Ministry of Housing commissioned a similar one from Peter Cock and Paul Goldstone (1984). Both indicated how state governments could assist low income earners in getting access to land and housing at an 'affordable price'.

The New South Wales report, in implicit accord with the opinions – or prejudices – of the Homeless Children's Association, argued that rural areas had a greater capacity 'to absorb young unemployed people in a lifestyle that does not produce the sort of costly social problems characteristic of more urbanized environments (prostitution, hard drugs, violence)'.[70] Multiple occupancy projects would have 'an extensive stimulatory effect on the existing rural economy', because new residents would generate local service jobs and increase demand on local timber mills and general stores.[71] Further, both studies assumed that land sharing communities would be economically viable in the long term. Land sharers would either find paid employment or their cash flow needs would be met by unemployment benefits. Dependence on unemployment benefits was emphasised, since the financial arrangements for purchasing the hamlets proposed that loan repayments be manageable within the dole. As the next federal report on communes (by Elizabeth Sommerlad *et al*) pointed out, such a feature

> presupposes however, that unemployment benefits are a civil right – a form of guaranteed income – rather than *a discretionary payment based on a work test as at present*. . . . Paradoxically, it seems that we have the

Federal Government exploring the idea of encouraging more people to adopt alternative rural lifestyles in the hope that this might represent a partial *solution* to unemployment while at the same time the two State Governments are considering schemes whose net effect might be to encourage more people to become dependent on the government for income support.[72]

And this was the nub of the federal–state conflict. The federal government's 'solution' to unemployment required that people on communes be prevented from participating in the labour market, both in order to reduce 'discretionary' dole payments and to leave job vacancies for others. So much for the conventional expectations of citizenship. Moreover the Sommerlad report, commissioned explicitly to investigate this, found that the commune movement was achieving neither. The brief was to learn whether communes provided 'a feasible supply side ameliorator to the current high levels of structural unemployment'. Criticising policy makers' 'romanticised image of rustic life', the Sommerlad report found that the implicit assumptions made by Hawke should be 'matters for further enquiry' rather than policy starting points. There may be 'little basis in fact' in supposing that 'the development of self-sustaining communities' is a goal or that they want to be 'economically viable through entrepreneurial activity'; or that young unemployed are 'interested' in this kind of lifestyle.[73]

The report's findings without doubt contradicted Hawke's assumptions. No commune was self-sufficient to 'the extent of operating independently of the formal market economy', nor did many see this as 'an achievable goal'. None could carry on without income either from welfare payments (received by a majority) or from conventional employment,[74] and two-thirds of those not in paid work wanted work. The average income was about half that of the Australian average. More commune dwellers had degrees (32.4 per cent) than the general population (4.2 per cent), and 64 per cent were employed up until their move to the country, mainly in the public, professional sector.

In sum, the report found that 'the financial viability of these communities was predicated on continued access to State welfare payments', and that this dependence was intentional; 'many had sufficient educational qualifications to find employment' if they left the communes. 'Their standard of living was equally dependent on their own labour and production' for housing and food, while low income status was also intentional 'because it was matched by an ideology of suppressed materialism'.[75] Since the federal government (e.g. the Department of the Attorney-General) found this an attractive feature of communes, the report initially queried whether such 'limited materialism' could be expected to continue to future generations, and even, 'as a social policy objective', whether it should be encouraged. This question remained unanswered in the report.

As for the vacancies left on urban labour markets, these were quite distinct from the jobs sought by the 'structurally unemployed'. Indeed, land sharers had such high qualifications and occupational status that 'it is debatable whether these people with valuable skills should be encouraged to withdraw from the labour market' onto welfare support at all, as this was a loss of investment in human capital. Finally, without more financial assistance, communes were likely to become 'economically depressed enclaves', since it was impossible for their inhabitants to save any cash. Transport costs were high and the properties were under-capitalised, while land resources were poor and over-used owing to a high density of population, and few commune members had practical skills. The 'multiplier' effect *might* rejuvenate rural economies, but any direct impact on local labour markets was marginal because commune dwellers were unable to create employment opportunities themselves, even if they were interested in entrepreneurial activities. They tended, rather, to displace the unskilled local workforce on account of their willingness to take on *any* paid work.[76]

So much for any effect of communes on the labour market. A further consideration in the report was the 'informal economy'. The concept has been used less in Australia than in Europe, where post-industrialists have enthused about its potential for social change, such as the debate over Pahl's research which was quickly acknowledged as an unviable form of self help for the unemployed.[77] Another stumbling block to informal economy ideas is the state's contradictory concern about tax revenue. That is, if all the productive activities not accounted for in GNP figures were somehow classified as 'economic activities', policy makers would face the dilemma of whether government purposes would be served better by taxing these activities or, if promoted as a survival strategy for the unemployed, by disregarding their tax potential. Since indirect taxation is a method of recouping revenue foregone in the 'black' economy, when does the 'black' economy shade into the 'informal' economy? The issue was raised in the wages for housework/mothers' allowance debate, because if housework were so productive it would be fairer to tax those who were *not* in paid work and *not* needing to spend their net income paying for childcare and household services.[78]

Possibly the Sommerlad report's emphasis on the informal economy was a way of softening the blow delivered to Hawke's idea. But an economist on the *Herald* was quick to complain of foregone tax revenue if that suggestion were to gain political favour. Failing to remember the media euphoria of only a year before, the article – called 'Yes Minister, we'll study communes' – derided the government for 'wasting its time and money studying the economics of hippidom': 'If I had come up with a bright idea like that, the bureaucrats would have laughed. "Ignore it minister, it's just another sun-crazed journo". But the bloke who thought of this little doozey was one R.J.L. Hawke.' Less frivolously, the especial condemnation was this:

> Dropping out is the ultimate form of tax avoidance. The government only taxes income, it can't tax psychic income and *it doesn't even tax work*. This principle is used by those people who give up their jobs to build their own home. Which is something the drop outs do too, of course. According to our intrepid researchers the popular belief that the commune-ists have abandoned the work ethic is wrong. . . . Because (their) productive activity is unpaid it isn't included in the Gross Domestic Product – just as housework isn't – and it isn't taxed. Almost 28 per cent of the land-sharers work more than 40 hours a week . . . Well, wasn't that interesting. You now know a lot more about middle-aged, middle-class hippies than you did. As for finding *a solution to unemployment*, you're no better off.[79]

In one sense this was correct, but it ignored what the Sommerlad report disingenuously called the government's more 'critical issue' of 'coping with high long term levels of unemployment' rather than merely 'finding solutions to unemployment', the latter being how both described Hawke's supply-side strategy. The report's argument on the informal economy implausibly tried to distinguish informal work from supply-side approaches: even if a majority on communes lived below the poverty line, these monetary concepts ignored 'the economic well-being accruing from informal economic activity'. The reason that informal economic activity is 'neglected' in GDP is due, the report hazarded, merely to the lack of status of communards, just as household work is dismissed for being 'predominantly' women's work.[80] A *proper* understanding of informal economic activity required a 'return' to a more 'obsolete' view of economics, where the demarcation between economic and social dimensions is more 'blurred', or, quoting Polanyi, a view where production and exchange is 'embedded' in social institutions. This optimistic discussion about resurrecting the past while disregarding the commodification of more and more household goods is common in the literature on the informal economy.[81]

The other reference to the informal economy concerned the number of hours worked in informal economic activities on communes. No existing community was totally sufficient in foodstuffs, so welfare benefits were necessary. The report discussed dole payments from the view of 'policy contradictions': either the dole is a discretionary payment (which the supply-side approach assumed) or the work test is 'anachronistic' in times of high unemployment. On communes the dole is often regarded as a 'civil right', and although people are meant to submit to the work test and actively look for employment, the report stressed that most beneficiaries *were* 'employed' – quite legally – but in the informal economy.[82]

In the 'longer term', if 'high structural unemployment' remained a feature of Australian society, communes had 'a great deal to offer' for 'a healthy and satisfying life' and for counteracting 'the damaging psychological and social consequences of unemployment'. With training, this lifestyle could be 'rendered' more attractive to the disadvantaged and be a 'desirable alternative to life on the dole'.[83] But it would require changes in social security policy. The report here assumed that the government 'recognises an obligation' for every citizen to receive a subsistence income (having queried it previously), and argued against the work test as limiting people's freedom to commit themselves to long-term 'useful activities' such as training or unpaid work. To support the informal economy, the government could either ease the work test in rural areas or introduce a guaranteed minimum income, an option favoured by land sharers. The report doubted that a guaranteed minimum income would gain political support 'as long as government policies are predicated on a return to full employment' (sometime). Another option was 'lump sum funding to communities in lieu of unemployment benefits to individuals', similar to a Community Development Employment Program (CDEP) administered by the Department of Aboriginal Affairs. The report considered this community work to be similar to land sharers' work, but 'the position of Aboriginal people in

Australian society justifies *special provision* which may be widely regarded as inequitable' if applied to communes. Despite such problems, the report finally recommended examining 'the implications of changing the fundamental nature of unemployment benefits in Australia' – which indeed they were.[84]

In brief, although the report revealed the limitations of the supply-side strategy, it ignored the issue of whether the Hawke government had abandoned full employment *de jure* as well as *de facto*. The report never clarified its meaning of 'solution' to unemployment, except for finding that the commune strategy was not a solution to removing people from unemployment figures or to reducing cash transfers. As for CDEP, this Aboriginal scheme (begun in 1977) was hardly a *'special provision'*. Instead of the entitlement then claimed from the Department of Social Security by all other unemployed Australian citizens, CDEP was and is paid from a fund 'meant to constitute special resources for reducing the disadvantages imposed on Aborigines'. It means that some Aborigines, if their community has volunteered, are the only people in Australia who have (in effect) worked for the dole, for over a decade. Volunteering is hardly a matter of community choice, moreover, since CDEP is virtually the only securely funded employment program available to Aborigines, who suffer high unemployment and lack the resources to build local service infrastructure and badly needed housing. It thus reduces Aborigines' unemployment rate and, once in the scheme, individuals are obliged to work if they are offered a job under CDEP because that constitutes a work test, *only* to receive 'dole' money.[85]

Following publication of the Sommerlad report the commune idea was abandoned at the federal level, not because the problems were insuperable but because casual employment prospects improved. The commune movement, no longer the object of government questionnaires, surveys and seminars, was now ensconced in the public arena as a legitimate lobby group. Its national lobby organisation – Sustainable Communities – even gained respect from the *National Farmer*.[86] But relations with local councils remained largely unresolvable. This is because councils assume that multiple occupancy, with its lower per capita rates, will make greater demands on local services while contributing less in rates than single blocks. Only a few New South Wales councils permitted Landcom rezoning, although some 'alternativists' managed to elect their representatives onto shire councils, both to promote multiple occupancy and to oppose large tourist developments and environmental degradation.[87]

In the process of gaining acceptance, 'alternative lifestylers' distanced themselves from counter culture communes, whose anarchist ideology was now judged, for example, as merely a 'disguise for privatism and social irresponsibility'.[88] Similarly, the Sommerlad report dismissed counter culture communes as relevant only in their 'failure' to be 'socially purposeful' because the 'personal fulfilment ethic' was too pervasive. A preferred 'self-reliance' developed later from the environmental movement.[89]

There are other interpretations. While most land sharers claim the dole, some original settlers became wealthy entrepreneurs and landlords, transforming from 'hippies to alternative lifestylers to trendies' of the Rainbow Region. Other developments occurred with multiple occupancy rules, whereby 'alternativist' developers (all male) set up 'packages' of sites with roads, a common dam and clearings, and sold shares at tidy profits to numerous divergent buyers.[90]

Multiple occupancy encourages this, because the individual ownership *rules* enshrined in local councils, which authoritarian councils upheld,[91] also defend individual *rights*. One critic asked whether this new ownership would be a 'slum in the making or an imaginative way to settle the battler on the land'. Often the land is steep and the soil poor, and, even if people find suburban kerbs unnecessary, multiple occupancy excludes the right to basic services like electricity, drinking water or sewerage. No safeguards can prevent 'crasser developers' from buying parcels of land and 'dumping the unsuspecting or idealistic poor on harsh unserviced terrain'.[92] Even Tuntable Falls (founded in 1973), which some left after finding the stress on community and co-operation 'oppressive', failed to mobilise members in collective improvements like building roads and dams. Package development with disparate buyers is even less likely to foster co-operation for building basic amenities. In the existing communes, a progressive decline in communality and a rising stress on personal privacy is widespread. Co-ownership of land is regarded by a majority solely as a means to achieve individualistic lifestyles.[93]

Interestingly, the other main study of Australian communes, by Margaret Munro Clark, commissioned at much the same time, was more attuned to New South Wales government concerns than to the labour market orientation of the Sommerlad report. Romanticism pervades this study.[94] Since cheap forms of housing had motivated the New South Wales government interest, the pictures described as 'beguiling examples of deep-drop cess-pit toilets' common in the Rainbow Region, do not dispel the hint of bias towards basic shelter, to put it mildly. The account, in any case, avoids a number of grim realities. For a start, after fifteen years of commune development, this north coast area is one of the most deprived in New South Wales. The population is growing at a far higher rate than that of Sydney's western suburbs, without receiving extra government aid as a 'growth area'. In 1987, 40 per cent relied on social security and the unemployment rate was 18.2 per cent. The rise in the number of single parent pensioners is due to the drawcard of lower rents in the region. One child in three is growing up in poverty, and even the social security inspectors sent to detect dole fraud found a smaller proportion there than in other areas.[95]

So much for the 'multiplier effect' to which governments and lobbyists attached such significance in their promotion of communes in rural areas. Others report that Nimbin settlers call the newly migrated unemployed people 'droogs', so displaying the same level of prejudice that the original communards endured.[96] Furthermore, the evidence of this new poverty area implicates the second generation of commune dwellers. It is not quite the case, as their parents assert, that 'some of them reject the value of poverty the same way as we rejected the value of materialism', in answer to a 1984 report that the children wanted BMX bikes, shoes and indoor toilets.[97] Their parents, if they wished, could return to highly paid jobs and 'materialism', but the children with their poverty ascribed, have less opportunity to do the same.

And if children face poverty, in communes or elsewhere, the same applies to women (or at least more women than men). In considering gender relations within communes, the Sommerlad report found that men 'predominated' in informal work and full-time employment, whereas women were 'constrained' by childcare.[98] The federally-sponsored content analysis of *Earth Garden*, like all other research on communes, found that women maintained 'traditional female attributes of motherhood, passivity, expressiveness and emotionality', while men maintained 'the more public and instrumental spheres'.[99] The two main studies found that decisions were mainly reached by consensus, which can disadvantage women. As Munro Clark observed, women on American communes often preferred a democratic vote because quick decisions were reached by this means, and essential work, like childcare, actually got done. A very small number of women in Australia have turned to all-female communities as a preferable strategy. There are three communal properties with ten or more women in New South Wales, one established since 1974, though none is any more self-sufficient than the mixed-sex communes studied above. The women either have paid jobs outside or rely on the dole or a private income.

COMMUNAL PROBLEMS

Without question, the fact that different ways of everyday life have now won some public acceptance is a social gain. And yet the original criticisms of the commune movement are also justified. The timing was unfortunate, as communes might have avoided state designs had the recession not occurred. Timing alone, however, does not explain all the problems, though their relation to the state does seem the most important factor.

On the question of social policy for communes, the British study by Abrams and McCulloch concluded that 'so far as communes as ends are concerned the right (social) policy for communes is to have no policy for communes'. That is, if communes are to be 'experiments in mutuality as such', social policy has no place because if they do achieve 'an alternative reality', despite constant failures, it is because they have 'forcibly separated themselves' from the dominant reality. State promotion of communes, even if communes were larger, richer, and legally secure as a result, cannot avoid being a means of 'containing the deviants from without'.[100] The only possible social policy for communes, according to these authors, lies in the promotion of communes as the means to give support to therapeutic communities, squatters and unsupported mothers. But *communes as such* can do next to nothing to change women's oppression – communal structures or the lack thereof neither helped nor hindered the attainment of more egalitarian gender relations.[101] Only when groups regard communal living *as a means*, by subordinating internal problems – such as maintaining satisfying relationships – to pursue outside goals, like political objectives, could the sharing of childcare and household tasks free women to participate more fully in the political world.[102]

Abrams and McCulloch admit the difficulty of separating ends and means. Communes as means – for sole parent pensioners – were regarded as suitable state policy for rural Australia in at least one government-sponsored proposal.[103] Communes in the Rainbow Region can hardly avoid being ends, due to their isolation and lack of employment opportunities. They cannot be supported as policy, although communal housing arrangements in cities are a different matter.

In addition, gender divisions on existing communes were hardly egalitarian. The fact that heavy construction and farming work is required does not adequately account for the widespread reproduction of the traditional sexual division of labour. Second-wave feminism quickly discovered that the original counter culture was essentially a male creation which rested on a 'hip' version of traditional sexual inequality, where women were 'earth mothers'. Also, housework is more burdensome when modern kitchen technology is rejected. Beliefs in children's autonomy, coupled with the sexual ethics of the early communes, often resulted in little paternal responsibility and left many middle-class women even more vulnerable to 'macho hippies' than in the cities.[104] Ironically, the gentler version of masculinity in the counter culture was an effective weapon in keeping women from asserting themselves, given strong norms against 'heavy' behaviour.[105]

These arguments did not convince one of those doing research for the federal government. William Metcalf argued that the only suitable approach for communes is to look at their internal structures, because applying 'our' criteria of 'liberation' and 'freedom' is a 'form of cultural imperialism'. If 'gender differentiation' is the predominant reality it 'frequently does not indicate inequality or sexual oppression'. Since the level of education of communards is so high in Australia, Metcalf suggested that this weakened the false consciousness argument, because many participants have 'with full "awareness" rejected feminist, Marxist and even liberal interpretations of "oppression" '.[106]

This 'education' argument not only assumes the gender neutrality of higher education,[107] but also assumes that all women on communes are familiar with theories of oppression and could change gender relations if they wished. The influences of external structures and their gendered subtexts, with which the most isolated commune has to contend, are also discounted. Extolling fixed gender roles on the grounds of an initial free choice obviates the necessity to look at the continuing internal power relations.

Furthermore, the search for self-liberation which the commune movement attempted, by trying to find new self-identities through a reciprocity of relationships (called 'collective self-seeking' in a non-pejorative way by Abrams and McCulloch) is problematic not only because these attempts often fail, but also because of the historically created way people in Western societies claim individual rights. As C.B. Macpherson shows, with the rise of individualism, individual rights were claimed on the basis that one owned one's own body and possessed one's own capacity to labour, as a supposed natural right. Those who do not sell their labour power and/or make contracts underwritten by state law as free and equal possessive individuals, have historically been treated as negative possessive individuals, as dependants.[108] Women and children were not 'individualised' by these liberal freedoms and rights initially, and still have fewer possibilities for self-determination.

Within communes, however, the appeal to 'natural' right is frequently the only way to claim individual rights (or be self-seeking), for communes encompass all levels of life: economic, political and personal. Every transaction and interaction is personal, there are no legal contracts to underwrite quite ordinary exchanges that would be impersonal, functional and often anonymous in mainstream society. If 'natural' right is claimed as a possession of one's own capacity to labour, it also means that one's labour and its productivity are things for which one owes no debt to civil society. Nowadays state welfare – imperfect and authoritarian as it is – ameliorates the very unequal effects of this fiction. But if there is no way of deriving a theory of political obligation – in mainstream society – from the assumptions of possessive individualism,[109] communes have even less scope for developing a theory of obligation. If one owes nothing to society, the claims of the social community over individual identity are undermined. There are no social obligations, so communes either frequently break up, or those 'possessing' more labour power (or capital or cultural capital or land) emerge 'insidiously' as leaders (insidiously because commune members attempt to reject explicit structural arrangements and do not formally alienate their labour power). Those with fewer 'possessions', or with less time to contribute labour power, do not. Women have not historically been able to derive individual rights from childbirth (ascriptive as this would be), and neither are their claims about caring for children usually recognised.

The most obvious conclusion to draw would be to question the notion that communes could be exercises in 'pre-revolutionary structure-making' (Theodore Roszak), or even exemplary alternatives in a positive radical sense. This is clearly expecting far too much of them (as Dennis Altman later saw).[110] The few that do manage to resolve the power relations are usually the most inward looking. Conversely, if consensus fails they frequently turn to religious, authoritarian forms, while gaining individual blocks was often an aim itself in Australia.

Other difficulties with the commune project concern the original arguments against 'monolithic system/corporate state' in preference to 'liberating our inner subjective condition'.[111] This conflated the bourgeois distinction between public and private which was to be opposed by a revolution of consciousness (new values) within alternative structures (new lifestyles).[112] From these presuppositions the commune movement opted for a private form of 'radicalism'. It was an alternative, radical subculture at the level of everyday life, not of political life, and it ignored the problem that alternative structures were an *effect* of the changed consciousness/new values involved in student radicalism rather than *a consequence of communal life*. Moreover, if problems ensued, most could easily leave (men in particular), assured of a space in mainstream, middle-class life.

To recall the criticism of how Altman, as much as the 'solely political' strategists of the traditional left, denied a 'dialectical nexus' between political, cultural and individual liberation,[113] this also failed to distinguish between political struggle and the state. By contrast, Altman's original defence of the counter culture welcomed its rejection of the traditional class politics either of revolutionary capture of the state or of the strategy of reformism through the state. As we saw, the new criticisms of industrial culture and individualism included the labour movement's consumerism and wage preoccupation, while 'direct' political action was too 'statist'. What Altman, and many others, eventually preferred to alternative structures for changing consciousness, was the 'personal is political' argument of the Black, gay and feminist movements. This meant that forms of oppression and diverse needs, formerly kept private, became politicised through new social movements. The counter culture rejected 'rationalist politics' (via formal electoral parties) only to become a radical, anti-consumerist subculture. In contrast, feminists, for example, turned to critical analyses of gender relations at the personal level, and feminist politics aimed to raise these matters publicly.

So, although the counter culture publicly criticised the manipulation of needs in the economy and the oppressive definition of needs by state bureaucracies, communes were an attempt to reprivatise human needs and stop debating about them. The justifications, drawn especially from Marcuse, were made on the basis that a clear distinction could be drawn between true and false needs. Instead of regarding needs as social/historical constructions, 'true' needs were identified as 'natural' and therefore not open to public dispute and contestation. The assumption is that needs are inherently non-political. Rather than *the politicisation of needs*, as Nancy Fraser puts it, the commune movement ruled out the possibility of a public political discourse on substantive questions of needs because it assumed that 'the system' was dominated by administrative and instrumental rationality. At the more authoritarian level, bicycles and indoor toilets could become 'false' needs.

By contrast, the social democratic insistence that needs are intrinsically political and open to questions of justice (exemplified by reformist governments like that under Whitlam) overlooks the counter culture's justified pessimism about the 'monolithic' state, because it cannot be assumed to be benign or 'neutral' to society. Bearing both problems in mind, the issue for Fraser is that needs are political not natural, and should be open to public interpretations within a participatory form rather than either reprivatised or administered and defined from the top down by the state.[114] To be fair to the Whitlam government, participatory politics had been a part of its political agenda, but this was rewritten by state administrative concerns, among other factors, and might have been undermined by a guaranteed income.

The anomalous case of communes, as well as the reason women and children are constrained generally from claiming rights (not less on communes), is bound to the definition of needs as private. When the production of goods moved from the private household, only later were the unequal effects of selling one's own labour power discussed in terms of public needs (e.g. workers' compensation or unemployment benefits). Other needs, historically supplied by women in the family have also become public concerns via the welfare state. This was intrusive and structured patriarchally, and complicated also because first-wave feminists had defined female needs as separate from male needs. It was much later that these issues were aired publicly with 'the personal is political' strategy. In communes the position is worse in principle, because the needs for care are reprivatised, and the needs for goods are retracted from the private official economy back to the private household, which therefore excludes the issues of needs from public debate. Needs are left to discussions between small communal groups.

There is no doubt that women's claims over needs and rights are neglected in mainstream society, because their work is still seen as *natural*. There are ascriptive consequences in claiming rights on the basis of biological child-rearing, and similar dilemmas obtain when speaking of women's capacities to 'alienate' their labour power expended in 'caring' at the personal level (e.g. mothers' allowances). But it is not made easier by the communal organisation being separated from the society at large. This is not to suggest that all communes necessarily turn to traditional ascriptive patterns, but the possibility is greater when needs and rights are once again a private concern judged internally by the members (for children too).

The commune movement was undoubtedly a genuine effort to restructure everyday life against the experience that needs (the Marcusian criticism) and public opinion (the Habermasian criticism) are manipulated in modern Western societies. But Marcuse's conception of manipulation neglects the potential for public participation in politicising needs. If needs are debatable, they are neither true nor false and therefore not available to 'objective' assessments, since that always raises the spectre of a judge or a vanguard to decide 'true' needs.

Marcuse's idea that individuals are indoctrinated to their instincts, and cannot find their true needs until they escape to alternative structures, was particularly influential with the counter culture.[115] As Patricia Springborg argues, however, if culture is a response to material needs, and if needs are historically determined over and beyond minimal survival needs, then genuine needs must also be culturally determined rather than true or false. The success of consumerism lies not in inculcating false, artificial needs (Marcuse's charge), but in the fact that modern advertising makes hidden appeals to genuine, if culturally determined, needs. People are not duped by these hidden appeals, but frustrated, as the vast majority lack the power to satisfy a variety of needs in ways other than via the consumer promise.[116]

Hence the alienation of consumer society, whereby individual-isation is expressed in terms of 'things' (you are what you have). Communes attempt to reduce alienation by collectively keeping the society at 'arm's length', but often develop into 'mechanical' com-munities where everybody is the 'same' and difference is ascribed according to sex. By contrast, both conservative and socialist traditions have tried to find mediations between the relation of the individual to society, through stressing the creation of freely chosen 'organic' communities, such as Durkheim's professional associations or, in a more conflict-oriented way, through social movements.[117]

Many communes, therefore, are doomed to fail, although this likelihood is important *above all* as an indictment of the Hawke scheme. The mainly middle-class inhabitants of a failed commune can view it as a transient learning experience, with mainstream life easily enough resumed. The consequences are different for the second generation – and far more so for the proposed 'communards': unemployed, unskilled teenagers earmarked for outback communes. Luckily in 1985 they were in a position to refuse.

There are consequences at another level too, because if communes *aim* to be free from outside economic and political structures – or their interference – they do not accomplish this in fact. They have to legitimise their reliance on welfare payments, and create new property laws as groups with communal needs, not as individuals with unique capacities or even 'possessions'. What happened here was that communes became legitimated as a result of administrative difficulties with unemployment. Likewise communes had to become politicised in order to exist at all in the face of local laws and local 'needs-talk' (e.g. fresh water) and 'rights-talk' (fairness to all rate-payers). Individual rights were then undermined by group claims. But communes can only talk about the need for communes *as such* in public discourse, not different needs.

The practical outcome demonstrates how communes, as singular projects, cannot accomplish wider social change. Theoretically the internal problems faced by communes reflect general constraints on political action. In this instance, many individuals from communes later joined the environment movement. But alternative structures in themselves gave no long-term outlet for the original voluntarism and new identities cultivated from the love-ins and rock festivals, except as a lobby group for commune interests. By being unable to identify an opponent, save as an amorphous concept – 'the system' –

the commune movement effected a social closure. Communes' internal practices included ascription, affirming possessive individualism in new guises, and an ahistorical and authoritarian view of human needs and forms of individuation. Transformation is always possible, but in order to survive *as communes*, they had to be shielded from the intrusive way that individual rights turn into harshly administered regulations. Indeed, solidarity was enhanced by early police repression, and hence communes became goals in themselves, rather than *vehicles* for societal change or individuation.

COMMUNES AND THE STATE VERSUS THE UNEMPLOYED

State interest became a cruel dilemma for the Australian commune movement. After federal and state approaches changed, the movement had little option but to negotiate in these administrative arenas, to attempt to change hostile local council policies. Yet alternative lifestylers understood the implications of the federal scheme for the unemployed, and their involvement with policy submissions, conferences and reports gave it an added, radical aura.

Still to be addressed are the reasons for the state's involvement in this particular alternative structure. A number of conclusions are drawn from this sorry tale after the discussion on worker cooperatives, the other plank of the state's hunt for alternatives to paid work. On the commune issue alone, however, those acting within the various state apparatuses and political processes cannot avoid the charge of being more cynically motivated about the commune solution than the other cases under review. Humphrey McQueen's response to Hawke's earliest proposal was that the expansion of self-supporting communes 'would be a sign of growing unemployment. Scores of thousands of people cannot live by growing dope, quilting and making candles out of yoghurt'.[118] Yet the government pressed on with the explicit presupposition that thousands of unskilled unemployed would indeed voluntarily evacuate the cities for rural poverty. This century's effort found no people as desperate as those during the recession of the 1890s, when a variety of communes and state labour farms emerged.[119] In the 1980s, claiming unemployment benefits in the cities was preferable to what would have been work-for-the-dole in communes.

An attempt to control young unemployed people was partly the impetus for state governments. Homelessness and urban violence were pressing public concerns, and criticisms were undermining legitimacy. Private enterprise also turned to the kibbutz idea when unemployment became a brief public concern, that is, when the captains of industry were attributed with responsibility for joblessness. But this typical bourgeois philanthropy speedily collapsed when local councils and rural residents successfully opposed the idea.

The federal government of the 1980s could not use counter culture communes in the same way as the 1890 commune fever was used by colonial states. Twentieth-century communes were largely a middle-class, student phenomenon which arose before the recession as an attempt to undermine labourism and 'the system'. The state could not conscript working-class teenagers to these communes. Nevertheless, the counter culture challenge and the spontaneous experiments, after several rewriting operations, still played a considerable part in easing major structural problems facing the state.

The redefinition of work was a long process, since the political climate and general prejudice towards the unemployed had been initially formulated by dominant groups making claims that 'dole bludgers' were synonymous with 'hippies' on communes. Once a relatively high level of structural unemployment was accepted as inevitable by the state (though not yet by the population), the new corporatist path – at least to halt wage demands – required union support. The unions demanded proper jobs, however, and rising male unemployment rates gave strength to oppositional demands to be in paid work rather than marginalised from society. Feminist demands were also taken into (electoral) consideration. In 1983 panic was endemic in federal bureaucracies: something had to be done about unemployment. 'Solutions' should be found that were seen to be sympathetic to the plight of the jobless but would also enable an admission or declaration that unemployment was not to be solved by proper job creation, without forfeiting union support, or being at the expense of work incentives, or by attacking women's workforce participation. The alternatives became the new supply-side 'solutions', of which the commune one proved a useful and apparently radical first step in shifting responsibility for teenage unemployment, until teenagers were removed from the supply-side altogether and the labour market changed.

At the same time as this rewriting process about the meanings of work and of the possible solution to unemployment was underway, the other major problem caused by unemployment – the blowout of the unemployment benefits bill – also needed urgent rethinking. The Whitlam government had made it more generous and more easily obtainable than in many other welfare states. The helpful 'solutions' to the state's problems caused by the demands for paid work, which were available from the commune movement's critique of wage labour and consumerism, were negated by the communes' reliance on unemployment benefits – hardly a 'solution' to the fiscal crisis.

Along with such failures in the commune plan there were also successes. For the government, the radical demands for the right to 'useful work' and to 'contribute' to the society without necessarily receiving remuneration were put to good use, chiefly in legitimising new definitions of work and unemployment benefits. This has reduced the federal government's responsibility to the unemployed, by eroding both the presumption that the dole is a right and the post-war belief in society's obligation to provide proper jobs to all who are able to work. Instead, the state now proposes that some people can contribute less than others, as second-class citizens if not in the lower tier of the new labour market, or in dole-work, or in 'training', then in some ill-defined 'informal' and marginalised areas.[120] Specifying that this should include communes, however, proved rather contradictory for the federal government, particularly when state governments were hoping that a small percentage of people would 'solve' their housing problems via the multiple occupancy path.

Meanwhile, the commune lobby achieved the legitimate space that before seemed impossible. Such was the fate of the most grass roots, popularly based attempt to carve out an alternative to mainstream society. With the worker co-operatives, by contrast, state apparatuses and private corporations played roles in their actual genesis in many parts of the Western world, once unemployment took off. This case, again in Australia of far more top down involvement than communes, will be considered next.

NOTES

1. P. Cock (1981), p. 140.
2. P. Ellyard (1975), p. 205.
3. *National Times* 30.7.73. Supposed scandals about Cairns' involvement with communes were regular media beat-ups.
4. J.S. Nalson (1977), p. 319.

5. See A. Harding (1985).
6. *ibid.*, pp 244-5.
7. B. Casey (1985), p. 20.
8. A. Harding (1985).
9. Australia. Social Security Review (1987), p. 15.
10. C. Wallace (1984), p. 32.
11. It could be argued, conversely, that opinion polls still advise the Liberal Party to try it every election.
12. C. Wallace (1984), p. 34; R. Sharp & R. Broomhill (1988), pp. 119-20.
13. See John Freeland (1987). In May 1987 the widows' pension and supporting parents' benefit was cut off for those whose youngest child was aged 16. Liberals have an equally harsh approach to sole parents, but the emphasis is more on enforcing private dependency.
14. R.J.L. Hawke (1979), pp. 40-3, 49.
15. *ibid.*, pp. 44-8, my emphases.
16. *ibid.*, pp. 48, 67.
17. Cited *Sydney Morning Herald*, 27.6.83; 'The saltbush eaters', *The Australian*, 3.12.79; 'Idylls for the idle', *Sunday Telegraph*, 2.12.79.
18. *The Australian*, 3.12.79.
19. *Sunday Telegraph*, 2.12.79.
20. Arena Editors (1979), pp. 1-4.
21. R.J.L. Hawke (1981), p. 56.
22. H.A. Nix (1981), pp. 73, 76-7.
23. Cock (1981), p. 139.
24. Australian Labor Party (1982), p. 56.
25. An Australian Institute of Political Science collection, 1981.
26. R. Sackville (1981), pp. 144-5.
27. Australia. Social Security Review (1987). ABS estimates exclude anyone who has worked for more than one hour a week.
28. J. Triado (1984), p. 49; H. Stretton (1987), pp. 8-9.
29. R.J.L. Hawke (1983).
30. R. Schneider, 'Communes as an alternative to the dole', *The Australian* 13.6.83, p. 1, my emphases.
31. 'Jobs for the boys and girls', *Sydney Morning Herald* 16.6.83, p. 10.
32. 'History is repeating its sad failures', *The Australian* 25.6.83.
33. *Sydney Morning Herald* 1.8.83.
34. G. Laurence (1983), p. 25.
35. T. Trainer (1983), p. 32.
36. Commune fever of the 1890s was discussed in chapter 2.
37. Y. Preston, 'The kibbutz dream: just a sad illusion?', *Sydney Morning Herald* 29.6.83, p. 22.
38. S. Rice, 'A kibbutz stirs the national psyche', *Sydney Morning Herald* 27.6.83, p. 7.
39. C. Cunneen (1984), pp. 34-7.
40. 'Hawke will get plan for kibbutzim', *Sydney Morning Herald* 15.6.83; *Sydney Morning Herald* 27.6.83.

41. C. Cunneen (1984), p. 46.
42. *Sunday Telegraph* 28.8.83.
43. 'Mangrove Mountain does not want kibbutz in its backyard', *Sydney Morning Herald* 26.9.83.
44. These were the terms used by the later report on communes commissioned by the Bureau of Labour Market Research, Sommerlad *et al* (1985), p. 11.
45. *Financial Review* 16.11.83.
46. Personal interview with John Butler, Attorney-General's Department, 2.8.84. The order was particularly made to the then Department of Employment and Industrial Relations. Also see 'Govts move cautiously on alternative lifestyles', *Sydney Morning Herald* 26.9.83.
47. Australia. Department of Employment and Industrial Relations (1983), my emphasis.
48. *Financial Review* 19.6.84.
49. *Sun-Herald* 8.4.84.
50. Personal interview with Bob Hogg, 20.6.84.
51. S. Williams (1984).
52. E.A. Sommerlad *et al* (1985), p. 12.
53. *Sydney Morning Herald*, country edition 21.9.83, p. 5.
54. Government expenditure on this particular research was set out in a letter from the Minister of Education and Youth Affairs (then Senator Ryan) to the Prime Minister, circulated to the Ministers of Employment and of Social Security, and the Attorney-General, on 7.6.84.
55. W.J. Metcalf (1984).
56. W.J. Metcalf & F.M. Vanclay (1984); (1985).
57. W.J. Metcalf & F.M. Vanclay (1985), p. 1.
58. Personal interview, Richard Gurney, Department of Education and Youth Affairs (DEYA) 2.8.84.
59. J.J. Butler (1984), p. 27; and interview with John Butler, 2.8.84.
60. Australian Council of Trade Unions (1984).
61. Sommerlad *et al*, p. 13.
62. *ibid*.
63. Personal interview, Adrian van Leest, DEIR 3.8.84.
64. Mentioned in a previous note, on Ryan's 1984 letter to the Prime Minister.
65. M. Munro Clark (1986), p. 195.
66. 'The crass voice of youth: cash and "coons"', *Sydney Morning Herald* 9.5.84, p. 1.
67. *Sydney Morning Herald*, country edition 2.12.79, p. 11; *Sydney Morning Herald* 4.12.79, p. 11.
68. M. Munro Clark (1986), p. 135; *Sydney Morning Herald*, country edition 21.3.80, p. 10.
69. Australia. Department of Employment and Industrial Relations (1983); 'Nimbin "droogs" may be kibbutz founders', *Sydney Morning Herald* 16.7.84.

70. Land Commission of NSW (1984), p. 5.
71. *ibid.*, p. 68.
72. Sommerlad *et al*, pp. 15–16, my emphases.
73. *ibid.*, pp. 1, 59.
74. Twenty communes with 216 adults were studied; *ibid.*, p. 183. 86% of the cash income not from welfare payments came from wages, salaries and casual jobs, and a mere 3.7% from the sale of goods or produce. A final 11.7% of all income was unearned or from royalties; *ibid.*, p. 113.
75. *ibid.*, p. 149.
76. *ibid.*, pp. 185–7.
77. See chapter 1, also, e.g., Burns (1975); Pahl (1980), (1984); Illich (1971); Offe (1984).
78. M. Edwards (1975).
79. R. Gittins, *Sydney Morning Herald* 16.1.85, my emphases.
80. E.A. Sommerlad *et al*, pp. 119, 189. The latter argument is discussed in my Honours thesis (UNSW, 1982) on the 'separate but equal' feminism of the nineteenth century. It was entitled 'The Campaign to Raise the Status of Housework', and found that the campaign failed.
81. E.A. Sommerlad *et al* (1985), pp. 21–3; see also R.E. Pahl (1984); L. Morris (1985).
82. E.A. Sommerlad *et al* (1985), pp. 129, 131, 133, 160.
83. E.A. Sommerlad & J.C. Altman (1986), p. 14; Sommerlad *et al* (1985), pp. 189–91.
84. E.A. Sommerlad *et al* (1985), pp. 191–7, my emphasis.
85. M. Mowbray (1986) p. 40.
86. 'Farm "trendies" seek new respectability', *National Farmer* 5.4.84.
87. Sommerlad *et al* (1985), pp. 16–7; see *The Australian* 23.11.85; *National Farmer* 5.4.84.
88. P. Cock (1982), p. 20.
89. Sommerlad *et al*, pp. 30, 40.
90. 'Mixing business with alternative life', *Business Review Weekly* 22.2.85; 'Dream of the free enterprise collective', *Sydney Morning Herald* 19.7.84.
91. P. Cock (1981), p. 140; M. Munro Clark (1986), p. 135.
92. A. Horin, 'The Nimbin experiment: rural slum or rural dream?', *National Times* 1–7.4.83.
93. M. Munro Clark (1986), pp. 130, 180.
94. The Faculty of Architecture, Sydney University, commissioned the work, and it in turn had also worked on communes for the NSW Department of Environment and Planning (M. Munro Clark (1986), pp. 9–10) as well as the old Homeless Children's Association.
95. 'North Coast poverty rising', *Sydney Morning Herald* 11.5.87.
96. *Sydney Morning Herald* 16. 7.84.

97. 'The Nimbin Hippies', *Sun-Herald* 1.4.84.
98. E.A. Sommerlad *et al* (1985), p. 152.
99. W.J. Metcalf (1984a), p. 49.
100. P. Abrams & A. McCulloch (1976), pp. 217–8.
101. *ibid.*, ch. 5.
102. *ibid.*, pp. 216–7.
103. S. Williams (1984).
104. B.M. Berger (1981), p. 151.
105. B. Donaldson (1975), pp. 433, 438.
106. W.J. Metcalf (1984a), pp. 49–50.
107. cf. M. Sawer & M. Simms (1984).
108. N. Fraser (1987).
109. C.B. Macpherson (1962), p. 275.
110. D. Altman (1973), p. 457.
111. Marcuse, cited by Cock (1975), p. 9.
112. D. Altman (1973), p. 723.
113. Peter O'Brien (1971), pp. 24–5.
114. N. Fraser (1987), pp. 1–7.
115. In the Australian debate, Peter O'Brien took Marcuse's position: for example, (1971), p. 27.
116. P. Springborg (1981), ch. 9.
117. Agnes Heller (1973) discusses the notion of community in modernity.
118. H. McQueen (1982), p. 219
119. The first commune fever is mentioned in chapter 2.
120. This will be discussed in chapter 7.

CHAPTER 6

Worker Co-operatives:
Supply-Side 'Solutions' to Paid Work

Official promotion of worker co-operatives was a recession-led phenomenon of the late 1970s. Nineteenth century co-operatives had been one response to the impact on workers of industrialisation and capitalist ownership. In the long term, however, consumer and credit co-operatives became far more extensive than worker co-ops. The latter were nearly always set up during depressions and most were short-lived, leaving no collective memory of worker co-operation other than the financial and emotional costs. With several notable exceptions, most Western countries have only seen co-operatives emerge through the attempts of workers to save their jobs in times of high unemployment.

In contrast to earlier, mostly spontaneous efforts on the part of workers, the most recent examples of worker co-operatives involved many governments and private corporations. On the one hand, the reasons for state interest in co-operatives were much the same as with communes. In Australia, the federal supply-side strategies that motivated state interest in communes also included worker co-operatives. On the other hand, a majority of the oppositional groups promoting co-operatives for their transformative potential were actually linked with state policies (quite unlike counter culture communes), and unemployment was already well entrenched. Many proposed the idea of a 'pure' co-operative development from within the lower echelons of bureaucracies, such as those in local British councils, especially the Greater London Council (GLC), and in Australia within the New South Wales and Victorian governments. But where in Britain the entire GLC was disbanded by the Thatcher government, co-op promoters in Australia merely sank into deep quandaries in trying to contend with diverse state and federal interest in co-operative schemes. Here no co-operative proponents were as committed to full employment as was the GLC. Each day the GLC used to raise a large black flag inscribed with the latest unemployment rate (in millions), as a provocation to the Houses of Parliament across the river. In Australia, by contrast, where radical co-op groups were not primarily concerned that there was no government commitment to employment creation, they shared with the federal government some elements of the post-industrial strategy. But even though governments funded co-operative development for years, the number of successful experiments was such that it would be an exaggeration to say that a worker co-op 'movement' exists in Australia. Co-ops remain marginal; to date, their promotion has had little success.

This chapter will describe and critically analyse the social processes through which particular models for co-operative development in Australia were elaborated from different centres within and outside the state by divergent social groups for their own interests and by the state for others. The evidence is of particular interest, for it shows the problems with two quite different models for promoting co-op development, as well as the reasons for the failures of the actual experiments. This has both theoretical and practical implications, not least for the post-industrial strategy. Theoretically, it may clarify a few aspects of the relation between ideas and policies. The formulation of ideas by oppositional groups and by those more directly concerned with state interests, their subsequent translation into various contradictory policies, and the progression of problems encountered were all closely related. The state played a central role, for few co-ops even began during the 1970s–80s without being fostered by governments in one way or another. The more practical evaluation of these experiments suggests that any similar promotion of co-ops via the state should be avoided in the future.

In discussing the whole project, it must be stressed that the experiments and debates did not move along any straightforward path. Among oppositional groups, numerous proposals emerged in a historical vacuum, since Australia had no worker co-operative tradition to influence local growth. These plans could be generalised as two basic models for co-operative development in Australia. They had different interests, goals and aims, and while the model closer to sources of money and power was implemented, it, in turn, faced other difficulties. Both models in fact suffered from being tied very closely to the state, to the extent that neither could survive very well without state support but that the designs of the state subverted both models.

Such a complicated picture cannot be introduced without an explanation of the two typologies. The first and earliest model was chiefly concerned with preserving the purity of principles of co-operation enunciated during the 1840s in Britain. The 1970s version would provide radical alternatives to conventional work organisations. Worker co-ops in this instance were promoted expressly in order to restructure power relationships by dispensing with management hierarchies and instituting direct democracy. The supporters of this model, many of whom had started as youth workers in government employment schemes, believed that if sufficient numbers of pure worker co-operatives were established, capital–labour relations could be subverted from within the market. The unemployed would suffer from neither state paternalism nor alienated wage-labour. Such an economic development would effect a 'third way', neither state owned nor privately owned. The recession was to be used as an ideal opportunity for this gradual restructuring. Their proposed model could be called a *left-libertarian* version, since the aim of this co-operative development was to avoid state interference by encouraging independence and individual 'motivation'. It was picked up, firstly in New South Wales, by a Labor led state facing criticism (now long past) about doing little to alleviate youth unemployment. The libertarian aspects of the model (that is, that co-ops should require little government expenditure) were appealing to a debt-ridden state. These same aspects also attracted economic libertarians (the new right), chiefly interested in co-ops for their potential to deregulate the labour market.

In opposition to this model, and against the increasing interest of federal as well as state apparatuses, which by then regarded the left-libertarian model as a cheap 'solution' to unemployment, another model emerged which could be generalised as a *left-labour* version. This model was proposed by various radical union-oriented researchers and supported by left wing junior civil servants. It was argued that oligarchical concentration and control, the hierarchical structure of the labour market and current levels of unemployment would adversely affect co-op members unless trade union safeguards were laid down by the state. Such state control, however, flies in the face of co-operative purity.

Both models did try to avoid the self-exploitative, incentive versions of worker-owner schemes – for a time – and the state designs for co-ops as a way of reducing the labour supply and legitimating the lack of commitment to full employment. But apart from these overwhelming difficulties, both models were themselves top down approaches and they suffered accordingly. Neither model generated grassroots support: few workers wanted to avail themselves of the opportunity of more control over their work lives, especially when these opportunities were imposed from above, at a time when jobs were under threat and material support was insufficient.

The following will trace the way that different governments in Australia tried to promote various models of co-operative development, and it will then evaluate the empirical and theoretical dilemmas that ensued. The problems with promoting democracy 'from above' and other distortions imposed by various state apparatuses reveal all too well the state's capacity to redefine progressive policy innovations for legitimising and administrative purposes. The state's role in both the commune and co-operative strategies will be established in the next chapter. It will deal with the subsequent period when 'acceptable levels' of unemployment rose higher and higher, a consequence, in part, of Australian governments' enthusiasm for the post-industrial solution.

THE PROMOTION OF CO-OPERATIVES
AND THE ROLE OF THE STATE

A steady stream of worker co-operative experiments began in the late 1970s, some years after the counter culture communes had been established. The situation by then was one of recession, revamped right wing ideology and a series of state and federal 'employment' policies and schemes which tried to divert attention away from the rapidly growing number of jobless at that time. The promotion of co-ops (initially in New South Wales) grew out of several government welfare-oriented job 'creation' schemes. These schemes were patronising and pointless, so much so that some of the more radical advisers and officers involved became strongly committed to the worker co-operative idea.

Before the state promotion got under way, only a few independent worker co-operative ventures (from the counter culture) existed in Australia, none to last the decade.[1] Conservative co-op supporters would include Fletcher Jones and Staff and other more conventional firms as worker co-operatives,[2] but purists would regard these as worker-owner incentive schemes, with workers owning only a tiny fraction of the firm. There are, of course, other types of co-operative enterprises, many of which have well established positions in the Australian economy, especially credit co-operatives like the building societies, and producer co-operatives such as the dairy farmers' co-operatives, which provide a marketing service. But pure worker co-operative enterprises – giving a service of employment to each owner-member – have a fleeting, intermittent history.

Indeed, even from the diverse approaches in what became yet another vast array of literature (like the commune saga) – from federal and state departments, politicians, state co-operative agencies, academics, trade unions and co-operative federations or lobbies – one can safely say that there is really no Australian tradition of worker co-operatives. There were several mining co-operatives in the 1860s and a few groups of printers and bootmakers formed short-lived co-operatives in Victoria during the 1890s recession.[3] Their scope is not to be compared with the commune fever of the time. Race Mathews (a Victorian Labor politician and an ardent co-op supporter) described them as mere 'attempts', 'sporadic and unsuccessful until 1976'.[4] Differing notes of optimism, quite removed from the realities of the recession, are discernible in all the co-operative promotional literature of the 1970s–80s. Yet the state-sponsored literature does little to explain those past failures, and there is no mention that the last desperate efforts to set up co-operatives occurred during the 1930s.[5] Worker co-operatives this time are presented as suddenly taking off with rising unemployment, but quite differently from those of past depressions.

The idea of promoting co-ops as a transformative, if gradual, strategy for the whole society grew out of particular disappointments and experiments within Community Youth Support Schemes (CYSS) in New South Wales around 1976, when unemployment was still relatively 'new'. CYSS, a federal-funded 'employment' initiative administered by state welfare departments, was not allowed to engage in job placement or job creation activities. Most CYSS groups attempted to help unemployed youth through the bureaucratic hurdles of other departments. Their brief was also to provide activities for them – that is, off the streets – and to provide what Windschuttle called 'therapeutic' relief.[6] Among these latter efforts, he described how various 'radicals' working in CYSS groups,[7] extended their official duties by explaining the structural and political causes of unemployment as a societal and not a personal failure. They had also arranged activities which deviated from the boy scout/papier mâché variety towards what Windschuttle considered were 'experiments which may lead them to establish models for alternative forms of community life'. In particular, a CYSS centre at Bondi Junction began running food and housing co-operatives, as well as experimenting with video, printing and permaculture.[8] From this the Bondi Collective was formed, consisting of people previously involved with the CYSS centre – 'frustrated CYSS officers', as a more senior bureaucrat described them.[9] They were determined to improve the situation of the unemployed *despite* the Fraser government's ineffectual though punitive schemes. At the state level, at least, there was hope of greater responsiveness from Premier Neville Wran's new ALP government, which had just taken over after long years of Liberal-Country Party rule in New South Wales. In November 1977 the people involved in the Bondi Collective made a request to the New South Wales Department of Youth and Community Services (YACS) for a grant to develop a work program for small house-repair contracts and odd jobs. In April 1978 YACS gave them money for some equipment and soon afterwards other co-operatives formed in Nowra and Ryde.[10]

A trickle of departmental reports – later to be an avalanche – ensued immediately. From the Deputy Premier's Policy Secretariat came 'Youth Resource Co-operatives: A Programme for Unemployed Youth' in July 1978. According to the civil servants involved, resource co-operatives were never supposed to be proper worker co-operatives but were instead regarded by the government as 'rescue operations', with the possibility that people could hire their own teachers and try to market the produce of their acquired skills. They were to offer a *'medium-term* role for the unemployed' – more, at least, than the CYSS guidelines, which still assumed that clean hair automatically ensured a job.[11] According to the submission, such co-ops would provide 'a stimulating environment for unemployed youth waiting to find permanent employment'. It was also critical that the New South Wales government had done nothing to cater 'for the welfare of over 50 000 unemployed youth in the state'.[12] Also at that time, YACS and the New South Wales Council of Social Service (NCOSS) produced a booklet called *Operation Co-operation* suggesting the advantages to be gained if young people formed work co-operatives. In December 1978 project officers in CYSS were sending memos to YACS about the 'natural inclination' they were finding among the young unemployed 'to utilize the skills which they had acquired' from CYSS 'towards constructive work with some remuneration'[13] – a cautious support indicative of the dole bludger accusations of the time.

Meanwhile the New South Wales government decided to implement the submission for resource co-operatives, now to be called the 'Youth Work Co-operative Programme'. Why was this decision taken? The welfare orientation is not disputed; these co-ops were to 'counter the serious dislocation caused by unemployment and to maintain motivation, self-respect and confidence' until jobs came along. Any 'problems encountered' would provide 'an important learning experience'.[14] On the one hand it was claimed that successive Ministers of YACS, Jackson and Stewart, were fairly 'slack', enabling juniors to have some freedom to press on amidst the lack of interest. On the other hand an inherent paternalism and meanness pervaded the scheme, later criticised by left-libertarians for merely providing halls with pinball machines and a phone: if any orders came through the kids could be sent out.[15] Indeed, YACS at that time was promoting the argument that the real issue facing youth workers was not how to prepare young people for work but rather 'how do we prepare them to handle life with little chance of employment'; that is, how do 'we' help 'them' from 'our' secure jobs.[16] Conversely, the press attributed the government's decision to 'the push having come from the community through the left of the Labor Party'.[17] For all those working on the New South Wales government's efforts to deal with unemployment it had become clear that there was little take-up of Wran's payroll tax deduction for employers to hire the young unemployed.[18] Perhaps more to the point for the New South Wales government was that the proposal involved relatively little money. So, despite the federal government's refusal to allow CYSS officers or premises to be used, or to relax the dole criteria for co-operative members, the Wran government allocated $3 million for the program, to start in January 1979 and end in June 1982.

The three-year saga can be told briefly.[19] The plan was 'envisaged to be *more than a "job creation" program*': it was to be a form of government support to independent community groups in self-help ventures designed to combat the effects of unemployment'.[20]

Of the twenty-one co-operatives established by 1981, however, only five were initiated by 'Local Citizens and the Unemployed'; the bulk were set up by CYSS project officers, social workers, charities and local councils.[21] So much for the spontaneous 'self-help' of 'independent community groups'. A 1981 report saw no co-operative as 'independently viable', and only two of these (a total of eighteen workers) still existed by 1985; others came and went. On the question of its being *more* than·job creation, the state's commitment to the scheme was much *less*. New South Wales had just faced heavy federal budget cuts from the Fraser government. The tensions between the welfare orientation, the cheapness of the program and the aims for self-sufficiency were marked features through to the present, though the welfare approach, all sides later agreed, was the cause of its eventual failure. As an example of the paternalistic approach, the YACS assessment – after the program had run for six months – noted 'signs of change in the attitudes of the participants'. It was optimistic that community attitudes to young unemployed would be more 'positive', when they could see 'the youth actively engaged in work and small business ventures'.[22]

The 1981 report found that young unemployed had used the co-operatives for picking up some casual work, for gaining skills or for trying to set up long term co-ops. Other research elicited that the co-ops had not been 'worker initiated' – the prime motivation was employment – and that before joining only 34 per cent knew much about co-operative principles.[23] Difficulties were noted with 'quality control' and unreliability of casual labour in terms of punctuality and work standards.[24] The Development Officer of Team Work Co-operative told the *Herald* of the problems of dealing exclusively with unemployed people, usually quite unskilled: 'Most employers get the pick of the crop; most co-ops get people who have difficulty finding work', she said. 'Some of our members thought nothing of mowing a lawn for three or four hours and walking away, simply leaving tools there.' Resources were strained by having to train so many members.[25] By the next year, promotional and educational programs were attempted and new goals now aimed to create 'permanent jobs within a co-operative framework'.[26]

With the three-year funding period setting a time limit, occasional press articles publicised their plight – 'Co-ops prepare to go it alone' – and the New South Wales Training Officer's approval that 'they are going to have to understand the 'real world' options open to them' once funding was over. 'It will go on even if we have to operate out of someone's bedroom – we are that committed,' claimed a member of Team Work,[27] a co-op which did indeed survive. In

March 1981 the YACS Co-operative Development Committee decided to change the program name from Youth Work Co-operatives to *Worker* Co-operatives 'on the grounds that the success of the co-operatives depended on workers' initiative and motivation, and not on the mere provision of work alone'.[28] This, of course, ignored the fact that the 'provision' could hardly have been called proper work. When the program ended (June 1982), it was restructured rather than abandoned and given another three years, but without the youth welfare approach.

Indeed it was to be a quite different, radically oriented model, the left-libertarian one. It was proposed by those project workers critical of the manipulative paternalism they had seen at first hand. They described their political outlook as libertarian socialist, but not anarchist, a position indicating their socialist commitment to the unemployed and their dislike of state 'workshops'.[29] The previous experiment should not be repeated, and this required that the state program be completely changed. The underlying belief was that co-ops might have an effect on existing structures, to become a 'third way' within the market while keeping as free of state direction as the perceived necessity for loans and training would allow. They were well versed in the co-operative literature from Europe, including the Basque nationalism inspiring the growth of the Mondragon co-operatives and the co-op traditions of France, Italy and Israel. The recent recession-reinforced growth of the British co-operative movement – emerging from private paternalism and state schemes – was also studied. The left-libertarians were under no illusions about the need for education programs for co-ops, given that Australia had no co-op tradition.[30]

The co-operative model chosen was based on the Rochdale Equitable Pioneers (set up in England during the 1840s). Co-operative membership is restricted to workers only, so as to exclude outside investors having any control, and is based on the principle of one member, one vote. The benefits of the surplus (profit) produced is based on work input rather than capital input and the rate of return to capital should be strictly limited, to prevent a degeneration into 'workers' capitalism'. Such worker co-operatives would reverse the capital–labour relation, since labour hires capital. Where the primary obligation of the capitalist enterprise is to maximise the return to shareholders, by contrast the major objective of a worker co-operative is to provide employment to worker-owners.[31]

This means that the co-op exists to promote the interests of its membership – 'only the members in any given situation can determine what their interests are'. This set of principles, for the left-libertarians, would locate worker co-operatives 'firmly within the ideological tradition which asserts that the surplus value created by workers' input belongs of right to the workers who create that surplus'.[32]

Left-libertarians interpreted the English tradition as an economic 'alternative' which was 'deliberately anti-capitalist', aiming 'to minimise the dominance of capital in economic activity' with a model of a 'practical alternative' (the exemplar argument): 'The co-operative model was not an alternative to the market economy. It was an alternative form of organisation within that economy which its proponents argued was more equitable, more likely to result in a range of social benefits, and to bring the economy under more direct popular control'.[33]

For left-libertarians, although this international tradition had never reached its 'potential', 'many observers are now claiming that current conditions (of unemployment, industrial conflict and pressures for industrial democracy) offer a unique opportunity for the movement generally . . . (and) for the development of a large-scale co-operative sector in Australia'.[34]

These co-op development officers came to view the objective of 'a permanent and significant worker co-operative sector (as an alternative to public and private sectors)' as a long-term goal, while far preferring co-operation to the mere stop-gap measures to date. They were not to find a particularly enthusiastic response, however, in their later research on worker-member attitudes towards its long-term future.[35] Despite this problem, left-libertarians still claimed that their interest was based not merely on what they saw as a 'job creation potential' but was

> also based on the potential of worker co-operatives to effect structural change within the market economy that may result in a new type of democratically controlled firm, with the provision and maintenance of employment as its central objective . . . The worker co-operative form does not challenge the existence of the market economy. Nor does it make . . . ideological claims beyond the level of the individual firm. However . . . worker co-operatives do operate on a set of ideological assumptions about the way in which the market economy, and individual firms within it, should be structured and operate.[36]

This potential would evolve slowly. They argued that although the approach was 'gradualist', it was possible to make 'significant gains over the right to appropriate surplus value *now*, in a capitalist economy for, after all, a revolution in Australia is not imminent'.[37] They stressed that their promotion of co-ops was mainly a 'micro-economic strategy' because the characteristics of co-ops were 'manifested internally'. Co-ops could only influence any industry policy (as was being formulated by the union movement) through 'arresting the rate of closure of firms' and 'creating new areas of industrial and commercial activity'. The danger of industry policies for left-libertarians was that 'a sectoral strategy runs far more risk of being a "top down" approach'.[38]

Nevertheless, their promotion was to take place within the state. There was, in fact, only one place in Australia where the push for worker co-operatives arose from outside any government bureaucracy. In Queensland a grassroots movement linked to communes had started a community-owned consumer co-operative at Maleny in the mid 1970s. Their newsletter, *The Co-operative Times*, sub-headed 'Co-operative Self-Development for Australia', warned about the difference in their approach, which

> seeks to promote the co-operative movement as a strategy to replace both capitalist and communist exploitation with a co-operative based socialist economy . . . Co-operatives have numerous benefits including job creation, ability to explore human inter-relationships, . . . alternatives to traditional worker alienation and so on. On the other hand it is during times of economic stringency, high unemployment and technological change, that co-operatives become appealing to capitalists and governments as labour intensive 'sweated trades' to fill essential gaps at the bottom end of the economy. Much of the current interest in co-operatives in Australia derives from this motivation.[39]

The luxury of being so explicit was a function of the Queensland group's autonomy, denied in the more moderate submissions of the left-libertarians in New South Wales. It was a far cry, as well, from the glossy brochures that later ensued from Victorian, Western Australian and federal government departments. The reasons given for fearing government and capitalist interest in co-operatives became all too apparent. But the risks of staying small, with insufficient government funds and little trade union support, were also fraught with those very same dangers, of the 'small business' kind, which deny co-operatives any survival rate beyond the sweated trade variety.

Particularistic 'group-individualism' can result in the very deregulation of the labour market that they warned against. What happened in New South Wales after Canberra's interest started to develop under the Hawke government, reveals this problem and shows how other states – notably Victoria and Western Australia – adjusted their co-op policies according to the saga of the New South Wales co-operative 'movement' (as federal bureaucrats later called it).

The way that the left-libertarian model became accepted as policy in New South Wales comprised a combination of factors. Near the end of the initial, welfare-oriented Youth Work Programme, YACS commissioned a report from the Social Welfare Research Centre of the University of NSW.[40] It gave cautious support to the 'co-operatives': 177 people were then employed – mainly full-time – and, despite the 'tenuous' economic viability of these co-ops, the scheme, they argued, was far cheaper than the cost of job creation in the private sector (such as a proposed alumina industry). After the program shifted away from hiring large numbers of unemployed young as casual labour, perceived as a 'welfare' measure, the co-ops built up permanent teams. The report suggested that, as a job creation scheme, the New South Wales Program 'has the advantage of operating on both the supply and the demand sides of the labour market. . . . [It] offers opportunities for skill development in "real work" situations; and it creates jobs by establishing business enterprises'.[41]

The report did warn, however, of the need for a realistic study of co-operatives' relations to the capitalist market place, to avoid underestimating the challenge of 'maintaining the co-operative ethos in a starkly competitive business world'.[42] And indeed, nearly all the later policy literature on co-ops agreed. The initial welfare-based program had 'limited success', 'poor success', was a 'failure', 'it failed to create sustainable economic activity', it encountered 'difficulties' or was 'characterized by a lack of coherent government policy and inadequate planning and support structures'.[43] What did all these various assessments actually mean by failure? More importantly, why did the program continue to the extent that it underwent three major restructurings, and why did other states in Australia jump on the bandwagon? The answer to these questions can be found in the rationales of politicians and other bureaucrats, including those at the federal level once the Labor Party took office. State apparatuses were facing new problems. From then on, state interest in co-ops became such that more promoters, researchers and civil servants were probably involved than were actual workers in co-operatives.

Possibly this cautious though hardly negative report, combined with the newly informed, radical approach of the left-libertarians, who wanted businesses owned and controlled by workers, influenced the New South Wales government decision to continue.[44] For, other than insisting on the fairly standard radical model, left-libertarians wanted workers to have some financial equity in their venture, to avoid what they saw as the 'dependency' and 'motivational' problems of the first, welfare-based scheme. High equity by workers was attractive as a cheap solution for the state, although from the left-libertarian view it was supposed to facilitate democratic practices and freedom from state direction, and to allow a choice of capital sources. They also argued that statutory agencies kept separate from, though funded by and accountable to, the relevant state department would protect the libertarian approach. In this way co-operative promotion would not be hindered by unworkable election promises (like suddenly offering to fund a co-operative) made by politicians currying favour with their own electorates. With these arrangements, the problems of the first scheme should be rectified.[45] In 1982 the Minister of YACS agreed to implement the left-libertarian proposal of slowly building a few more stable co-ops, though yet again on the same minimal funds.[46] And until 1985 the left-libertarians worked carefully on their project in New South Wales.

At this point, however, various threats to the left-libertarian vision arose. In Victoria, a more union-oriented, *low* equity co-op program was beginning. More seriously, the new ALP federal government's interest in co-ops posed one threat, while another came from the union movement's opposition to Hawke's supply-side scheme and its preference for the Victorian model. As we saw in the case of communes, the 'hunt for alternatives to paid work' had included worker co-operatives as part of Prime Minister Hawke's strategy. In one sense the title was even more ominous than for communes, but nobody pointed out that from the radical perspective (let alone that of a co-op member), a worker co-operative was meant to be an alternative to wage labour, not an alternative to the *receipt of pay*. Whether workers would receive pay was hardly a concern in Canberra, which was shifting its unemployment policies in the face of demands for jobs. Separate federal research on co-ops was carried out at the same time as the investigations of communes. This new interest and the unions' harsh criticisms of Hawke's co-operative tactic eventually destroyed the left-libertarians' program.

The main efforts within the bureaucracy in Canberra were the following. In the Attorney-General's Department, an Assistant Secretary reviewed the legal measures for facilitating both 'co-operative and communal enterprises'. He was optimistic for co-ops but from the viewpoint that the New South Wales left-libertarians' vision was 'strict and doctrinal: co-ops appeal to the entrepreneurial spirit but their plugging of the union line, allowing for no erosion of standards, would knock this spirit'. (On this issue, unions argued the reverse.) Nevertheless, he also disliked the motives of the Department of Employment and Industrial Relations (DEIR) to reduce workforce participation, preferring to hope that here were the 'incipient stages' of what in twenty years' time might be 'different social and legal structures'.[47]

The Office of Youth Affairs was busy for some time with brochures, submissions and funding outside reports, such as $24 000 spent on a study of training options carried out by the Co-operative Federation of Australia.[48] Here again were divisions. One report on co-op agencies was sympathetic towards the left-libertarian model, whereby agencies were structurally independent from government and political pressures on resource allocation. It also presumed that an independent agency would encourage self-sufficiency rather than dependency. Most importantly, it did not consider that co-ops were a solution to 'short-term youth unemployment'.[49]

This report went unheeded in Youth Affairs. Preference was given to a 'broad approach' – now being mooted in Western Australia – towards the whole area of 'co-operative, community and self-employment business ventures' as well as a 'social enterprise option for *the meaningful involvement* by young unemployed people in their communities'.[50] Youth Affairs supported this welfare approach 'because there is no single solution to unemployment and Hawke and Ryan favour trying a lot of innovative solutions'. The left-libertarians had a 'narrow, purist model' which pushed them into a corner: they were 'prejudiced' against looking elsewhere by insisting that it was 'hard enough to establish credibility as a legitimate, soundly-based alternative within the labour market without being lumped in with the brown rice and sandals set'. Left-libertarians had indeed been alarmed at being equated with communes. According to Youth Affairs their approach was 'ideological' in its stress on ownership and control. Despite these criticisms, Youth Affairs was being cautious, given the scepticism of DEIR and the failures in New South Wales. It favoured a pilot training scheme, 'networking' of co-ops rather than government direction, and loans rather than grants.[51]

This, then, was the range of rewriting operations occurring within the administration. Outside the bureaucracy, the Australian Democrats were also promoting their version of co-operatives, with an Industrial Democracy Bill attempted in 1982–3 by Senator Siddons (whose Siddons Industry Ltd encourages worker ownership, but more as an exploitative 'incentive scheme' like that of Fletcher Jones and Staff Pty Ltd).[52] An Employee-owned Co-operative Bill was proposed in 1984 and 1987. The Bill allowed for creditors and others to be members with workers, an anathema to left-libertarians then, because workers would lose control and risk being sold out. It also envisaged that 'in hard times the owner-employees of a co-operative would strive to keep the organisation viable' rather than cutting their losses.[53]

All these Canberra-based proposals had, by then, thoroughly appalled the New South Wales left-libertarians, since their plans were being redefined by other arms of the state for supply-side reasons. For them, the federal approach of combining communes with worker co-ops was particularly worrying, because this implied that working in a co-op would take one out of the workforce, which is actually the case in some respects. The New South Wales government had interests (the young, the company closures) other than Canberra's urgent need to find immediate 'solutions' to unemployment, which had given the left-libertarians a leisurely space in which to operate. This was suddenly being destroyed.

At the very same time a quite different threat to left-libertarian plans emerged from the Secretary of the Australian Council of Trade Unions (ACTU), Bill Kelty. The co-operative–commune plans were particularly criticised in Kelty's broad rebuttal of the Hawke-DEIR proposals to the Economic Planning Advisory Council (EPAC). 'Supply-side' approaches should not be introduced 'to generate employment opportunities as an alternative to active and comprehensive demand policies', nor 'detract from fiscal and monetary policies designed to maximise economic activity', he maintained. Work co-operatives, enterprise allowances and small businesses, as 'labour-supply measures' were unacceptable to the ACTU and inappropriate for welfare objectives. If such a sector were to be built up, it must be 'much more than a refuge for those who drop, or are pushed, out of the 'normal' labour market'.[54] For the ACTU, moreover, far from having a 'purist' model, left-libertarians were by no means sufficiently oriented to the union approach, given the high equity workers would need. As for the 'hyperbole' from Canberra about co-ops, the ACTU wanted to stop it, being well aware of a few cases in Victoria where publicly funded co-ops had undercut commercial ventures, putting employees of the latter out of work.[55]

The left-libertarian model was now being attacked from many sides. The mere existence of these experiments was perhaps not manna but at least a crumb from heaven for those weighed down by the unemployment issue and the responsibility for the rising welfare bill – namely the federal government. But the left-libertarian emphasis on autonomy and egalitarianism, so attractive in itself, was far too 'narrow' and 'ideological' for welfare/supply-side measures. The union response was an attack from the opposite position. How then could state (Labor) governments justify continuing with co-op experiments in the face of the ACTU line? The federal (Labor) supply-side plan for co-ops was dropped rather soon, given the need to maintain the Accord. But how could co-op supporters accommodate these problems and still keep promoting their cause?

EMPIRICAL DILEMMAS: RADICALS VERSUS THE STATE, THE ECONOMY

The debate, as could be expected, moved to more defensive ground. Radicals became far more concerned with devising structural principles for co-operatives that would appropriately stave off both Canberra's approach and the ACTU's concern with protecting workers. As it turned out, the dilemmas ensuing from the questions of structure, especially of worker equity and the relation of co-operatives to government, were not amenable to solution. Reshaping to avoid one trap only landed a different co-operative model in others. Hence New South Wales politicians suddenly switched to a model favoured by the new Labor government in Victoria, where direct funds had been given to start a few co-operatives, in a low equity, state directed version. This became what I have called the *left-labour* model, which took into account the union opposition. A report, commissioned by both state governments in 1984, strongly criticised the left-libertarian model and substituted proposals for this strict left-labour model.[56] Debates between the two radical sides thereafter became more intense.

There was one area of mutual opposition, however, concerning Canberra's supply-side approach (where worker co-operatives were virtually indistinguishable from communes). Left-libertarians argued that co-ops must be seen as viable by customers and creditors, which would not be the case if they were identified with 'sub-economic' or 'non-economic' forms of activity. Government support should be founded on the former basis or not at all.[57] The left-labour report added that 'alternative lifestyle co-operatives' emphasise personal fulfilment rather than commercial efficiency and tend towards 'subsistence operation and inadequate safeguards against self-exploitation'. The federal interest reflects 'a move to encourage workers out of the workforce (when there are no jobs) into a fringe employment sector. Opportunities to re-enter the labour market may be diminished by the lack of marketable skills' and so forth.[58]

But beyond these disclaimers the problem sank far deeper. How were any of the co-op supporters going to prove that worker co-ops would not suffer a similar fate? Government funds were needed badly, yet state control is at odds with co-op principles. Papers with titles such as 'Co-ops Are Working' merely asserted that 'viability' was possible.[59] By failing to address key problems, particularly the fact that 90 per cent of small businesses were failing in the first eight years, the bulk in their first, the arguments remained unconvincing. Co-op promoters had to find other reasons for reassuring unions, politicians and the bureaucracies that co-ops were special. Simultaneously, co-operatives must not be implicated in welfare-workshop or supply-side measures.

Hence, the left-labour model stressed the possibilities for industrial democracy and that a proper 'industry policy' could be promoted as well, because this, to them, was a necessity if co-operatives were to survive. (The ACTU proposed an industry policy as the pathway to restoring employment.) Consequently, close connections must be kept with government and because of the need for low equity to prevent capitalist, owner-boss 'mentality' and practices from emerging. The model should incorporate the union position because 'self-help' approaches to job-creation were usually allied with anti-union attitudes and practices, and substandard wages and conditions. Moreover, the model recognised a real danger that . . . pressures (from the market, towards economic marginalisation) will draw worker co-operatives into a wider process emerging through the economy of breaking up the work-force into 'self-employed' groups who work harder because they work 'for themselves'. This is the context in which conservatives support worker co-operatives.[60]

With close government supervision and restrictions on opportunities for personal capital gain, this fate could be averted. The payment of a nominal joining sum by worker-members – that is, low equity – would end union fears about any plan like that of the left-libertarians, for high equity really 'involves employees paying for their employment, or expects employees to reinvest part of their wage as a condition of getting a job'.[61]

The problem here, of course, was that the New South Wales government was unconcerned about high equity. Low equity would need lots of money from somewhere. The left-labour model proposed funding contracts from the state for capitalising 'selected' co-ops,[62] though 'non-compliance with the . . . contract could result in cessation of funding'. In sum, state 'collaboration' would ensure that anti-union and discriminatory practices would not occur and *could* also enable co-ops to be incorporated into an industry development strategy.[63]

The *left-libertarians* naturally took exception to a new proposal so critical of their own model. The restrictions, they felt, would drastically limit the ability of co-ops to survive. Meagre shareholdings would leave the co-operative 'open to undue influences by outside lenders' and turn co-operatives into 'a form of State Enterprise': 'Nominal shareholdings could be viewed as token shareholdings as, with state direction, it would be found necessary for the Worker members to have only token power'.[64] By wanting to put a brake on the 'capitalist' motivations of workers, the 'left-labour' model was really trying 'to legislate for changes of attitude'.[65]

Another factor, about which little has yet been said, is the potential for industrial democracy supposedly implied in the structure and principles of co-operatives. The two different models, both sides argued, could hinder and facilitate workplace democracy in different ways. But there was mutual agreement that democratic practices must be taught. Worker-members needed management skills as well as lessons in co-operative principles: the co-op structure was not sufficient. The left-libertarian's experience was that democratic practices depended on workers gradually coming to understand their roles, rights and responsibilities. This required training and internal mechanisms to 'maximise information flow' and participation.[66] The left-labour group, however, warned that in trying to achieve commercial viability co-operatives did not necessarily extend democratic ownership into democratic organisations: 'In fact the contrary would appear to be the case. Without an initial commitment to industrial democracy principles, it is difficult to overcome the conventional management structure'.[67] Co-ops also need a 'supportive environment' from unions, government departments, customers and creditors. The services of Technical and Further Education (TAFE) colleges and the Trade Union Training Authority (TUTA) were frequently alluded to in all the literature. In one, high schools should be drawn into the task, and in another, 'cultural traditions and attitudes' were cited as the chief cause of the failures of Australian co-operatives.[68]

The problem at the core of these debates was that the difficulties that the left-libertarian and the left-labour models attempted to address cannot be embraced simultaneously. The conflicts that arose from so many contradictory designs by the state apparatuses made compromises difficult to find. The dilemma for the left-labour model was that co-ops might indeed resemble 'state enterprises' where workers lost control and grass roots spontaneity. But left-labour promoters saw such co-ops as vehicles for promoting 'industry policy', since to them it was unthinkable that governments would promote co-operatives as a 'viable' alternative without some plans to foster industrial development. Moreover, with their democratic structures, they might enhance the cause of industrial democracy. Industrial democracy, however, has yet to be instituted in existing state sectors, and the only comprehensive proposal for industry policy came in 1987 from the ACTU (in *Australia Reconstructed*). Why did the promoters imagine that state support for worker co-operatives might draw the federal government into implementing these path-breaking policies? Low equity co-ops would need vast loans or grants from the state to avoid the fate of the previous state-owned, youth 'workshops', so rightly derided by all sides. But the chances of government financial and structural support, to the extent that co-operatives became a significant 'third sector', were slight – especially in the case of state governments. The chances were slight, in fact, because acceptance of rising unemployment and problems of budget deficits were the reasons for state interest in co-operatives in the first place. This did not change. The New South Wales government supported the third co-op program (which left-labour adherents took on), only in terms of the 'austere times' that severely constrained state spending.[69]

Conversely, independent co-ops requiring high worker equity, as in the left-libertarian model, are remarkably similar to a partnership, or any small business. Those who found 'nothing socialist here' approved of their assumption of 'the normal commercial risks of industry'.[70] This may be all very well for professionals like lawyers and doctors, but co-operative policies were directed towards the least powerful in the labour market. Workers in co-ops do indeed pay for their own jobs, often with their redundancy pay, and they may compete against other co-ops and other workers. Such co-ops might also deny a role for unions and oppose the hiring of new members, especially the even less skilled and low income earners, generally women and migrants. An abhorrence of state supervision meant that the slightest chance of decent state funding was forfeited. In this way, the model lent itself to the federal supply-side approach as well as right-libertarian support, as another self-employment scheme to add to the deregulation of the labour market.

Following debates during 1984, the New South Wales program was redesigned to allay union fears about Canberra's intentions. With this third restructuring, left-libertarians bowed out of the state program. More closely aligned with the incentive schemes of Siddons, Fletcher Jones and so forth, the third promotional agency was called the Association for Employee Ownership in Australia: for them, 'worker co-operative' was a name of the past. Tax-free trust funds set up by each corporation were thereupon regarded as the way to 'build an employee-owned sector', since nobody would pay for it. Anti-union attitudes and mistrust of the left-labour co-op 'takeover' in New South Wales, which tried to prevent workers gaining profits (or suffering losses), were readily apparent at their promotional conferences. The group turned to Canberra, via Siddons and the enthusiasm of Race Mathews, to lobby for enabling legislation for debt-financing trusts and tax incentives so that corporations could be 'given away' to workers. Having a stake in the enterprise might change workers' attitudes. An 'ownership-income psychology' would 'empower' workers, enthusiasts were told by an expert on the legislation for 'Employee Stock Ownership

Plans' in the United States in 1986. And, despite these different ownership structures, education was still necessary to inculcate democratic practices.[71]

For left-libertarians, having faced the past problems, survival seemed to dictate a redefinition of workplace democracy to *worker ownership* through tax incentive schemes. But, it need hardly be said, this was even more of a top down approach. It may boost productivity but it changes little, except that workers effectively earn less in poor years. The libertarian model would now be controlled by the individual corporation which might sell it off. Conversely, with privatisation on the federal agenda since 1987, worker-ownership could be facilitated by a state assets sale to its employees. In Britain, these sales resulted in low-income workers selling their few shares at the first opportunity.[72]

Ultimately, then, the dilemmas about creating a co-operative movement in any of these diverse ways are insoluble at the practical level, save in the unlikely event that governments are required to provide a proper job for all those able and willing to work. Job subsidies could be provided accordingly, to worker co-operative proposals as much as any other that might create or retain jobs. Worker co-operatives cannot be given responsibility for job creation, but those who want to set up co-operative structures should have the same support as other work organisations. Since 1975, as we know, there has been no federal government with a *de facto* commitment to full employment: the high rate of unemployment has fluctuated only marginally during this time. Consequently, it is hard to see a path for co-operative development which does not involve conflicting state policies about reducing the supply of labour, about workers paying for their own jobs, and about labour market deregulation and other anti-union practices.

Hence, any development must be totally divorced from employment creation. A very tentative possibility could be to convert small state-provided services into worker co-operatives. Again, however, the dangers of redefinition could result in assets sales to hard-pressed worker-owners. It would be feasible only for small state sectors that were already viable, such as specific local community services, but again only if workers wanted it. Such an alternative could provide independence for employees and improved relations with clients. If it could be effected, this sort of co-operative development would not be privatisation of state services – an assets sale – but a denationalisation which would reduce the worst effects of bureaucracy and line management, while making some services more accountable to citizens. Such an avenue, however, has never been proposed. These speculations are provided in order to stress that any optimism for a viable co-operative development should be based on the reality of these conservative times – however genuine the commitment to the ideals of industrial democracy. In particular, the future promotion of co-ops should not again rest on their supposed potential for job creation or retention.

Viability was the chief problem for the actual co-operative experiments and this is hardly surprising, given the state of the commodity or service markets with which co-operatives also had to deal and which ultimately affected their prospects, however provocative and emancipatory their internal structure might or might not have been. In markets where so many goods are produced offshore or by machines, where distribution and marketing is controlled by multinational firms, and the market in labour is becoming increasingly deregulated, the problem is whether any co-operative, especially if promoted from above, can avoid a short life of self-exploitation if it is not backed properly by the state in a clearly viable niche. To give one example from the last decade, the then Labor Minister of Employment in New South Wales argued that the third attempt at promoting co-ops would be more successful where they developed as takeovers from 'structural sackings'.[73] The reason given reveals the wishful thinking that was widespread in various sectors of the state: 'Because worker's [*sic*] co-operatives don't require justification through high rates of return on capital they can thrive in circumstances where corporate accountants would merely call in the receivers'.[74]

Such statements overlooked, among other things, that production in these goods had not necessarily slowed down, nor were there market shortages. Learning from past experience, the state merely preferred establishing co-ops from 'structural sackings' rather than as 'start-ups' because it was a way of coping with political pressures after sudden job losses from closedowns. Also start-ups invariably suffered from a lack of skills and were more expensive.

In 1985, newly installed left-labour promoters sought to persuade union officials of the benefits of co-ops under the New South Wales Worker Co-operative Programme. The Australian Commercial Glassblowers at Newcastle was presented as a good example of a 'conversion' co-operative – from a 'structural sacking'. The case was not just a matter of attempting to preserve a dying craft skill. More than their inability to compete with the 'scientific methods' of big, British-made machinery being installed elsewhere, the workers faced enormous marketing problems. As a Glass Workers' Union official said at the time, Australian Consolidated Industries (ACI) had most of the glassmaking in Australia 'sewn up'. British Crown Corning owned 51 per cent of one big ACI plant. It marketed and distributed for the Newcastle co-operative but there were suspicions about the percentage returned to the worker-members.[75] In 1986, the Glass-blowers Co-operative folded, having lasted for two years.

The left-libertarians also remained attracted to rescue operations. At their conference in 1986 many were disappointed that the unskilled, low-paid female workers at Rank Industries (a whitegoods firm in Sydney's western suburbs) had voted against contributing nearly $4000 each to save their jobs. Conference members suggested that future closures could be forestalled by better promotion of co-operatives. The lack of enthusiasm at Rank was attributed to the fact that the women may not have liked dealing with an all male cast of unionists and co-op promoters.[76] Aside from the expense for workers in 'rescue' operations, there was also no reason to assume, as the left-labour model had, that in the present climate government departments might be more kindly buyers from co-operatives, nor that private firms could be forced by unions to employ 'labour-hire' co-operatives to counteract the labour-hire practices occurring now. Apart from the Mudginberri meatworkers' dispute, anti-union legislation in several states and Liberal Party proposals to deregulate the labour market, the OECD view of concentrating on 'increased labour market flexibility' had been promoted for over a decade.[77] These views were not without influence in the Labor government.

In any case, anti-union employment practices were already widespread. The growth of the 'flexible' firm is well documented, showing how small firms are bound to the strategies of large enterprises which have access to finance, and maintain and expand the import/export links, the market share, and efforts to influence government policies: 'The new owners of production, . . . are the small private competitive sector business people, contractors, outworkers, freelancers who are now controlled and regulated by the large firm. Franchising exemplifies the above development'.[78] Such was the climate for even newer 'owners of production' in

Australia – worker co-operatives. The promotion of co-operatives in New South Wales from 1979 resulted, by 1985, in fifteen co-operatives – others came and went – with just over 200 people working as co-operative members.[79] With the exception of some English-language teachers, most were skilled tradesmen. In 1985, one co-op did motor repairs and another engineering, and there was a commercial refrigeration plant and a computer software firm. These had the greatest numbers of workers, others had only four or five members. Victoria had far fewer co-operatives, and its state promotional program was wound down in 1986.[80] The New South Wales program followed suit in 1988.

THEORETICAL DILEMMAS

In evaluating such an unsuccessful story, there are a number of theoretical questions involved. From the very beginning, promoters of both models were beset by two related problems the solutions to which, they hoped, would be found by partially complying with the interests of the state apparatuses. The first is that any ownership of the means of production faces inevitable restrictions and uncertainties from the market in a capitalist economy. The private efforts of workers are no match for monopolies, as Marx, among many others, recognised long ago.[81] As far as state supply-side strategies were concerned, this was hardly a problem. Workers could pay for their own jobs while the unemployment numbers and the state deficit from cash transfers would be reduced. Co-op promoters tried quickly to distance their projects from this kind of state 'support'. But the second problem was the lack of a worker co-operative tradition in Australia and opposition to co-operative development by the union movement. This would hinder all efforts to build grass roots enthusiasm.

Hence, in the efforts to establish a co-op movement 'from above', both models required help and, for sheer survival in the market, the actual co-operatives needed state or corporate funds and other support structures. Such help, however, usually comes with different forms of influence or control. In the context of a recession, the only available state support was based on the appeal of co-operatives as potentially job creating or saving, or as an activity for the unemployed young. The corporate sector and various economic libertarians gave ideological support to the co-op movement because of the potential for greater productivity and for weakening labour market regulations and the unions. While neither gave much material support, both top down approaches alarmed the unions: therefore, co-operative structures were endlessly adjusted in response to these dilemmas.

A 'prefigurative' argument, that co-ops were 'pioneers of a new exciting territory', a 'testing ground' for socialism that 'we practise along the way',[82] formed the basis of one Labor politician's support, among others. It is an interesting position for a professed Fabian socialist to hold, given Beatrice Webb's harsh judgement that co-operatives were associations of small capitalists as fraudulent as any other.[83] More to the point – given that this was clearly not the view held by such promoters of industrial democracy as Race Mathews – is that co-ops cannot be any testing ground if they suffer from problems of commercial viability, as Judy Wajcman concluded in an English study of a failed shoe-making co-operative set up by women after a 'structural sacking'. If most co-ops collapse or survive only at workers' expense, then this is the economic reality which shapes people's experience. Feeling anxiety throughout, it was found that after the failure the co-op members sensed an increase in powerlessness and in the sense of 'the apparent inevitability of the capitalist system'.[84] Moreover, being a grass roots experiment, it had none of the dubious benefits of the state promotion faced by Australian co-operatives.

Economic viability is clearly a prime necessity, but viability was also related to a problem with the whole saga of state promotion in Australia, of trying to impose democracy from above. This is a complex issue, and if a few remarks are relevant in this context, they do not arise from any lack of sympathy with the ideals of industrial democracy. The analysis merely suggests a recurrence of the well known problem that the means of approaching an ideal have a tendency to influence the outcome. What seems to have happened in this case was that the promoters of worker co-operatives made an assumption that the need to control one's whole life – in the broad sense including the workplace – was a popular need. The economic situation and consequent state interest could be used to set up the participatory structures of worker co-operatives and thus transform industrial authority structures.

Not only was the timing incorrect, so that many of the workers involved faced the sole 'choice' of a co-operative job or joblessness, but the promotion was an imposition itself. Leaving aside, for the moment, the economic circumstances previously discussed, worker co-operatives are not *necessarily* unviable provided there is a grass roots interest in controlling the work environment (which may be exemplified by the Basques in Mondragon,[85] although their nationalist movement was the more determining inspiration). Genuine control requires commitments of a lot of time, energy and trouble – ultimately a wish to restructure the relation of work to the rest of one's life. For example, depending on the material circumstances, people who are self-employed may take a day off work if they feel like it, and ordinary employees can often do the same via sick leave. Depending on income, this may be spent on the beach or at the golf course. Wajcman found with the all-female co-operative that tensions arose between single women and those who could not put in what rapidly became a fifteen-hour day, because of conflicting demands from husbands and children. In this sense the structure of a co-operative involves a shared commitment which precludes taking a day off and so forth: work and life are less separate.

Hence, if these 'prefigurative' testing grounds are introduced from above, the form has an effect on the content such that they are felt as impositions, however emancipatory the intent. In this sense they are also unlikely to succeed, *even if* the economic niche is relatively favourable. The dilemma is part of the far wider problem of how to translate into practice the theories of participatory democracy of humanists such as J.S. Mill and G.D.H. Cole. Democratic participation in the workplace is here viewed as having a most important educative function as well as being a form of political participation in its own right.[86] The educative function not only serves the purpose of gaining practice in democratic skills and procedures, but also has another socialising aspect. Instead of 'passivity' (J.S. Mill) within a 'servile' industrial system, which Cole maintained inevitably reflected itself in 'political servility' even with universal franchise, these theorists considered that confidence in one's effectiveness to control one's life and environment, and a belief that one could be self-governing, might be acquired through industrial participation.[87]

In stark contrast to pseudo forms of industrial participation (where workers may 'advise' or have a token representative), pure worker co-operation is a form of participation that requires an enormous input from each member. The outcome of this participation would be both the policies or decisions arrived at by all and the 'development of the social and political capacities of each individual', as Carole Pateman points out.[88] This is the humanising aspect of socialisation for democracy. But, in the case of Australian co-operatives, it appears that not many people wanted to take this opportunity. The extreme example was that of process work, clearly most likely to engender apathy and feelings of ineffectiveness, such that, expense aside, the unskilled female workers at Rank Industry could hardly have been expected to want to run their own factory, or rather, to own the conveyor belt that ran them.

In respect of the whole range of work, however, if the need for the sort of control over one's life that co-ops offer is not widely popular, a co-operative movement cannot grow. The development of such demands for control – another vexed question – may come from political action or from a wish for autonomy. Many aspects, it need hardly be said, are affected by income level and gender. The major problem, however, is that for all the confidence and freedom that may be gained through taking on more work and shared responsibilities, the will to make such a high level of commitment cannot be imposed from above.

In conclusion, this case not only exemplifies the capacity of the state to turn oppositional demands to quite different purposes, but also specifies the mechanisms through which this process took place. The reasons for the failure of the promotion of worker co-operatives were multifarious, as we have seen, even if the state's role was decisive. Many had sincerely hoped that this would be a possible path to greater workers' control and less alienated working conditions. Most of the demands were based on these assumptions, but the lack of a worker co-operative tradition here – save in times of unemployment – and the attitudes of the union movement, were hardly auspicious signs. Even less so was the economic situation and the interest taken by politicians and the bureaucracies. It is highly unlikely that agents of the state would have ever extolled the virtues of co-operation without the impetus of the employment crisis and the turn to deregulation and privatisation. At the federal level co-ops served similar purposes to those we saw with communes. State governments supported co-ops for different reasons, but never with the intention or even the possibility of providing adequate finance: the states have been progressively starved of federal funding.

Given this context, which was somehow to be manipulated towards fostering a co-operative movement by the oppositional groups, it is hardly surprising that insuperable conflicts between the two different though radical models would ensue. The assumption that state support could be redefined for radical purposes proved to be a mistaken one. Staving off conservative designs from either libertarian or statist interests was never adequately achieved. Visions about the effects that co-operatives might have on existing structures, or a contrary worry that these structures would adversely affect co-operatives, created the conflicting models, neither of which could ever have addressed *all* the supply-side and welfare problems, a possible labour market deregulation and the risks inherent in a capitalist economy. The other dilemma was that such schemes, the post-industrial one included, proposed for whatever emancipatory motives, were imposed on workers – most of whom had not wished for such democratic and time-consuming structures. The fact that very few women work in any of the existing co-ops is indicative not only of the general constraints on women's labour-force participation, but also of the added difficulties imposed by worker co-ops. Even the workers actually involved in co-operatives were consistently regarded as needing further education on the benefits of co-operation. The constraints faced by women were not even considered by co-op promoters.

More practically, the promoters of co-operatives *might* have been able to manipulate state support if it had been grounded in a federal commitment to full employment. This, of course, was not the case. Co-operatives were promoted by governments merely as vehicles for cheap job creation or as job retention schemes or, worse, as supply-side methods to reduce workforce participation. With the aims of co-operation redefined in a number of contradictory directions, the results, for those at the least powerful end of the labour market, were hardly good. Such an outcome was far from the intentions of the original co-operative promoters. They had seen the devastating effects of unemployment on the young, and were harshly critical of the paternalistic state 'workshops' – those early youth co-operatives. If unemployment could be ameliorated *at all*, at least proper co-operatives were preferable to those. Thus the promotion of co-operatives was determined by previous policies. Given that a dramatic improvement in state employment policies is the basic (if still improbable) solution, there seems only one conclusion to be drawn about any further development of worker co-operatives: it should depend primarily on the initiatives of workers themselves, especially if they can elaborate their own working relationship with, and gain acceptance from, trade unions (whose fears were justified). Such development should not depend on negotiations with state apparatuses. In the light of past failures, co-operatives also need to be sufficiently viable to attract skilled workers. Above all, co-ops cannot be regarded as alternatives to paid work. Given the past experiments with state-promoted co-ops and the present wider climate, the outlook is hardly promising.

NOTES

1. Both emerged from the counter culture: one was in Maryborough, Victoria, around 1976, another at Nimbin in 1978; neither were well organised or long lived. Personal interview, Alan Greig, NSW CODA, 26.3.85.
2. Siddons Industries and W.L. Allen Foundry are the other more well known examples in Australia.
3. Western Australia. State Employment Task Force (1983), p. 24.
4. R. Mathews (1983), p. 13.
5. This information came from a different source, an organiser at an unemployed workers' centre in Melbourne, Greg Pettiona, personal interview, 31.8.84.
6. K. Windschuttle (1980), pp. 223–4.
7. Cited in A. Jamrozik (1981), p. 136.
8. K. Windschuttle (1980), p. 224.
9. Personal interview, Richard Persson, NSW Ministry of Housing, 14.9.84.
10. A. Jamrozik & R. Beck (1981), p. 19.
11. Interview R. Persson, 14.9.84.
12. Cited A. Jamrozik & R. Beck (1981), p. 19.
13. Cited A. Jamrozik (1981), p. 19.
14. Cited A. Jamrozik & R. Beck, pp. 20–1.
15. Interview A. Greig, 26.3.85.
16. K. Windschuttle (1980), p. 274.
17. *Financial Review*, 'Workers Unite and Become Bosses All' 28.1.83.
18. Western Australia. State Employment Task Force (1983), p. 24; Interview R. Persson, 14.9.84.
19. See A. Jamrozik & R. Beck, for a detailed report, commissioned by the NSW government.
20. A. Jamrozik & R. Beck (1981), p. 53, my emphasis.
21. *ibid.*, p. 55.

22. Cited A. Jamrozik & R. Beck (1981), p. 27.
23. J. Carruthers (1981), pp. 13-14.
24. A. Jamrozik & R. Beck (1981), p. 27.
25. *Sydney Morning Herald* 1.6.81.
26. Cited A. Jamrozik & R. Beck (1981), p. 29.
27. *Sydney Morning Herald* 1.6.81; *Sydney Morning Herald* 17.9.81.
28. Cited A. Jamrozik & R. Beck (1981), p. 36.
29. Interview A. Greig, 26.3.85.
30. A. Jamrozik & R. Beck (1981), p. 28.
31. J. Carruthers (1981), p. 8.
32. CODA (1984), pp. 1-2.
33. *ibid.*, p. 5.
34. J. Carruthers, p. 18.
35. *ibid.*, p. 14.
36. CODA (1984), p. 6.
37. Personal interview, Malcolm Rodgers, NSW CODA, 26.7.84.
38. CODA (1984), pp. 14, 16.
39. *The Co-operative Times*, Summer 1984-85.
40. A. Jamrozik & R. Beck (1981).
41. *ibid.*, p. 78.
42. *ibid.*, p. 124.
43. Respectively, NSW Worker Co-operative Programme (1985); Western Australia. State Employment Task Force (1983), p. 25; Australia. Office of Youth Affairs (1983), p. 5; CODA (1984), p. 33; Australia. Department of Education and Youth Affairs (1984), p. 6; TransNational Cooperative (TNC) (1984), p. 24.
44. One other argument was that the Minister so uninterested that the left-libertarian group had the space to continue and to have their own way. Interview R. Persson, 14.9.84.
45. The three NSW state-run programs all had separate titles: Youth Work Co-operative Programme, 1979-1982; Common Ownership Development Agency, (CODA) 1982-1985; NSW Worker Co-operative Programme, 1985-1988.
46. Interviews with A. Greig, 26.3.85; M. Rodgers, 26.7.84 & R. Persson, 14.9.84.
47. Personal interview J. Butler, 2.8.84.
48. Minister of Education and Youth Affairs, Senator Susan Ryan, in a letter to the Prime Minister, 7.6.84, about state spending on commune and co-op research projects.
49. Australia. Department of Education and Youth Affairs (1984), pp. 10, 4.
50. Western Australia. State Employment Task Force (1983), p. ii, my emphasis.
51. Interview R. Gurney, 2.8.84.
52. Interview, M. Rodgers, CODA, 26.7.84. The scope of worker ownership in the two firms is as follows: the employee share trust owns about

18.5 per cent of Siddons' issued stock. About 700 of the 1,600 employees at Siddons Industries own shares. Worker representatives are on the board and can only advise on efficiency and productivity. In 1986, staff of Fletcher Jones who had bought $1 shares (70 per cent of the 2000 employees) received about 5.6 per cent of the company's $6 million share issue, the method of annual distribution of the profits. This averages at $240 per annum each, as a bonus issue to relatively low-paid employees. *Financial Review*, 22.7.87.

53. Senator Jack Evans, Corporations (Employee-owned Co-operatives) Bill, Canberra, Commonwealth Government Printer, 1984.
54. ACTU (1984) pp. 2–4.
55. Interview D. Landsley, ACTU Research, Melbourne, 30.8.84.
56. TransNational Co-operative (1984).
57. NSW Worker Co-operative Development Committee, 'Government Support for Worker Co-operatives', undated discussion paper (in answer to Australian DEIR paper to EPAC of Dec 1983), p. 4.
58. TransNational Co-operative (1984), p. 20.
59. CODA (1984).
60. TransNational Co-operative (1984), pp. 4–5.
61. *ibid.*, p. 37–8.
62. *ibid.*, p. 42.
63. *ibid.*, p. 95.
64. Appraisal of the TNC Report on Worker Co-operative Policy in NSW and Victoria, unpublished document (possibly September 1984), from CODA.
65. CODA, discussion document on the TNC Review, unpublished (September, 1984).
66. CODA (1984), p. 22.
67. TransNational Co-operative, p. 59.
68. Personal interview B. Rawlinson, Co-operative Federation of Victoria, 31.8.84; Victorian MACC Seminars, unpublished papers, 1984.
69. Bob Debus, Speech by the NSW Minister for Employment and Housing at the opening of the Worker Co-operatives TUTA Seminar (Sydney, 28 June 1985).
70. Des Keegan, *The Australian* 18.1.85.
71. Conference, Association for Employee Ownership in Australia, University of Sydney, November 14, 1986, which was attended by Siddons, Mathews, the left-libertarian group, one union enthusiast, a representative from the later left-labour NSW Co-op Programme (who did not speak) and a variety of co-op workers. Another conference was held in November 1989 at the University of Sydney, but the new trajectory towards employee share plans is evident in the September 13 1990 Conference, held at a far more upmarket price and location, namely the Inter-Continental Hotel, Sydney.
72. *Sydney Morning Herald* 25.6.87.

73. Debus argued that here they are 'potentially very valuable indeed', but failed to mention how far more 'valuable' they would be to politicians than to the redundant workers involved.
74. Bob Debus, 1985.
75. Personal interview GWU Official, 28.6.85.
76. University of Sydney Conference, 14.11.86.
77. P. Patterson (1985), p. 12.
78. TransNational Co-operative (TNC) Workers Research (1985), p. 3.
79. Information from NSW Worker Co-operative programme: papers issued at TUTA seminar, Sydney, 24 June, 1985.
80. J. Burke & D. Griffiths (1986).
81. R.C. Tucker (1978), pp. 517–8.
82. J. Thornley (1981), p. 178. The latter are R.W. Connell's words, cited by Race Mathews, Victorian Labor politician and Fabian (1983, p. 25).
83. Cited in A. Jamrozik & R. Beck (1981), p. 98.
84. J. Wajcman (1983), p. 182.
85. A recent study explains how the Mondragon co-operatives have conventional line management and indirect forms of democracy. It has been questioned how pure they are as co-operatives: M. Mellor, J. Hannah & J. Stirling (1988).
86. C. Pateman (1970), p. 35.
87. *ibid.*, p. 38.
88. *ibid.*, p. 43.

PART III

The Citizen/Work Nexus

CHAPTER 7

Dole-Work and 'Acceptable Levels' of Unemployment: Rights for Citizens and Duties for the Rest

The question of whether the separation of income from work could be a progressive solution to unemployment is no longer a matter of guesswork. Analytic shortcomings of post-industrial theory are illustrated in depressing detail by empirical examples of its failure in practice. Even though the stories just told are obviously nationally specific, the counterfactual arguments to be derived from them apply more generally against the hypothesis.

Alternatives to wage labour have served to undermine the citizenship of whole categories of the populations involved. This suggests, as my more encompassing argument, that a nexus between pay and work is a less decisive political and social issue than the nexus between citizenship and paid work. That is, the basic conditions for political participation in modern societies are strongly linked to mainstream employment.

The evidence shows that governments can indeed be interested in alternatives to paid work, to say the least, mainly as supply-side strategies to remove people from making claims for cash and conventional work. In the case of guaranteed incomes, governments have been chiefly concerned to reinforce the cash/work nexus and reduce social wages. The fact that governments have not extensively implemented such policies is no cause for relief, however, for their legacies in Australia, for example, are now embedded in other policies that have marginalised unemployment more permanently and redefined the meaning of work.

Other than communes and worker co-operatives, the only remaining alternative kinds of work that have interested both post-industrialists and governments during the last twenty years have come to little as government strategies. Enthusiasm in this case was for vaguely defined and quite disparate urban activities, ranging from domestic to 'black' work, usually grouped under the concept

199

of 'informal economy'. Policies, however, were impossible to formulate, so government promotion, in Britain for example, was limited
to propaganda directed at the unemployed about the wonders of 'self-
help'. The question of what might constitute non-economic or
informal work is difficult enough,[1] but clearly an 'informal economy'
would not be informal if governments supported or regulated it (an
idea supported by Claus Offe)[2]. Unless proper employment ensued,
it is unclear how this could be done, since governments will never
simply *permit* those forms of exchange (goods, labour or cash),
which are formally subject to fiscal control. Across the OECD,
political parties and the media frequently use contentious claims
of a 'hidden economy' to launch crusades against the 'working
unemployed' claiming benefits.[3] Similarly, broad-based consumption
taxes (regressive though they are), which collect revenue at the point
of purchase, are often justified as a way to tax 'underground'
activities. But while consumption taxes do not necessarily *reduce*
black activities, no government would legalise black work, a tack
favoured by Bill Jordan.[4] That would undermine the entire basis
of tax collection from profits, wages and the sale of goods and
services. Governments have enough difficulties as it is in taxing
profits, without permitting other forms of barter and exchange. The
state could provide specified resources to the unemployed, like
allotment gardens, but a vegetable supply in no way constitutes a
socially acceptable modern existence.

The informal work idea is therefore as dubious as the commune
one, because a proper income and tools, facilities, contacts and skills
are the *preconditions* for many self-help or 'self-servicing' activities.[5]
In the case of informal, or rather illegal, activities undertaken for
enterprises, the segmentation of the formal labour market is mirrored
in the informal one. The latter is characterised only by greater
exploitation and vastly reduced wages in the weakest segments, like
the illegal clothing workshops that employ mainly women.[6] Hence,
anyone who sees potential for survival, let alone radicalisation, in
the notion of abandoning the unemployed to informal work is
deluded. Offe and Jordan insist that a guaranteed income is also
necessary. But as we have seen, the state has only promoted
alternative work in order to *avoid* providing incomes, although even
the more 'formal' self-help structures of mandatory co-operation or
communality were beyond the capacities of the Australian government to enforce. Nevertheless, that government thereupon dispensed

with alternative work ideas and simply *abandoned* some groups, by reducing the categories entitled to unemployment benefits. This caused an immediate rise in the number of homeless teenagers.

The abandonment represents the culmination of a series of strategies aimed to alleviate pressure on a government in so-called crisis over its responsibility for an expanding dependent population. Furthermore, the state's response to this problem, in legitimating new forms of non-participation, ultimately constitutes a redrawing of the boundaries of citizenship. In Australia, restrictions to unemployment benefit entitlements, and later changes to the scheme, represent more brutal examples of this trend.

The marginalised and passive second-class citizens thus created by such governments stand in bleak contrast to the naive optimism of the post-industrialists. Their proposals for governments to guarantee incomes and provide alternative work assume a benign, democratic state as a starting point. In reality, the alternative plans enabled the Australian government to become even less accountable to marginalised populations, as I will here demonstrate. A passing review of employment and dependency patterns shows the impetus for the government's hunt for alternatives to paid work. As for the outcome – proposals to break the cash/work nexus led directly to the government enforcing it more harshly than before. Hardly a year after Hawke abandoned the post-industrial strategy he proposed work-for-the-dole, and a year after that, the benefit restrictions began.

The implications of dole-work and its widespread popularity were indications of a clear shift in the parameters of citizenship and reveal, in a broader sense, another misconception in the post-industrial thesis. The problem is this. It is well known that 'workfare' or dole-work has powerful conservative advocates in Britain, the United States and elsewhere. The policy provides punishment via increased surveillance, and recipients would constitute a class of indentured labourers. In Australia its implementation was too difficult, although it proved very effective as a threat. Importantly, the Labor government only proposed dole-work *after* the distortions to conventional meanings of work and obligation were already accomplished. (The more conservative governments of Thatcher or Reagan could be more blatant than a party of the labour movement.) This, in turn, was made possible partly because of the intellectual climate fostering the alternatives to wage labour theme. It was also possible, far more importantly, because beliefs about independence, about living off one's own work and about avoiding 'bludging' on others *on purpose* are deeply embedded, not just in people's heads but also in the material manifestations of citizenship.

What will also be argued here, then, is that if the state is to be effectively criticised for removing rights and for blaming the victims of unemployment, governments' ideological 'success' with dole-work should be better understood in order to reassert the opposite, namely proper employment. Dole-work proposals were to impose a drastically restricted conception of 'citizenship' on the excluded, which reduced rights as it imposed duties, such as 'training' or 'make-work'. None of this is, of course, exclusive to Australia. In general, a slippage between duties and obligations lies at the heart of state impositions from above, and this ambiguity is embedded in most state policies. A universal, inclusive conception of citizenship (as a defence from below) involves a close relation between rights and freely assumed obligations. The latter are *not* duties, for obligations involve choice. The expansion of rights to all is only possible when proper employment opportunities are also available, to enable all to assume obligations as and when they choose.

FROM FULL MALE EMPLOYMENT TO CHRONIC UNEMPLOYMENT

Capitalism has, of course, never provided employment opportunities to all. The clearing mechanism of unemployment is an inherent feature of labour markets, and decommodification of labour was only partially achieved through union struggles and state regulations, commitments and provisions. Many of these, of course, have recently been dismantled and, as the century comes to a close, the long boom after World War II seems more an aberration than a lasting trend. As post-industrialists point out, however, that era of full employment and employment-related security concerned only men. This accurate premise is part of their more questionable conclusion that full employment today is both impossible and undesirable. But how has the labour market changed?

In Australia, as elsewhere, the economic regime of the boom involved considerable expansion of industry and state infrastructure, with demand sustained by increased public expenditure during slumps. A vast system of tariffs and subsidies also developed in Australia, but this tended to relieve foreign owned manufacturers from the need to develop stable export markets. The present economic regime, however, has involved recessions, deficits, vulnerability to international markets and a decline in productive investment. Popular debates in Europe about a shift to 'post-Fordist' work practices are hardly relevant here, except for groups of skilled male workers. Fordism refers to conveyor-belt manufacturing techniques and mass consumption of similar goods – a hallmark of the boom – yet post-Fordism, with high technology industries and a flexible, multiskilled labour force has not developed much beyond ingenious new arrangements to enhance the 'flexibility' of low-paid workers. Changes are more as a result of the growth of Fordist mass production techniques in service areas such as chain restaurants, and developments in microelectronics and telecommunications which have significantly altered the composition of the labour market.[7]

Australia's economic malaise since the 1970s has, along with other social changes, eradicated the old compromises where Australian-born men and boys formed the permanent workforce, and female and migrant labour were a semi-reserve army. The fulltime labour market for teenagers had collapsed well before the recession of 1974, but after that teenage unemployment rates grew to double the overall rates.[8] The old career paths for teenagers, in banking and postal services for example, were removed, and a credentialling explosion and changes to the apprentice system were also important factors. Teenage girls suffered higher unemployment rates than boys, and casual employment of school students in the retail and service industries grew rapidly.[9]

By 1978–79 Australia had moved to the highest rate of unemployment since the depression, and this change in the labour market was greater, relative to past trends (such as the unemployment rates in the United States), than in any other Western country during the years 1973–79.[10] The collapse of full employment was accompanied by a radicalisation of the right, a widespread phenomenon in many countries. In 1978 *The Australian* newspaper ran a popular tax revolt campaign and 'new' right-libertarian political parties erupted and fundamentalist movements grew.[11] But if principles of free market and small government were preached, they were hardly practised. The state, instead of intervening *less*, merely changed the form of intervention and tightened discipline.[12] Despite efforts at cost cutting, the Liberal government did not succeed in reducing welfare expenditure. This was because, while favouring existing rebates and other fiscal and occupational welfare to promote 'free choice' and 'self-help', and destroying Medibank and other Whitlam government innovations in welfare services, 'residual' state payments increased. The growing dole bill resulted in the social security and welfare bill advancing from 17.7 per cent of federal spending in 1970–71 to 27.9 per cent in 1978–79.[13] Propaganda against unemployed 'hippies' expanded into accusations that married women were taking jobs from teenagers.[14]

Fifteen years after full employment was abandoned, the Hawke government had reshaped the state's responsibilities for unemployment into a set of punitive surveillance strategies, while a different kind of labour market became segmented by age, sex and ethnicity.[15] To take the latter first, the striking change is in the numbers of women *permanently* in paid work, rather than in a reserve army where they could be laid off and sent 'home' with relative ease. Labour forces in most industrial societies are now becoming feminised, although this is less so in the secure, 'core' labour market than in an expanding casual, low-paid or 'contingent' sector.[16] This permanent participation of women makes the representativeness of the labour movement dubious, with so many male union leaders.[17] Many unionists have concentrated on restructuring other work sectors rather than securing better conditions for the 'contingent' workforce.[18] State policies, unions and work practices do not even acknowledge women's dual burden: the duties of paid work and the domestic work duties imposed by social constraints and individual men.[19]

In relation to this new employment regime, which was emerging by the 1980s, the idea that there is also a new welfare regime in Australia is shown in a significant decline in the numbers of private dependants and an equivalent rise in social dependants, although the *proportion in employment* has remained constant. John Freeland shows that well before the 1974 recession until the present day, 'approximately 42 to 43 per cent of Australia's population has, in terms of the money economy, supported approximately 57 to 58 per cent of the population . . . In the broad sense nothing much has changed in terms of economic dependency/population ratios'. The significant changes lie rather in the patterns of dependency. From 1971 to 1986 the social dependency ratio (those relying on cash transfers from the state) increased from 10.4 per cent to 25.6 per cent, and the private dependency ratio (those dependent on support within families, such as spouses and children) fell from 47.4 per cent to 31.3 per cent.[20]

So, although the overall participation rate altered little between the full male employment era before the 1970s and the contemporary unemployment era, social dependency doubled, while private dependency declined more markedly. This indicates a major social change. Recipients of unemployment and related benefits and their households account for over half the increase in social dependency, due to structural changes involving full-time job losses. Also, a larger proportion is active in the labour market (that is, employed, under-employed or registering as unemployed). The massive reduction in private dependency is about women. Women's labour force partici-pation rate in April 1991 was 52.3 per cent, compared with the male rate of 75.4 per cent;[21] the stereotype of breadwinner man with dependent woman and children now comprises only 13 per cent of all households.[22] Put differently, married women had a workforce participation rate of 6.5 per cent in 1947 but by 1987 it was 48.6 per cent.[23]

In the later 1980s there was significant job growth, but it did not reduce the social dependency rate because expansion was in the casual, low-paid segments of the labour market and these jobs were primarily taken by those in households that already had employed members. High levels of unemployment persisted and long-term unemployment increased.[24] With the emergence of a 'core' and 'contingent' labour force, the proportion of Australians defined as living in poverty has increased,[25] as has the number of working 'poor', who are either not protected by centralised wage fixing and not in unions, or who are in weak unions.[26]

Meantime, discourse on restructuring on the part of the Labor government, unions and the corporate sector – complex though it is – stressed technical, economistic solutions to modernise industry and move labour towards post-Fordism.[27] This tack was implicitly about full male employment but, even then, union leaders became insulated (and therefore ineffectual?) inside new corporatist struc-tures, emphasising tax reductions and investment 'bribes' in traditionally masculine, environmentally suspect areas. Financial deregulation in 1985, however, further weakened the potential of the state to encourage any investment and profits were subsequently repatriated overseas and/or used for speculative rather than productive investment.[28] Overseas borrowing, some to pay for an 'unprecedented concentration of economic power in Australia', exacerbated balance of payment problems and was financed by monopoly pricing.[29] Some of the big corporations that evolved went into liquidation later.

The 1990s began with deepening recession, and unemployment rose again to match the Fraser government peak of January 1983. But job creation is no longer the volatile issue it was when the Labor Party won office on its corporatist platform in March 1983. Concern for the unemployed is confined now to party manoeuvres and Liberal Party faith in classic economic orthodoxy rather than genuine calls for job creation. The right to participate has been so reduced that the unemployed can no longer claim unemployment benefits but only 'allowances', as will be discussed later. They must now prove that they are searching for nonexistent jobs, and if that takes too long, must join Newstart, the misnomer for tighter work tests and spurious contracts for enforced 'training' with no employment prospects.

FROM THE HUNT FOR ALTERNATIVES TO PROPOSALS FOR DOLE-WORK

The general social, economic and political context, therefore, has considerably changed. What was the part played by the debates about worker co-operatives and communes? High unemployment levels were still unacceptable to the public in the early 1980s, despite the assumption by more and more policy makers and dominant groups that unemployment was a stable component of the economic structure. Hawke was among the many who made this plain. Yet a full employment policy of promoting overall growth and the restructuring of industry, even with the phenomenon of 'jobless growth' via new technology, was still promoted by the labour movement: the old vision of full male employment. It did not accommodate the young, women and older men. Disenchantment with the labourist version of full employment grew among diverse ranks, and demands for proper work were not made consistently or with lasting conviction.

The pessimism from the left that developed during the Hawke governments was based partly on the correct perception that the capacities of state intervention have been significantly reduced, particularly with a long-term contraction of the tax base and state-owned assets, and the deregulation of finance capital. Right wing movements, from Tax Revolts to the Festival of Light, became more influential in the political arena. New media concentrations made it difficult for dissident voices to find a hearing, and the ALP's turn to corporatism and away from the ideals of the Whitlam era was another cause for pessimism or, among ALP loyalists, a cause of awkward defence of this new male unionism. Oppositional groups were led to doubt that full employment was possible, while those favouring the post-industrial thesis seriously questioned whether paid work was desirable.

It is no wonder, then, that the alternative proposals could be launched with relative ease. And yet the fanfare occurred just when a demand for jobs developed quite spontaneously from below. The unemployment figures played a major part in bringing down the Fraser government, but whether job creation ever stood a chance at that moment is irrelevant because the new ALP government turned instead to the alternative solution. Meanwhile the labour movement was institutionalised via the Accord. If sovereignty was being devolved to the market during the Fraser era, it now partly devolved to a corporatist structure *as well*, making a curious combination. Corporatism, it has been argued, is more a form of 'simulated politics' than actual debate, with bargaining occurring behind the scenes.[30] So, in Australia's case, there was no way of knowing whether the unions' defeat of a consumption tax plan in 1985 was not bought at the price of the bank deregulation of that year. A large price it was too, given that the unions had already acceded to wage freezes in the Accord on the understanding that employment policies would ensue. Deregulation further removed that possibility. Conversely, and while utterly excluded from the new tripartite arrangements, there were some groups, notably feminists, who won a brief space in the political arena (at least to the point where married women were no longer 'officially' blamed for the unemployment of others). Hawke's speeches demonstrated this change, which allowed co-op and commune supporters to gain minute spaces as well.

At this stage, the main directions of these policies were to reduce the supply of teenage labour and to 'manage', and also win public acceptance of, long-term unemployment and new forms of under-employment as permanent fixtures. These were achieved by policy makers' success in changing the meaning of conventional notions of work, obligation and participation. The hunt for alternatives to paid work demonstrated that the government was concerned with employment and *work*. The promotion of co-ops and communes was not dissimilar from the way the guaranteed income debate progressed through those institutional processes and arenas dealing with *poverty*. The similarities lie in how the state managed the communication between the dominant and anti-establishment forces engaged in the debates, and channelled the ideas in various directions.

The result of the government activity, it must be reiterated, was that neither communes nor worker co-operatives were successful as alternatives to labour market participation. Virtually no commune dweller either went off the dole or gave up formal employment. By 1985, after the New South Wales government's co-op schemes had operated for seven years, there was a total of 224 people employed in worker co-operatives.

Along with the later 'work-or-no-dole' plan, the press consistently attributed the commune idea to Hawke alone, for which he was eventually the object of considerable media derision.[31] Such treatment of ideas taken seriously by that same press only a few years previously, serves merely to mask the actual social problems, while simplistically insinuating that a better leader would come upon real answers.

This is, however, hardly the case. Unemployment, one of the major problems arising from existing organisational structures, has multiple effects on political and institutional structures. The fact that commune and co-operative plans were taken seriously by the state is primarily an indication of the difficulties in searching for solutions to unemployment without far-reaching structural changes within society as a whole. The new corporatism was, if anything, achieving the reverse.

As far as the legitimising role of state policies was concerned, however, the plans were effective. It was necessary to be seen to be doing something (*anything*) about unemployment, especially at a time when unemployed groups were unusually active. This was the primary reason why hitherto repressed 'alternatives', especially the commune movement, received such attention. And this sudden solicitousness came just when their presence would make the broader attempt to reduce the supply of labour, including part-time work and early retirement, look more attractive. It obviated the need to draw on the wornout rhetoric against women. In any case, women were not an employment problem for the state, in that they had no choice (given male refusal to share responsibility for children) but to take the new casual jobs created in the 1980s. Women were already far too overworked to demand full-time jobs. The future of low-income, jobless teenagers was the primary concern, even though organised redundant male workers were the more politically embarrassing.

Also, in the same way as the guaranteed income idea, commune and co-op proposals were supported by completely diverse groups, from small businesses and big corporations to socialist libertarians and environmentalists. The ensuing competition within the political arena led to adjustments to the proposed models, and ultimately the realisation for co-op supporters that the small business lobby would not allow exclusive subsidies for co-operatives and that state governments could not 'deliver'. Similarly communes would find few public resources available after conventional farming groups became politicised in the late 1980s, when the depression hit the rural sector. Local governments and more traditional rural groups remained opposed to any commune development, whether by individuals, the state or private charity. Marginalisation of the new underclass may be in the interests of some dominant groups and it may ease the problems of the state, but intervening groups and conflicting levels of government can make the implementation of such policies too difficult.

Another facet of the process was the Accord itself. The labour movement was now in a position to make itself heard, at least where these plans were concerned. It was in the union's interest to protect arbitration, at the time subject to heavy criticism, from subversion by these schemes for alternatives, which from the union perspective amounted (correctly) to exit routes from the formal economy into fringe employment, renewed forms of self exploitation and poverty, which would only further aid the deregulation of the labour market.

The state's interpretation of these conflicts, subsequent to its tentative plans and discussions between senior civil servants and representatives of co-op groups and communes, was to call for further research. Young people did not want to live on communes, and commune dwellers did not leave the labour market since they claimed unemployment benefits, nor create job vacancies as most were professionals. Finally, worker co-operatives could be restructured more to union principles, but minimal state subsidies seriously restricted their growth. At the federal level both schemes died, though certain legal forms were changed, to the extent that 'multiple occupancy', for example, is a new form which may be detrimental to some universal rights.

In the process, the state achieved a further erosion of the notion that people have a right to paid employment. Although work-for-the-dole ideas (of 1986) were unlikely to be implemented, the right to unemployment benefits became increasingly tenuous: teenagers lost eligibility in 1987 and the benefit was replaced entirely in 1990. The fate of each particular proposal demonstrates the complexities involved in this type of 'incorporation'. It should be seen as a less one-way process than some co-opting arguments allow, because the state was involved in contradictory roles, and had to contend with conflicts from a plurality of groups and the inertia of historically produced constraints of past labour market and social policies. In addition, the capacity of the state to use spontaneously created inputs from below, shows how, as in the United States, Australian society is less rigidly stratified than in Europe and how the whole state edifice is relatively open to demands, particularly in times of crisis and dissension. Oppositional groups, from feminists to the fleeting organisation of the unemployed had left their mark, as well as these radical challenges against wage labour which the state was unable fully to implement as conservative policies. Through these debates the state managed particular changes and itself changed, the outcome of which had not been previously apparent.

DOLE LABOUR: UNEMPLOYMENT AS A FIXTURE

Having established this interplay between the state and opposing social groups and movements, we have still to consider the question of the desirability of full employment, so disputed by the post-industrial thesis. That is, it has been argued that post-industrial ideas represent a general struggle to move *beyond* wage labour, a move to which no government would ever accede unless it were moulded to state interests. But discussion is still required about whether the strategy for separating income from work is misguided in other respects.

The first issue is compulsion, and here I am concerned with the way governments became more unaccountable and authoritarian towards the unemployed, a key problem neglected by post-industrialists. Immediately following Hawke's political redefinition of obligation, the dole-work idea was introduced. Although post-industrialists argue rightly that wage labour inherently involves compulsion, and dole-work is therefore the most extreme enforcement of the cash/work nexus, the question remains: does wage labour still enhance citizenship in *other* ways, where dole-work clearly does the reverse?

What happened in Australia was that the meaning of work and the right to unemployment benefits were both redefined in order to reduce the state's previous commitment to provide employment or, failing that, cash support as a universal entitlement. This created a climate where the notorious issue of 'bludging' could re-emerge. It is worth considering in some detail for, without question, the 'bludger' charge was and is a patently unfair but popular exercise in blaming the victims of unemployment that first emerged when the Whitlam government raised the rate of benefits. 'Bludger' attacks reached new depths with the dole-work proposals. As an imposed duty to work, dole-work highlights exactly what should be meant by its opposite, that an obligation to work is only that which can be freely assumed, as the following sections will argue. I will briefly discuss the dole-work debate before considering the differences between duty and obligation and the rather complex relation between obligations and rights. This leads to the conclusion that full employment rather than the reverse has the potential to reduce compulsion or duty, and in that respect to enhance citizenship.

In Australia, the payment of very meagre unemployment benefits was introduced in 1944. The Whitlam government's 1973 introduction of a comparatively generous level – in that benefits were raised to pension levels – meant an element of choice was included. Hence, the benefit became based on the individual's right to choose (*relatively* freely) the sort of work she or he wished to do, and on the right to have needs met.[32] In other words, the dole became a right that the society owed its members as a duty or at least a commitment, when it failed to provide a minimum standard of employment. Furthermore, between 1973 and 1975, pensions and benefits for single adults and young people were at the same (increased) rate, thus assuming that sixteen-year-olds were, just like adults, in financial need when without work.[33] The post-war promise to maintain full male employment was the other commitment, undertaken by the Chifley government when women's labour force participation was slight. With the onset of the recession, however, this promise was broken, partly because the original full employment policy was never armed with effective mechanisms to maintain employment,[34] and partly, as we have seen, after the Whitlam government's path to reformism was abruptly halted.

Hence, as unemployment became long-term and benefits (paid from general revenue rather than specific contributions by workers) became increasingly costly for the government, the state developed an urgent interest in reducing its responsibilities. Anyone over sixteen had a right to receive the dole on leaving school, although from 1975–6, the sixteen-to-eighteen-year old rate was held down and steadily reduced. Much as the government tried also to increase school retention rates, there were few reasons for teenagers to stay at school (other than the growing minority who entered universities) because there were by then too few job opportunities or job schemes (for the 25 to 30 per cent of unemployed teenagers), to give training any end result. While teenagers wanted to remain in the labour market, the government wanted them to withdraw from it. Because it had no commitment to creating jobs to give a purpose to training, the supply-side strategies aimed to reduce the supply of teenage labour in any way possible. As we saw, the commune and co-operative plans faced problems – these were not necessarily insoluble, and at the very least, the plans showed that the government was concerned about the future of teenagers. This sympathy did not last.

By 1985 the overall unemployment rate crept down below the 8 per cent mark, and by the next year the previous 'soft' stories about alternative lifestyles and kibbutzim were replaced with hard ones about welfare fraud and 'dole bludging'.[35] The government claimed in June 1986 that it had created over half a million jobs, although many were part-time or casual positions.[36] The low-paid contingent workforce was now expanding, and conditions were not improved by a two-tiered wage settlement with the trade unions in 1986.[37] Accordingly, the previous supply-side solutions of removing groups from the workforce – as it had been conventionally understood – were now redundant. There were apparently lots of 'jobs'. In a reflection of the new hard line, that same month in 1986, the prime minister suggested the time had come to recognise that the unemployed, particularly young people, had 'a responsibility to undertake some community work' in return for the dole. In other words, society no longer had a duty or responsibility to pay it and, far from suggesting people had a right to receive support, the payment was to be even more discretionary or conditional than before. Instead of the work test, where payment depended on proof that you were *looking for work*, Hawke proposed that benefits should be paid in exchange for the *performance of community work* which might become compulsory.

The media's coverage of unemployment swelled with renewed virulence, most notoriously in a round of attacks on dole fraud, television debates on dole-work and a fascination with similar American 'workfare' schemes.[38] The revival of the popular 'bludger' theme was not just a journalist beat up, however. The federal Department of Employment and Industrial Relations insisted that the voluntary community work currently being planned for unemployed young people would not involve any substitutions in 'the usual areas of paid employment'.[39]

Such a denial only highlights what Hawke and others envisaged for dole-work. Dole-work itself cannot provide the sense of having a useful social function that paid jobs tend to give (whether this perception of usefulness is right or wrong). If the work is not to be done through normal employment, the question that immediately arises is whether it is worth doing at all. Once it is regarded with suspicion, and especially since the explicit compulsion does not give even an illusory sense of control, there is no learning of the 'work habits' frequently stressed by conservatives. Instead it represents a form of surveillance: people are not to be trusted to look for work (however little work there may be), they must be forced to do meaningless work. With dole-work not only would the unemployed be stigmatised even further, but they would also lose the individual right (a civil right, T.H. Marshall might have said) to sell their labour power. It is not 'free' wage labour but a primitive form of state conscription or indentured labour.

There are numerous ways that dole-work would deprive people of the property right to sell their labour power. If implemented, *no-one* would then have a right to withdraw from the labour market and to even a minimum of control over the conditions for entry into the labour market, particularly of choice, location and price. The employed would be severely constrained by the threat of dole-work, but those 'working' for their unemployment benefit could neither leave dole-work nor look for other work. With the dole-work proposals, the widespread disapproval of 'bludging' is used even more cynically and hypocritically than usual, given that 'bludger' campaigns have occurred with monotonous regularity since the recession.

The initial arguments against dole-work in 1986 mainly arose from traditional defenders of the unemployed, such as the welfare agencies and elements of the labour movement. The work-for-the-dole plan was criticised for devaluing the principle of voluntary work, which of course it does. It would create invidious divisions between the fortunate superiors who *choose* to volunteer and the conscripts. Moreover, the distinction between criminal offenders on community work orders and those merely in the state of unemployment would be blurred, given that both programs were predicated on the idea of a 'repayment of a debt to society'.[40] Community organisations would be overburdened and suffer further if time had to be expended on training and 'supervising' young and inexperienced unemployed people: as it is, they are usually unable to find suitable places for most ordinary volunteers.[41]

Some Labor politicians and unionists argued that young people on dole-work would be exposed to even more exploitation and harassment than they were already suffering. It was, in effect, a 'woolly make-work scheme'.[42] This was certainly the case, for dole-work would place those subjected to it in a greater position of dependence than before. Without the availability of socially acceptable work, the work test cannot prove whether or not anyone is *choosing* to live off the work of others (this is what 'bludging' means). The work test has been unable to *prove* this for at least twenty years, since the numbers out of work have exceeded the number of vacant and suitable jobs. But dole-work would force people to live off 'make-work' – socially useless work provided by the state. Hence, the actual futility of the work test for the past decades would be 'resolved' by imposing non-work on all those forced to 'live off' others. It would, of course, also deter many from applying for benefits at all – the covert, primary aim of both requirements.

Despite criticisms, the federal 'community work' program was one of the few to enjoy an increase in the 1986 budget. Soon after, the ACTU presented a scheme whereby all income support for the young should be tied to a school, job or training program. The proposal to abolish their unemployment benefit was used at the time as a bargaining counter for more involvement in investment paths.

The idea was modelled on Swedish policy, but with nothing like Sweden's training programs and active employment policies for adults, such that actual jobs have existed in Sweden for all but 3 per cent of the population aged over twenty, during the recent past. Hence, it was little different from the original dole-work proposal, especially given that the ACTU was concerned that the dole was the one payment to teenagers that had 'no strings attached'.[43]

Nevertheless, individual union pressure about the potential of 'make-work' to undermine proper jobs and wages, as well as cost estimates, eased the government from compulsory dole-work to a voluntary scheme.[44] After that, the 'work or no dole' demand was heard less frequently, although Aborigines (as we saw) have been subjected to dole-work for a decade, and the conservative parties keep it on their political agendas. It is obviously favoured for its punitive, disciplinary aspects, while right wing libertarians support dole-work more for its potential to undermine those in paid work, both in terms of wages and of rights to bargain on the labour market.

Meantime the dole-work debate was not merely a slanging match. Its immediate effect was that eligibility for unemployment benefits became less and less regarded as a right. Dole fraud investigations were stepped up, with Department of Social Security inspectors able to remove from the files many of those still eligible for benefits by convincing them that the dole was not worth the harassment.[45] The application of a stricter work test, irrational as it was with eleven unemployed for every one job (in 1987), has always had less to do with whether cheats and 'bludgers' *really* exist and more to do with reducing workforce participation and claimants.

Many young people polled at this stage even considered dole-work as a way to end the increasing stigma confronting welfare recipients.[46] But what, in the event, proved to be easier and cheaper for governments – having become so distanced from the old idea of full employment, first via plans to abandon and second to completely enforce the cash/work nexus – was to remove unemployment benefits completely from teenagers aged sixteen to eighteen. The following year, 1987, they were proclaimed ineligible, and the $50 payment was replaced with a $25 job search allowance, with a further $25 available subject to a parental means test. Teenagers could search for work from a position of private dependency, rather than, as before, participants in the labour market; the assumption was that unemployed young people lived at home and could be supported by their parents. Evidence, it need hardly be added, shows otherwise: most parents of unemployed teenagers have lower incomes and thus a limited capacity to support an unemployed child.[47]

In addition, rather than increase education allowances to make training more enticing, those who were least able to continue with education were then faced with the job search allowance being held down so that student allowances could overtake it.[48] Having created more 'children' who must stay at home and school, the government simultaneously decreed sixteen-to-eighteen-year-olds to be independent adults if they lived with a sole parent pensioner. Vocational training was only proposed for under 700 single parents each year, hardly adequate, to say the least, for the 20 000 people expected to be removed annually from these pensions when their youngest 'child' reached 16.[49] The number of homeless teenagers rose immediately after they lost the right to workforce participation.[50] Unemployment had been removed from the political agenda, to be replaced in the media by homelessness, 'dole bludging' and drugs.

In such a hostile environment, the Australian left has remained as divided as many in Europe and the United States about the employment crisis. The labour movement continued to press for 'productivist' strategies to create male jobs (note the ACTU's 1987 vision in *Australia Reconstructed*), which is not in any way the same as arguing that opportunities to work should be extended in principle, since the meaning of returning to 'full employment' in their strategies is never so clearly defined.[51] The ACTU document also abandoned support for the right of young people to unemployment benefits, given that the ACTU's enthusiasm for Swedish policies ignored the different conditions for teenagers there. Elsewhere, in contrast, the post-industrial argument for the separation of income and work reappeared in public and academic debates, to become popular amongst those left wing elements most critical of the corporatist trends, some of whom were attempting to form 'new left' or 'left-green' political parties.[52] Despite past failures in searching for alternatives, the logic of post-industrial alternatives to wage labour was at that stage following the left-wing intellectual debates from West Germany and Britain about guaranteed or basic incomes.

By the end of the 1980s, the Social Security Review, a major undertaking of the Hawke government, brought out its main recommendations. It disagreed explicitly with the basic income plans of British intellectuals such as Bill Jordan, and instead stressed an 'active' social policy to draw pensioners and beneficiaries into employment and job-training programs.[53] This meant that even more benefits would be redefined. It assumed that full employment and participation were desirable, and while the resulting Active Employment Strategy was based on an assumption of an expanding labour market, the review was all along undermined by the classic liberalism pursued by the federal government. Despite the ACTU's belief in industry policies, the government had no intention of creating proper employment programs. In addition, fees were introduced for vocational training at technical and further education (TAFE) colleges; the sweetener of paying fees later through tax was considered only for university students (who might have a chance, eventually, of gaining employment). In New South Wales the Greiner government led the way in making TAFE virtually inaccessible, although the federal government toyed with similar plans.[54]

In relation to these contradictions between recommendations for an 'active' basis to cash transfers and the lack of active support by governments to ensure this (to say the least), the 1990 election offered further harsh measures for the adult unemployed. There was a notable lack of public criticism, presumably because by then unemployment appeared to have been *solved*. The Labor Party's promised 'reforms', to force the unemployed into training, were seen merely as a minor variation on the Liberals' standing promise to remove unemployment benefits altogether after a recipient had had them for nine months. John Elliott, then President of the Liberal Party depicted this as a policy for the 'workers' against the 'bludgers' – who would be rendered destitute. Federal Treasurer Paul Keating's defence of the unemployed on that occasion was memorable for its rarity on the part of the ALP.[55] Labor's threat of training or no dole was again explicitly based on Hawke's more ingenious concept of a 'reciprocal obligation' to 'society' for dole payments.[56] The contradiction here was hardly noticed politically, for if training were out of reach, there was at that stage (albeit briefly), a lot more work. It was far easier to make quite unrealistic work tests and remove more claimants, for work had become defined as any work in the contingent labour market, no matter how casual. Should anyone *voluntarily* leave this work, there is now a wait of up to three months for benefits.[57] The growing proportion of working poor and underemployed was nearly as marginalised as the 500 000 people or more counted as unemployed (or rather, as working for less than an hour a week) during each year since 1983.[58]

A new polarisation had therefore set in. Although women's claims to labour force participation were at last recognised (in contrast with a renewed virulence in the conservatives' 1990 electoral campaign, aimed at returning women to private dependency),[59] the Hawke government succeeded in cementing a dual labour market and in restricting the criteria whereby clients could make claims on the state. These two strategies were interconnected, because after 'work' took on new meanings, fewer of the already marginalised were eligible for state support. Through attempts to reduce the supply of labour (which became redundant after the contingent workforce developed), the Hawke government succeeded in changing everyday ideas about full employment and obligation and incorporated these new ideas into policy. When the jobless were transformed into the homeless, even the idea of moving to 'full employment' reappeared during the 'best' year, 1989, employment meaning now a casual job reserved mainly for prime-age adults.

In 1990, after Labor was re-elected, unemployment benefits were abolished and substituted with Job Search and Newstart allowances. Effective in 1991, Newstart has increased welfare officials' discretionary powers by being deliberately vague about the kind of 'work' or 'training' recipients would be expected to perform. As a Brotherhood of St Laurence report put it

> the post-war objective of making unemployment benefit an entitlement and a compensation from the community to the unemployed person for the failure of the labour market to provide adequate employment is gone. The removal of this objective meshes with the consistent vein of public opinion holding that unemployment is due to individual deficits and the failure to look hard enough for a job.[60]

At the end of 1990, unemployment rose sharply. The 9.9 per cent rate was presented as a deviation from, rather than the culminating trend of, the Hawke government's lack of commitment to employment.

OBLIGATIONS AND CITIZENSHIP

The groups with the most tenuous links to a labour market that is increasingly a segmented buyers' market are, therefore, more and more constituted as lacking the ability to fulfil their 'obligation' or, more correctly, *duty* to the society. There is no reciprocity, for the government is less and less required to fulfil duties towards those it now isolates as the 'citizens'. The state is no more committed to proper jobs or meaningful training (and even, possibly, old age) than it is to decent support for child-raising.[61]

What is the difference between duty and obligation? A government imposes an individualistic set of 'contractual obligations' to the state that the unemployed must fulfil (such as to 'train') in order to receive cash transfers. Those within the labour force, however, do not have any 'obligations' imposed on them – far from it, they are left to act from self-interest alone,[62] and receive work-related rights and benefits into the bargain. This spurious contractual argument, where the unemployed are to repay a 'debt' to society, has given further scope for liberals and conservatives (particularly men) to constitute the 'real' citizen as a tax-payer.

Tax-paying, however, is not strictly an 'obligation' assumed exclusively by workers but a compulsory duty imposed on all. Even in Australia, where there are relatively few consumption taxes (at the time of writing), everyone does pay indirect tax, and there are some taxes on pensions. In an increasingly regressive system, the highest income earners and wealth owners also *avoid* a greater proportion of tax than anyone else, through fiscal welfare like rebates, imputation schemes, concessions and subsidies. The extent of fiscal welfare is estimated to be higher than that paid out as social welfare.[63]

Newstart or the proposed dole-work are imposed duties too, but they also involve *restrictions on rights* and hence do not constitute the unemployed as citizens at all. Who, then, are the recognised citizens? The so-called 'tax-payer' hardly fits a *formal description* when systems of rebates and minimisation schemes become rights that seem to prompt an obligation to 'evade'. That means taxes are less of a duty for some. It suggests that the constitution of the citizen is of an individual with both rights and obligations, with the problem being that liberal democratic governments formally acknowledge only rights and duties (in various combinations). When labour, Fabian or social democratic parties have held office and urged the extension of *rights* to workers, there has never been the same concentration on obligations. Furthermore, when it did happen, with the full employment commitment, it was only ever extended to men – Norway and Sweden are possible contemporary exceptions. (Likewise, the difference between a conscripted army and a volunteer army, that is, between duty and obligation in the face of war, has so far also only concerned men.)

The argument here is the following.[64] Modern citizenship evolved with the development of capitalist markets, but was legally constituted by such new laws as, in Britain, the Poor Law Amendment Act of 1834. Such legislation created a new division between paupers (deserving and undeserving) based on a capacity to *work*. Although, as we know, wage labour was subsequently decommodified to allow those who could not find work to become 'deserving' (of support), the dividing line remained between citizens, with rights and obligations, and the rest – whose duties were imposed and whose rights were fewer and often ignored, especially in the case of women in private dependence on men. Moreover, rights were removed altogether by incarceration in workhouses.

T.H. Marshall is taken as offering a classic statement of modern citizenship, yet Marshall failed to make a distinction between duties and obligations. He mentioned duties only in passing, as those tasks that are done *voluntarily*. Although 'the duty to work' was of 'paramount importance', it was hardly discussed beyond mentioning that duties appeared 'remote and unreal' when the community was so large.[65] His Whig view of the historical development of 'welfare citizenship' neglects the problem that, despite population size, accusations of 'bludging' or 'cadging' have been so effective. Marshall's notion of citizenship, or its (smooth) evolution by the 1950s, was in fact based solely on three kinds of rights: civil, political and social. Civil rights comprise freedom of the person from harm; the right to free speech, thought and faith; equality before the law; and the rights to own property and make contracts. Political rights concern the rights to vote, to join political parties and to stand for elections. Social rights are about the quality of life, whereby the state should provide the opportunity, through health, education and welfare services, for everyone 'to live the life of a civilised being according to the standards prevailing in the society'.[66] Marshall opposed the liberal position that all rights are derived from property, whereby everyone *by nature* owned at least their capacity to labour. As he suggested, even though the right to vote, for example, was exclusively held by those with market rights of private property (that is, based on wealth), with universal suffrage it became based purely on personal status.

More pertinently, Marshall's chief objection to the liberal view was that when civil rights became the sole rights of citizenship during the nineteenth century, they entrenched class inequalities because capitalists and workers were presumed equal in their rights to enter into market exchanges and contracts.[67] Marshall argued that a key civil right introduced in Britain was 'the right to work where and at what you pleased under a contract of your own making', which removed the old regulations over mobility and wages.[68] At the same time social rights were totally removed from citizen status with the Poor Law reforms. The 1834 Amendment divided all former 'paupers' into the 'undeserving poor', that is, the unemployed (who should not gain welfare support), and the 'deserving poor' or destitute (who should).[69] Henceforward, the free citizen was 'undeserving' of support and acquired the freedom to starve, because through the process of 'deserving' state support, civil and political rights were lost. In principle, a destitute person's claim for poor relief would be met by internment in the new workhouses – a loss of personal liberty and political rights (if any). With the Factory Acts, the citizen became a legal entity with exclusive masculine rights because the civil right to conclude a free contract was restricted for women and children.[70]

Marshall, writing during post-war reconstruction in Britain, argued that the political and social citizen rights gained during the twentieth century – that is, the current forms of political participation and state welfare provisions – had ameliorated the social inequalities of property or civil rights. After trade unions had asserted 'collective civil rights' so that workers could gain 'basic rights', social rights appeared to be entrenched in the contract system. In 1949 Marshall suggested that citizen status was subordinating 'market price to social justice'.[71]

Several problems with this conception of citizenship help to explain (in part) why the systematic denigration, contraction, privatising and removal of state provision since the 1970s has been relatively easy for many governments.[72] First, the gendered nature of welfare and market-related or fiscal provisions has resulted in a divided defence. Where Marshall saw a universal status in the citizen, he accepted its paternalism towards women, and neglected the precariousness of social rights. The latter proved to be far more politically vulnerable than, say, the right to vote. His conception has also been criticised for ignoring the fact that the promotion and creation of welfare institutions were not as open to political participation from below as labour and welfare historians assumed.[73]

The welfare tradition of social engineering and 'dependency and depoliticization of second class citizenship' that developed was, therefore, easily attacked by liberals.[74] In contrast to Marshall, contemporary progressives argue that welfare rights should *only* be defended in so far as they enhance civil and political rights, such as freedom and autonomy. Independence, it is suggested, should be fostered by removing the taints of altruism, compassion or benevolence from any justification for welfare provision, and by claiming instead that enhanced autonomy and active political involvement require resources and opportunities, a more adequate basis for defending social rights.

This assumes, however, that an ideal citizenship of *rights* is a sufficient condition to transform and limit both the state and the market. By contrast, Fraser has pointed out that those with a close relation to the market are the principal citizens.[75] That is, if citizen status still 'invades' contract at least for 'core' workers, it is not clear even now if this benefits women as much as it does men. Similarly, Pateman suggests Marshall ignored the extent that paid employment became the key to citizenship within the welfare state.[76] The 'market citizen' is also masculine, in that men's right to independence and self-respect through the capitalist market was upheld in principle by the previous full male employment policies and employment-related benefits, to save them from being the 'undeserved exiles from society'[77] or bereft of resources for social participation. Women, by contrast, were always treated as the 'natural' social exiles and consigned to private patriarchy 'behind closed doors'. Pateman sees the contemporary solution lying in the construction of women (and men) as public rather than private dependants.

That is, Pateman agrees with the post-industrial diagnosis of chronic unemployment as permanent, and the promotion of a guaranteed income as the way to constitute a universal citizenship free of gender divisions.[78] This avoids the problem that state welfare is not the public political forum for claiming women's rights that Pateman assumes. Rather it comprises arenas of paternalism or tutelage that treat the 'targeted' objects as administered clients with other doors closed. Furthermore, as Anna Yeatman points out,[79] although the distinction between contract and tutelage is still a gendered one, women's increasing participation in business and professional sectors is changing this distinction to an extent. In some countries, notably the United States, a new development of class differences is occurring, between those women who can buy their way out of feminine dependency and imposed duties (by employing nannies and cleaners) and claim masculine, freely-contracting status, and those who cannot.

In other words, the issue which is not articulated by such defenders of a more progressive citizenship is the actual nature of citizens' 'duties' (compared with rights). And yet the idea is central to the conservative discourse of the new right and, as we have seen, to many welfare states, which have uncovered new so-called obligations (meaningless duties and punishments) for clients to perform in exchange for welfare benefits. Such problems indicate that citizenship can not be adequately defined purely in terms of rights. Rights can be negated by other rights claims, and be used to entrench marginalisation. Those who are excluded from the market (through unemployment and discrimination) have less chance to claim rights because of a very ill-defined relation between rights and obligations. Similar difficulties arise from the rights gained by the civil rights and feminist movements, which are frequently counteracted with rights claims by those already privileged – such as the rights claimed by fathers, whites or men against anti-discrimination laws or child protection acts.[80] Such political problems with an exclusive rights strategy mean that a concept of obligation is equally as important, and its effect lies in making a critical distinction between duty and obligation. Duties are embedded in the contractual aspect of liberalism: they are prescribed and require obedience. Duties reduce rather than enhance people's rights and opportunities for social, economic and political participation; that is, they restrict rather than expand citizenship. By contrast, obligations rest within liberalism's radical humanism; they are the key to participation and form the basis of rights claims.

A distinction between work as duty and work as obligation illustrates Pateman's influential discussion on political obligation.[81] The problem she identifies there is that citizens, in general, claim rights and protection through Western political institutions *only* by exchanging them for obedience. She attributes this to classic liberal democratic theory's failure to keep its sole radical element, that citizens' obligations are only freely assumed. Liberal theory is ideological because obligations were only ever a possibility for the few. The rest had to perform duties but this was presented as an 'obligation' made through a contract, particularly because the liberal notion of self interest could never be a strong basis for gaining obedience. It may not always be in a person's self interest to obey.[82] Instead, the classic liberal notion of the social contract had to be retained so that, for example, with universal suffrage there is an assumed contract with the state through the tacit 'consent' of our voting. As Pateman explains, liberal democratic theory treats the contract as a promise, but it is a special kind of promise to *obey*, not a promise that could enlarge freedom and equality by citizens assuming *their own, rationally and voluntarily created obligations*. Instead 'substantive political freedom and equality . . . are given up or exchanged for the protection of the liberal state', just as other contracts involve giving up freedom in return for protection and subsistence (note the traditional marriage contract, the employment contract or the contract of slavery).[83]

Pateman makes a conceptual distinction between 'ought' and 'obligation',[84] which shows how a citizen's *duties* cannot be voluntary. She suggests that various forbearances and practices exist that we 'ought' to perform – certain duties – for without them social life would be unthinkable. Liberal theory's abstract individualism denies all the ways we are bound by rules, duties and oughts, and concentrates instead on the 'individual's capacities to create obligations' and to rise above them. But the conservative *and* socialist assumption that duties exist in a social and historical context, does not *necessarily* have to exclude the liberal idea of individual creativity. A new obligation, freely assumed, holds the promise of a new relationship. If the autonomous individual is a social and historical construction, so too are relationships of obligation. These relationships, Pateman stresses,

> depend upon, and arise from, the complex web of inter-subjective meanings and constitutive rules of social life, but they also transcend them. Individuals are not completely submerged in their rules, meanings and oughts, but are also superior to them, and use them as a necessary basis from which they judge, choose and act, and create and change their social relationships.[85]

Duty, therefore, plays no part in the practice of self assumed obligation but rather is embedded in the prevailing culture. A citizen, presumed equal, free and rational, cannot be forced to obey duties and conform to norms and rules without denying these presumptions of citizen rights. If the case of women poses extreme difficulties for liberal democratic theory, it is also hard to locate any 'free and equal individuals' among working-class men, despite male authority over women. Indeed there are very few of these abstract individuals, which is why obligation is a 'problem' for liberal democracies.[86]

So, rights are lost when duties are imposed, and while rights remain neither universal nor sufficiently enhanced by social welfare, a defence of rights is insufficient. Important though the extension of rights is, democratic citizenship concerns obligations as well. The potential for free and equal participation in a political community requires that we recognise this argument that obligations are only legitimate when freely assumed. Even if their background and history lies in duties and societal prescriptions, obligations only mean the same as duties performed obediently when citizens' freedoms are removed. At worst, this puts citizens at the mercy of the state.

Accordingly it is possible to argue that we all 'ought' to work when we can and have the opportunity to work and to participate in the work of society, and thus be 'independent' of governments or spouses. Women *and* men also 'ought' to raise and care for the future generation of citizens, for societies cannot survive without this. But only citizens have rights safeguarded by having the unrestricted opportunity to make and create obligations like work and caring for children, and to change them or not, as individuals, to assume them at all. This is the basis of our social and political participation, for rights can be removed by other rights claims and lead to exclusion, but obligation enhances participation and provides a basis for rights claims through erasing the prescriptions of duties.[87]

It is, therefore, a problem whether the welfare state actually embodies or provides for the practice of the liberal concept of obligation rather than obedience to imposed duties. In this sense, the liberal claims are not valid, for they cannot be realised through such a state. Whether the claims have been socially effective at different times, in legitimating and justifying liberal democratic practices, is another matter.[88]

What does this tell us about the post-industrial proposals? According to the above distinction, there are grave problems in neglecting the issue of obligations and defending only rights. That is, the alternatives to wage labour theme assumes that obligations are unnecessary, whereas the dole-work idea and the Newstart 'contract' do not mean obligation at all, but strict duty. The opportunity to fulfil an obligation to work exists – at the very least – only when proper jobs are fully available *and* when unemployment benefits are a right. By contrast, when there is no state commitment to full employment, governments have numerous options: setting dole-work prescribes a duty which removes the civil right to make a work contract of your own choosing, 'where and at what you please'. This civil right is of course also meaningless when there is chronic unemployment. Even if the state guaranteed an income, it could always reduce the level and thus force people to take the jobs 'going begging'.[89] A 'right to cash' is very easily undermined when there are no chances to fulfil obligations.

Conversely, the dole-work debate illuminates a full employment position not worthy of any support if it fails to make a distinction between the authoritarian imposition of make-work and a properly autonomous choice of socially useful work. Upholding the distinction requires that the right to unemployment benefits is as necessary as the opportunity to work. In many places, of course, both of these have been lost.

The constitution of a progressive citizenship is possible only if it emerges through demands from below, but it seems essential that this include a 'politics of full employment'. Although a full employment policy obviously requires state implementation, a combination of rights and obligations provides citizens with defences against both the state and the market, as will be discussed in the final chapters. On the question of rights, Barbalet points out that in creating and enforcing the rules and laws, the state 'constitutes the principal expression of political power in national societies'.[90] Hence at different times the state may promote some rights and enforce and safeguard a particular combination of rights at the expense of others that are more or less in conflict with market principles. States can remove rights, or ignore, accede to or repress the groups demanding change. The outcome of any dealings with the state from below depends on the relative strengths and weaknesses of social movements. An exclusive emphasis on rights often weakens a social movement, because rights easily lose their collective nature in the legalistic construction of rights as individual possessions, whereas obligation implies co-operation with the collectivity. People's political participation is enhanced if they participate in the market and are not merely clients of the state. The reason, therefore, why rights are a necessary but insufficient condition for universal citizenship is because they are protected, expanded and defended only when there is the potential to assume obligations, and reduced or lost when obligations are turned into imposed duties. Hence, *breaking* the cash/work nexus removes obligations whereas *weakening* the nexus moves a little way towards creating obligations.

NOTES

1. See especially N. Redclift (1985).
2. For example, C. Offe (1984).
3. P. Harding & R. Jenkins (1989), p. 6.
4. B. Jordan (1982), p. 221.
5. See the discussion in chapter 1 about Ray Pahl's work.
6. J. Godschalk & J. Mevissen (1989).
7. R. Mahon (1987), p 6; B. Hindess (1990), p. 32.
8. Australia. Social Security Review (1987), p. 55.
9. R. Sweet (1980).
10. P. Stricker & P. Sheehan (1981), p. 48.
11. M. Sawer (1982), pp. 1–19.
12. See, for example, A. Harding (1985) on the Fraser government's alternating 'hardline' and 'softline' responses to unemployment.
13. B. Head (1982), p. 114; S. Macintyre (1984), pp. 91–3.
14. K. Alford (1979). Overall the unemployment rate increased from 1.4 to 8 per cent between 1970 and 1986, reaching 9.9 per cent in 1983. Australia. Social Security Review (1987), p. 54.
15. An increase in segmentation by sex is shown in T. Karmel & M. MacLachlan (1988); also J. Schofield (1990), pp. 20–6. On the exclusion of old and young, see Australia. Social Security Review (1987), pp. 13–33.
16. *ibid.*; J. Jenson *et al* (1988).
17. J. Schofield (1990), pp. 14–15.
18. Australia. Department of Employment, Education and Training, Women's Bureau (1989).
19. M. Bittman (1991); (1990); L. Peattie & M. Rein (1983).
20. J. Freeland (1987), p. 8.
21. Australia, Department of Employment, Education and Training, Women's Bureau (1991), p. 12.
22. F. Maas & P. McDonald (1989), p. 36.
23. R. Sharp & R. Broomhill (1988), p. xii.
24. P. Saunders (1990). In 1979, 37% of the retail industry comprised casual labour, 19% part-time and 44% full-time; in 1988, 59% was casual, 13% part-time and 27% full-time. H. Glezer (1988), p. 34.
25. The number of Australians in poverty has risen from 8 to 13 per cent between 1972–3 and 1981–2, and of children in poverty from 8 to 19 per cent; R. Sharp & R. Broomhill (1988), p. xi.

26. This is in comparison to that found by Henderson's poverty research for the 1960s; R.F. Henderson (1971). See also J. Schofield (1990), pp. 34–68. B. Bradbury *et al* (1988), show a rising number of employed in poverty since the Henderson Poverty Inquiry, especially self-employed and part-time workers.

27. A. Yeatman (1990), pp. 101–18; K. McDonald (1988).

28. H. Stretton (1987), pp. 7–11.

29. Max Walsh, 'The great carve-up of Australia's economic cake', *Sydney Morning Herald* 10.8.87.

30. Z. Bauman (1982), pp. 136–40.

31. *National Times* 20.6.86.

32. M.T. Lewis (1975), p. 17.

33. J. Trethewey & O. Burston (1988), p. 5.

34. R. Watts (1987), pp. 119–24.

35. Australia. Social Security Review (1987); A. Farrar (1986), p. 12.

36. Ralph Willis, Minister for Employment and Industrial Relations, claimed this in June, 1986, avoiding the rates of part-time job creation. See J. Wajcman & S. Rosewarne (1986), p. 15. The largest rise in jobs between 1983 and 1986 was in government and wholesale and retail; Peter Freeman, 'Economic slump', *Sydney Morning Herald* 18.8.86, p. 26. Opposition spokespeople claimed that the number of people unemployed for more than two years had gone up by 33% during the first Hawke government: Charles Blunt, 'The Task is to Restore Incentive', *Sydney Morning Herald* 12.6.86.

37. The two-tier wage system was introduced at the end of 1986. See R. Sharp & R. Broomhill (1988), pp. 72–5.

38. See, typically, Des Keegan, *The Australian* 12.8.86 and *Sydney Morning Herald* 8.7.86. Channel 9's '60 Minutes' followed this theme heavily too, staging a debate at Rooty Hill, Sydney in September 1986.

39. Principles, Community Volunteer Programme, obtained from Department of Employment and Industrial Relations, August, 1986; personal interview, A. van Leest, DEIR, 19.8.86.

40. V. Sheen (1987), p. 8.

41. *ibid.*, p. 13; Petition Package by Rozelle Community Youth Support Scheme, 1986.

42. John Halfpenny, Victorian Secretary of the AMWU, *Sydney Morning Herald* 21.7.86; Bob Debus, NSW Minister for Employment *Telegraph* 16.6.86.

43. Union investment was to be through superannuation funds. Kate Legge, 'ACTU wants to end youth dole', *Times on Sunday* 12.10.86. The idea of modernising the workforce along Swedish lines, which was so stressed in the ACTU/TDC's *Australia Reconstructed*, forgot that while Sweden totally excludes people under 20 from the workforce, it also has a commitment to full employment for all adults, and proper training schemes with real jobs at the end of them. Australia. Department of Trade (1987).

44. Milton Cockburn, 'Dole work remains a matter of choice', *Sydney Morning Herald* 3.3.87.
45. A. Farrar (1987), pp. 27–8.
46. Ross Dunn, 'Youngsters back plan to work for the dole', *Sydney Morning Herald* 7.3.87.
47. J. Trethewey & O. Burston (1988), pp. 2–5.
48. B. Cass & A. McClelland (1989), p. 20; Fred Gruen, 'Poor Australia', *The Independent Monthly*, February, 1990.
49. J. Freeland (1987), p. 9.
50. Fred Gruen, 'Poor Australia', *The Independent Monthly*, February 1990.
51. *Australia Reconstructed* (Australia. Department of Trade/ACTU, 1987) makes few references, for example, to job creation in women's traditional work areas.
52. For example, J. Mathews (1986); (1988); compared with D. Altman (1988), and, from the Rainbow Alliance, Camilleri, J., P. Christoff *et al* (1989).
53. The chief opponent cited was Bill Jordan: e.g. B. Cass & A. McClelland (1989); and Australia. Social Security Review (1988).
54. Paola Totaro, 'Business to fund half of new TAFE', *Sydney Morning Herald* 9.6.90; Paola Totaro, 'TAFE enrolment facing 'collapse', *Sydney Morning Herald* 10.2.90, and TAFE National Centre for Research and Development (1990).
55. Alan Ramsay, 'Elliott brings fight to street level', *Sydney Morning Herald*, 21.10.89.
56. Milton Cockburn, 'Labor plans crackdown on dole', *Sydney Morning Herald*, 21.2.90.
57. Brian Howe, Social Security Changes – 13 May 1987, News Release, Minister for Social Security, BLH 35/87.
58. This was even the case when the rate went down to 6.0% in 1989. See the ABS figures in the Social Security Review, Occupation Unemployed', and DEET, Women's Bureau, *Women at Work*, issues of 1987, 1988, 1989, 1990.
59. In the late 1980s, the Liberal Party machine turned out propaganda with male breadwinners and female dependants behind picket fences and television dramas about women being forced to work and *therefore* unable to have babies: 'It's not right', according to the voice-over.
60. V. Sheen & J. Trethewey (1991), p. 30.
61. Child maintenance collection via taxing the non-custodial parent, and wage rises through superannuation, further individualise and privatise societal responsibilities.
62. B. Jordan (1989), p. 105.
63. A. Jamrozik, M. Hoey & M. Leeds (1983).
64. For an extended elaboration, see J. Pixley (1992).
65. T.H. Marshall (1965), p. 129.
66. *ibid.*, p. 78.
67. J.M. Barbalet (1988), p. 9.

68. T.H. Marshall (1965), p. 87.
69. K. Polanyi, (1957), p. 224.
70. The removal of citizenship was effected by the Poor Law Amendment of 1834: T.H. Marshall (1965), pp. 88–9.
71. *ibid.*, p. 122.
72. In Australia the backlash came before very much welfare or social citizenship was instituted.
73. For example, M. Roche (1987), p. 369.
74. *ibid.*, p. 381.
75. N. Fraser (1987a).
76. C. Pateman (1988), pp. 238–9.
77. *ibid.*, p. 235. Pateman is here citing Hegel.
78. *ibid.*, p. 256.
79. A. Yeatman (1990), pp. 141–3.
80. This issue is well covered in C. Smart (1989).
81. C. Pateman (1979).
82. *ibid.*, p. 165.
83. *ibid.*, pp. 169–70.
84. Pateman's aim is to shows how, in principle, a theory of participatory democracy has no need of the liberals' social contract myth.
85. C. Pateman (1979), p. 29.
86. *ibid.*, pp. 171–2.
87. C. Smart (1989), pp. 153–9, discusses the example of fathers claiming rights to custody of their children, and contrasts it with the fairer, more realistic but also gender-neutral criterion of primary caregiver for child custody cases. In that case, it is less a matter of rights than of the person who has freely chosen the obligation. See also J. Elster (1988). He suggests that the right to free speech does not imply a duty to talk, even though public debate might wither unless it is exercised by some. The duty to vote is a case in point in Australia: enforcement does not enhance the electoral process, for political parties do not have to persuade the electorate to actually want to vote, and the 'donkey vote' can be more easily dismissed by parties, as the term suggests.
88. See G. Markus (1982), for this distinction.
89. This phrase was a Freudian slip of the Shadow Treasurer of Australia, Peter Reith in regard to 'Fightback!'. *Sydney Morning Herald* 29.8.91.
90. J.M. Barbalet (1988), p. 109. Barbalet's argument concerns only rights.

CHAPTER 8

The Politics of Full Employment
Versus the Separation of Income and Work

In a small number of OECD countries relatively healthy rates of employment have been maintained fairly consistently through the 1970s and 1980s. Sweden is not the sole, shining example; Austria, Norway, and Japan are also notable employment societies. The reasons for this vary considerably, as do the causes of chronic unemployment in other countries.[1] In Australia's case, growing mass unemployment was shaped by a cluster of factors and policies, including the post-industrial experience. The historical landmarks already identified created a climate where high unemployment rates became more and more acceptable. As a return to *market solutions* gathered apace, the guaranteed income debates and commune and co-operative movements, although in some respects grass roots attempts to seek emancipation and control over everyday life, were fatally constrained and compromised by government interest. The state was interested only in controlling the marginalised populations and in using the alternative ideas for fiscal and legitimation problems. Moreover, governments were not unchanged after these dialogues and experiments, emerging as they did with various institutional structures that were less accountable and more authoritarian towards those sections of the population which had, during the 1960s, demanded inclusion.

My argument has been that the state's redefinition of work, obligation and unemployment benefits was facilitated in the Australian case by a specific use of the radical proposals. This remains the major problem with all the alternatives to wage labour. There is, however, another side to the issue, one which the next two chapters will address. The post-industrial position is that the separation of income from work is not only desirable but also permanent. This is critically analysed by questioning the notion that unemployment is irreversible and by arguing against the idea that unemployment

231

could have a transformative potential. It is both questionable theoretically and mistaken as a social strategy, as it neglects the social consequences of dualising any society which, above all, has affected the groups already excluded from or disadvantaged within the social division of labour.

These are slightly different arguments to the previous ones. On the one hand, as already discussed, the post-industrial thesis is that alternatives to wage labour constitute a progressive challenge to the employment system that would be desirable and possible. The evidence presented has shown that these predictions are neither desirable nor progressive because the implementation of various parts of the schemes is all too possible. No existing government considers a challenge to the prevailing political-social system to be an acceptable aim. But governments can certainly implement post-industrial ideas in accordance with state interests, as has, of course, already been the case.

On the other hand, post-industrialists suggest that full employment is not desirable, and is anyway impossible. The previous chapter suggested that opportunities for employment are an essential component of citizenship; in addition, it is necessary to investigate whether full employment is desirable for any other reason: the topic of the final chapter. This chapter will consider whether full employment is impossible, or if it is more feasible than a guaranteed income.

THE DEBATE ABOUT CHRONIC UNEMPLOYMENT

Although there are the exceptions, this period has seen sporadic demands for the creation of jobs unable to counteract an increasing pessimism about any *return* to full employment in most OECD countries. Among the numerous explanations of the employment crisis, those who actually *promote* the separation of income and work are often as convincing as any about the causes of the crisis. The way their analyses conclude with this remedy as a desirable development is the problem I will concentrate on here.

Since the 1970s the number of positions emerging about the future of work have appeared to be more constrained than the variations in actual employment trends. While it is clear that manufacturing employment has declined, Gøsta Esping-Andersen, for example, points to three different 'post-industrial' trajectories, produced by differences in the 'packages' or clusters of state welfare and labour market policies of various OECD countries. Although these models do not account for more specific variations (Australia's wage-earner welfare fits none too well), he identifies a 'Swedish' model of near-full employment, with men working mainly in the private sector and a high participation rate of women, mainly in welfare services. The model represented by the United States has witnessed an expansion of both business services ('good jobs') and 'fun' services (mostly 'junk jobs'). In what was West Germany, women's workforce participation is lower than elsewhere, and there has been little post-industrial development, partly because wage policies prevent 'junk job' development.[2]

Walter Korpi and Göran Therborn identify other profiles of high employment countries that include the Finnish and Swiss experiences and the Japanese 'model' on different grounds to those explaining full employment in Austria, or Sweden and Norway. These countries' institutional constraints and relative power balances all vary, and their policies (especially those of Switzerland) are therefore not easily transferable nor always desirable. Nevertheless this comparative work on the actual divergence of rates in OECD countries indicates that mass unemployment is not a 'fatality' about which we can do nothing.[3] The question of improving the situation is very difficult, and one that cannot be properly dealt with here. It is not, however, *the impossible task* that pessimists from both right and left assume.

Bearing this in mind, let us look more closely at the positions taken by post-industrialists on the one hand, and several proponents of full employment on the other. It is my contention that where debate has appeared to be polarised between those in favour of and those against full employment, there are more like four different positions, two of which are less concerned with the fate of marginal-ised populations. None is related to a fifth position which in many countries has been the prevailing right wing orthodoxy for the past twenty years. The revival of classic economic liberalism actively promotes the lash of unemployment as *the* way to drive down wages and inflation, and to enhance profits. According to the fifth position, labour markets will clear when union defences or 'wage rigidities' are broken and populations have little option but to work for poverty wages. (Monetarist concepts like a 'natural rate of unemployment' assume that all unemployment is voluntary.) The United States' trajectory is taken as exemplifying this position, although the ill-informed often identify Taiwan or Singapore as examples of low-wage countries, where in reality state decommodification, control of prices and provision of infrastructure are more extensive than in many liberal democracies (and some wages are higher).

Returning to the four different positions on employment, the first full employment position objects the most strongly to the systematic attack against union defences across many OECD countries. The labour movement traditionally supports full employment as its source of bargaining strength in what is then a sellers' labour market. Involved in this position are, however, the 'loyalists' who not only cling to the old ideal of full employment but also expect these jobs to be created mainly in the 'productive' sector on a forty-hour week.[4] Moreover, it presupposes that the industrial sector generates jobs, but that it is not generating enough jobs because the business cycle is in a downturn. As we saw, the ACTU in Australia has favoured reviving productive industries by using a post-Keynesian strategy of corporatist management, with wage restraints in a newly segmented centralised wage-fixing structure (the Accord). Investment enticements and other macro-profit-led employment policies along with microeconomic reforms, are regarded as a way for Australia to develop a post-Fordist industrial sector of multiskilled jobs. It regards the low-paid service sector with alarm, pointing to antiunion practices in fast-food chains like McDonald's. However it has done little to engage with workers in these services, it has supported removing teenagers from the labour market and it has shown little concern for those already excluded or enthusiasm for changing work-practices so that men might share in caring for children or doing housework. Men predominate in union leadership and theirs is a nostalgic vision of full male employment with upgraded skills in a 'clean' but still industrial environment. This could be called a 'strong' approach to full employment.

The 'strong' post-industrial position against full employment gradually lost adherents (except within governments) as the unemployment plague spread. It developed from the technological determinism of the original post-industrialists who asserted that industrial decline was due to a system change. Another influence here was the counter culture's partiality for the 'why work?' theme. When the recession began, this position tended to welcome the permanency of unemployment on the rather simplistic grounds that huge societal wealth would permit a satisfying exit from a wage-labour system that merely disciplined workers. On the one hand, it accepted Harry Braverman's argument (against the optimism of Daniel Bell) that the majority of 'post-industrial' jobs evolving in the service sector were low paid, often insecure and menial, and therefore considered unemployment to be preferable. On the other hand, it was now argued that these jobs, meaningful or not, did not substitute for the number of positions lost in the process of so-called 'deindustrialisation', automation and so forth. Accepting this 'new reality' as excluding any possibility to reverse these trends, a change of theoretical and political perspectives was urged. (The early work by Fred Block and Barry Jones is fairly representative.) The assumption was that unequal power relations could be *solved* by escape from wage labour and that industrial growth only brought ecological destruction. A new utopia could be inaugurated through increased leisure and different ways of living and working in alternatives like communes and co-operatives.

This strong or 'dry' post-industrial version (like its strong full employment counterpart) has never considered the problem of transition for the marginalised groups.[5] The Hawke government, while using the lash of unemployment more consistently, also displayed a tendency to pursue *both* strong policies simultaneously. This resulted in a contradiction between its attempts to solve unemployment by returning to the ACTU's full employment policies, or to solve it by predicting that the full employment era was over and by devising radical new policies more attuned to this post-industrial trend. Either way, those in marginalised positions were further excluded.

There are, however, two moderate or 'wet' versions of both the full employment and the post-industrial positions which have been, above all, concerned to improve the situation of marginalised groups, and in a less grandiose way than either of the strong counterparts (see figure 2, page 236). During the 1980s it was unfashionable to defend any Keynesian alternative, thus depriving the employment position of some important policy tools. Both accept, however, the 'reality' of the decline in the industrial sector, but the 'wet' full employment position emphasises micro-policies for *specific* job creation at the local level, on the grounds that this is less expensive and more effective in improving and conserving the employment situation of marginal groups than the labour movement's grandiose schemes. By contrast the 'wet' post-industrial position urges that a guaranteed or basic income is the answer to protecting the excluded.

Figure 2 The contemporary employment debate

For Full Employment		Against Full Employment	
'Traditionalists'	'Realists'	'Realists'	'Post-Industrialists'
Full employment dogma.	Agree with 'realities'.	Stress social reasons for unemployment.	Stress technical and economic reasons that unemployment here to stay.
◦ Since jobs are demanded, full employment must be supported.	◦ Stress the efforts to conserve and to improve the situation of the already under-privileged groups.	◦ Much more sympathetic than the post-industrialists to labour movement and the excluded, and about the meaning of 'work'.	◦ Argue that work merely disciplined workers, so it is desirable to abandon and undermine wage labour.
◦ Traditional dogma looks for jobs mainly in the 'productive' private sector.	◦ Maintenance of the marginalised groups via a 'progressive' full employment, with emphasis on service jobs.	◦ Jobs in the service sector are even more exploitative than in manufacturing.	◦ Huge societal wealth which can easily be shared equitably.
◦ Only requires 'political will'.	◦ Not alternatives to wage labour.	◦ Search for a structure of alternatives for those already excluded.	◦ Neglect existing marginal groups.
◦ The usual demand is for a paid 40-hour week.	◦ Not full employment dogma, but ideological shift to a 'right to a job'.	◦ Against the 'Politics of Full Employment'.	
◦ Neglect existing marginal groups.			

Both 'Realists' agree the Full Employment 'dogma' is:
◦ inflationary
◦ corporatist
◦ sexist
◦ ecologically damaging
◦ governments cannot deliver
◦ further dualising the society.

Both 'Realists' agree to:
◦ reduction in work hours
◦ paying for parental child care from welfare
   cash transfers (and so forth).

These are the two positions with which this chapter will deal. The moderate post-industrial group's preference is to reorient the debates towards alternatives to employment rather than to maintain the illusions of the full employment position which they consider neither possible nor desirable. At the same time, these theorists oppose the simplistic post-industrial assumptions about leisure and wealth for all. Being sympathetic to the unemployed and to the labour movement in general, this group's perception of the powerless situation of those already excluded from work prompts their stress on political restructuring to provide the alternatives to gainful employment.

Equally they disagree with macro-Keynesian policies and union plans for job creating industry policies. These are criticised for being inflationary or corporatist and statist, as well as environmentally unsound and exclusive to white males. Left wing post-industrialists argue that under the changed social and economic conditions, governments are unable to satisfy expectations for job creation, and to maintain them means only the further marginalisation of certain groups and the dualisation of the society as a whole. Maintaining the illusion for a return to full employment, they argue, only postpones the search for alternatives which both are realistic and could prevent further deprivations for the groups excluded from the labour market. Broadly speaking, their arguments are based on two basic assumptions. First, the circumstances on which full employment policies could be based are unrealistic and economically unsound, and contradict basic developmental trends. Second, either leisure and some employment or alternative work is said to be more liberatory than just employment, as long as incomes are guaranteed. That is, the crisis of 'employment society' is regarded as having a progressive potential to undermine wage labour, if not industrial society as such.

During the 1980s, another set of 'realists' entered this debate on the pros and cons of full employment.[6] Closer to post-industrial 'realists' than to the full employment dogma, as figure 2 (p. 236) shows, they nevertheless support full employment. The argument is that even if the employment situation is poor, job creation efforts must be made to conserve and improve the position of already underprivileged and marginalised groups.

According to this stance, it is the maintenance and restructuring of paid work, not alternatives to it, which is essential. While proper

support for part-time work and leave from work with cash transfers
for the caring of children, for example, are as necessary in this vision
as for the post-industrial 'realists', it would occur within a
restructuring of employment rather than either abandoning a right
to work *or* simply continuing with the current macro-policies to
stimulate growth that still marginalise parts of the population,
especially women. Writers in the United States (Juliet Schor) and
Britain (Michael Rustin), for example, have argued that the provision
of 'proper jobs' for all who wish to work is a fundamental and
necessary aim. They also suggest that this is strategically possible,
as long as it is tackled in different ways to the more dogmatic
full employment responses of the last fifteen years. Instead of
stressing only the societal obligation to provide jobs to all, these
authors also make an effort to clarify the other side of the obligation
as well, of the members of the society to each other. Rustin and
Schor argue, in effect, that even though the normative disapproval
of living off the work of others is both widely held *and* unfairly
applied to the unemployed today, it could be reshaped in terms of
justice into a demand for jobs. This political strategy would hence
involve an ideological reorientation towards the employment
question. If governments were required to provide proper jobs for
all adults who were able and willing, notions of 'fairness' could be
appropriately applied.

This argument for the opportunity to work opposes the post-
industrial thesis that full employment is neither attainable nor
desirable. It makes several quite substantial contributions to two
issues which are central within this chapter, namely the thesis of
irreversible job losses and the political and economic efficacy of
implementing job creation, as compared with what seems to me
are serious problems for implementing a guaranteed income.
Nevertheless it is difficult to deny that a 'right' to work proposal
entails a potential for more compulsion, which I alluded to in
discussing the distinction between duty and obligation. If a 'politics
of full employment' cannot defend the rights of the unemployed
more *inclusively*, it runs an obvious risk of giving ideological
support to the 'bludging' charges laid against those who are
excluded from the workforce. Without the explicit and emphasised
right to unemployment benefits at the least, it is easy to imagine
new forms of state surveillance emerging. Indeed, a freely assumed
obligation is quite different from a 'right' to work, which could be

rapidly transformed into a compulsory duty.[7] Both the opportunity to work and the right to withdraw to unemployment benefits are inseparable.

THE ECONOMICS AND POLITICS OF FULL EMPLOYMENT

The selection of literature dealt with here, on the 'potential freedom for employment' versus the 'alternatives and guarantees within unemployment' debate, by no means pretends to be comprehensive. Various arguments of Claus Offe, John Keane, Andre Gorz, and Bill Jordan will be compared with those of Rustin, Schor and others.[8] No author takes quite the same position, but both positions refer to social reality and both reject, as a matter of principle, all right wing monetarist and economic liberal policies. Both tend to agree that Keynesian fiscal policies on their own are unable to restore full employment, although among full employment proponents, a resurgence of Keynesian-based proposals has emerged in the 1990s. The main areas of dispute in this debate lie elsewhere. They are, first, over *the efficacy and political consequences* of a guaranteed income system compared with post-Keynesian schemes aiming for full employment (with controls over supply as well as demand, following Kalecki, Robinson, and so forth), that would be combined with direct job creation policies. Second, there is conflict over the projections of future employment losses from technological change and from 'deindustrialisation', and also considerable dispute over the nature of the service sector. It will be maintained that while conjecture is hardly certainty, it often predetermines the arguments. The third aspect of the debate is the general problem of the physical and social limits to growth, and the fact that some post-industrialists tend to augment the employment crisis into a crisis of industrial society as such, or of the whole 'Modern Project'.[9] The more basic disagreement (which is dealt with in the last chapter) is over the desirability or otherwise of re-establishing and fully extending to women the connection between income and work performed in the formal economic sphere. Obviously these four themes are closely connected, but a close identification with one aspect is apt to limit implicitly the arguments put for or against the other issues. For example, the argument that favours breaking the cash/work nexus tends to be pessimistic even about modest job creation schemes. First, then, let us turn to some of the debates about the economic and political efficacy of various full employment schemes.

As far as Keynesian approaches are concerned, neither side has had much faith in expansionary fiscal policies, except in so far as the underlying concern is with defending and preserving the welfare state and ameliorating the problems facing the unemployed. Post-industrialists in particular argue that budgetary stimulation of demand to raise the total number of available jobs is not just insufficient but also has adverse effects. For example, reflationary fiscal policies attempt to manipulate the aggregate demand for labour so that it balances the supply of labour, mainly by increased public investment and reductions in taxation. As Offe has argued, such policies *on their own* cannot ensure that private investment will occur at all, let alone in labour intensive areas. The same could be said for monetarist and supply-side provisions of 'favourable frameworks' for investors,[10] but they, of course, cut welfare as well. Even standard Keynesian public investment, however, may enhance job losses, especially in high technology sectors.[11] More generally though, balance of payment difficulties, inflation and government borrowing are all exacerbated by budgetary reflation, and neither wage–price spirals nor capital flights can be prevented by fiscal measures – they only become more likely.

Up to this point, then, Keynesian approaches to unemployment have mainly been seen by both 'realist' positions to be deficient. It is in the subsequent arguments that paths diverge. Since Keynesian programs deal only with demand, supporters of full employment usually stress that the problems of supply must be tackled as well. For example, from Britain, Andrew Glyn argues that 'expansionary policies are doomed to failure unless trade is controlled, capital flight prevented and investment planned'.[12] Glyn's program, however, is hardly a modest one (calling as he does for nationalisation), whereas Juliet Schor suggests an incremental approach. A full employment program that considers both demand and supply conditions is, according to her,

> one that addresses basic relations of power. That is, it alters conditions of supply by instituting measures such as democracy in the work place, popular control over investment decisions, and political rather than market determination of wages, profits and prices. . . . Ultimately, . . . a progressive response to the crisis is to argue that corporate power should be curtailed. A full employment program is a step in that direction.[13]

Such policies are attacked by post-industrialists on a number of counts. The criticisms to be dealt with here are of a different order to the controversies over projected unemployment figures (especially those that question whether industrial society is really over) or over the reliance on growth, which will be discussed later. What is at issue in this instance are the methods for pursuing full employment favoured by labour movements, and the consequent pessimism of post-industrialists about the likely form that such supply and demand strategies would take. Since this would be a corporatism that has already been found wanting it is, therefore, futile to search for any political support for such a path.

For example, John Keane and John Owens[14] provide a comprehensive criticism of the British system of full male employment followed after the war. In *After Full Employment* they predict that the current British Labour Party programs would suffer much the same fate as Beveridge's version – but more seriously would be unable to deliver on employment. They catalogue the well known rise of unaccountable bureaucracy and the risk of political unpopularity from failing to meet citizens' expectations. Hopes would be much higher, in fact, with Labour's promise to extend full employment to all adults and not just white males as in the post-war commitment.[15] The promise would fail because tripartite arrangements between capital, the state and labour are too fragile to control either management investment prerogatives or trade union wage demands. For example, they rightly point out that British trade unions have historically been unwilling to use their pension fund investments; moreover, union proposals for industrial democratic rights are only envisaged for those in paid work. Other critics expand on this point arguing that, given the exclusivity of their members, corporatist arrangements have an inherent tendency to marginalise those outside paid employment.[16] Keane and Owens maintain that a further dualising of British society would occur well before the slow reductions proposed in the unemployment figures took place, although they doubt that job losses are, anyway, reversible.[17]

As we have seen, Australia's attempt at the corporatist path has indeed further marginalised the unemployed (although supply controls, over finance capital, for example, were actually lost, and employment creation policies, such as they were, were based on fostering investment). In his paper on the future of the labour market, Claus Offe takes the problem a step further by asking whether the 'strategic actors' concerned – namely capital, labour and the state – really do regard economic growth and full employment as primary objectives. Capital, he argues, gains huge advantages from unemployment and can externalise its attendant social costs. The only concerns of capital are the risk of creating permanent 'dropouts' from the labour market and the possibility of social unrest. At the same time, Offe suggests, even while full employment actually does suit the state's financial, economic and political interests, the costs for the public sector of implementing job creation oppose those same state economic and financial interests. For trade unions, full employment is their most basic interest, but Offe points to the difficulties in its implementation, while being most sympathetic to the problems involved. It is unfair to expect from an interest group the level of altruism required to bring in, as German unions attempted, a reduction in work time with attendant wage cuts: workers were expected to make sacrifices in order that those outside the union movement might be employed.[18] Bill Jordan takes this view too,[19] although a similar argument could also be made for 'taxpayers' in supporting a guaranteed income *or* job creation. Offe claims that his position on the grim future of employment is a realistic one and projects the creation of politically secured alternatives for those excluded, a point I will come to later.

By contrast, Michael Rustin's proposal for a statutory right to work aims to counteract such conclusions but does so by actually agreeing with much of the above analyses. Rustin acknowledges that politicians' cautious bidding – at election time – to reduce the jobless rate by this or that implausible figure always suffers even more attrition with the experience of government. The 'political will' called for by some full employment supporters (such as Andrew Glyn) is hardly sufficient. Hence Rustin's right to a job scheme would have to place an 'absolute obligation on governments, instead of being a contingent aim depending on trade offs with other economic objectives'.[20]

Rustin's argument about the British experience runs as follows: The post-war manipulation of aggregate demand initially created only a *de facto* right to a job, because the principles of market and economic contract remained dominant. Keynesian policies do *not* provide 'work' as an entitlement or a 'benefit'. Other legal entitlements to citizens' social rights, such as education, health and minimum subsistence, can be so claimed by individuals (up to an elusive 'point', one has to add). But *work* was provided in the interests of employers (and indirectly the tax office). This post-war system of allocating labour according to the needs of the market has now broken down. Rustin has doubts about whether Keynes' method of *saving capitalism* by achieving full employment could work again, so too about whether a governmental responsibility to provide proper jobs would seriously *threaten capitalism*. For him, the latter would at least reverse the present grim trends, exacerbated as they are by present policies and in some countries by corporatist exclusivity. Rustin suggests a 'specific and local' socialisation of the market economy – a 'limiting planned condition' of providing a job 'for each individual who chooses to work'.[21]

In an effort to counteract the pessimism that the state's interests may not be served by full employment due to costs and political unpopularity with taxpayers, Rustin urges caution. The labour market should be only minimally regulated because it is the unemployment issue, rather than socialism in general, which is likely to have popular appeal. He assumes that support would arise from arguments about citizens' rights to a job and to moral assumptions about reciprocity. Minimal regulation would also avert opposition from the labour movement, since trade unions' functions depend on the contractual labour market. But the substantial addition to workers' rights involved in this right to work could be the tradeoff, Rustin suggests, in achieving greater union co-operation with the income policies required to counteract the inflationary wage demands that full employment could bring.

As for the implementation of a statutory right to work, Rustin does not pretend to have a comprehensive economic policy but again questions the pessimism exemplified by Offe or Jordan. Since unemployment varies across regions, it would be more appropriate to give regional agencies the duty to find a job for all those out of work for more than six months in their area. His scheme assumes the continuation of existing job creation programs, especially subsidies to private firms and public sector employers. These should be more strictly controlled, however, with appropriate punitive sanctions to prevent well known distortions and manipulations by employers. Failing these, direct job creation would be funded through the agencies. The jobs would all be paid at market rates while being conditional on workers fulfilling the tasks.[22]

On the thorny issue of cost, Rustin argues that the state would act rationally when its 'expenditure in supporting employment in the market sector . . . [does] not exceed expenditures made and revenue foregone in relation to the unemployed'.[23] Direct job creation should be computed similarly to justify economically the greatest possible part of the increased expenditure.

Of course, this might amount to considerable expense (as so many governments maintain), but it is instructive to compare the post-industrial position on this question of costs. The guaranteed income idea, proposed (rather vaguely) by Offe and Keane among others, involves greater state expenditure unless it is set at (or later reduced to) an unacceptably low level (as favoured by right wing proponents). More recently, Bill Jordan has written extensively on the same 'basic income' idea. He prefers it on the grounds that employment creation is difficult to justify in terms of competitive self-interest unless it contributes to economic growth and efficiency, while in terms of 'fairness' it expects 'too much' of workers and is not feasible.[24] Yet he accepts that a basic income should be set at two levels (one much lower), because the '*pure* basic income principle' could not prevent poverty among all groups *even if* the tax rate (in Britain) were set at 86 per cent! Hence, instead of the same level for all, a more 'just' scheme would need to reflect different needs by specifying that certain categories (such as the elderly or the disabled), received a first tier or better 'basic income'.[25] But if a basic income has two tiers, the notion of a stigma-free citizen entitlement is already lost. As for relative costs, to fund a similar two-tier scheme in Australia, it has been estimated that the current top marginal tax rate (at least) would have to be applied to those at the *bottom* income level. If income support became an automatic right of citizenship, even a two-tier system would be 'a radical and costly departure from the existing income support system', that would certainly tax the wealthy more than now (an attractive thought), but also involve higher taxes for those on below average incomes. Since Jordan's costing rules out the lower tier being high enough to provide a subsistence standard of living, there would be no 'disincentive effect' (except, he suggests, for married women). Peter Saunders suggests that equity and adequacy tend to take second place to simplicity in these schemes.[26]

Jordan's assumptions about the possible effects of a basic income are similar to those discussed in chapter 4. Most are market-based predictions about the greater 'flexibility' employers would gain by employing those on the lower-tier basic income. This is to agree with the classic argument that the labour market does not clear because wages are too high and the unemployed are not *trying* to undercut existing wages. Bowles and Boyer show, on the contrary, by combining Keynesian aggregate demand and Marxian labour process approaches to 'employment regimes', that the wage may be too high or *too low* for profitability, accumulation and employment. Evidence of involuntary unemployment is provided by studying the hiring policies and labour discipline of individual enterprises. Given existing work conditions, and even with atomistic competition and flexible prices and wages, employers are not likely to believe that those offering to work for less would actually work as hard.[27] So what employers would do with basic income recipients might be a variation on that or, worse, they might simply use them opportunistically. Jordan himself admits that the potential for 'reintegrating' the 'oppressed underclass' arises only by providing this 'limited' incentive for economic participation (but here 'limited' really means that second tier recipients would be desperate to get any casual, substandard work, or to qualify for the more favoured categorical tier), and he makes highly contentious claims about likely improvements to gender relations in the household.[28] Even Andre Gorz, who favours 'some' employment and leisure, has recently argued that a 'guaranteed minimum functions as the wages of marginality and social exclusion'.[29]

To sum up the debate over the politics of full employment so far, both sets of 'realists' find it unlikely that full employment could be achieved *merely* by macro-economic policies to stimulate growth (though employment proponents do not dismiss these out of hand). Jordan argues that even when the British economy was growing at the fastest rate for a century (in 1988), and manufacturing output was at 5.5 per cent, manufacturing employment was still declining and service growth was slow, with the jobs therein 'characteristically' part-time and low-paid. The other side also agrees that certainly in comparison with regional job creation efforts, macro-policies to foster growth by tempting investors, such as tax reductions, are very expensive, in addition to being frequently counter-productive, if not futile, when tax concessions are used for mere speculation.[30] The relevance of growth in itself is anyway not clearcut. Comparative research shows that the relation between unemployment and GDP growth is virtually insignificant: countries with low unemployment have had widely differing rates of growth. And growth in industrial output is not a sufficient condition for maintaining industrial jobs. Employment creation and protection policies, as well as avoidance of wholesale redundancies, are also important.[31] Britain notably lacked a commitment to employment, even when oil revenue eased its international constraints.

Moderate proponents of full employment do not rely on predictions based on analyses about where future job growth might be located under existing market conditions – with or without policies like tax reductions. The position is, for instance, at odds with Jordan, who sees market trends in the OECD only as tending towards low-paid service jobs, or maintaining a 'unified' labour market with a small workforce by accepting high unemployment with generous benefits. There has been greater divergence than this, and in any case the modest full employment side asserts that state intervention is essential to *change* the specific market conditions. It is justified economically by discounting the cost to governments of unemployment benefits and expenditure in controlling (and punishing) the unemployed, as well as state tax revenue losses, when adding up the costs of job subsidies.

On the latter issue, it is instructive to compare Sweden's expenditure mix. A low percentage of state revenue is spent on unemployment benefits or 'passive support' while the equivalent to the percentage that Denmark spends on unemployment benefits is spent on public works, subsidised jobs and retraining, or 'active support'.[32] Sweden has an unemployment rate of 3 per cent. There is little research in the mass unemployment countries on the comparative overall costs of maintaining the unemployed as opposed to creating localised jobs. But in Australia, using 1987 jobless figures, the total direct cost to the federal government (alone) of dole payments and tax revenue foregone was estimated at between $5 and $6 billion. If a tenth of those then unemployed had found jobs, budget outcomes would have improved by $600 million.[33] In a defence of Keynesian public spending and the multiplier effect, calculations for 1992 have been made on the effects of an initial Australian government outlay of $1 billion in generating nearly 120 000 jobs for one year. On the minimum adult unskilled wage rate, 103 446 jobs would be directly generated, perhaps for urgent council works, and the remaining 16 125 would be induced through the multiplier process in the private sector. After one year, the net outlay would be reduced by $370 million, from increased tax revenue and reduced outlay on unemployment benefits. This modest measure would not *cure* unemployment, but the cost to the Budget of doing nothing is estimated as twice as high as the job creation these economists propose.[34]

Post-industrial arguments, therefore, tend to neglect the potential viability of a requirement on governments to create and conserve jobs. They concentrate on how macro-policies are too expensive, given budget deficits. Keynesians dispute this and, in making a distinction between 'profit-led policies' and 'wage-led policies', political economy approaches draw attention to a diversity of Keynesian 'macro' tools. Depending on the conditions, high wages may cause a profit squeeze, but in today's climate, and given that wages are *also* a source of demand, profitability (and hence 'business confidence') may actually flow from wage-led policies.[35] The post-industrial pessimism about the effectiveness of any employment policy, moreover, has for some time been rebutted by the 'star performers', even if the models involve too many historically and socially specific components to be simply 'taken over' by other countries.

There are, indeed, widely varying grounds for optimism where job creation is concerned which cannot be discussed here. For instance, any attempt to predict the likely developments from the Economic Community (EC) is complicated further by the collapse of the Soviet system. The Australian labour market is much more regulated than Britain's, although that could change for Britain since its entry to the EC. Rustin's concern to persuade the labour movement to accept labour market regulation, in order to stem inflationary pressures from tight labour markets, is less applicable in Australia. The Accord has stringently held down real wages (though not salaries) for the past eight years, even when there was no government commitment to full employment. Arbitration, however, still sets wages based on need, not profit alone. It is not the further socialisation of the labour market which is threatening Australian trade unions, but its deregulation.

In some countries the more modest proposals may at least be a start. The more Keynesian-oriented proposals reject, for example, job subsidies, for that assumes that unemployment is due to excessive real wages, rather than a lack of demand in the economy.[36] Rustin suggests that proper job creation is part of a medium-range socialist economic policy. He defends it for taking an ideological initiative when there are few political programs committed to universal employment:

> It seeks to pre-empt hostile denigration of the poor and workless by proposing that the state, rather than providing inadequate benefit for those able to work, instead ensures or provides properly paid work. It seeks to link the social needs for more goods and services (the reconstruction of cities, for example) to the abysmal waste and deterioration of worklessness.[37]

In view of the economic problems with the grandiose corporatist methods of achieving full employment (let alone the havoc caused by neo-classical liberal orthodoxy), a new commitment to employment – if it came – could be encouraged by some such state regulation, appropriate for the specific country.

Thus far we have considered the economics of full employment. Rustin and Schor both stress the notion of obligations as important ideological gains in a *politics* of full employment. Certainly it is more appealing than Jordan's argument that the political popularity of a basic income could be based on its greater efficiency, particularly in creating labour market flexibility.[38] And yet Rustin and Schor's emphasis on obligations has authoritarian overtones, as Keane and Block insist.[39] The notion has been used so often against the unemployed that its use on their *behalf* may well not be worth the political and social risks. The previous chapter considered the distinction between duty and obligation in order to highlight the punitive nature of dole-work and the unfounded accusations that dole recipients are choosing to live off the work of others. The opportunity to work and the right to withdraw onto unemployment benefits were considered essential preconditions of full citizenship. The question here, however, is whether the obligatory nature of work could be efficacious as a *political* strategy. The norm against bludging still has a firm hold with the unemployed as well, even when the charges are blatantly unfair. The underlying cultural value of paid work involves quite separate elements neither revealed in public opinion polls nor addressed by post-industrialists. With Rustin too, ideas of obligation are identified with duty, but a *right* to work, unlike having *opportunities* to work, is a dubious basis for enhancing citizenship. These confusions conjure up spectres of dole-work, useless make-work and harsh employment enforcement. Defenders of full employment are also accused of extolling the work ethic. Some post-industrialists suggest that the beliefs inherent in these attitudes towards work and bludging are fundamentally misguided. They also argue that the full employment position ignores women's unpaid work, although they refuse to consider whether women require paid work.

Let us take first the work ethic, which Gorz has criticised in particular. It is now an overused, vulgarized concept, given that Weber himself argued that what may well have been a religious motivation for changing the habits of the Protestant bourgeoisie lost its efficacy long ago. More to the point, Simo Aho suggests, is whether the working class ever believed it. Certainly coalminers, shearers and male workers in other heavy industries last century espoused machismo values about their strength, but most workers simultaneously devised a multitude of strategies *against* their employers, such as 'go-slow', work-to-rules and demarcation lines. These were hardly examples of the work ethic. By contrast, industrial society created the normative demand to live off one's own work even if this presupposes an instrumental submission to routine and dull work. It can also be empirically verified that most modern populations have not given up this value, a point amply demonstrated in the Australian dole-work debate. Some of the unemployed themselves favoured working for their dole.[40] Gorz's claim that the unemployed are 'allergic' to paid work is, therefore, mistaken. Keane and Owens, in taking issue with Gorz on this, agree that most unemployed have a 'passion' to engage in paid work. Nevertheless, they mainly set this down to the undoubted poverty and isolation suffered when unemployed.[41]

Here, the issue of obligations and the possibility that new needs can be created through the work that people do tend to be avoided in the face of their argument that the unemployed are misguided in wanting paid work rather than proper alternatives to employment. This latter, work without pay in a dependent situation, is something women have experienced far more than men since industrialisation. Why do people want paid work?

In modern societies, to be dependent on the paid work of others can take the form either of an impersonal dependency on the state, whereby the taxes supposedly from the work of others provide bare subsistence, or of personal dependency. A full-time housewife is usually considered (especially by men) to be *living off* the paid work of a husband. She usually writes down 'household *duties*' on occupational forms. I will briefly clarify this issue in order to consider whether the independence of employment has any significant political appeal.

Housework and caring for children are two separate activities, if difficult to distinguish in practice. Men are 'free riders' or hotel guests in the household when women alone do the domestic work. This is the prevailing situation for the vast majority of Western households even now, when most women have taken paid employment.[42] Whether women only do unpaid work or both, they can rarely choose to withdraw openly from domestic work because men still retain *de facto* rights to violence, and male control over domestic finance is maintained in inverse proportion to women's wages. While a proportion of men may not *choose* to exercise these extreme rights, a vicious circle still operates that can only be broken by men collectively relinquishing their power. As long as men, and likewise society in general, refuse to take a shared responsibility for children, individual women must take casual work and thus subsidise the high pay of men. This leaves women in a position of economic dependence. While women cannot approach the men's income contribution to the household, their claims for equal sharing of domestic tasks are usually rejected by men, and their choice of leaving a male partner is financially difficult. Where a couple is unemployed (a frequent situation with long-term unemployment), there is no evidence that men share household tasks, as post-industrialists assume, but rather the opposite.[43]

The rearing of children is certainly socially useful *work*, but in modern societies this involves sacrifice, isolation and low status. Women cannot change this powerlessness from a position of economic dependence: the possessive individual shifts for himself and the grownup children must do the same. Household units no longer reciprocate at the individual level to the extent of pre-industrial units. How, ideally, could obligations become reciprocal between the society and those who care for the new members who will contribute to the future society? The caring for small children puts some limit on the extent that the particular caring adults can participate in modern employment but so far caring has been rewarded with lifelong female dependency and reduced opportunities for women in the labour market. To foster independence, the present feminist movement insisted (by and large) that women should have greater choices than domestic work and its freedom from an income, and instead have the opportunity to take employment. Feminists have tried to remove sex-specific tax advantages like wife rebates and to replace them with cash transfers for children and the main adult carer/s and parental leave rather than maternity leave; along with decent, easy to obtain child-care. These demands basically assert the principle that a freely assumed obligation enhances the relation between child and parent. Housework is rather different, but proper childcare and equal opportunity in employment have been starting points for women to gain independence.

A basic income would not reverse the prevailing male resistance, because women's links with children (and elderly or disabled relatives) – entrenched since industrialisation – mean that women primarily need opportunities to vacate the domestic arena instead of being tied further to it. Post-industrialists ignore the fact that women's greater workforce participation initially provided the possibilities to discover new needs, to attempt to change the gendered nature of paid work, to gain independence from men and to argue for equal sharing of housework and parenting.[44] In sum, the idea that society could recognise its obligations to the future generation *and* provide the preconditions for women to be free from either state or private dependency is an appealing ideological argument. Most women only face imposed duties under either form of dependency; having the opportunity to *choose* obligations is, for most, still our utopia.

So, if women's potential independence remains unresolved, to say the least, in the post-industrial vision, what about the prospect of obligation being recast as duty and the risk of further surveillance with a full employment policy? The only test about whether the unemployed are purposely living off others, even if it is authoritarian to require such a test, is the provision of socially necessary and appropriate work with an element of choice. This logically excludes the make-work that is implied in work-for-the-dole, since if work has been imposed simply to keep the unemployed 'busy' (like moving sand back and forth), they would still be 'living off' the socially useful work of others, much as prisoners do. (For this reason, people may well resist, so it is likely that dole-work would be impossible to enforce.) Nevertheless, even a full employment policy could produce other *social* costs, above all an increase in the authoritarianism of the state. The previous Eastern Europe and Soviet full employment policies are inapplicable, because there were no workers' rights whatever, and the organisation of all facets of social life was imposed from above.[45]

In Sweden, however, where active employment policies have extended labour force participation to women as well as men, in socially useful work, there are severely punitive aspects. The right to claim unemployment benefits may be suspended if a person quits work voluntarily or refuses to take an assigned position in another region, for example. The length of exclusion from benefits varies between five and fifty-six days, depending on the duration of the job refused. Interpretation of suspension rules is usually very harsh, so that people are often forced to accept any work offered to them. Indeed, the whole welfare system is extremely punitive for those who want, or are forced, to avoid wage labour. The disincentive effects of the social wage that Offe suggests, hardly apply in contrast to the whole system of actual work enforcement.[46] So what case could be made for a politics of full employment that did not give credence to harsh work tests?

The only possibility lies in the notion of obligation that encompasses the values of individual freedom and equality in the sense that obligations can only be *self-assumed*. This requires recognising the right to withdraw from the labour market (that is, to claim unemployment benefits). But it is only a beginning, for it is important to emphasise Pateman's distinction between horizontal obligations (to one's fellow citizens) and vertical duties (imposed from the top down). Even in a full employment context, 'free' wage labour would be still imposed in various respects: the stratification of the labour market, the unfreedom of wage labour and the inability to define what is socially necessary work remain unresolved. That is, whether employment should meet social needs, like popular demands for nursery childcare or public transport, or be *only* available in the interests of profit, is linked to this conception of *horizontal* obligations.

While it can be argued that *some* profitable enterprises have arisen from collective demands (the recycling industry?), further elaboration is necessary. Post-industrial 'realists' are so pessimistic on this score that obligation is ignored. Instead they argue on behalf of the unemployed for the removal of the stigma attached to unemployment. As a political strategy this holds out less well than employment. First, we cannot imagine machines doing *all* the work: even if it were technically possible, the necessity and desirability of a particular type of technology is anyway a social decision. There will always be some people doing society's work (and being paid for it). Second, if social life is unthinkable without mutual aid, the social pressure – the 'ought' – for all to contribute is fair from the point of view of communality and equal sharing but is nevertheless authoritarian. It is erroneously and unjustly applied as a norm when proper work and unemployment benefits are denied to so many. This is a quite different argument from saying that people need not contribute or be useful but that those excluded should be helped to feel better about this. In the more authoritarian example, Barry Jones suggests an intellectual elite might be the sole contributors to society, who would patronisingly attempt to provide 'meaningful alternatives' for the rest, or rather the 'less gifted'. Dahrendorf calls this process an inversion of the frontline of class struggle, where those who were previously forced to work for those who lived off their labour are no longer allowed to do so.[47]

By confusing notions of the work ethic with other reasons for working, therefore, post-industrialists imply that that this normative demand to live off your own work is outmoded. But this is an individualist position at odds with the social conception of human existence. The opportunity to engage in paid work is a prerequisite for everyone to fulfil this norm – the *ought* – and thus to achieve independence. Conversely, individuals cannot be free if they are coerced into work by the loss of rights (especially as was the case in Eastern Europe) or the threat of real poverty without unemployment benefits, which is virtually the case in Sweden. For an *obligation* to be freely assumed, paid work cannot be compulsory. These are the bare starting points for a democratic weakening of the contractual relations of the cash/work nexus.

Justification of 'economic' obligation (following Pateman) has to involve – at the very least – control over the choice of work individuals wish to do, and at what price and location, which is implied by full employment and the right to withdraw from the labour market. Full employment improves workers' bargaining position. Given the nature of wage labour and the stratification of the labour market, however, this hardly amounts to an obligation. Without the chance to participate *effectively* in decisions about the content of the work and of society's work – in the form of industrial and economic democracy – obligations are not freely assumed. Only if such participatory conditions existed would people be choosing to submit themselves to a fair judgement that they were 'free riders' on unemployment benefits. That is, if the nature of employment were created and decided horizontally between different social groups, there would be an opportunity to freely take on obligations in the world of work. In this way we would know the usefulness of our own work to the society, based on fairer, more democratically achieved understandings than those so prevalent today. The likelihood of creating anything like such an obligation is impossible, however, unless everyone has the opportunity to participate in economic life.

In contrast to the 'alternatives within unemployment', the above arguments could serve as ideological backings to a politics of full employment. But they are only that. Post-industrial 'realists' have argued that alternatives to paid work would facilitate far greater control and democratic participation than would wage labour. Worker co-operatives are exemplary in this respect; the possibility that a guaranteed income would permit the free assumption of obligations is, however, totally remote. Only a maximum income set above minimum wages could achieve this, and even Jordan admits that to be unthinkable. Nonetheless, post-industrialists ask where could *proper* jobs actually come from in the wake of what they perceive as a technological revolution.

THE THESIS OF IRREVERSIBLE JOB LOSSES

Post-industrialists stress that full employment is not feasible because technical changes are removing jobs that cannot be replaced elsewhere. I will not dwell on the complicated predictions about the rate and particular sectors of future job losses. It was some time ago when Giddens criticised Andre Gorz' predictions as prime examples of the 'perils of punditry'.[48]

Nevertheless, the post-industrialists' most 'realist' and telling argument – whatever the other costs – is that job creation can *only* be make-work because there are no job growth areas. 'Deindustrialisation' processes are seen by Keane and Owens as so irreversible that counteracting measures like import and exchange controls and industry policy are not just naive but display 'a lamentable nostalgia for a bygone past'.[49] Moreover, the 'microelectronic revolution', it is suggested, will probably result in the loss of as many future jobs in the service sector as those currently being lost in manufacturing.

Post-industrialists insist that the bulk of new jobs, especially in the United States, are part-time service 'junk jobs', their workers virtually incapable of unionising to enforce better conditions.[50] Barry Jones goes as far as arguing that many of the new and old service jobs would not exist if they were not cheap.[51] In terms of Europe, an opposite problem is also cited frequently: that the service sector has a limited capacity to compensate for manufacturing job losses because of its low productivity growth. A 'cost-disease' occurs because service sector labour tends to out-price itself.

The cost-disease prediction is based on the assumptions that wages in services match those in the productive manufacturing sector and, more importantly, that productivity growth can be measured in the same way as manufacturing output. Esping-Andersen suggests the case is unproven because the cost-disease model depends on a restrictive definition of productivity (two tables versus one cared-for person?) and, in contrast, because high wages depend on unions' ability to impose wage regulations (which occurs less in the United States) and governments' willingness to support good wages. Also it is impossible to look on services as an 'undifferentiated mass'. Apart from many services being pre-industrial work and others expanding with industrialisation, even so-called post-industrial services cannot be divorced from the manufacturing economy. As he says, 'we still have no coherent definition of what are services', but, in his view, even in the United States, where services have expanded significantly, there is a mixture of 'good' and 'bad' jobs.[52]

The pessimism about the lack of jobs presupposes an absolute dearth of potential job growth areas for socially useful work. On this question, post-industrialists do not seem to listen to collective demands from below: these are not imaginary job areas. They arise from numerous and existing unmet needs for public transport, childcare amenities, paid home services for the sick and old, local media outlets, the resurrection of community work, prevention of environmental degeneration, the easing of crowded school classes, nursing shortages and the collectivisation of such domestic tasks as laundries. Gorz has recently argued strenuously against the commodification of what he calls 'work-for-oneself', to counteract (rightly) the resurrection of jobs like shoe shining.[53] Yet even at the luxury, trivial end, which is often a function of cheap labour, some personal tasks depend on the technology available: a barber was a key local figure until adjustable razors were invented (what else do men do?). Of course, many but not all such proper jobs would be in the public sector *and* to the advantage of women: there is a dubious moralism against the idea of takeaway food. Moreover, much of this pessimism is flawed if state intervention in job creation is *not* taken into account. For many post-industrialists, the welfare state is represented as incapable of finding or paying for job creation (or replacing controls on capital movements), but quite able to guarantee incomes. These are obviously self-contradictory assumptions.

The moderate full employment defence demonstrates a close relation between the quality of service jobs and unemployment. Juliet Schor not only stresses the traditional advantages of full employment accruing to labour, but also questions the post-industrial analyses of the causes of unemployment. The dispute concerning the question of whether it is a case of cyclical or permanent trends is a complex one. Both 'realist' positions give little weight to the optimistic account that unemployment is mainly due to downturns in the business cycle, and both recognise international changes in capital movements.

Technological change is presented by post-industrialists as a basic cause of irreversible job losses. This has often been questioned. First, what is not always made clear is whether the *aggregate* number of jobs indubitably falls during periods of major technological change, since new skills are also created, or whether *particular* groups of workers lose jobs, skills, community ties and support, which happens with wholesale retrenchments and can be counteracted by government policies for gradual change and retraining. Schor is concerned to stress traditional left wing arguments about how technological change has always been used to control workers and alter the qualitative content of jobs.[54] Such an emphasis may well be at the expense of admitting the enormity of the long-term job losses from microelectronics, as people like Keane and Gorz contend – in any case, neither side in the 'realist' debate has any illusion about the extent of the shift from manufacturing to services.

More to the point is whether the structural shift to the service sector is to be regretted because the lower levels of this sector are made up of inherently menial jobs, as is so strenuously claimed. In counter-acting such arguments, Schor does admit that it is too much to claim that the nature of the commodity being produced is irrelevant to the social relations characterising its production. For example, union organisation may well be more difficult in some service areas.

But it is still valid to separate cause and effect. Gorz has depicted the service sector as consisting mainly of exploited 'servants'. He argues that this is really a trend towards the 'South Africanisation' of societies like the United States.[55] Schor contends, however, that these facts of low pay, insecurity and poor working conditions in 'reproduction' work are mainly the result of gender discrimination and/or minority status and not something intrinsic, as Gorz would imply. To quote Schor's remarks:

> First, the idea that manufacturing industries have 'good' jobs and services have 'bad' jobs is not in general true and obscures the origins of job structures. What is 'good' about some jobs results from workers' struggles to raise wages and improve working conditions. . . . Second, men have historically been much more successful in obtaining 'good' jobs than women on account of discrimination and probably because of higher levels of unionization among men.[56]

As she says, the destruction of organised bases of workers' power with the decline of manufacturing has weakened unions (especially in the United States), so that workers as a whole will suffer. She is as opposed to relying on industry policy (reindustrialisation) as post-industrialists. It may not be aligned with prevailing consumption patterns, and will also mainly benefit men – if it is not a case of more jobless growth. Reindustrialisation will not counteract the exploitation of new sectors and populations. Schor's point is that only full employment, rather than just protection against losses, can do anything to improve the ability of the new workers to organise to improve wages and working conditions.[57] Likewise, Esping-Andersen notes that affirmative action in the United States has led to greater participation by women and blacks across all employment sectors, although blacks and Hispanics most lack union protection and are overrepresented in 'junk jobs'.[58]

In countries like Australia, where far more workers are unionised (than in the United States), the union movement has failed to defend weaker workers. Poor conditions in the lower levels of the service sector are also connected to the character of the workforce and hence to whom is available to fill these jobs (e.g. guest workers, unskilled migrants, women with childcare difficulties) rather than the character of the jobs. For example, after a job is feminised, it often drops in status.

But these arguments are insufficient, according to the post-industrial argument. Even if the service sector could provide better working conditions through improved union activity, it is also under threat of job losses from the 'micro-electronic revolution'.[59] In the next twenty years it will be unable to compensate for the losses in the primary and secondary sectors. These long-term predictions insist, therefore, that present unemployment levels are irreversible.

Such a long-run argument begs Keynes' answer that in the long run we will all be dead. A labour market perspective on unemployment, in contrast, is less concerned with sectoral changes and more with the effects of the structure of the whole labour market. In times like these, the costs of unemployment *in whichever sector* are shunted down the hierarchy of the labour market and experienced by those least able to bear it and with the least capacity to resist, especially women and young people. The issue of discrimination here is the way the whole labour force is stratified by class, race, nationality, sex and age. The divisions are both created and reinforced by discrimination, unequal access to education and training and by professional associations, trade unions and employers' associations. What happened after unemployment took off in the 1970s was a general 'downgrading' of labour, whereby the new arrivals at the bottom levels of the employment hierarchy were pushed out. For example, in a 'service' area like education the teachers remain, but the government-employed school cleaners are dispensed with and replaced by fewer, subcontracted casual workers. But subcontracting has emerged in all sectors rather than being a phenomenenon exclusive to the service sector, as many post-industrialists imply.[60]

So the problem of whether the trends are permanent or cyclical has no simple answer. But the labour market perspective counterbalances the stress on how calamitous the shift from industry to service is. In times of high unemployment, it is the structure of the labour market, and not the divisions within the economy itself, which mainly determines which groups of people will be the most severely affected. A marginal position in the labour market during such times results not just in losing a proper job, but also in being forced to take any work whenever and wherever possible. Subcontracting and the growth of the black economy have their equivalents in the sweated trades which were banned at the end of last century.

The latter issue relates to the changes in labour force participation this century. Before that, the majority of populations in industrialised countries were outside wage labour, and domestic servants of the nineteenth century were not, strictly speaking, free wage labourers. Now women are participating more than ever before and the young and the old are the chief groups excluded from the labour force. Post-industrialists seem gravely concerned about women's employment conditions, yet do not point in the direction of improving them.

This deep pessimism is closely related to doubts about whether the labour movement could again 'move'.[61] Post-industrialists are not alone in expressing disappointment with the failures of corporatism in some countries (Australia being one) and with the exclusive practices of organised labour (vis-à-vis the unemployed). Many unions have failed to include female workers in their strategies and leadership structures. Union support for worker superannuation in Australia is a prime example of women's intermittent work history being ignored. Yet the actual principle of unionism is not one of my criticisms. There is much that a united union movement could do to improve service jobs, and improve union membership at the same time.

On this question, a recent comparison of three different 'profiles of marginalisation' in Western Europe is pertinent. This identifies not only Sweden but also Denmark as exhibiting fewer tendencies of dualisation and polarisation than (West) Germany and Britain. On the first kind of marginalisation, from the labour market, Denmark is little better than Britain, with higher rates and longer term unemployment than even Germany. The second level concerns marginalisation from average wages, and here Denmark scores the best. Because the workforce is tied to the labour market through insurance benefits or active labour market policies, the unemployed have a greater chance of keeping away from poverty or becoming social clients. A very interesting third level of marginalisation is that of union membership. The study proposes that rates of union membership are not just related to the potential for workers to engage in social and political struggles but also for counteracting marginalisation in the labour market and declining living standards. It is in Denmark and Sweden where a majority of unemployed stay in unions. This is because the unemployment insurance funds are administered by the unions, so that to become a member of a fund is the same as joining the union. Also, membership of both has expanded during the last fifteen years (unlike in Britain), because of the growth in female labour participation and higher unemployment levels among women.[62] And yet this far closer link between the unions and the unemployed is possibly one of the reasons that unemployment is a much greater concern to these societies than to those in Britain or Australia. Such an enhanced unionism which includes women, even when unemployed, not as 'clients' but as union members out of work, also has the potential to put pressure on the political parties.

In sum, the numerous post-industrial predictions about the future of employment are just that – only 'long-run' predictions. The worst may eventuate but it also might not, though the additional danger is the one of self-fulfilling prophecies. For example, without state intervention aiming for full employment, there certainly will be much greater unemployment when the excluded and desperate can be used structurally to replace even more full-time workers, as a 'contingent' army. Particular technologies and work practices are developed according to the availability of cheap or expensive labour and not vice versa. Full employment, in this respect, serves to alter the power balance where the introduction of new technology is concerned, for it removes a potential source of servile labour to twiddle new knobs. Without intervention and regulation in the labour market, moreover, it is those at the lowest levels who suffer, irrespective of whether they actually work in the primary, secondary or tertiary sectors. Unemployment rates now, for women as well as men, are still way below the catastrophic male levels of the 1930s depression, yet post-industrialists tend to see similarities in the figures.

SYSTEM CHANGE OR EMPLOYMENT CRISIS?

This pessimism about irreversible job losses from technological change is also linked by post-industrialists to predictions that more widespread societal change is taking place. The present employment crisis is a sign of the end of 'employment society', welcomed both for heralding a system change and for bringing an end to growth.[63]

I will briefly discuss a few of the well known problems with blanket criticisms of growth before turning to the possibility that these theories are confusing what is clearly a differently structured labour market with a general decline of industrial society itself. The contemporary employment crisis does not necessarily signal a complete degeneration of the labour market or an end of employment society. Hence, the search for alternatives to wage labour, in my view, only contributes to the prevalent splitting of the labour market, in which capital and organised labour face the marginalised groups and the whole society is further dualised.

Criticisms of growth are widely recognised as sound. The principle and ideology which has sustained capitalism – growth – has bred a materialism which substitutes distributive claims for democratic control and ties populations to the socio-economic ascription of wage labour. Fred Hirsch's striking argument is that growth has both physical and social limits. There are inherent conflicts today between the way individual preferences, such as a preference for driving a car, are impossible to satisfy, when the sum of all these individualistic actions results in, say, the choking of roads.[64]

Hirsch's analysis of the way the free market can oppose or inhibit free choice is very persuasive.[65] Nevertheless, several criticisms of the anti-growth argument are important to the employment debate. Anti-growth has a reverse side which is elitist, puritanical and even authoritarian. Who is to judge whose and which needs should be met? Zygmunt Bauman suggests that the ecological movements tend to forget that it is only the rich who discover that 'money does not bring happiness'. The poor and insecure find these slogans hypocritical. Proponents of 'small is beautiful' have neglected the fact that their self-respect was gained from public status and intellectual activities. If the only path to social status and personal fulfilment is through the consumer promise, the question is how growth can be equitably limited and natural resources preserved, when activities which a short time ago were only available to the elite few are now extending to the many.[66] The Hawke commune plan clearly hoped to confine the limits to growth to the people who had no choice – the unemployed young. Once again, it is a problem of who decides. A fairer strategy to reduce the importance of the consumer promise and to impose an equitable limit on growth would be based on the extension of democratic participation and the provision of public goods accessible to all citizens. The onus on placing limits can hardly be born by the individuals expelled from the existing wasteful and polluting economic system – they are not even in it to have some effect.

More recently, environmentalists have become far more aware that the environment is likely to be better controlled when workers' livelihoods are not at risk. At best, of course, a full employment policy would actually win workers' support for the anti-growth cause.[67] And workers' support in the celebrated case of the green bans in New South Wales was the basis of successfully halting destructive development. Conversely, the current battles over logging Australian rainforests are directly attributable to workers' fears for their jobs, an issue with which environmentalists have become very concerned. The timber industry has exploited the job question as much as the forests, for their opposition to environmental protection is actually based *against* employing greater numbers of workers on recycling and farming timber on cultivated plantations.

In addition, not all growth is environmentally damaging or socially counter-productive. The post-industrialists under review have tended to substitute negative signs for Bell's positive acclamation of the growth of the service sector, seeing 'junk jobs' everywhere. But with regard to natural or social limits to service sector growth, questions should be asked about whether *all* service work damages the environment or is individually achieved at the expense of community. Education, arts, public transport and childcare, to name a few, are crying out for expansion, and even Fred Block recently admitted that the growth debate is too polarised between all or nothing. Qualitative growth is quite different from mere quantitative expansion.[68]

The end to growth debate has been usually linked with the prediction that employment society is over. The crisis of employment society is assumed to be a crisis of the whole growth project rather than a crisis more specifically for the unemployed. Not only was former productive growth destructive, but the 'microelectronic revolution' is regarded as so different from past technological change that Block proposes an abrupt break has occurred, with a shift to a new social structure of accumulation. Full employment is a false necessity because the 'fantastic advances in productive technology' render old institutional arrangements and former beliefs about work obsolete. An 'historical discontinuity' means a new situation must be faced.[69]

Few people could dispute that dramatic changes have occurred over the last twenty years. But it is important to be precise about what can be said confidently about this change, because there are no definite indications that it amounts to a general social crisis. Extrapolating this from the employment crisis tends to obscure the fact that societies in which wage labour is the predominant form of labour are not necessarily losing this basic 'ordering principle', as Simo Aho calls it.[70] So far it is only clear that parts of the population have suffered a decline in living standards. Full employment has in any case never been a necessary condition of these societies that are also capitalist. Even if full employment is dismissed as utopian, it is important to see, as Aho says, that 'Rational control of nature and society can be lost without losing social order based on wage labour, and vice versa: the abolishment of wage-labour is not inevitably in contradiction with the "Positive Utopia".'[71]

In other words, this crisis certainly explains the dualisation of the population but it cannot necessarily be linked with anything else. The quite different question, however, is whether it would be possible to guarantee the social integration and reproduction of the population by converting what was the labour force into a 'leisure force' of consumers. As Aho goes on to say, such a dubious outcome would still be functional for 'labour society'.[72]

So, instead of hoping for employment society's disappearance, of which there are no indications, the more important considerations are the social problems caused by unemployment and the further concentrations of power that have developed over this period, into communication systems, for example. A far more gloomy 'post-industrialist', Alain Touraine, stresses that it is more a matter of looking to the social movements that can resist these growing forms of domination. The criticism of the original post-industrial thesis is still sound: if the new technology entails a narrower distribution of power, it is questionable whether this is a 'revolution'. It may well be no more than the general tendency that both Marx and Weber were describing long ago.[73]

In conclusion, this chapter has attempted to address a series of predictions about unemployment. A prediction, of course, is only that, but if post-industrial 'realists' attack a politics of full employment for its authoritarian corporatism, the full employment argument can counter this with the social, political and economic costs of a politics of separating income from work. Full employment would not be authoritarian if a restructuring of work recognised the rights of the unemployed. The opportunity to work has to entail appropriate work that can be refused, for the imposition of make-work disallows the possibility of contributing to society as much as does the exclusion from work. As things stand now, the unemployed are increasingly penalised. If exclusion leads to particular forms of surveillance, full employment does not inherently lead to others. The political costs of the increased state intervention required for job creation are not necessarily greater than the political costs of a guaranteed income, which also cedes further control to the state. Those who are disillusioned with socialist types of intervention neglect that feminists or environmentalists also make demands on the state: in general there is a greater need to render the state more accountable than ever before. Full employment is a step in that direction, with social and political gains, especially of solidarity, labour market strength and protection of union rights. Provided that the opportunity to work came with a right to withdraw, obligations could be more freely assumed in paid work and could actually reduce authoritarian and paternalistic state intervention.

As for the question of economic costs, a guaranteed maximum income would be far more expensive than the cost of providing proper jobs, while a minimum basic income, still very expensive, is not likely to increase the number of jobs except those 'going begging'. Post-industrialists assume job losses to be irreversible partly by denying the possibility of a growth of *proper jobs* in the service sector and partly by neglecting the fact that the unemployed comprise those at the lower levels of the labour market across all sectors. The employment crisis may well be no more than that – arguments about a system change are hardly, as yet, convincing, especially in the light of comparative evidence of widely differing employment experiences. 'Labour society' still exists, the point is rather that high levels of unemployment have been politically acceptable in many countries for some time.

The benefits of pursuing a modest full employment program seem, therefore, to far outweigh those of plans based on pretending to know the future. And support for the opportunity to participate does not arise from a naive optimism about the merits of wage labour. Greater democratic participation within the world of work seems the more appropriate position towards wage labour than to call for its abolition. And it is to this issue that I will turn. I have attempted to question one aspect of the post-industrial thesis. Many post-industrialists, however, do not rely solely on the predictions that a politics of full employment would be futile and authoritarian. They also argue that the abolition of wage labour – by separating income from work – is actually preferable, and it is this assumption that will be discussed now.

NOTES

1. Indicators, *The OECD Observer*, December 1991/January 1992; W. Korpi (1991); G. Therborn (1986); and B. Rowthorn & A. Glyn (1990).
2. G. Esping-Andersen (1990), pp. 222–6.
3. G. Therborn (1986), p. 16.
4. See, for example, P. Beilharz (1987) for an analysis of ALP and union documents.
5. Margaret Thatcher proclaimed that only the 'wets' consider the poor and powerless.
6. Figure 2 (page 236) sets out the four positions under review that are against and in favour of full employment.
7. J. Elster (1988).
8. For example: C. Offe (1984); J. Keane & J. Owens (1986); A. Gorz (1985a); F. Block (1985); M. Rustin (1985); J. Schor (1985a); B. Jordan (1989); and A. Gorz (1989).
9. S. Aho (1986).
10. C. Offe (1984), p. 82.
11. J. Keane & J. Owens (1986), p. 156.
12. A. Glyn (1985), p. 9.
13. J. Schor (1985a), p. 79.
14. Their general position is that the unemployment crisis has the potential to create a socialist vision of a new 'post-employment' society, partly along the lines proposed by Andre Gorz; J. Keane & J. Owens (1986), p. 178.
15. J. Keane & J. Owens (1986), p. 152.
16. Bauman (1982), p. 136.
17. J. Keane & J. Owens, p. 157.
18. C. Offe (1984), pp. 86–7.
19. B. Jordan (1989), p. 114.
20. M. Rustin (1985), p. 152.
21. *ibid.*, pp. 149, 152.
22. *ibid.*, pp. 157, 161.
23. *ibid.*, p. 162.
24. B. Jordan (1989), p. 109.
25. B. Jordan (1987), p. 163.
26. P. Saunders (1988), pp. 28–31.
27. S. Bowles & R. Boyer (1990), pp. 188–91; 201.
28. B. Jordan (1989), p. 121.
29. A. Gorz (1989), p. 205.
30. Contrast C. Offe (1984), p. 81, on this point with the job creation argument of K. Windschuttle (1986), and see B. Jordan (1989), pp. 112–3 and 109 on British growth rates and the futility of job creation.
31. B. Rowthorn & A. Glyn (1990), pp. 233–7.
32. S. Marklund (1986).
33. D. Dixon (1988), pp. 22–4.

34. R. Green, B. Mitchell & M. Watts, 'It's time to rethink job creation', *Sydney Morning Herald* 18.11.91; and R. Green, B. Mitchell & M. Watts (1992).
35. S.A. Marglin & A. Bhadouri (1990) p. 175.
36. R. Green, B. Mitchell & M. Watts (1992), p. 43.
37. M. Rustin (1985), p. 171.
38. B. Jordan (1989), p. 115.
39. F. Block (1985) an answer to Schor; and J. Keane and J. Owens, 'Like the poor, the jobless will always be with us', *The Guardian* 30.4.86.
40. S. Aho (1985), p. 59. The demand for work, *any* work, was repeatedly stated on the '60 Minutes' television debate, Sydney, 1986.
41. J. Keane & J. Owens (1986), p. 171.
42. M. Bittman (1991).
43. See L. Peattie & M. Rein (1983), ch. 4; and L. Morris (1990), ch. 10.
44. A. Gorz (1989), pp. 150-2, provides the ultimate in eulogising mothers while mentioning not one word about fathers.
45. F. Feher, A. Heller & G. Markus (1983), pp. 73, 96.
46. S. Marklund (1986).
47. Cited in S. Aho (1985), p. 60; see also B. Jones, (1982), pp. 198-207 in particular for his criticism of the work ethic.
48. A. Giddens (1987), ch. 12.
49. J. Kean & J. Owens (1986), p. 155.
50. R. Baiman (1986), p. 32.
51. B. Jones, (1982), pp. 202-5; 240-1.
52. G. Esping-Andersen (1990), pp. 193-5; 205.
53. A. Gorz (1989), pp. 153-60.
54. J. Schor (1985a), pp. 71-2.
55. A. Gorz (1985), pp. 104-5.
56. J. Schor (1985a), p. 75.
57. *ibid.*, p. 76.
58. G. Esping-Andersen (1990), pp. 225-6.
59. For example, R. Baiman (1986), p. 16.
60. C. Craig, J. Rubery *et al* (1985), pp. 115-20; TransNational Cooperative Workers Research (1985).
61. I am grateful to my PhD examiner, John Keane, for suggesting this issue.
62. J. Larsen (1991), pp. 38-9.
63. J. Keane & J. Owens (1986).
64. F. Hirsch (1977), p. 10.
65. C. Crouch (1983), p. 186.
66. Z. Bauman (1982), p. 178.
67. J. Schor (1985a), p. 87.
68. F. Block (1990), p. 197.
69. F. Block (1985), pp. 97-8.
70. S. Aho (1985), p. 57.
71. S. Aho (1986), p. 71.
72. S. Aho (1985), pp. 60, 72.
73. N. Birnbaum (1971), p. 397

CHAPTER 9

Participation, Work and Social Movements: The Defences against the State

A well known impression of unemployment was established in a study of Marienthal during 1930, which found that within this unemployed community, 'the few who are still politically active are those who still have work'.[1] Today some argue that this need not be an effect of unemployment, and that the lack of work in the late twentieth century could actually help in expanding people's political life. One of the main distinctions in the debate on the future of work is between the feasibility and the desirability of a full employment policy. The post-industrial claim that unemployment is irreversible was disputed in the previous chapter. We turn now to the desirability of a politics of full employment (as a trend), and suggest that the opportunity to participate is a basic condition of being a citizen. Even though the extreme form of full employment is unacceptable if it reduces rights, the opposite (libertarian) argument for the separation of income and work has greater difficulties.

The (moderate) post-industrial position forcefully denies that the aim of full employment is desirable, on the grounds that citizenship has virtually nothing to do with participation in mainstream employment. The basic conception of political life underlying this claim is as follows. First, paid work in modern societies provides little if any potential for self-formative experiences, or for formulating demands, democratising work and politicising new needs. Second, even if there were some potential for these gains, the social integration maintained through employment would never transform society: full employment is a policy for social control and integration, in order to avoid social unrest. Third, the existing, powerless situation of the unemployed must be transformed, for active politicisation is only possible through a proper separation of income from work. The desirability of the decline of 'employment societies' is, therefore, strongly qualified by attaching the normative condition of guaranteeing distributive justice.² It turns out that there are usually three conditions attached which depend on state implementation, while the result depends on an assumption about human action.

The three conditions are: that all citizens should be granted the right to a basic income; that the availability of 'freely chosen' work must be supported and enhanced by the state; and that new political arenas should be created or expanded. The assumption is that, as a result of these new state guarantees, people's vastly extended free time will be spent in political engagement, thus enlarging the public sphere and strengthening citizenship. There are considerable variations in the preferences for informal work or increased political action. Some, like Habermas, find little need to defend any sort of work, and though his theoretical turn from the production paradigm is very influential, other post-industrialists still attempt to hold that unpaid work activities are equally important.

Andre Gorz, for example, draws distinctions between the right to a job, the right to work and the right to income: it is the paid job which is mere necessity.³ Claus Offe presents a much broader conception of work than Gorz's notion of 'heteronomous' work. A mere 'uncoupling' of the cash-work nexus even with *generous* income guarantees would, according to Offe, 'fundamentally violate the human need for meaningful, useful and purposive activity'. This means that a guaranteed income scheme should not only be the new form of distribution of the means of subsistence but should *also* be the basis for providing 'the appropriate institutional and material resources' which would then enable people 'to carry out their self-chosen activities' as alternatives to wage labour in an 'informal economy'.⁴ Keane, Offe and Gorz are all aware that guaranteed income and informal economy proposals have been favoured in Europe by new right libertarians because they could further cheapen the existing marginalised sector of what would become a permanently dual workforce.⁵ Instead, Offe believes that a combination of *both* proposals, for a guaranteed income and the informal economy to form the basis of a 'politically justified and reinforced *dual economy*', would be a model diametrically opposed to that of the new right. 'The limited sphere of informal, self-organized independent labour' should be promoted and institutionally extended, he argues. This is vital because, if the unemployed have to 'invent' their own work with no support, they will face 'the hopelessness of an economy of lifeboats'.⁶ Although it all sounds very promising, further elaboration by Offe on this point, particularly on the ways that it could be practically implemented and so forth, only arrives at a gradualist solution directed to the already employed. In it we find no especial commitment to those already unemployed and marginalised. The same could be said of Block's recent work supporting a basic income.[7]

Despite the above conditions and qualifications, it is my contention that to be excluded from either the political *or* the economic sphere is to be denied the possibility for even minimal participation in both. Regardless of its emancipatory intentions, there are serious difficulties with this challenge to the chief means of social integration in modern societies. The discipline of wage labour is undoubtedly an integrative force, but accepting this fact does not rule out the importance of quite different processes. Indeed, there are social and political conflicts that may not occur otherwise if one considers wider meanings of work and politics. Equally there are positive and liberating aspects that may accrue through a politics of participation, partly based on the modern differences between leisure, housework, work and employment. So far, these distinctions have mainly been enjoyed by men. Further, if it is accepted that the transformation to capitalism involved a switch from society being served by the economy to society being subordinate to the economy (as Karl Polanyi argued)[8], it follows that modern social reality is partly created, shaped and affected by paid work. Even if this rarely provides any control or active participation in the process, its transformation cannot be achieved through being excluded. Here I will emphasise that the potential for learning experiences and for the formulation of demands from the workplace are more significant than the proposed alternatives. A more active, inclusive conception of citizenship recognises that *neither* a government *nor* a labour market can be made more accountable (or less authoritarian and discriminatory) unless there is independent participation in both arenas. This strengthens people's capacity, as full citizens, for involvement in social movements. From this it seems clear that the expectations of an enhanced politics through the greater 'free time' of being unemployed are quite unfounded. It is, therefore, important to demand full employment as an aim and a trend.

The wider meanings of work and participation must be contrasted with the problems posed by the post-industrialist view of leisure, labour and politics. First a comparison of several views of labour and leisure will be considered. Second, the distinction between housework and paid work – both forms of labour – is shown to lie in the much greater potential of employment than housework for politicisation. Third, exclusion is less likely than participation to give rise to social movements. And finally, the claim that alternative structures could provide a framework for politicising needs is disputed. In themselves, communes, guaranteed income schemes or informal and domestic work cannot render either the state or the market more accountable to the majority below.

LABOUR AND LEISURE

The historical emergence of surplus labour gave rise to a new form of leisure or play no longer intermingled with work. This leisure was enjoyed initially only by those who had been in a position to relieve themselves from paid labour. In this way the Marxian tradition distinguishes the modern form of leisure from labour, with labour having analytical primacy. In contrast to the significance of labour in Marxian theory, most post-industrialists characterise wage labour as just one human activity among others, given undue importance from 'false necessity',[9] from indoctrination into regular work habits and from the ideological hold of the work ethic.[10] Rather than call for increased leisure, however, which will only bring more manipulation from the leisure industry, most of the post-industrialists maintain that unpaid, freely-chosen *work* holds liberatory, self-formative potential.[11] Some seem to suggest that a reintegration of work and leisure is possible, though Gorz insists that all socially useful labour is heteronomous or imposed from above, and based on necessity or organic needs. For Gorz, it must therefore continue, but be drastically reduced in favour of auto-nomous, 'free-time', non-necessary activities that are somehow not leisure, nor, one might add, housework or childcare.[12]

Leaving aside, for the moment, the question of domination in both wage labour and unpaid domestic labour, the Hegelian-Marxian conception of the internal aspects of work speaks quite differently of historical needs, rather than mere necessity or organic needs. It regards all work as mediation in comparison with the immediate, *passive acceptance* of organic needs by animals. Following from this, work is not just one of many human activities which because of the necessity to satisfy organic needs is therefore unfree (à la Gorz), but a 'fundamental event' of human existence,[13] whereby people become conscious of what they 'truly' are, as historical beings. The satisfaction gained from this formative activity is through the objectivity and permanence given to consciousness outside of itself. In the independence of the object, as Hegel states, 'consciousness, qua worker, comes to see . . . its own independence' which those who direct, use and benefit from the labour of others do not experience.[14]

According to Marcuse's early formulations, work is not just any activity, but 'the doing of human beings as the mode of one's being in the world: . . . winning one's "permanence" and at the same time making the world "one's own".'[15] In this way, even some of the negative and unfree aspects of work are at least partly self-formative and have a liberating and humanising possibility.[16] Yet, as post-industrialists (among many others) have suggested about the dilemma of industrialisation, if work is this process of constructive objectification it must entail direct control of production, following the view that artisans supposedly controlled fully their work process. Creative, independent skilled work is, as we know, the very kind of work that is continually rationalised and routinised in modern workplaces, particularly with the introduction of microelectronics and robots. Cybernation provides added force to Gorz's leaning towards Marx's alternative conception of the future of work, where freedom is possible only outside socially necessary labour time (in contrast to the other Marxian view, which stresses that the realm of freedom is coexistent with that of necessity).

While in no way wanting to underestimate the processes of rationalisation and the fact that most workers lack control over the work process, it is still possible to defend the normative conception of work where historical necessity has liberatory aspects. Participation in the world of paid work is frequently devalued, partly because both Marxists and post-industrialists focus either critically or otherwise on manufacturing, which is now in decline. Both schools of thought treat service work sceptically, drawing on Harry Braverman's deskilling hypothesis, which privileges artisan trades exclusively. Braverman assumes there is something inherently wrong with the growth of services, in their destruction of 'the older forms of social, community and family co-operation'.[17] Equally well known, Habermas has been very influential in 'watering down' the concept of labour in favour of communicative interaction, an issue I will address later.

Yet, to return to Marcuse's view of objectification,[18] the relation of subject to object is not limited solely to the relation between humans and things (or nature). He argues that the process of objectification can involve any being or entity 'other than the self', thus including relations between people which in paid work means primarily the service sector. It is not to say that service work is superior (as Daniel Bell has it), but just that in Marcuse's approach to objectification the emphasis is on the 'independence of the object' (Hegel) in the relation *either* of subject-to-'thing' or of subject-to-'other person'. This does not imply an inherently instrumental and merely manipulative approach to the object, but simply objectifies any thing or person other than the self. An instrumental approach (such as one works only to make money) may ensue from the power relations in the workplace – hospital, school or restaurant as well as factory. This is a matter of the lack of control over the process or, as Braverman explains, of the separation of conception from execution as an instrumental means to discipline workers. But, in both service *and* manufacturing sectors, whether serving at a table or making a table, teaching children or writing books, there is an inherent 'lawfulness' of the task which is imposed on the worker.

The possibility for self realisation entailed in this imposition of work is exemplified in Marcuse's comparison of work with the freedom of play. It is is a quite different view from that of Gorz, where the work of necessity is imposed as to be so 'heteronomous' that it is quite separate from the 'sphere of autonomy' of free time. Instead, Marcuse speaks of how, in play, no one has to conform to and therefore learn to respect the 'actuality' of the objective world – of everything other than oneself, other human subjects included – which happens with work. Instead, 'one does entirely as one pleases with objects'. Play is to do with events of the ego, of 'self-distraction' and 'forgetting oneself'. In this sense play is not self sustaining, it cannot present a lasting and continually repeated possibility for self-fulfilment, however 'burdensome' *work* may be. Play is directed away from itself, pointing towards work, in the sense of a 'self-recovery' for work and from work.[19] What this implies is that there is actually no work, even of the most privileged, professional kind, which does not involve an onerous imposition from which leisure provides a vital respite. But in the meaning of one's life, leisure remains just that – a respite – though it does suggest that the social meaning of leisure should be expanded rather than contracted. Conversely, if it is possible through work to learn to respect the world other than the self and therefore also to respect oneself, the potential of work is far beyond mere manipulation and necessity.

The distinction, then, that Marcuse makes between the subject and the 'other', which argues for self realisation being attainable primarily through work, seems to provide a sound basis for a sociological defence of work.[20] Nevertheless, it may appear that my support for the concept 'labour' is based upon a positivistic conception of instrumental reason, especially by avoiding the issue of the subjectivity of the human 'other'. I will attempt to argue otherwise, that the overcoming of social domination through technical reason within the workplace *and* the wider society does not lie in *abandoning* the sphere of paid work. It is rather a matter of industrial democracy, accountability structures for 'other subjects' like clients and further participatory and representative democracy (to also include concerns about the relation of the society to the natural environment).

Hence the burdensome nature of even the most emancipatory, 'autonomous' form of work is one defence against Gorz's arguments about heteronomous or imposed work.[21] Equally, the argument supports leisure as an important contrast with participation in paid work. This is related to another contentious issue, namely the work ethic. Post-industrialists claim that moral attitudes to work – the work ethic as imposed duty at the sacrifice of leisure – are reversing for the better. But what do these continual attacks on the work ethic actually mean? When Weber introduced the concept, he aimed to demonstrate that money making as a calling or an ethical obligation stimulated the development of the 'self-made man', or the self-employed in small business. In his fable of the putter-out, fortunes were made but always reinvested:

> The old leisurely and comfortable attitude toward life gave way to a hard frugality in which some participated and came to the top, because they did not wish to consume but to earn, while others who wished to keep on with the old ways were forced to curtail their consumption.[22]

Weber also, however, argued that this work ethic rapidly became its opposite with the development of capitalism. He quotes Wesley's horror that religion had produced industry and frugality but also, inevitably, riches and 'pride, anger, desire of the flesh'. If there had formerly been a religious and ethical meaning to the 'pursuit of wealth', this 'spirit of religious asceticism' had long ago escaped from a materialistic capitalism that had become determining.[23] Bearing this in mind, perhaps some post-industrialists actually prefer the original meaning of the work ethic, except for its pecuniary element.

Indeed, the conception that time in paid work *prevents* the constructive enjoyment of unpaid activities results, it seems to me, in a gross neglect of the lived experience of unemployment. Protestants may have attempted to outlaw leisure and consumption but Gorz (and even Offe) is hardly less puritanical about needs, given that they follow the more problematic aspects of Fred Hirsch's anti-growth argument (discussed in the previous chapter). By contrast, as Sean Sayers argues, the Marxian tradition values leisure as well as the civilising aspects of the growth of leisure. The most inspirational aspects of Marx's view of a fulfilling life involve valuing work and leisure, production and consumption, activity and idleness – of humans rich in needs. Sayers points out that the growth of modern leisure, of all that is 'not work', was eventually extended to wage labourers through a reduction in work hours and the development of new needs and capacities (like education, travel, hobbies, sport and entertainment). These new needs were clearly interrelated with the vastly expanded consumer needs deliberately fostered by capitalism during this century. But modern leisure is not the same as the *lack of distinction* between work and leisure in pre-industrial societies. Sayers suggests, with understandable impatience, that it is 'grotesque' to think of unemployment as offering the realisation of leisure, autonomy and freedom. This is not simply because of the economic hardship involved (which, in all fairness to the post-industrialists, is at least addressed if not solved with their concept of a guaranteed income). What it does not address is, for example, the following problem put by Sayers:

> Activities like reading, gardening, knitting, watching TV or meeting friends in the pub – pleasurable and fulfilling in the context of a life of work – outside that context are not capable of providing a satisfactory filling for life. What may be enjoyable and rewarding as a hobby is insufficient as the central activity of life. For such pursuits have value primarily in contrast to work, and precisely because they are not work, but engaged in simply for the pleasure they bring.[24]

If leisure or non-necessary activities are promoted at the expense of labour, both conceptions become caricatures that do a disservice to the unemployed. Leisure is not necessarily inhibited by work, even if Weber was correct about the work *ethic* in its original form. But leisure is, I would argue, far more inhibited by the condition of worklessness.

At worst, then, the current promotion of leisure or 'non-essential' activities, even combined with a guaranteed income, is authoritarian and manipulative. But even the most sympathetic view, such as that of Gorz and especially Offe, may be coloured by educational experience. Intellectuals with a broad, humanised education are far more likely to perceive – and to experience themselves – the liberatory aspects of leisure than are those having only a narrow, technical preparation for the workforce. While the workforce is shrinking, it is even more necessary to make distinctions between the 'education for leisure' schemes imposed from above and the 'grammar school education' where one interest may become a profession or trade (music) and another a leisure pursuit (physics). Leisure classes for the unemployed are also vastly different from freely choosing to learn about a whole variety of leisure pursuits in one's free time as an adult. (*Voluntary* participation in leisure education for hobbies and amateur sports is remarkably high in Sweden, a phenomenon which has been directly related to its active full employment program during the 1980s.)[25]

Furthermore, studies show that the meaning of work to a person's life is closely related to the ability to use free time.[26] The more the job is felt to be intrinsically satisfying, the greater is the pleasure derived from free time. This means that the emphasis should not be on 'leisure', but on exploring ways to extend possibilities for self realisation and to create new needs within the world of work, and for freer choices of the sorts of work people would like to do. Following from this, instead of free time – for those with jobs – typically offering the greater 'choice' of overtime or other ways of 'making money' – a ubiquitous phenomenon in Australia as elsewhere – free time could also have the potential for its own kind of self-fulfilment.[27] But this enhanced sense of leisure would be difficult to achieve at the expense of work.

HOUSEWORK, WAGE LABOUR AND POLITICS

According to the above 'internal' aspects of work, leisure is a necessary complement to work, though not in itself a sufficient purpose in life. Nevertheless, the idea that the negative aspects of work may be self formative is only one potentially liberating facet. Housework has the 'burdensome character' that Marcuse ascribes to 'labour', and the inherent 'lawfulness' of the objects impose specific demands on the labouring activities. The same cannot be ascribed to craftwork as leisure (even if it produces use values), because housework is not a contrast to work, in the sense of leisure being 'not work'. In fact housework and child rearing do not appear to be modern, because they are 'never done' or completed, and so cannot make a contrast with leisure. (A picnic is strenuous work for the responsible adult.) Hobbies are less constrained by time: for example, the pleasurable vegetable garden can be left to grow weeds but the dinner cannot be left unprepared. What can be 'wrong' with housework as an *exclusive* alternative to paid work that would also apply to hobbies?

My defence of employment up to this point has not addressed Braverman's idea that the 'artisan' aspects of housework are preferable to the degradation which accompanied the commodification of household products and the growth of the service sector, especially since he sees this as destroying 'the family' in the process.[28] The post-industrialists take his criticism to its logical conclusion by claiming that housework as well as 'freely chosen activities' – as objectification – would be sufficient for self-fulfilment and could be liberating if everyone had a guaranteed income. Following the more problematic aspects of the domestic labour debate, some argue that the Marxian conception of labour is sexist because of its implicit assumption that the responsibility for childcare and housework lies with women and its ignoring the barriers against women's full participation in the labour market. But if women's actual work participation is generally viewed favourably within the Marxist tradition, post-industrialists find the unpaid nature of women's traditional 'craft' skills in bread and jam making a matter of special significance in terms of their proposals.

Some post-industrialists are quite sympathetic about the low status of and lack of remuneration for housework,[29] but I shall argue that the cure – that we do more of it – is misplaced. Leisure cannot be the prime filling for a life, but housework is not leisure: it is usually burdensome even if sometimes fulfilling. The question here is whether, for both women and men, participation in the world of paid work is an improvement on being confined to the private 'informal' sphere, even if economic 'independence' were provided to all via state guaranteed incomes.

The first dubious idea is that we can all return to an era where the distinction between work and leisure was blurred. The problem, as those responsible know all too well, is that many houseworkers do not enjoy the modern distinction between work and leisure. When hobbies are pursued in the home they often only add to the dull chores for the person responsible. Cleaning up the carpentry mess or the budgie cage is hardly pleasurable. The devaluation of housework is partly due to the fact that it takes place in what is for other, non-responsible household members, the site of leisure. Indeed, it is not clear whether houseworkers enjoy any leisure, if we consider the principle behind Mother's Day. Contemporary time budget studies show an increase in home-centred leisure but that the 'division of labour in the household [remains] between those who do a lot (women) and those who do very little (men)'.[30]

One answer here is that housework is purely private. It is often suggested that the recognitions and comparisons of all kinds of work only occur with their 'publicity'.[31] Feminists have reinterpreted Hegel's notion that the three different spheres of the modern social world have their own principle of association or their own 'virtue'.[32] Because Hegel excluded women, his is a male model, where participation in political, economic and personal spheres provides different but closely related intersubjective recognitions. The three spheres offer separate avenues for individual identity formation: a person is recognised as an equal citizen by the state, as an independent agent with skills that can be contrasted in the world of paid work or contract, and as a unique individual in personal or private life.[33] These persons, however, are privileged men, for each sphere has a patriarchal structure. Until women participate in all three arenas, Anna Yeatman suggests, none will be transformed.

Yet in the employment arena, post-industrialists quite understandably see no potential publicity or contrasts in work. If work is more dull as a result of technological change, and if (almost) everyone is deskilled, there is nothing different to be contrasted in public and thus the individual identity formation that may be gained through paid work does not occur. Hegel had a point, but it was a bourgeois masculine one because, as Maria Markus argues,[34] the economic sphere was never a 'public of participants' where evaluations and comparisons could be formed publicly in open debate. Offe has convincingly demonstrated that the rise of capitalism was based on the 'achievement principle', but it was distorted as new

forms of workplace organisations developed. The original claim was
that the social status and integration of an individual within a
capitalist industrial society was to be based upon a person's functional status within the world of work, rather than the ascribed
(inherited) status of people in previous forms of community. Modern
status is meant to be based on achievement and effort but, given that
the functional relation to the economy is manipulated and organised
by the few for profit, a person's 'success' in employment societies
actually rests on ascribed characteristics, privileges and 'loyalty'.
Hence the achievement principle has become perverted and
repressive, and serves as a means of social control. It ranks the
powerless groups by criteria outside public control (like lack of
loyalty or of expensive credentials, or too much 'femaleness'), and
suggests that they are unsuccessful because they do not put in
sufficient 'effort' in the workplace.[35] Markus further demonstrates
that, apart from the implications for men and the whole society, the
fact that women are still 'failing' at work, despite their double effort,
can be partly attributed to their tendency not to 'present themselves
as successful', according to the way the achievement principle now
operates.[36] The subversion of, rather than submission to, the achievement principle is the strategy preferred in feminist politics today,
so that wider meanings of merit (than maleness and obsequiousness)
encompass achievement.

Post-industrialists argue, however, that a guaranteed income
would enable people to avoid this workplace hypocrisy altogether.
This is not an argument over predictions of job losses or the internal
satisfactions that some people may experience in paid work even if
it is dull. What they argue is that, since dull work cannot offer a
positive source of identity, alternatives to wage labour are more
humanising and provide preferable sources of identity formation.
It is pointless to try to resurrect or create more powerless jobs. Post-
industrialists regard the expanding service sector as merely drawing
large numbers of women into the most exploitative conditions
which none consider are likely to improve.

Their criticism of wage labour, therefore, implies that the failings
of the domestic labour debate could be turned into successes. The
predicament for feminists during the 1970s was that merely to
praise housework and even to demand wages for it only paralleled
the 'separate-but-equal' strategy of first-wave feminism. Wages for
housework, everyone quickly saw, would similarly lock women into

the private sphere and naturalise their sole responsibility for all these tasks. Post-industrialists would reverse this, if incomes could be guaranteed, by having men join women in a network of households.[37] That is, the work activities in the private 'informal' sphere should be generalised to both men and women, where distinctions between work and leisure could still be maintained. Men would at last see that housework and voluntary work were really work. In sum, social integration through the cash/work nexus is not worth supporting, since the achievement principle only legitimises modern inequalities while distorting individual identity formation.

There are a number of problems with the above arguments. On the question of the individual's connection to society, the modern source of identity does indeed depend to a large degree on a person's place in the division of labour. Despite the power and inequality that has come to be legitimated by the achievement principle, the onus is still on the post-industrialists to show where other sources of identity formation might lie, ones that do not rest on ascriptive criteria. For a start, a guaranteed income in no way improves this problem of individual integration into the society. Since there is no community implied at all in the state provision of incomes to all, the relation to society becomes even more abstract as the collectivity does not exist.

Second, it can easily be pointed out that returning men and women to the home, by itself, only creates a superficial form of equality – one that confines both men and women to the private sphere while not changing its patriarchal structure. This problem has yet to be satisfactorily addressed by the post-industrialists. Similarly, another problem with the wages for housework debate was its assumption that capitalism would be undermined without the unpaid support of women. But South African capitalism flourished quite nicely by keeping indentured labourers in barracks. Keane and Owens do point out that Gorz's depiction of a homogeneous political identity of the unemployed may rest upon the ascribed common interests of the permanently marginalised. Instead, the basis of their support for more free time depends, for them, upon the 'politically difficult' problem of developing solidarity between the unemployed and other groups within society.[38] Offe's solution to the risk of marginalisation is an 'institutionally reinforced' structure of alternatives, though his sympathetic defence of the meaning of work tends to neglect the political problems: there is no strategic way that the already powerless may be heard.[39] Habermas, by contrast, waters down the concept of labour because he sees no conflict potential, nothing political in work. Despite qualifications about industrial democracy, Keane similarly suggests that full employment 'crowds out' other social and political activities.[40] Habermas' argument for the separation of income and work recognises that a guaranteed income is insufficient, but posits that the greater free time would enable a more 'political' participation in the public sphere.[41] Post-industrialists propose, therefore, that policies must be implemented to ensure, for example,

> equal access to the means for voluntary economic, social, political or cultural activity. . . . More emphasis, energy and time must be given to the 'public sphere' of democratic politics, and to nonexchange value based social and cultural activity, so that the blind and self-destructive domination of technocratic 'instrumental reason', closely allied with the culture of 'productivism' and 'industrialism' would recede in favor of more truly rational and reasonable social values.[42]

In effect, then, full employment could be abandoned if political structures were vastly enhanced, so that marginalisation would not occur or would somehow be mitigated. Clearly no-one who favours the extension of participatory and representative democracy could disagree with an expansion of the public sphere. The serious question is rather one of how it could be achieved strategically, when the conception of political action regards employment as so irrelevant that exclusion from paid work has more potential in this respect. The theoretical argument against productivism is that participation in paid work is an instrumental activity carried on at the expense of other, more politically explicit facets of the human potential. The social theories criticising productivism arose from a more general downgrading of a normative conception of work so prominent in Marxist and socialist thought. These critiques were partly in response to the rise of state socialism and the mechanisation of industrial work, whereby the emancipatory significance of labour appeared to be lost.

The meaning most often given to productivism – namely a lack of concern for, if not glorification in, control of nature and destruction of the environment – is the 'productivism' I have no wish to defend. But in the broader sense also used, it is not an innocent term. Is it necessary to equate productivism with participation? Are there no politicising potentials in the world of work? It appears to me otherwise, that the 'watering down' of labour, conceptually, has serious consequences, and not just for denying any relevance to economic and industrial democracy strategies, public political debate on needs and struggles over workers' rights. It also theoretically evades the problems with exclusion from work. This has been extremely influential. Several philosophical positions underlie these post-industrial analyses. Hannah Arendt, in particular, based her influential criticism of the 'life and labor philosophers' such as Marx on a three-fold distinction between labour, work and action. According to her, action is the most 'human' form of activity.[43]

Arendt argues that modern society is a 'laborers' and consumers' society', above all concerned with producing abundance.[44] This sacrifices 'the political' because theories of life and labour are merely concerned with natural needs which cannot be political, because needs are biological. (Gorz has a similar understanding of necessity: needs are not regarded as historically specific.) As Arendt saw it, when political structures do become concerned with life and labour – that is, substantive questions of need – they can easily become totalitarian.

Arendt herself refused to countenance that conceptions of labour and production could provide the bases for understanding societies. She instead defined politics as quite separate from production, using the philosophical distinction between action (praxis) and production (poiesis), or doing and making. Praxis is a pure action which has no 'product' and is meaningful in itself. In light of the tragic developments of the twentieth century, modern social theory has tended to turn away from the production paradigm. This was understandably important in pointing to major deficiencies in Marxism. Nevertheless, as an argument influencing post-industrialists to abandon full employment, the position also has serious deficiencies. The problems with our society are now frequently attributed to the degradation of all forms of intentional activity to some form of making or mere instrumental control, at the sacrifice of praxis in the 'political' world (as Gyorgy Markus points out).[45]

On the empirical level, the arguments against productivism and heteronomous (or imposed) labour appear to be self evident. In liberal democracies there is an ideological discrepancy between the formal acknowledgment of freedom, equality and property for each citizen, and the actual and complete lack of formal rights for each worker. While free to make contracts on the labour market, wage labour is totally unfree in work.[46] Where, then, is the space for praxis or doing, when the work is not even in the maker's control, and worse, when the labour movement appears to have little option but to support the logic of capitalist development while merely bargaining over the terms? Theoretically, however, this rather aristocratic dichotomy between praxis and poiesis has several effects, in narrowing *participation* in paid work to mere productivism, and in viewing exclusion from it as relatively unproblematic.

In Habermas' use of the praxis–poiesis distinction, for example, work is instrumental action, whereas only from communicative action (his form of praxis) can come any moral insights which could lead to liberation from social domination. Axel Honneth suggests that in this way Habermas discounts the 'conflict potential still available in social labour' from his theory of action. By removing the dimension of consciousness from his concept of work, Habermas leaves out the possibility of a moral learning which can occur as a reaction to the loss of control of the work process. This 'practical rationality', as Honneth identifies it, 'gives inner logic to the breaches of standards and acts of resistance which have become daily practice in capitalist industrial work'.[47]

Not only that, however, for if there is a possibility of *resistance*, there must be other possibilities for political action within participation in paid work. The making–doing distinction has wider problems which include the way that relations between subject–other–subject (in service work) could be defined. Gyorgy Markus suggests that the distinction between praxis and poiesis is really one between *accomplishments*, where the end is internal to the action's own course (praxis), and *achievements*, which refers to an object or end-state as a result (poiesis). But, as he says, an accomplishment may range from eating to helping someone in distress (a nurse?); and achievement can result from a cobbler making a shoe but equally from Van Gogh making the painting of a shoe. There can be little theoretical or moral significance derived from these distinctions, when many of our makings are doings (or actings) and many actings are makings.[48]

Markus thus questions the use of the praxis–poiesis dichotomy, pointing to the fact that even the original Aristotelian distinction itself was not clear and that even more difficulties appear in modern formulations of the dichotomy. On the crucial question of politics, which was regarded as the main field of praxis, Aristotle also described successful political behaviour as *techne* or skill. But skill was supposed by him only to concern making, not doing. What has happened to the dichotomy now, according to Markus, is that in the search for an activity which can oppose the supposedly entirely instrumental activities of production, some new praxis concept modelled on speech or communication can be found. But it then lacks any of the traits of *active intervention* which are necessary for realising particular intentions in whatever concrete event or situation.[49] It is also difficult, therefore, to suggest how and where those excluded from production are to act, and with whom against what.

Take, for example, Habermas' notion that moral knowledge may ensue from the experience of systematically distorted structures of communicative interaction within *any* repressive form of organisation. Such a notion obviously applies to participation in a *work* organisation. But it excludes the possibility of any moral learning from the actual work process. Thus it gives no especial significance to participation in the world of work, even work which is itself communicatively structured like much of the service sector, and it has nothing to say about exclusion from employment, even though formal workplaces represent the major arenas of interaction in modern society. Citizenship and political life, for the post-industrialists, have nothing to do with paid work and the labour market, and neither appear to be capable of progressive change.

On this issue, Habermas' use of the praxis–poiesis distinction parallels his theoretical distinction between system and lifeworld. The earlier definition of the 'public sphere' has slightly shifted, so that it is now part of the 'lifeworld'.[50] His previous conception saw the old bourgeois public sphere being undermined by bureau-cratisation and opinion making after universal franchise was attained, because the public sphere was no longer homogeneous. The outlook for reconstituting public life along emancipatory lines appeared to require a public body of organised private individuals to legitimate political compromises.[51] While in no way disagreeing with his call for the expansion of autonomous public spaces, like the other post-industrialists he now expressly prefers that the participants of the public sphere need not also engage in paid work.[52] This is regardless of the fact that the original public sphere was made up of bourgeois men participating, to say the least, in the new economic sphere and indeed partly motivated to scrutinise state activities for economic reasons. It was also undermined by workers (from chartists through to feminists) demanding the vote. Although Arendt also relegates action or praxis to the public–political sphere alone, particularly in the form of voluntary associations, she at least admits to interesting exceptions, like the spontaneous, if short-lived workers' councils (such as the Soviets in 1917 and those in Hungary in 1956).

Further difficulties occur in Habermas' formulation that the steering media (power and money) of the contemporary system are 'invading' the lifeworld. Communicative interaction is not exclusive to the lifeworld, and neither is instrumental manipulation to system, if the forms of traditional domination in private households are considered. Insulating system from action (lifeworld), as Habermas has done, neglects, for example, the fact that modern sexist norms are embedded in system, and imposed from the top down as well as the reverse, in a two-way process.[53] Contesting the 'naturalness' of these norms, or challenging 'technocratic domination' and the 'culture of productivism' may well be very hard to achieve, but if we accept that resistance occurs in the work process, then even greater control over the structure and content of work is in principle possible. These possibilities for action, however much they also require social movements, are logically denied if system is abstracted from lifeworld. No-one can deny that *some* work will always continue and even though it is usually alienating, as a felt experience alienation itself holds out the opportunity for change. Similarly, without the chance to be independent agents on the labour market, individuals must face the state as passive clients.

Against such theoretical divisions, it seems preferable to take the view emphasised by Markus, that life is a combination of action *and* production. If social roles are not, in principle, to be fixed ascriptively, then the criteria for the 'good life' cannot be just the accomplishment of 'good and noble actions' throughout one's life, as in the Aristotelian conception of praxis, important though this is. These actions would be prescribed unless life were also 'a matter of making, achieving competences, recognitions and results', the ends of which should be freely chosen. None of this, of course, is available to the unemployed or, one could add, to the second generation of the commune movement, who resent their ascribed position. Nor was it available to women, who gained the vote at the turn of the century and who aimed to raise moral concerns at the political level. Because most women were simultaneously denied an economic position and confined to the private sphere, their demands were largely ignored. Moreover, given that most of our lives more generally are a series of responses to unpredictable events over which we have no control, it is more important to ask how to find ways for everyone to achieve some freely chosen goals and accomplish something uniquely meaningful.[54] This cannot be considered while accepting the present widespread exclusion from the world of work and positing 'political' action as being possible solely in a separate political sphere. Such action is intended, presumably, to counteract ascription and dependency for those confined to the private sphere, but it is difficult to imagine how it could become widespread or effective.

From the world of paid work, workers' demands have arisen that are not only 'economistic' but also 'political' – workers' battles for the franchise, for example, are hardly reducible to productivism. In addition, as Nancy Fraser argues, the politicisation of needs has included demands for the health and safety of workers and now for childcare: social needs arising from life and labour that Arendt denies political status. These are demands that became part of public political debates and historically gained rights for workers, tenuous though they may be.[55] When women rejoined the labour force in significant numbers, issues that had previously not been defined as such were formulated, given new metaphors and named in public: they were therefore politicised.

There is, moreover, another aspect to employment that a few post-industrialists have belatedly admitted.[56] It is well known that the argument about dull work and deskilling tends to underestimate the capability of workers to influence the definition of what 'skill' is.[57] The effects are vastly uneven and depend on factors like mobility, the level of union organisation, labour market shortages or the ability to control labour supply. Women do not score highly on these factors. Dentists, however, seem to do increasingly narrow, specialised, 'dull' work but no-one can ignore their competences, income, social recognition and status. Outworkers confined to home responsibilities for childcare find it difficult to resist exploitation or to define their skills *as such*.

Indeed, the separation of income from work holds no promise for women. Feminists have challenged traditional understandings of productive work and thereby shown that the previous views of what properly belongs to employment as distinct from what counts as non-employable or extra-employable work is not natural, but arbitrary and inequitable. The predominant feminist agenda is to undermine all the assumptions that those who work, rather than being employed, *choose* this condition and its freedom from a wage or salary. Instead the aim is to challenge the achievement principle and introduce a new politics of skill definition into the workforce. To the extent that it has been effective so far, this strategy has required a combination of political demands directed at both the state and the market.

So, it is undeniable that the proposals about the public sphere were pathbreaking steps, at the time, against the statist tendencies of socialism. New emphasis was placed on resistance, dissent and demands against the state, and defence of civil rights (all somehow 'praxis'), allied with the action of a plurality of social movements (other than the labour movement) within the political world. From this, many theorists have rightly pointed to forms of social liberation which have less authoritarian consequences than those which history has revealed about aspects of the Marxian theory of revolution. But the question remains whether this theoretical turn to 'new' social movements should be gained *at the expense* of finding any possibility of resistance, let alone participatory democracy, political demands and self-fulfilment, in people's taking a 'position' within the historical world of work.[58] Indeed, the extent that some of these social movements, such as the modern feminist movement, have managed to politicise economic needs also requires theoretical consideration. Accordingly, rather than welcoming exclusion as the harbinger of greater free time for *more* political action when not busy in the private sphere, it seems likely to me that resistance, the defining of new needs and skills and other political activity is instead enhanced by inclusion.

PARTICIPATION OR EXCLUSION

Even if it is accepted that political action does occur through participation and is not just the wage bargaining which can often accept existing power structures, it could still be argued that other, equally fruitful kinds of political action could be anticipated from the excluded groups. That is, participation could be granted *some* political potential, while alternatives to wage labour might still be the more radical strategy if there were a political structure whereby exclusion from paid work became relatively unproblematic. From the evidence of the fate of alternatives to wage labour, this seems highly unlikely, for it ignores modern realities that strictly limit the opportunities for articulating conflicts and fighting them out in public. There are some problems with exclusion that express this more generally.

Although Alain Touraine is well known as a post-industrialist, his neo-Marxian perspective provides a perspective on participation in work and politics that is different to that of other post-industrialists. For example, Touraine's formulations are certainly less identified with the praxis–poiesis distinction (that is, work is mere instrumental action, politics is communicative action). At face value, though, Touraine also appears to water down the concept of work. Social movements are at the centre of his action theory and the labour movement has less relevance in post-industrial society, being either fractured or incorporated into state structures. The presence of other social movements is given primary importance. They are not reduced to secondary epiphenomena on account of their members' functional class position – a typical problem with classical historical materialism, which can brand feminists or ecologists as merely petty bourgeois.[59] Touraine's stand is similar in this respect to the most fruitful aspects of other social movement theorists.

In addition, on the contested question of system change, Touraine, like most other modern social theorists, points to the way that 'social domination' has 'penetrated' beyond production into information, consumption and so forth.[60] Habermas, as I have mentioned before, speaks of the steering media of power and money. In contrast, and in trying to avoid system theoretical approaches which emphasise contradiction, not conflict and action, Touraine prefers to stress dominant or 'ruling class' social movements while also noting the increasingly diverse nature of the modern state.[61] Accordingly, 'the popular class' now is the class of consumers, and 'the principal field of class relations and conflict' lies in the area of culture. 'Work', therefore, *seems* less important:

> Manipulated both at his work and in his consumption, the postindustrial society man [*sic*] is opposing himself to this domination both at work and outside his work and relying more and more on life outside work to demonstrate the conflict of interests opposing his personal and

collective identity to the great apparatuses that are the managers of change.[62]

Despite these similarities with other post-industrialists, to a certain extent his theory suggests a path that avoids the dichotomy of work versus interaction or making and doing, which leaves other post-industrialists arguing that if nothing 'political' can come from participation in paid work there is no theoretical or practical reason to support it. This is not just because Touraine disclaims, for example, against underestimating 'defensive reactions and protests in the work situation'.[63] These are mere assertions. On this point he denies setting leisure in opposition to work. Life outside work has increased, however, as leisure has developed and as the young and old are increasingly excluded from work. The field of class conflict, therefore, has simply broadened. It is not a change from a society where the 'problems of labor' are dominant to one where 'life outside work' is more important. Instead, he maintains:

> that we are moving from *a domination centred on work* to another, more general kind in which the problems that appear within the work framework are bearers of social movements only to the degree in which they are linked with the totality of the problems arising from *a domination now extended over a system of production* that integrates manufacture, communications, training, and consumption much more closely than before.[64]

More importantly, it would be illegitimate to suggest that Touraine's schema does reduce the importance of the concept of work. Touraine suggests that society 'produces' itself, even though its 'work upon itself' is not now confined to economic production but extends to all areas of culture.[65] Action – seen as conflict (not purely as contradiction) – creates or changes the prevailing set of social forms and structures.[66] Above all, work is not organic necessity and manipulation or domination of nature, but society's self production. The process is riven with historical conflicts between social movements over its control.

This is not a 'productivist' conception, partly because a society's action is not on a 'supposedly external nature' but concerns its own self production.[67] The actual cultural patterns a society takes are formed partly by the work of knowledge (which is now science and was previously religion), and this *defines matter* as some particular state of nature, so that 'nature' is a social construction. But the prevailing pattern also encompasses accumulation – the type of economic activity and investment of a society – as well as a 'cultural model' by which a society 'reflects' upon its own 'totality'.[68] Even if dominant groups control the cultural patterns, it does not mean that subordinate groups who contest this control would necessarily change the actual patterns.

In general, it seems to me that much of the disillusionment with 'labourism' and workers' movements centres on the fact that too much has been expected of them. The critique of reductionist class analysis rightly shows that the system category of wage labour is not the same as the social category of proletariat or worker, in that system conflicts do not lead to emancipation,[69] but rather to accumulation 'problems'. Now very little is expected of workers' movements, on account of the statist consequences of revolutions to capture the state and new forms of corporatism emerging in OECD countries. In contrast with both the previous optimism for class conflict and the present pessimism about it, Touraine points out that the industrial culture developing in the West was eventually accepted by the popular class last century. It was the *form* of class relations and capitalist control over industrialisation that was continually contested by all kinds of popular movements, not industrialisation *per se*. Touraine, correctly it seems to me, denies that the workers' movement or, one could add, a dominant movement could ever change the form of the society (the state does that).

Since Touraine analyses action according to different levels, the workers' movement may, among others, be a 'catalyst' for change but unionism in itself is not necessarily this kind of action. A brief elaboration shows the extent to which this is not a 'productivist' position. The prevailing cultural patterns are 'expressed' through various traits in social organisations and by the level of productivity and technical division of labour. Touraine's three-tiered 'systems of action' are not concrete divisions of the social world, such that *work* exists only in the economic sphere whilst *interaction* is reserved for the political realm. Touraine speaks of human interaction of various kinds which are analysed on increasingly abstract levels – of everyday organisation, political institutions and finally of cultural patterns. The movement is in both ways, so while forms of investment and knowledge shape society and are controlled by the dominant class, this control is continually contested and resisted. Resistance *may* occur at the main historical level through social movements, but more usually there are relations of competition and influence

operating at political–institutional levels, or individuals can try
questioning the norms and expectations (defined institutionally)
which control the social organisation.[70] Because social organisation
is the closest to everyday life, all three levels of interaction may be
involved. For example, although bargaining for wages or trying to
retain one's job still presupposes an acceptance of the particular
norms and constraints defined and imposed on that organisation,
certain strikes or resistance to those norms may involve 'political'
conduct or even historical struggle through social movements.[71]

So, to the immediate question in hand, of exclusion in comparison
with participation in the world of 'work', Touraine defines organisations as the 'concrete manifestations' (i.e. the least abstract) of
cultural patterns and class domination, regulated by political
decisions and institutionally defined norms. ('Social organisation'
can refer to a national society or an enterprise or a hospital.) While
defined and legalised at the institutional level to carry out specific
goals, organisations can decide on policies to the extent that an
education department can decide on forms of education but cannot
avoid reproducing inequalities, and a firm can decide on what goods
to produce but not whether to make a profit.[72]

Private networks of households or personal relations like 'the
family' are not social organisations.[73] Given Touraine's definition,
this is partly self-evident despite his avoidance of a detailed
justification. But it can be argued that private life in modern societies
is controlled in many ways by institutional mechanisms and
decisions which are rarely gender or class neutral, by the authority
of many organisations and by patriarchal and ethnic traditions; the
family is involved in socialisation, but not like a school with a set
of legally defined functions such that it can also be analysed
institutionally or even at an historical level. The private household
engaged in domestic labour – of whatever members – does not carry
out technical functions prescribed from above;[74] it is now a con-
suming unit. There are possibilities of resistance motivated by
household problems (for example with neighbourhood or consumer
associations and consumer boycotts), but all children must attend
school and it is cheaper to buy bread than to make it. The private
household cannot change institutional norms: though some may
be able to introduce relations like gender equality from within, this
will not alter the position of women in general and it will not be
easy to maintain in the face of external constraints. If the private

household does attempt to set goals for itself – as communes and the 'informal' economy suggest – then those members will not be participating in social organisations and will be outside class domination and society's self production. As we saw, commune members could only compete for political influence on behalf of communes as such.

The argument for the separation of income from work, however, regards private households as having transformative potential. By contrast, Touraine's schema emphatically denies that *escape* from organisations could increase the power of individual or collective actors. It is only within organisations that there is the possibility of *influence* at the institutional level or even at the level of class relations, however much the opposition also requires a social movement.[75]

And while 'creative forms of conduct' to contest the form of the social order is initiated within social movements, this action occurs through participation in the instituted social forms. Touraine argues for this in the following way. The individual actor commonly experiences a sense of crushing domination inside the organisation from the whole social and historical framework. The actor tries to escape, 'to confront the laws, the rule, the traditions with an appeal to creativity centred upon himself as an individual or upon willed social interactions'.[76] (To correct the masculine vision, one could think here of Mary Daly's appeals to an inner femininity and of all-female communes.) But such revolts, as opposed to participation, are ambiguous. Even if the revolt directly challenges the cultural patterns, such as rejecting a male-dominated society or capitalist production, it is empty of content and ahistorical, since it has to make appeals to human needs outside the historical framework. The commune movement's appeal to 'natural' needs exemplified this problem. It denied that needs are socially constructed, needs which, as Touraine says, 'cannot be lived outside social relations of domination, of decision, and of organisation'. Spontaneous creative rebellion is little different from marginality and, like the ghetto, risks reinforcing the very social order against which revolt is posed. The dilemma of participation however, is this:

> Social participation does not succeed in bringing the actor into relation with the system of historical action, for it binds him [*sic*] both to the interests of domination and power and also to a historically formed and bequeathed order. . . . The actor cannot reach the system of historical

action directly within the social organisation; he can do no more than manage, with greater or lesser success, the dialectic of *engagement* and *disengagement*. He can only escape from this by moving up from the social organisation level to the upper levels, first by becoming a political actor and, even better, by transforming himself into a producer of society, through social movements and through art. . . . The relation of actor to historicity cannot exist outside the dialectic of revolt and participation.[77]

Touraine constantly speaks of the workers' movement in industrial society contesting the domination and control of the production organisations. All those excluded were left with 'no influence at all', being at the same time subjected to the relations of authority and repression from organisations in which they have no part.[78] This gradually became women's position, so pronounced in Australia with the arbitrated family wage and a decline of women's participation in public associations with the end of domestic service. Typically, Touraine finds no place for 'first-wave' feminism although, from the perspective of participation, 'separate but equal' was indeed problematic as a long-term strategy, despite political gains and however much women were constrained by previous mechanisms. Moreover, the increasing inclusion of women at the organisational level since World War II directly interrelates with the institutional changes accomplished by the feminist movements that emerged by the 1960s. Limited though these reforms may be, they have still challenged the political functions of organisations. Participation still implies control but also the possibility of redefining norms and creating social movements.

As for the problems of actual participation, Touraine employs his own definition of alienation. It is *the lack of capacity for action*, resulting from the 'disorganising effects' of the contradiction between dependent participation and conflictual participation in the organisation.[79] But this 'deprivation of consciousness' is never total. The limited opportunities for conflictual participation are still preferable to the impotence and anomic conduct which is a consequence of exclusion and total dependency, again most clearly exemplified by the unemployed and also suburban women, atomised and isolated and without even the internal leverage of producing use-value, with the increasing commodification of household goods. But it cannot be said that exclusion from social organisations *rules out* the possibility of action in the political arena, nor could one even say that action by the excluded is unlikely. First-wave feminism is a partial example of the latter, although women's relative successes then (such as gaining the vote) *may* have been more due to the previous level of their participation in the prevailing economic life. In colonial Australia women with influence were economically more productive than in Britain. British suffragettes' demands were repressed and women won the vote only in 1918, after their participation in wartime industries.

Touraine, however, does admit that the social problems which arise as a result of exclusion may turn out to be 'weakened' forms of social movements which engage in some conflictual action and leave indirect effects.[80] This cannot be predicted. Nevertheless, Touraine argues convincingly that the options for the creation of social movements via exclusion are extremely limited. Exclusion makes it difficult for any consciousness of subordination and of a real adversary to emerge. On this point I regard the feminist slogan, 'the personal is political', as an effort to overcome such a lack of consciousness, but it was also an argument for altering norms at the institutional level. Touraine's argument, when applied to these problems with 'personal politics', is clearly relevant to the alternatives to wage labour. The counter culture's suggestion that a radical, politicised consciousness might emerge from participation in different work structures, supposedly outside class and state domination, is explicitly opposed by Touraine's formulations. The excluded, with no possibility of influence, face authority.[81] This helps partially to explain how governments were able to use these spontaneous structures for their own purposes. The same process occurred with the exclusion of women at the turn of this century, with the state's use of the separate but equal strategy to increase its policing of families.

For Touraine, actual participation within a social organisation means that class consciousness – which is a function of participation, not exclusion – *may* develop into class action, especially when such action is not just aiming to shuffle positions around an organisation whose authority is not questioned. Australia's most unusual example of this was the green bans in the late 1960s, whose success was due to the workers' refusing to build or destroy. Demands made through social movements that are not directly related to particular functional interests are certainly voiced by those excluded from organisations. Nevertheless, our chief historical examples of action by those with the self-created identity of 'unemployed' are of the hunger marches.

The only content possible – as I see it – for demands made from without, is the demand for inclusion, for jobs and the right to participate. Inclusion makes it possible to engage in conflictual relations. Revolt and flight, as just discussed, only reinforce the existing exclusion, for there is no clear opponent. On the other hand, as Touraine warns, when conflict is not present, 'forced unity, violence and withdrawal prevails'.[82]

To deal with this question in the Australian case, when unemployed groups set up soup kitchens outside the clubs of the rich and powerful, protesting against the Fraser government in 1982–3, this was just when the numbers of men losing jobs had risen. The political responses were highly ambiguous, even when the level of debate about unemployment and exclusion forced some political sympathy. The corporatist management brought in by the Hawke government while the hunt for alternatives to jobs took place led to further exclusion. As we have seen, the trend since then has been to punish exclusion further, by redefining unemployment benefits and proposing dole-work. Enforced participation in dole-work, unlikely though it is, could lead to conflict, even the possibility of twisting the debate to demands for proper jobs. Impoverishing young unemployed people – to return them to parental authority – more likely results in an increase in homelessness, violence and involuntary incarceration in prisons and asylums which, unlike organisations, have no internal dynamic but are ghettos which permanently reproduce exclusion.[83]

A progressive argument against exclusion could be formulated as follows. Exclusion from organisations denies the chance for any influence, as a day-by-day opportunity presented by recurring participation in paid work. While not wanting to suggest that excluded groups and individuals would *never* be likely to engage in conflictual action in the political arena, other social movement theorists like Melucci argue that it is rare.[84] There are certainly fewer possibilities for opposition from 'without' and therefore participation in paid work is preferable, however alienated the work, to facing the authority of the state apparatuses from the position of marginality. It is *participation in society's self production* which implies opportunities for conflict, even if slight, which could lead to an expansion of control from below.

Otherwise, as far as the post-industrialist thesis is concerned, Touraine's prognosis is by far the most gloomy, though his pessimism is mitigated by a realistically limited optimism for social movements' continual struggles and a refusal to accept that alienation is total within the world of work. As he says, domination today is more widespread. From this it follows that there is no area of paid work – industrial production included, but just as importantly now, communications, training, the service sector generally, whether public or private – where the internal opposition to the modern 'managers of change' is not a far more significant question than the options posed by revolt, flight and certainly by exclusion.

POLITICISATION OF NEEDS AND EXTENSION OF RIGHTS

Alienation is a fundamental concern of post-industrialists. Having attempted to argue against the separation of income and work – against exclusion and against according *primary roles* to leisure and houseworking – a final issue remains. This is that spontaneous initiatives to create alternative structures could themselves be regarded as a form of politics.

The creation of alternative structures was an attempt at politicising needs for greater control over everyday life than that of wage labour. In the case of the guaranteed income proposals, of course, these were demands directed at the state that required state implementation. The same could be said of the way worker co-operatives were promoted in Australia. But in the sense that all the alternatives to wage labour were to be *exemplary,* the demands and experiments were to have political effects. Co-operatives would create a third way in the market, neither public nor private; 'employment society' and the false equation of effort and success would be undermined by guaranteed or basic incomes. The commune movement was initially even more ambitious. Related to this, the creation of alternative structures was a strategy, at least on the part of its leftist supporters, that assumed that the new structures would radicalise the participants.

We have seen how the state used these demands for quite different purposes. But there is still the question of whether there were *inherent* failings with this form of politics. Two issues seem to be involved here. First, there are the more general social costs in what Nancy Fraser calls the 'dynamics of need-politics',[85] and second, in the case of the specific proposals, their actual content is not intrinsically concerned with public–political debate. Thereby, the possibility for resistance is closed off because these alternative structures are supposedly 'autonomous' and free of opponents.

The dynamics of need-politics is a general account of state incorporation and formalising processes. So, in the cases presented here, a series of operations were set in train whereby oppositional demands were redefined by the state into non-participatory and administrable kinds of needs. Even in the case of the democratic co-operatives, the co-op workers were transformed into passive clients who had to be 'educated' in the skills of co-operation and who must appeal to the state for more money. Different kinds of co-op structures were needed in order that motivation could be improved or, conversely, that anti-union practices leading to worker capitalism could be avoided. Bureaucratising and formalising procedures were set in train by the state, which could, at best, only be paternalistic. The state in this way redefined the meaning of *alternative* through a process whereby demands formerly regarded as illegitimate, because of work incentives and the evasion of the control of wage labour, were converted into legitimate areas of state intervention because alternatives to paid work as a source of income (for those involved) might aid the state's crisis of employment. This has nothing to do with the crisis for the unemployed. Local state policies also engaged in rewriting operations so that communes, for example, were legalised into 'multiple occupancy' titles to become cheap, unserviced housing. Attendant upon this process, rights previously won – to clean water or to state welfare services (in the case of the guaranteed minimum income) – might run the risk of being lost. These are social costs even when there are gains, in the face of bureaucratically defined needs.

The second problem alluded to refers particularly to the guaranteed income, though other alternatives are implicated as well. Demands are made *on the state* for the creation of alternative structures. In the content of the demands, however, there is no demand which attempts to make the state more democratically accountable. These demands are to change *work* and the system of wage labour. If the state implements or legalises these new structures, they then assume a place in free markets. The commodity markets, however, can easily accommodate guaranteed incomes, co-operatives, the informal economy and communes. The private economy is underwritten by the state. The fewer controls and state regulations on the commodity markets in land, labour and goods, the more easily the alternatives can emerge and the more options become available to the biggest in the markets. We saw the fate of co-operatives, like all small business partnerships in this respect. The big land developers now have increased opportunities where multiple occupancy is concerned, and a guaranteed minimum income may reduce bargaining capacity in the labour market.

Furthermore, many post-industrialists regarded the guaranteed income as the answer for undermining the coercion of wage labour. This can only operate if the income is set at *above* average wages, a point few post-industrialists admit. But there is still the matter of the social cost of a guaranteed income in respect of the state. Rather than offering accountability structures or the possibility that socially-defined needs would be set from below by all the excluded (the working poor and the workless poor), a guaranteed income does the opposite. Since a guaranteed income can only be implemented by the state, the state can then define the need, set the income and decide the standard in the interests of *state problems*. These could be various: to cure inflation the income might be lowered; to remove public services and reprivatise health or education or to bring in indirect taxation, the income might be raised slightly.

These are both strategic and theoretical problems that need to be considered in the light of present constraints, exclusions and forms of powerlessness. It can still be argued that defending paid work – dull powerless work – from an emancipatory viewpoint is contra-dictory. But the onus is also on the alternative structure thesis to prove that the flight from wage labour will not make the situation worse. Rather than being contradictory, mine is merely a position which recognises first, that alienation is never absolute and second, that 'being there' holds the greater possibility to intervene than 'being absent'. At the same time this defends all projects of revitalising the public sphere.

What the cases showed, in this latter respect, was that although the counter culture in general was defining and attempting to politicise needs that the labour movement had ignored, there were two paths taken: one into the marginalism and separatism which the state has now turned to its own uses, the other into more specific social movements – feminists, gays, environmentalists and others. The latter entered the public debates, the former were quiet. Rights have been won and needs made public, and various political structures have been set up to scrutinise the state bureaucracies and the world of mainstream employment (for example, anti-discrimination legislation). Instead of taking a defensive position, this was 'offensive' action to extend the field of political activity. Through all these efforts of the social movements, civil society was being preserved and extended. In the harder times of the 1990s, the newly achieved structures of accountability have been dismantled, right wing social movements hold much of the public sphere and the rights and needs of many have been eroded. If social and individual rights are threatened any further, the alternative structures will become the economic libertarian's dream.

This final chapter has made out a case against the desirability of separating income and work, the most important part of my argument. I have attempted to demonstrate firstly that leisure and work are not mutually exclusive and that worklessness is highly unlikely to enhance leisure. Furthermore, the conception of labour that regards formal paid work as only instrumental, screens out resistance, the possibility of some control and of political action in the world of work. If participation in work, in the sense of merely 'being there', is alienating for the vast majority, exclusion, as houseworkers know, is a far more powerless position and holds few chances for identification of opponents and involvement in social movements. Finally, it appears that setting up alternative structures results in the very opposite to that which was intended. Making public various needs and rights to greater control over work lives was certainly an important project, even when it came through the rejection of wage labour. It is not a matter that work should be a privilege, because it is stratified and there is nothing meaningful about work at the lower end. But it is more a question that the society should try to define work rather than have definitions imposed from above. The attempt to do this through setting up alternative structures, however, seems only to result in the quest for greater control becoming private again, if not redefined into quite the opposite by governments.

NOTES

1. M. Jahoda, P.F. Lazarsfeld & H. Zeisel (1972), p. 41.
2. J. Keane (1988), pp. 71, 94–6.
3. A. Gorz (1985a), p. 34.

4. C. Offe (1984), p. 95.
5. A. Gorz (1985).
6. C. Offe (1984), pp. 92, 95.
7. K. Hinrich, C. Offe & H. Wiesenthal (1988); F. Block (1990), pp. 189–218.
8. K. Polanyi (1957), pp. 56–7, 68.
9. F. Block (1985).
10. A. Gorz (1985a), p. 35.
11. J. Keane (1988), p. 83.
12. A. Gorz (1985a), p. 57.
13. H. Marcuse (1973), p. 13.
14. G.W.F. Hegel (1977), p. 118.
15. H. Marcuse (1973), p. 13.
16. S. Sayers (1988).
17. H. Braverman (1974), p. 359.
18. The following discussion will leave aside the problem of Marcuse's theory of revolution – the collective worker – which one could compare with Gorz's of the supposedly homogeneous 'non-class of non-workers' (*Farewell to the Working Class* 1982).
19. H. Marcuse (1973), pp. 14–15.
20. My discussion here centres on the 'other' as other human subjects, so the problem on which Habermas (1971, p. 88) took issue with Marcuse, of extending subjectivity to the natural world, is not immediately relevant.
21. For example, see Giddens' 1987 criticisms of Gorz, p. 283.
22. M. Weber (1976), pp. 68; 163.
23. *ibid.*, pp. 175, 181–2.
24. S. Sayers (1986), p. 92.
25. G. Rehn (1984).
26. M. Markus & A. Hegedus (1976).
27. *ibid.*, p. 106.
28. H. Braverman (1974), ch. 13.
29. J. Keane (1988), p. 73.
30. M. Bittman (1990).
31. For example, S. Sayers (1986).
32. C. Pateman (1984).
33. A. Yeatman (1986).
34. M. Markus (1986), p. 437.
35. C. Offe (1976), p. 98.
36. M. Markus (1986), p. 438.
37. The network suggestion was made by Offe in an interview with Boris Frankel discussing 'Post-industrial Politics', Radio 2FC, Minders, Sydney, ABC, 14.3.87. See also K. Hinrich, C. Offe & H. Wiesenthal (1988).
38. J. Keane & J. Owens (1986), p. 171.
39. See K. Hinrich, C. Offe & H. Wiesenthal (1988), p. 242.

40. J. Keane (1988), p. 79.
41. J. Habermas (1986).
42. R. Baiman (1986), p. 10, his emphasis.
43. H. Arendt (1958), p. 174.
44. *ibid.*, p. 126.
45. G. Markus (1986), p. 30.
46. And, as Marx pointed out, 'has nothing to expect but – a hiding' (1954), p. 172.
47. A. Honneth (1982), p. 181.
48. G. Markus (1986), p. 42.
49. *ibid.*, p. 34.
50. J. Habermas, see for example, 'New Social Movements' (1981).
51. J. Habermas (1974), p. 55.
52. For example, Habermas (1986).
53. N. Fraser (1985).
54. G. Markus (1986), pp. 44–46.
55. N. Fraser (1987).
56. For example, A. Gorz (1989); F. Block (1990), pp. 85–8.
57. As Giddens (1987) points out in relation to his debate with Gorz, p. 287.
58. As Marcuse (1973) describes it, p. 27.
59. See R. Eyerman (1984).
60. A. Touraine (1977), p. 161.
61. A. Touraine (1985), p. 76.
62. A. Touraine (1977), p. 162.
63. *ibid.*, p. 161.
64. *ibid.*, p. 164, my emphases.
65. This is reminiscent of Raymond Williams' arguments about culture.
66. A. Touraine (1981), p. 62.
67. A. Touraine (1977), p. 13.
68. *ibid.*, pp. 17–19.
69. For example, J. Cohen (1982).
70. A. Touraine (1977), p. 20.
71. *ibid.*, pp. 55–6.
72. A. Touraine (1977), pp. 238–9, 241; (1981), p. 74.
73. A. Touraine (1977), p. 267.
74. Much as the evidence shows attempts to enforce the nuclear form from above, the unmarried person, for example, has never been outlawed and population drives have not usually met with great success.
75. This last form of opposition is his definition of 'class action' or a 'class subject', as compared with class consciousness which is always present at the organisational level, however limited: A. Touraine (1981), pp. 69–71; (1984), p. 9.
76. A. Touraine (1977), p. 275.
77. *ibid.*, p. 276, Touraine's emphasis. If one substitutes 'she' for 'he' the dilemmas of women in male-dominated organisations become all too

apparent, and the feminist demands within work understandable via the social movement perspective.

78. A. Touraine (1981), p. 67.
79. A. Touraine (1977), p. 169.
80. Touraine is only making a general argument here: *ibid.*, p. 353.
81. A. Touraine (1981), pp. 67–8.
82. A. Touraine (1984), p. 13.
83. A. Touraine (1977), p. 254.
84. A. Melucci (1989), pp. 35–7.
85. N. Fraser (1987a), pp. 20–1.

Conclusion
In place of post-industrial dreams

Over the course of two decades now, the employment issue has bobbed up intermittently to gasp for life amidst indifference and fatalism in far too many countries. This in itself constitutes an additional injury for those many millions who are disqualified from social and political life by unemployment. Whether even higher levels of unemployment will continue to gain political acceptance is unanswerable, much as many of us would like to hear otherwise. For if we want to reverse the situation of marginality, meaninglessness and lack of control that is inherent to unemployment, hardly anything has yet been done. The political, economic and social changes required are considerable, even though the depth of change varies in proportion to the extent of mass unemployment in a country and to numerous other important factors. But in many places public debate is limited, research is scattered and concrete policy proposals for job creation are few and seldom heard.

It is quite beyond the scope of this book to make any such recommendations – which would necessarily be nationally or regionally specific in order to be realisable in the prevailing context. A renewed enthusiasm for these kinds of explorations would indeed be timely. All that this book has attempted to say is that there can be no refuge in 'soft' options to proper employment policies, because they rapidly transform into harsh options for marginalised groups. In place of what has merely been a dream, the only progressive solution to contemporary joblessness lies in genuine employment opportunities for all who want them. Any alternative path restricts and undermines the citizenship of those people already unemployed.

My argument has consisted of positive and negative elements. A positive case for full employment as *an aim in principle* has rested, above all, on a negative answer to the question of whether an alternative to wage labour could be desirable. This question has been tested theoretically and practically. The cases where specific governments have used the post-industrial strategy illustrate several general features of the idea. First, the strategy requires state implementation, but no contemporary government takes the proposal's intention to subvert the existing political and economic power structures to be an acceptable aim. Second, the similarities in a strategy supported for such opposing motives are far greater than the almost imperceptible differences. Third, even where a government might start out with vaguely 'post-industrial' intentions, such as in Australia where the strategy took off on a basis more of concern than indifference for the unemployed, there is no structural component of the strategy that could empower the 'underclass'. Once within an alternative to mainstream participation, governments are even less constrained by the marginal groups than before.

This, it seems to me, is a general argument about the way the idea neglects the facts of any state's power. Of course, there are also specific circumstances and differing institutional mechanisms which additionally shape or distort a proposal in any one country. For example, the very existence of a large commune movement in idyllic rural areas in Australia is not unique but certainly unusual. Similarly, a guaranteed income can have varied effects, depending (as in the United States) on regional labour markets and so forth. But the general case against alternatives to wage labour is still applicable.

The same cannot be said for proposals for employment creation in different countries, for there is no one general solution. Indeed, a further problem with the post-industrial strategy is its assumption that certain *contradictions* facing welfare states are both universal and the key to understanding contemporary unemployment trends. At a very broad level of generality, it is possible to agree that the problem facing most welfare states, of requiring but being unable now to maintain full employment, is due to their lack of power over capital. But this does not explain the notable exceptions, nor the fact that in Australia, for example, the original state regulations for protected wages, tariffs, control of capital movement and progressive taxation were introduced much earlier than in some countries. These state controls did not give rise to an inevitably 'contradictory' set of demands on the state, as the system line from Offe would suggest. Circumstances certainly changed and, as it turned out, Australia's commitment to full employment was abandoned during an extremely volatile period. Conservative and neo-classical liberal movements had mounted a vast attack on 'welfare', state regulations and formal democracy itself, with the sacking of a popularly elected government. These were no mere contradictions. Moreover it is ironic that the *anti-labourist* strategy of the Whitlam government, of increasing *social welfare* rather than wage-earner welfare through state control of mineral resources instead of protected manufacturing, also contributed (in its failure) to the beginning of a decline in state controls over capital (such as they were). The problem identified by Habermas that the limitations of 'the welfare state' are due to its 'feeding' on the image of 'laboring society' is, therefore, not applicable to Australia in any clearcut way.

This implies that contemporary mass unemployment was not *created* by welfare states committed to full employment but eventuated from right wing mobilisations and reduced or nonexistent state regulations on capital, among other factors. Such actions are historically and geographically more specific and less due to a logic of systemic contradictions than the anti-employment position would have it. The new prospect in Australia is a further deregulation of the labour market, to the increasing detriment of those already discriminated against in lower stratas of the labour force. It will be a return after eighty years to wages being determined *not by need at all*, but by profit and bargaining strength alone. It is a situation where state sovereignty is increasingly devolving not towards participatory mechanisms but to market and corporate structures. The concentration of power in the latter belies the democratic rhetoric of the propaganda for privatisation.

These are potentially grim outlooks which still face little opposition. The intellectual climate that fostered a post-industrial path, despite its concern for marginal groups, lacked the grounds to set any obstacles against the re-emergence of classic economic liberalism as the spurious new orthodoxy. A serious consequence is the dearth of research on potential job policies in numerous countries. We still mainly rely on comparative work, from the research of Korpi, for example, and Glyn, Rowthorn, Schor and Therborn, research that shows how varied are the contexts and policies that have maintained full employment among the few 'star performers'. So far such exceptions have mainly acted to falsify the global prognosis about the permanency and irreversibility of unemployment, but in the meantime few moves towards reversing the trends have been made, and some 'stars' are faltering under the impact of the European Community's present position.

There are, however, numerous arguments against supply-side and monetarist doctrines; some, too, are wary of the 'dry' corporatist experiments in parts of Europe and Australia. Analyses emerging in political economy, sociology, the 'regulation school' of French economics and other diverse views that draw partly on Marxian and Keynesian traditions provide realistic and not excessively optimistic recommendations. Many dismiss as absurd the ideas held by neo-classical theory that unemployment is *voluntary* and that 10 per cent may be a 'natural rate' of unemployment. In general, none offer a return to a Golden Age but they provide a number of suggestions for flexible new policies to conserve and expand employment.

The reason these analyses are convincing is above all because they recognise that the situation of marginal groups depends not on following orthodox economic theory to the letter but, far from it, on the differing balances of power, which need to be considered at international, national and regional levels. Accordingly, the *sine qua non* of any recommendation actually coming to fruition relies on the relative strengths and weaknesses of social movements. The intellectual climate clearly can play a part, however, whereby the more realistic and relevant are the suggestions, the greater the chance of their gaining a wider public. Every country has particularities: markets and sectors vary; institutional mechanisms, international links and ownership structures differ; business cultures range from competitive to co-operative; economic, fiscal and debt constraints are not the same, and neither is the extent of environmental degradation. Those who have experienced neo-classical policies first hand, as United States, New Zealand, British (and also Australian) populations have, will not depart from the same problems, to say the least, as those from the more social democratic or labourist models.

There again, if certain significant countries were to change course, cross fertilisation could occur. The attempts by various social movements in some places to reach reconciliation through constructing new visions is further ground for hope. In Australia, so far, this has not come to much. The major environmental organisations recently issued concrete job creation programs; feminists have turned to union leadership structures and some male unionists have genuinely embraced affirmative action. Others, unfortunately, have not. And the logging saga is a case in point, where the timber unions and environmentalists were unable to create any shared ground. While several countries have been planting eucalypt plantations for years, the timber industry in Australia works through the last natural forest before it is outpriced by the overseas eucalypts.

This is where I come full circle. The main problems with the 'productivist' understanding lie within its definition of human beings as only those beings who *produce* and who have instrumental control over nature. This narrow understanding has primarily been at the expense of constructing other relations with the environment *and* at the expense of less masculinist conceptions of humankind. It is truly ironic, then, that the idea of separating income from work is supported on the basis that the workplace is irredeemably productivist, just when the limitations of feminism's previous 'separate but equal' strategy have been recognised by so many women. We are now trying to redefine these conceptions of human nature through participation in the workforce and through the feminist movement to change the structures and culture of work and everyday life.

If we deny the potential of one major facet of contemporary social life, namely paid work and all its possibilities for greater participation in other arenas, we deny women and men the chance for a multi-faceted life. On the one hand, even if a dependent sort of participation is the more common experience in all forms of paid employment, it is possible to oppose this domination collectively. On the other hand, exclusion means denying all access to even dependent participation from where the opportunity to 'act out' a conflict might arise. So, although the limitations of 'productivism' are evident in all industrial societies, they are quite different from the potential for action and greater control that can emerge from 'participation'.

References

Abrams, P. & A. McCulloch (1976) *Communes, Sociology and Society*, Cambridge: Cambridge University Press.

Aho, S. (1985) 'Labour Society in Crisis? A Discussion', *Acta Sociologica*, vol. 28, no. 1, pp. 55–61.

Aho, S. (1986) 'Labour Society and its Crisis as Sociological Conceptions', *Acta Sociologica*, vol. 29, no. 1, pp. 55–61.

Alford, K. (1979) 'Cramming the Workforce and Neglecting their Children?', *Journal of Australian Political Economy*, no. 6, (November) pp. 58–72.

Altman, D. (1970) 'Students in the Electric Age' in R. Gordon (ed.) *The Australian New Left*, Melbourne: Heinemann, pp. 126–47.

Altman, D. (1970a) 'The Politics of Cultural Change', *Other Voices*, vol. 1, no. 2 (Aug–Sep), pp. 22–8.

Altman, D. (1973) 'Revolution by Consciousness' in H. Mayer & H. Nelson (eds) *Australian Politics*, third reader, Melbourne: Cheshire.

Altman, D. (1975) 'The Quantum Leap' in M. Smith & D. Crossley (eds) *The Way Out*, Melbourne: Lansdowne Press.

Altman, D. (1977) 'The Counter-Culture: Nostalgia or Prophecy?' in A.F. Davies & S. Encel (eds) *Australian Society*, 3rd edn, Melbourne: Longman Cheshire.

Altman, D. (1988) *A Politics of Poetry*, Sydney: Pluto Press.

Arena Editors (1979) 'Ruled out of Society', *Arena*, no. 53, pp. 1–4.

Arendt, H. (1958) *The Human Condition*, Chicago: University of Chicago Press.

Australia. Commission of Inquiry into Poverty (1975) *Poverty in Australia*, First Main Report, vol. I, R.F. Henderson, Chairman, Canberra: AGPS.

Australia. Department of Education and Youth Affairs (1984) 'A Review of Worker Co-operative Development Agencies in Australia', by Brian Greer, Canberra: AGPS.

Australia. Department of Employment and Industrial Relations (1983) '"Supply-side" Approaches to the Unemployment Problem', unpublished paper prepared for the Economic Planning Advisory Council (meeting of 12 December).

Australia. Department of Employment, Education and Training, Women's Bureau (1989) *New Brooms: Restructuring and Training Issues for Women in the Service Sector*, Canberra: AGPS.

Australia. Department of Employment, Education and Training, Women's Bureau (various) *Women at Work*, newsletter Canberra: AGPS.

Australia. Department of Trade (1987) *Australia Reconstructed*, ACTU/TDC Mission to Europe, Canberra: AGPS.

Australia. Office of Youth Affairs (1983) 'Commonwealth Government Policy on Communities and Co-operatives', unpublished discussion paper prepared by R. Gurney.

Australia. Social Security Review (1987) 'Occupation: Unemployed. trends in Unemployment in Australia, 1970 to 1986', by Erica Fisher, SSR Research Paper no. 36, Canberra: DSS.

Australia. Social Security Review (1988) 'Income Support for the Unemployed in Australia: Towards a More Active System', by Bettina Cass, SSR, Issues Paper no. 4, Canberra: AGPS.

Australia. Taxation Review Committee (1974) Preliminary Report (Asprey Committee), Canberra: AGPS.

Australian Council of Social Service (ACOSS) (1975) 'Guaranteed Minimum Income: Towards the Development of a Policy', (August), Sydney: ACOSS.

Australian Council of Social Service (ACOSS) (1976) 'Poverty Commission's Guaranteed Minimum Income Proposals – Questions and Issues Raised' (April), Sydney: ACOSS.

Australian Council of Social Service (ACOSS) (1977) 'Whatever Happened to Full Employment?', Sydney: ACOSS.

Australian Council of Trade Unions (ACTU) (1975) 'Survey of Young Workers', Research Report for the Commission of Inquiry into Poverty, Canberra: AGPS.

Australian Council of Trade Unions (ACTU) (1984) 'Labour supply policies and employment', unpublished member's discussion paper for Economic Planning Advisory Council, by W.J. Kelty.

Australian Labor Party (1982) Platform Constitution and Rules.

Baiman, R. (1986) 'The Economic Argument for Increasing Technological Unemployment in the U.S. – and the 'Full Employment Politics' Debate within the U.S. Left', unpublished paper presented at the Conference of the Union of Radical Political Economists, Cape Cod, Massachusetts, USA (15 August).

Barbalet, J.M. (1988) *Citizenship*, Milton Keynes: Open University Press.

Barbalet, J.M. (1989) '"Old" Social Movements in the West', in C. Jennett & R. Stewart (eds), *Politics of the Future*, Melbourne: Macmillan.

Bauman, Z. (1982) *Memories of Class*, London: Routledge & Kegan Paul.

Beilharz, P. (1986) 'The Left, the Accord and the Future of Socialism', *Thesis Eleven*, no. 13, pp. 5–21.

Beilharz, P. (1987) 'Reading Politics: Social Theory and Social Policy', *Australian and New Zealand Journal of Sociology*, vol. 23, no. 3 (November), pp. 388–406.

Beilharz, P. (1987/88) 'Class Theory and its Discontents', *Thesis Eleven*, no. 18/19, pp. 166–78.

Bell, D. (1973) *The Coming of Post-Industrial Society*, New York: Basic Books.

Benhabib, S. (1981) 'Modernity and the Aporias of Critical Theory', *Telos*, no. 49 (Fall), pp. 39–59.

Berger, B.M. (1981) *The Survival of a Counterculture*, Berkeley: University of California Press.

Birnbaum, N. (1971) *Towards a Critical Sociology*, New York: Oxford University Press.

Bisset, D. (1975) 'Working for Change' in M. Smith & D. Crossley (eds) *The Way Out*, Melbourne: Lansdowne Press.

Bittman, M. (1990) 'Division of Labour in the Household', Research Discussion Paper, no. 11, Melbourne: Centre for Applied Research on the Future, University of Melbourne.

Bittman, M. (1991) 'Juggling Time', Canberra: Office of the Status of Women, Department of Prime Minister and Cabinet.

Blewett, N. (1973) 'Labor in Power', *Meanjin* (December) pp. 357–66.

Block, F. (1985) 'Full Employment as False Necessity', *Socialist Review*, vol. 15, no. 84 (Nov–Dec), pp. 93–8.

Block, F. (1987) *Revising State Theory*, Philadelphia: Temple University Press.

Block, F. (1990) *Postindustrial Possibilities*, Berkeley: University of California Press.

Boggs, C. (1976) *Gramsci's Marxism*, London: Pluto Press.

Bookchin, M. (1971) *Post-Scarcity Anarchism*, London: Wildwood House.

Bowles, S. & R. Boyer (1990) 'A Wage-Led Employment Regime' in S.A. Marglin and J. Schor (eds) *The Golden Age of Capitalism*, Oxford: Clarendon Press.

Bradbury, B. *et al* (1988) 'Poverty in the Workforce' SWRC *Reports and Proceedings*, no. 72 (March), Sydney: University of NSW.

Braverman, H. (1974) *Labor and Monopoly Capital*, New York: Monthly Review Press.

Braybrook, I. (1970) 'Negative Income Tax in Australia', *Australian Journal of Social Issues*, vol. 5, no. 2 (July), pp. 120–31.

Brennan, T. (1977) 'Women and Work', *Journal of Australian Political Economy*, no. 1 (October) pp. 34–52.

Bryson, L. (1977) 'Poverty', *Current Affairs Bulletin*, vol. 54, no. 5 (October), pp. 4–17.

Bryson, L. (1977a) 'Poverty Research in Australia in the Seventies: Unmasking Noble Terms', *Australian and New Zealand Journal of Sociology*, vol. 13, no. 3 (October), pp. 196–202.

Burke, J. & D. Griffiths (1986) 'Democracy at Work', *Australian Society* (November).

Burns, S. (1975) *The Household Economy*, Boston: Beacon Press.

Burton, C. (1985) *Subordination*, Sydney: George Allen & Unwin.

Butler, J.J. (1984) 'Preliminary Report on Co-operative and Communal Enterprises', Canberra: Department of the Attorney-General, unpublished.

Camilleri, J., P. Christoff *et al* (1989) *New Economic Directions for Australia*, Centre for Australian Social Policy Analysis, Phillip Institute of Technology.

Campioni, M., L. Jacka *et al* (1975) 'Opening the Floodgates: Domestic Labour and Capitalist Production', *Refractory Girl*, no. 7 (November), pp. 10–14.

Carruthers, J. (1981) 'The Emergence of Worker Co-operatives in NSW', *Work and People*, vol. 7, no. 3, pp. 8–18

Case, J. & R. Taylor (eds) (1979) *Co-ops, Communes and Collectives*, New York: Pantheon Books.

Casey, B. (1985) 'Active Labour Market Policy: An International Overview', *Bulletin of Labour Market Research*, no. 14 (March), pp. 19–21.

Cass, B. (1978) 'Women's place in the Class Structure' in E.L. Wheelwright & K. Buckley (eds), *Essays in the Political Economy of Australian Capitalism*, vol. 3, Sydney: ANZ Book Co.

Cass, B. & A. McClelland (1989) 'Changing the Terms of the Welfare Debate', paper presented at Social Welfare Research Centre, National Social Policy Conference, University of NSW (5–7 July).

Castles, F.G. (1985) *The Working Class and Welfare: Reflections on the Development of the Welfare State in Australia and New Zealand, 1890–1980*, Wellington: Allen & Unwin.

Catley, R. & B. McFarlane (1983) *Australian Capitalism in Boom and Depression*, Sydney: Alternative Publishing Cooperative Ltd.

Cock, P. (1975) 'Radical Change – an Alternative Strategy' in M. Smith and D. Crossley (eds) *The Way Out*, Melbourne: Lansdowne Press.

Cock, P. (1981) 'Alternative Lifestyles for the Unemployed?' in J.T.O. Kirk (ed) *When Machines Replace People. What Will People Do?*, Canberra: Society for Social Responsibility in Science.

Cock, P. (1982) 'The Rainbow Region – Centre of the Alternative Australia', *Current Affairs Bulletin*, vol. 58, no. 9 (February) pp. 16–22.

CODA (1984) 'Co-ops are Working', Submission to the NSW Government Review of Worker Co-operative Policies.

CODA (1984a) Discussion Document on the TNC Review, unpublished.

Cohen, J. (1982) 'Between Crisis Management and Social Movement', *Telos*, no. 52, Summer, pp. 21–40.

Cohen, J. (1982a) *Class and Civil Society: The Limits of Marxian Critical Theory*, Amherst: University of Massachusetts Press.

Connell, R.W. & T.J. Irving (1980) *Class Structure in Australian History*, Melbourne: Longman Cheshire.

Craig, C., J. Rubery *et al* (1985) 'Economic, Social and Political Factors in the Operation of the Labour Market' in B. Roberts, R. Finnegan & D. Gallie (eds) *New Approaches to Economic Life*, Manchester: Manchester University Press.

Crouch, C. (1983) 'Market Failure: Fred Hirsch and the Case for Social Democracy' in A. Ellis and K. Kumar (eds) *Studies in Fred Hirsch's Social Limits to Growth*, London: Tavistock.

Cunneen, C. (1984) 'Capitalism, the State and Youth: Initiatives in the Containment of the Homeless and Unemployed Young of NSW' in D. Cottle (ed.) *Capital Essays*, Sydney: University of NSW.

Davitt, M. (1988) *Life and Progress in Australia*, London: Methuen.

Dean, M. (1990) *The Constitution of Poverty*, London: Routledge.

Dixon, D. (1988) 'Unemployment: the Economic and Social Costs', *Research for Action*, no. 2, Melbourne: Brotherhood of St Laurence.

Donaldson, B. (1975) 'Women's Place in the Counter Culture' in J. Mercer (ed.) *The Other Half*, Melbourne: Penguin.

Edwards, M. (1975) 'Financial Assistance to Mothers: A Critical Appraisal', *Australian Quarterly*, vol. 47, no. 1 (March), pp. 90–4.

Edwards, M. (1978) 'A Guaranteed Income Scheme: Implications for Women' in A. Graycar (ed.) *Perspectives in Australian Social Policy*, Melbourne: Macmillan.

Elliott, G. (1978) 'Two Steps Forward, Two Steps Back: An Australian Welfare State?', in A. Graycar (ed) *Perspectives in Australian Social Policy*, Melbourne: Macmillan.

Ellyard, P. (1975) 'Alternatives and the future – a legitimate role for government', in M. Smith & D. Crossley (eds) *The Way Out*, Melbourne: Lansdowne Press.

Elster, J. (1988) 'Is There (or Should There Be) a Right to Work?' in A. Gutman (ed.) *Democracy and the Welfare State*, New Jersey: Princeton University Press.

Esping-Andersen, G. (1990) *The Three Worlds of Welfare Capitalism*, Princeton: Princeton University Press.

Eyerman, R. (1984) 'Social Movements and Social Theory', *Sociology*, vol. 18, no. 1 (February) pp. 71–82.

Farrar, A. (1986) 'Looking behind the scandals', *Australian Society* (September).

Farrar, A. (1987) 'The carrot-and-stick strategy', *Australian Society* (October), pp. 26–8.

Feher, F., A. Heller & G. Markus (1983) *Dictatorship over Needs*, Oxford: Basil Blackwell.

Fitzpatrick, B. (1944) *A Short History of the Australian Labor Movement*, Melbourne: Rawson's Bookshop.

Flinders University Marxist-Leninists (1973) 'The Counter-Culture' in H. Mayer & H. Nelson (eds) *Australian Politics*, third reader, Melbourne: Cheshire.

Frankel, B. (1978) 'Marxian Theories of the State: A Critique of Orthodoxy', *Arena Monograph*, no. 3, Melbourne: Arena Publications Association.

Frankel, B. (1987) *The Post-Industrial Utopians*, Cambridge: Polity Press.

Fraser, N. (1985) 'What's Critical About Critical Theory?' *New German Critique*, no. 35 (Spring–Summer), pp. 97–132.

Fraser, N. (1987) 'Social Movements vs. Disciplinary Bureaucracies: The Discourses of Social Needs', CHS *Occasional Papers*, no. 8, Centre for Humanistic Studies, University of Minnesota.

Fraser, N. (1987a) 'Women, Welfare and the Politics of Need Interpretation', *Thesis Eleven*, no. 17.

Freeland, J. (1987) 'Behind the welfare crisis', ASW *Impact*, vol. 17, no. 5 (August), pp. 6–9.

Friedman, M. (1962) *Capitalism and Freedom*, Chicago: University of Chicago Press.

Fry, K. (1985) 'Soldier Settlement and the Australian Agrarian Myth after the First World War', *Labour History*, no. 48 (May), pp. 29–43.

Furniss, N. & T. Tilton (1979) *The Case for the Welfare State*, Bloomington: Indiana University Press.

Gershuny, J.I. (1979) 'The Informal Economy: Its role in post-industrial society', *Futures* (February).

Giddens, A. (1984) *The Constitution of Society*, Berkeley: University of California Press.

Giddens, A. (1987) *Social Theory and Modern Sociology*, Cambridge: Polity Press.

Gil, D.G. (1973) *Unravelling Social Policy*, Cambridge, Mass.: Schenkman Publishing.

Gill, G. (1974) 'Back to Mother Earth', *Arena*, no. 34, pp. 7–12.

Glezer, H. (1988) 'Mothers in the Workforce', *Family Matters*, AIFS Newsletter, no. 21 (August).

Glyn, A. (1985) *A Million Jobs a Year: The Case for Planning Full Employment*, London: Verso & NLB.

Godschalk, J. & J. Mevissen (1989) 'Informal labour', unpublished paper, International Sociology Association Conference, June, Madrid.

Gordon, R. (ed.) (1970) *The Australian New Left*, Melbourne: Heinemann, pp. 3–39.

Gordon, R. & W. Osmond (1970) 'An Overview', in R. Gordon (ed.) *The Australian New Left*, Melbourne: Heinemann.

Gorz, A. (1982) *Farewell to the Working Class*, London: Pluto Press.

Gorz, A. (1985) 'The American Model and the Future of the French Left', *Socialist Review*, vol. 15, no. 6, pp. 101–8.

Gorz, A. (1985a) *Paths to Paradise: On the Liberation from Work*, London: Pluto Press.

Gorz, A. (1989) *Critique of Economic Reason,* London: Verso.

Gramsci, A. (1971) *Selections from the Prison Notebooks,* New York: International Publishers.

Graycar, A. (ed.) (1978) *Perspectives in Australian Social Policy,* Melbourne: Macmillan.

Green, D. & L. Cromwell (1984) *Mutual Aid or Welfare State,* Sydney: George Allen & Unwin.

Green, R., B. Mitchell & M. Watts (1992) 'Economic Policy in Crisis: A proposal for Jobs and Growth', Evatt Foundation Impact Series, Sydney.

Habermas, J. (1971) *Towards a Rational Society,* London: Heinemann.

Habermas, J. (1974) 'The Public Sphere', *New German Critique,* no. 3, pp. 49-55.

Habermas, J. (1975) *Legitimation Crisis,* Boston: Beacon Press.

Habermas, J. (1981) 'New Social Movements', *Telos,* no. 49 (Fall), pp. 33-7.

Habermas, J. (1982) 'A Reply to my Critics' in J.B. Thompson & D. Held (eds) *Habermas: Critical Debates,* London: Macmillan.

Habermas, J. (1986) 'The New Obscurity: the Crisis of the Welfare State and the Exhaustion of Utopian Energies', *Philosophy and Social Criticism,* vol. 11, no. 2 (Winter), pp. 1-18.

Habermas, J. (1987) *The Theory of Communicative Action,* vol. 2, Cambridge: Polity.

Hall, S. & D. Held (1989) 'Left and Rights', *Marxism Today* (June), pp. 16-23.

Hancock, K. (1970) 'The Economics of Social Welfare in the 1970's', in H. Weir (ed.) *Social Welfare in the 1970's,* Sydney: ACOSS.

Handy, C. (1982) 'The Informal Economy', ARVAC Pamphlet no. 3, Wivenhoe, Essex.

Harding, A. (1985) 'Unemployment Policy: A Case Study in Agenda Management', *Australian Journal of Public Administration,* vol. XLIV, no. 3 (September), pp. 224-46.

Harding, P. & R. Jenkins (1989) *The Myth of the Hidden Economy,* Milton Keynes: Open University Press.

Hawke, A. & D.E. Lewis (1989) 'Evaluation of an Alternative Income Maintenance Scheme', paper presented at National Social Policy Conference, University of NSW.

Hawke, R.J.L. (1979) *The Resolution of Conflict: 1979 Boyer Lectures,* Sydney: Australian Broadcasting Commission.

Hawke, R.J.L. (1981) 'Generating Employment Options for Government' in J.T.O. Kirk (ed.) *When Machines Replace People,* Canberra: Society for Social Responsibility in Science.

Hawke, R.J.L. (1983) Prime Minister's Speech to the International Labour Organisation, Geneva (June 10).

Head, B. (1982) 'The New Right and Welfare Expenditures' in M. Sawer (ed.) *Australia and the New Right,* Sydney: George Allen & Unwin.

Hegel, G.W.F. (1977) *The Phenomenology of Spirit*, Oxford: Oxford University Press.

Held, D. & J. Krieger (1983) 'Accumulation, Legitimation and the State' in D. Held *et al* (eds) *States and Societies*, Oxford: Martin Robertson.

Heller, A. (1973) 'Individual and Community', *Social Praxis*, vol. 1, no. 1, pp. 11–22.

Heller, A. (1976) 'Marx's Theory of Revolution and the Revolution in Everyday Life' in A. Hegedus, A. Heller, M. Markus & M. Vajda (eds) *The Humanisation of Socialism*, London: Allison & Busby.

Henderson, R.F. (1971) 'The Relief of Poverty: Negative Income and Other Measures', *The Economic Record*, vol. 47, (March), pp. 106–14.

Henderson, R.F., A. Harcourt & R.J.A. Harper (1975) *People in Poverty: A Melbourne Survey*, Melbourne: Cheshire, with supplement. (First published 1970.)

Higgins, W. (1974) 'Reconstructing Australian Communism', *The Socialist Register*, pp. 151–88.

Higgins, W. (1978) 'State Welfare and Class Warfare' in G.C. Duncan (ed.) *Critical Essays in Australian Politics*, Melbourne: Edward Arnold.

Hindess, B. (1990) 'The Post-Fordist Persuasion', *Australian Left Review*, no. 117 (May).

Hinrich, K., C. Offe & H. Wiesenthal (1988) 'Time, Money, and Welfare-State Capitalism' in J. Keane (ed.) *Civil Society and the State*, London: Verso.

Hirsch, F. (1977) *Social Limits to Growth*, London: Routledge & Kegan Paul.

Hobsbaum, E.J. (1962) *The Age of Revolution*, London: Cardinal.

Hollingworth, P. (1975) *The Poor: Victims of Affluence*, Melbourne: Pitman.

Honneth, A. (1982) 'Work and Instrumental Action', *Thesis Eleven*, no. 5/6, pp. 162–84.

Horne, S. (1970) 'A Comparative Note on Guaranteed Annual Income', *Australian Journal of Social Issues*, vol. 5, no. 2 (July) pp. 117–19.

Illich, I. (1981) *Shadow Work*, London: Marion Boyars.

Jahoda, M, P.F. Lazarfeld & H. Zeisel (1972) *Marienthal: The Sociography of an Unemployed Community*, London: Tavistock.

Jamrozik, A. (1981) 'Worker Co-operatives: Do they have a Future?', unpublished SWRC Seminar paper, Sydney, August.

Jamrozik, A. & R. Beck (1981) 'Worker Co-operatives: An Evaluative Study of the New South Wales Worker Co-operative Programme', SWRC *Reports and Proceedings*, no. 12, August.

Jamrozik, A., M. Hoey & M. Leeds (1983) 'Occupational Welfare: Supporting the Affluent?' in A. Graycar (ed.) *Retreat from the Welfare State*, Sydney: Allen & Unwin.

Jenson, J. *et al* (1988) *Feminization of the Labour Force*, Cambridge: Polity Press.

Jones B. (1982) *Sleepers Wake! Technology and the Future of Work*, Melbourne: Oxford University Press.

Jones, M. (1974/5) 'A Critical Appraisal of the Australian Assistance Plan', *Social Security*, vol. 2, no. 3 (Summer), pp. 23–33.

Jordan, B. (1982) *Mass Unemployment and the Future of Britain*, Oxford: Blackwell.

Jordan, B. (1987) *Rethinking Welfare*, Oxford: Blackwell.

Jordan, B. (1989) *The Common Good*, Oxford: Blackwell.

Karmel, T. & M. MacLachlan (1988) 'Occupational Sex Segregation – Increasing or Decreasing?', *Economic Record*, vol. 64, no. 186 (September).

Kasper, W., R. Blandy *et al* (1980) *Australia at the Crossroads*, Sydney: Harcourt Brace Jovanovich.

Keane, J. & J. Owens (1986) *After Full Employment*, London: Hutchison.

Keane, J. (1988) *Democracy and Civil Society*, London: Verso.

Kennedy, R.E.W. (1968) 'The Leongatha Labour Colony: Founding an Anti-utopia', *Labour History*, no. 14 (May), pp. 54–8.

Kewley, T.H. (1980) *Australian Social Security Today: Major Developments from 1900 to 1978*, Sydney: Sydney University Press.

Kingston, B. (1977) *My Wife, My Daughter and Poor Mary Ann*, Melbourne: Nelson.

Korpi, W. (1990) 'Political and Economic Explanations for Unemployment: A Cross-National and Long-Term Analysis', *British Journal of Political Science*, vol. 21, no. 3 (July).

Kumar, K. (1978) *Prophecy and Progress*, Harmondsworth: Penguin.

Land Commission of NSW (1984) 'Multiple Occupancy Development', Feasibility Study, Sydney.

Larsen, J. (1991) 'The Welfare State and Unemployment in Denmark and other European Countries', *SPRC Reports and Proceedings*, no. 91, Kensington: Social Policy Research Centre, University of NSW.

Laurence, G. (1983) 'Communal Problems', *Australian Society* (June), pp. 25–6.

Lemert, C.C. (1981) 'Literary Politics and the Champ of French Sociology', *Theory and Society*, vol. 10, no. 5 (September) pp. 645–69.

Lewis, M.T. (1975) *Values in Australian Income Security Policies*, Commission of Inquiry into Poverty, Canberra: AGPS.

Maas, F. & P. McDonald (1989) 'Income Splitting', *Family Matters*, AIFS Newsletter no. 24 (August).

Macintyre, S. (1983) 'Work or Starve', *Australian Society*, vol. 2, no. 5, (June).

Macintyre, S. (1985) *Winners and Losers: The Pursuit of Social Justice in Australian History*, Sydney: Allen & Unwin.

Macintyre, S. (1986) 'The Short History of Social Democracy in Australia', *Thesis Eleven*, no. 15, pp. 3–14.

Macpherson, C.B. (1962) *The Political Theory of Possessive Individualism*, Oxford: Oxford University Press.

Mahon, R. (1987) 'From Fordism to?: New Technology, Labour Markets and Unions', *Economic and Industrial Democracy*, vol. 8, no. 1.

Mahony, J. & J. Barnaby (1973) 'Assistance to families with children', *Social Security*, DSS, vol. 1, no. 1 (Winter), pp. 6–14.

Malos, E. (ed.) (1982) *The Politics of Housework*, London: Allison & Busby.

Marcuse, H. (1973) 'On the Philosophical Foundation of the Concept of Labor in Economics', *Telos*, no. 16 (Summer), first published 1933.

Marglin, S. (1990) 'Lessons of the Golden Age', in S.A. Marglin & J.B. Schor (eds) *The Golden Age of Capitalism*, Oxford: Clarendon Press.

Marglin, S.A. & A. Bhadouri (1990) 'Profit Squeeze and Keynesian Theory', in S.A. Marglin & J.B. Schor (eds) *The Golden Age of Capitalism*, Oxford: Clardendon Press.

Marklund, S. (1986) 'Is the Welfare State Irreversible?', unpublished paper delivered at SWRC Seminar, University of NSW, Sydney (19 September).

Markus, G. (1982) 'A Radical Theory on Classical Political Obligation', *Radical Philosophy*, no. 32 (Autumn).

Markus, G. (1986) 'Beyond the Dichotomy: Praxis and Poiesis', *Thesis Eleven*, no. 15, pp. 30–47.

Markus, M. (1986) 'Women, Success, and Civil Society: Submission to, or Subversion of, the Achievement Principle', *Praxis International*, vol. 5, no. 4 (January) pp. 430–42.

Markus, M. & A. Hegedus (1976) 'Free Time and the Division of Labour' in *The Humanisation of Socialism*, by A. Hegedus, A. Heller *et al*, London: Allison & Busby.

Marshall, T.H. (1965) *Class, Citizenship and Social Development*, New York: Anchor.

Marx, K. (1954) *Capital*, vol. I, Moscow: Progress Publishers.

Mathews, J. (1986) 'Rethinking the Safety Net', *Australian Society* (November).

Mathews, J. (1988) *A culture of Power*, Sydney: Pluto Press.

Mathews, R. (1983) 'Building the Society of Equals: Worker Co-operatives and the ALP', *Victorian Fabian Society*, pamphlet no. 39, Melbourne: Victorian Fabian Society.

McDonald, K. (1988) 'After the Labour Movement: Strategic Unionism, Investment and New Social Movements', *Thesis Eleven*, no. 20, pp. 30–50.

McDonald, K. (1990) 'Social Welfare: Reconstituting the Political' in A. Jamrozik (ed.) Social Policy in Australia, SPRC *Reports and Proceedings*, no. 81 (April).

McGregor, C. (1975) What Counter Culture?' in M. Smith & D. Crossley (eds) *The Way Out*, Melbourne: Lansdowne Press.

McLuhan, M. (1967) 'Guaranteed Income in the Electric Age' in R. Theobald (ed.) *The Guaranteed Income*, New York: Anchor Books.

McQueen, H. (1982) *Gone Tomorrow: Australia in the 80's*, Sydney: Angus & Robertson.

McQueen, H. (1970) 'Laborism and Socialism' in R. Gordon (ed.) *The Australian New Left*, Melbourne: Heinemann.

Mellor, M. *et al* (1988) *Worker Cooperatives in Theory and Practice*, Milton Keynes: Open University Press.

Mellor, M., J. Hannah & J. Stirling (1988) *Worker Cooperatives in Theory and Practice*, Milton Keynes: Open University Press.

Melucci, A. (1989) *Nomads of the Present*, London: Hutchinson.

Mendelsohn, R. (1979) *The Condition of the People: Social Welfare in Australia 1900–1975*, Sydney: Allen & Unwin.

Metcalf, W.J. (1984) 'Alternative-Lifestyle Research in Australia', Institute of Applied Social Research, Griffith University.

Metcalf, W.J. (1984a) 'Gender Differentiation within Alternative Lifestyle Groups', *Social Alternatives*, vol. 4, no. 3, pp. 47–51.

Metcalf, W.J. & F.M. Vanclay (1984) 'Government Funding of Alternative Lifestyles: an opinion survey', Report to the Australian Department of Education and Youth Affairs, Institute of Applied Research, Griffith University.

Metcalf, W.J. & F.M. Vanclay (1985) 'Social Characteristics of Alternative Lifestyle Participants in Australia', Report to the Office of Youth Affairs and Department of Prime Minister and Cabinet, Institute of Applied Research, Griffith University.

Mills, C. Wright, (1956) *White Collar*, New York: Oxford University Press.

Mingione, E. (1978) 'Capitalist Crisis, Neo-dualism and Marginalisation', *International Journal of Urban and Regional Research*, vol. 2, no. 2, pp. 212–21.

Morris, L. (1988) 'Employment, the Household and Social Networks' in D. Gallie (ed.) *Employment in Britain*, Oxford: Blackwell.

Morris, L. (1990) *The Workings of the Household*, Cambridge: Polity.

Mowbray, M. (1986) 'Work-for-dole in action', *Australian Society* (September), p. 40.

Munro Clark, M. (1986) *Communes in Rural Australia: The Movement since 1970*, Sydney: Hale & Iremonger.

Nalson, J.S. (1977) 'Rural Australia' in A.F. Davies *et al* (eds) *Australian Society*, 3rd edn, Melbourne: Longman Cheshire.

Nix, H.A. (1981) 'The Rural Solution?' in J.T.O. Kirk (ed.) *When Machines Replace People*, Canberra: Society for Social Responsibility in Science.

NSW Worker Co-operative Programme (1985) Explanatory Papers issued at the TUTA Seminar on the NSW Programme, Sydney, 24 June.

O'Brien, Patrick (1973) 'The Left Liberation Myth', in H. Mayer & H. Nelson (eds) *Australian Politics*, third reader, Melbourne: Cheshire.

O'Brien, Peter (1970) 'A Comment on Dennis Altman's "The Politics of Cultural Change"' in R. Gordon (ed.) *The Australian New Left*, Melbourne: Heinemann.

O'Brien, Peter (1971) 'Culture and Revolution', *Arena*, no. 24, pp. 22–31.

O'Connor, J. (1973) *The Fiscal Crisis of the State*, New York: St Martin's Press.

Offe, C. & V. Ronge (1979) 'Theses on the theory of the state' in J.W. Freiberg (ed.) *Critical Sociology: European Perspectives*, New York: Irvington.

Offe, C. (1976) *Industry and Inequality. The Achievement Principle in Work and Social Status*, London: Edward Arnold.

Offe, C. (1978) 'The Future of European Socialism and the Role of the State' in Proceedings of the 3rd International Colloquium on the Future of Socialism in Europe, Montreal, pp. 67–75.

Offe, C. (1984) 'The Future of the Labor Market', *Telos*, no. 60 (Summer), pp. 81–96.

Offe, C. (1984a) *Contradictions of the Welfare State*, Cambridge, Mass.: MIT Press.

Offe, C. (1987) 'The Utopia of the Zero-Option. Modernity and Modernization as Normative Political Criteria', *Praxis International*, vol. 7, no. 1, pp. 1–24.

Pahl, R.E. (1980) 'Employment, work and the domestic division of labour', *International Journal of Urban and Regional Research*, vol. 4, no. 1.

Pahl, R.E. (1984) *Divisions of Labour*, Oxford: Blackwell.

Pateman, C. (1970) *Participation and Democratic Theory*, Cambridge: Cambridge University Press.

Pateman, C. (1979) *The Problem of Political Obligation*, Chichester: John Wiley & Sons.

Pateman, C. (1984) 'The Shame of the Marriage Contract' in J. H. Stiehm (ed.) *Women's Views of the Political World of Men*, New York: Transnational.

Pateman, C. (1985) 'The Patriarchal Welfare State: Women and Democracy' in A. Gutman (ed.) *Democracy and the Welfare State*, New Jersey: Princeton University Press.

Patterson, J.T. (1986) *America's Struggle against Poverty, 1900–1985*, Cambridge, Mass.: Harvard University Press.

Patterson, P. (1985) 'Labour Market Analysis at the OECD', *Bulletin of Labour Market Research*, no. 14 (March), pp. 11–14.

Peattie L. & M. Rein (1983) *Women's Claims: A Study in Political Economy*, New York: Oxford University Press.

Piven, F.F. & R.A. Cloward (1982) *The New Class War*, New York: Pantheon Books.

Piven, F.F. & R.A. Cloward (1987) 'The historical sources of the contemporary relief debate' in F. Block *et al* (eds) *The Mean Season*, New York: Pantheon.

Piven, F.F. & R.A. Cloward (1971) *Regulating the Poor*, New York: Pantheon.

Pixley, J. (1991) 'Citizen, client or worker? State, class and welfare' in M. Muetzelfeldt (ed.) *State, Society and Politics in Australia*, Sydney: Pluto Press.

Pixley, J. (1991) 'Wowsers and Pro-Woman Politics: Temperance against Australian Patriarchy', *Australian and New Zealand Journal of Sociology*, vol. 27, no. 3 (November), p. 293–314.

Polanyi, K. (1957) *The Great Transformation*, Boston: Beacon Press.

Polanyi, P. (1971) 'An End to Poverty' in R. Boyson (ed.) *Down with the Poor*, London: Churchill Press.

Pym, D. (1980) 'Towards the Dual Economy and Emancipation from Employment', *Futures* (June), pp. 223–237.

Quadagno, J. (1990) 'Race, Class and Gender in the U. S. Welfare State: Nixon's Failed Family Assistance Plan, *American Sociological Review*, CV, 1 (February).

Redclift, N. (1985) 'The contested domain: gender, accumulation and the labour process' in N. Redclift & E. Mingione (eds) *Beyond Employment: Household, Gender and Subsistence*, Oxford: Basil Blackwell.

Redclift, N. & E. Mingione (eds) (1985) *Beyond Employment: Household, Gender and Subsistence*, Oxford: Basil Blackwell.

Rehn, G. (1984) 'The Wages of Success', *Daedalus*, vol. 113, no. 2 (Spring), pp. 137–68.

Risstrom, E. (1972) 'Negative Taxation as an Aid in Tax Reform', *The Chartered Accountant in Australia*, vol. 43, no. 1 (July), pp. 17–27.

Roche, M. (1987) 'Citizenship, Social Theory, and Social Change', *Theory and Society*, vol. 16, no. 3 (May), pp. 363–400.

Roe, J. (1975) 'Social Policy and the Permanent Poor' in E.L. Wheelwright & K. Buckley (eds) *Political Economy of Australian Capitalism*, vol. I, Sydney: ANZ Books.

Roe, J. (1976) 'Perspectives on the present day', in J. Roe (ed.) *Social Policy in Australia*, Sydney: Cassell.

Roszak, T. (1970) *The Making of a Counter Culture*, London: Faber & Faber.

Rothman, D.J. (1985) 'Social Control', in S. Cohen & A. Scull (eds) *Social Control and the State*, New York: St Martin's Press.

Rowley, K. (1970) 'Ideology in the Electric Age' in R. Gordon (ed.) *The Australian New Left*, Melbourne: Heinemann, pp. 148–60.

Rowthorn B. & A. Glyn (1990) 'The Diversity of Employment Experience since 1973' in S.A. Marglin & J.B. Schor (eds) *The Golden Age of Capitalism*, Oxford: Clardenon Press.

Rubinstein, L. (1976) 'Do You Have a Job? Wages for Housework', *Journal of the Communist Party of Australia* (October), pp. 8–14.

Rustin, M. (1985) *For a Pluralist Socialism*, London: Verso.

Ryan, E. & A. Conlan (1975) *Gentle Invaders*, Melbourne: Nelson.

Sackville, R. (1981) 'Summation' in J. Wilkes (ed.) *The Future of Work*, Sydney: George Allen & Unwin.

Salmon, J. (1975) 'Passing the Buck – An Australian Guaranteed Income Scheme' in Proceedings of a Seminar on Guaranteed Minimum Income, Sydney: ACOSS.

Saunders, P. (1978) 'A Guaranteed Minimum Income Scheme for Australia?' in A. Graycar (ed.) *Perspectives in Australian Social Policy*, Melbourne: Macmillan.

Saunders, P. (1988) 'Guaranteed Minimum Income Revisited: Paradise Lost or Guiding Light', *Economic Papers*, vol. 7, no. 3 (September).

Saunders, P. (1990) 'Employment Growth and Poverty', SPRC Discussion Paper no. 25, Sydney: Social Policy Research Centre, UNSW.

Sawer, M. (ed.) (1982) *Australia and the New Right*, Sydney: George Allen & Unwin.

Sawer, M. & M. Simms (1984) *A Woman's Place: Women and Politics in Australia*, Sydney: Allen & Unwin.

Sayers, S. (1986) 'Work, Leisure and Human Needs', *Thesis Eleven*, no. 14, pp. 79–96.

Sayers, S. (1988) 'The Need to Work: a Perspective from Philosophy' in R.E. Pahl (ed.) *On Work*, Oxford: Basil Blackwell.

Schofield, J. (1990) 'Freezing history: Women Under the Accord, 1983–1988', Industrial Relations Research Centre Monograph, no. 20, Sydney: University of NSW.

Schor, J. (1985) 'Full Employment as Justice', *Socialist Review*, no. 84, (November–December), pp. 98–100.

Schor, J. (1985a) 'The Economics and Politics of Full Employment', *Socialist Review*, no. 81, (May–June), pp. 65–92.

Sharp R. & R. Broomhill (1988) *Short Changed: Women and Economic Policies*, Sydney: Allen & Unwin.

Sheen V. & J. Trethewey (1991) 'Unemployment in the Recession', *Brotherhood Comment*, no. 1, Melbourne: Brotherhood of St Laurence.

Sheen, V. (1987) 'Community work for unemployed young people', *Policy in Practice*, no. 1, Melbourne: Brotherhood of St Laurence.

Shields, J. (1982) 'A Dangerous Age: Bourgeois Philanthropy, the State and the Young Unemployed in the 1930s' in *What Rough Beast?*, by Sydney Labour History Group, Sydney: George Allen & Unwin.

Siedlecky, S. & D. Wyndham (1990) *Populate and Perish: Australian Women's Fight for Birth Control*, Sydney: Allen & Unwin.

Smart, C. (1989) *Feminism and the Power of Law*, London: Routledge.

Smith, M. & D. Crossley (eds) (1975) *The Way Out: Radical Alternatives in Australia*, Melbourne: Landsdowne Press.

Smith, P. (1974) 'Guaranteed Annual Income', ACOSS Background Paper, no. 3 (July), Sydney: ACOSS.

Sommerlad, E.A., P.L. Dawson & J.C. Altman (1985) 'Rural Land Sharing Communities: An Alternative Economic Model?', Bureau of Labour Market Research, Monograph Series no. 7, Canberra: AGPS.

Sommerlad, E.A. & J.C. Altman (1986) 'Alternative Rural Communities: A Solution to Unemployment?', *Australian Journal of Social Issues*, vol. 21, no. 1, pp. 3–15.

Souter, G. (1968) *A Peculiar People: The Australians in Paraguay*, Sydney: Angus & Robertson.

Spooner, S. (1973) 'Relationship between Work Incentives and Receipt of Welfare Benefits', *Social Security Quarterly*, DSS (Winter), pp. 22–5.

Springborg, P. (1981) *The Problem of Human Needs and the Critique of Civilisation*, London: George Allen & Unwin.

Steinfels, P. (1979) *The Neoconservatives*, New York: Touchstone, Simon & Schuster.

Strasser, S. (1977) 'Never Done: The Ideology and Technology of Household Work', unpublished PhD, New York State University, Ann Arbor: Michigan University, Microfilms International.

Stretton, H. (1987) *Political Essays*, Melbourne: Georgian House.

Stricker, P. & P. Sheehan (1981) *Hidden Unemployment: The Australian Experience*, Melbourne: Institute of Applied Economic and Social Research, University of Melbourne.

Summers, A. (1975) *Damned Whores and God's Police: The colonisation of women in Australia*, Ringwood: Penguin.

Sweet, R. (NSW Department of TAFE) (1980) 'A Labour Market Perspective on Transition Programs', unpublished paper, Conference of Tasmanian High School Vice Principals (July).

TAFE National Centre for Research and Development (1990) 'National review of training and development needs of TAFE teachers', Newsletter no. 1, Leabrook SA (February).

Theobald, R. (ed.) (1967) *The Guaranteed Income: Next Step in Socioeconomic Evolution?*, New York: Anchor Books.

Theophanous, A.C. (1980) *Australian Democracy in Crisis*, Melbourne: Oxford University Press.

Therborn, G. (1986) *Why Some Peoples Are More Unemployed Than Others*, London: Verso.

Thompson, E.P. (1968) *The Making of the English Working Class*, Harmondsworth: Penguin.

Thornley, J. (1981) *Workers' Co-operatives: Jobs and Dreams*, London: Heinemann.

Tierney, L. (1970) 'Social Policy', in A.F. Davies & S. Encel (eds) *Australian Society*, 2nd edn, Melbourne: Cheshire.

Toffler, A. (1970) *Future Shock*, New York: Random House.

Touraine, A. (1971) *The Post-Industrial Society*, New York: Random House.

Touraine, A. (1977) *The Self-Production of Society*, Chicago: University of Chicago Press.

Touraine, A. (1981) *The Voice and the Eye*, New York: Cambridge University Press.

Touraine, A. (1984) 'Social Movements: Special Area or Central Problem in Sociological Analysis?', *Thesis Eleven*, no. 9 (July), pp. 5–15.

Touraine, A. (1985) 'An Introduction to the Study of Social Movements', *Social Research* (Winter), pp. 749–88.

Trainer, T. (1983) 'Reconsidering Communes', *Australian Society*, (October), pp. 31–2.

TransNational Cooperative (TNC) Workers Research (1985) 'Anti-Union Employment Practices', Summary and Recommendations, (Sydney, 22 May).

TransNational Cooperative (TNC) (1984) 'Worker Co-operatives in New South Wales and Victoria: A Policy Review', Commissioned by F. Walker, NSW Minister for YACS and Housing & J. Simmonds, Victorian Minister for Employment and Training.

Trethewey, J. & O. Burston (1988) 'Changing Entitlements for the Young Unemployed', *Research for Action*, no. 3, Melbourne: Brotherhood of St Laurence.

Triado, J. (1984) 'Corporatism, Democracy and Modernity', *Thesis Eleven*, no. 9, (July), pp. 33–51.

Tucker, R.C. (ed.) (1978) *The Marx-Engels Reader*, New York: W.W. Norton.

Tulloch, P. (1979) *Poor Policies: Australian Income Security 1972–77*, London: Croom Helm.

Tulloch, P. (1983) 'The Welfare State and Social Policy' in B. Head (ed.) *State and Economy in Australia*, Melbourne: Oxford University Press.

Wajcman, J. (1983) *Women in Control: Dilemmas of a Workers' Co-operative*, Milton Keynes: Open University Press.

Wajcman, J. & S. Rosewarne (1986) 'The 'feminisation' of work', *Australian Society* (September).

Walker, R.B. (1970) 'The Ambiguous Experiment: Agricultural Co-operatives in NSW, 1893–1896', *Labour History*, no. 18, (May), pp. 19–31.

Wallace, C. (1984) 'The Statistical Alchemy of Women's and Youth Unemployment', *Journal of Australian Political Economy*, no. 17 (November), pp. 31–42.

Ward, R. (1973) 'The End of the Ice Age', *Meanjin* (March), pp. 5–13.

Watts, R. (1987) *The Foundations of the National Welfare State*, Sydney: Allen & Unwin.

Weber, M. (1976) *The Protestant Ethic and the Spirit of Capitalism*, London: George Allen & Unwin.

Western Australia. State Employment Task Force (1983) 'Co-operative, Community and Self-Employment Business Ventures', prepared by P. Kenyon.

Williams, S. (1984) 'Sustainable Rural Resettlement', Armidale: Australian Rural Adjustment Unit, University of New England.

Windschuttle, E. (1974) 'Should the Government pay a mother's wage?', *Social Security*, vol. 2, no. 1, (Winter), pp. 12–17.

Windschuttle, K. (1980) *Unemployment*, Ringwood: Penguin.

Windschuttle, K. (1986) 'Local Employment Initiatives and Labour Industry Programs', unpublished paper delivered at DEIR Conference on Local Employment Initiatives, Canberra.

Yeatman, A. (1986) 'The Social Differentiation of State, Civil Society and Family Life: A Working Model of Post-patriarchal Structures of Citizenship', paper presented to the SAANZ Conference, University of New England, Armidale, (9–12 July).

Yeatman, A. (1990) *Bureaucrats, Technocrats, Femocrats*, Sydney: Allen & Unwin.

Index

323